Microfinance and Rural Development

ABOUT THE AUTHOR

Mithilesh Kumar Jha, Asstt. Prof. and Head, Deptt. of Economics, Yingli Govt. College, Longleng , Nagaland. He obtained all his degrees from BRA BIHAR UNIVERSITY, MUZAFFARPUR, namely B.A, M.A, Ph.D., LLB. He had served earlier three consecutive terms as an executive member from Nagaland in NORTH EASTERN ECONOMIC ASSOCIATION (NEEA). He is the life member of Indian Fconomic Association, North Eastern Economic Association (NEEA), and BOOK CLUB of NBT, INDIAN RED CROSS SOCIETY. He is the academic counsellor of IGNOU for MEC and BA programme for BECE at IGNOU study centre, Longleng. At present, holding the various posts to function the college smoothly, viz. Prof In-charge, Career Guidance and Counselling Cell, Convenor, Internal Quality Cell, Prof In-charge of Consortium for Educational Communication, Environmental studies and to organise the elocution and Essay competition sponsored by FORUM OF FREE ENTERPRISE, Mumbai. He has presented more than thirty research papers in regional and national level seminars and conferences. He has contributed about ten research papers in different leading journals of Economics and edited books.

Microfinance and Rural Development

Role of Self-Help Groups

Mithilesh Kumar Jha

CONCEPT PUBLISHING COMPANY PVT. LTD.
NEW DELHI-110059

ISBN-13 : 978-81-8069-855-2

First Published 2012

Published and Printed by

Concept Since 1974

Concept Publishing Company Pvt. Ltd.
A/15-16, Commercial Block, Mohan Garden
New Delhi-110059 (India)
T: 25351460, 25351794, *F*: 091-11-25357109
E: publishing@conceptpub.com, W: www.conceptpub.com
Editorial Office: H-13, Bali Nagar, New Delhi-110 015, India.

Cataloging in Publication Data--*Courtesy:* D.K. Agencies (P) Ltd. <docinfo@dkagencies.com>

Jha, Mithilesh Kumar.
Microfinance and rural development : role of self-help groups / Mithilesh Kumar Jha.
p. cm.
Originally presented as the author's thesis (Ph. D.)—Babasaheb Bhimrao Ambedkar Bihar University.
Includes bibliographical references (p.) and index.
ISBN 9788180698552

1. Microfinance—India. 2. Self-help groups—India. 3. Rural development projects—India. I. Title.

DDC 332.0954 23

Preface

The book is designed for use in courses that focus on Microfinance, SHGS and Rural Development in developing countries especially in India. It is structured and written both for students who have had some basic knowledge and training in rural development, microfinance, and SHGs and for those novice with little or no formal cognisance about aforesaid subjects. For both the groups, essential principles and concepts on the topics that are particularly applicable to the problems of developing countries are explained candidly. It lucidly presents *ad rem* suggestions of the discussed problems too. Thus the book should be of special value in Rural Development courses that attract students from a variety of disciplines. Yet the material is sufficiently broad in scope and rigours in coverage to satisfy any quench of Microfinance, Rural Development and Self Help Groups. The book is resulted from author's seven years research for his Ph.D.

Approach

It is said that *sanghaih saktih kalayuge*. It means that in modern time (*Kalyug*) power endowed in groups. It is tested by time too. Thus it is obvious that Power lies in group and savings boost the power to perform in its optimum level. Contribution of the group makes it more viable through self help. Ergo, it is said that Self-help is the best help and self-employment is the best employment. This is the central point of the philosophy of the self-help group. It proves its applicability in modern world where unemployment, poverty, malnutrition, hunger, etc., are prevailing. It is felt that individual effort is too inadequate to improve their fate. This brings about the necessity for organizing them in a group by which they get the

benefits of collective perception, collective decision making and collective implementation of programmes for common benefits; the organization holds power and provides strength; it can be an antidote to the helplessness of the poor. Savings of the group brings the multiplier effect of investment to break the vicious cycle of poverty, income and employment. It can be vividly demonstrated in a credit programme for the rural poor through the continuous expansion of their economic base. Incomes also rise, soar with additional investment through borrowing. The vicious cycle of low income, low savings, low investment and low income can be broken by injection of credit in the cycle. More credit, more investment, more income, more saving, more investment and more income are the results.

From the time immemorial, India is divided into urban and rural India. It is the urban dweller and our policy makers who have had utilised the rural wealth to build the urban domain more prosperous and glittering glitz and neglected the source of prosperity (rural areas). This deprivation continues even today, rural credit delivery mechanism also did not fulfil the long cherished desire of the deprived people. Though pompous speeches, speechact, robust planning, and active involvement of the functionaries etc. did not bring the remarkable effect. It still looks futile. Rural credit is still in the crunch of usurious usury and money lender. There is a lack of philanthropist and maximum institutional sources are in the firm grip of the *dalals* of the rural areas. In the midst of this juncture MF and SHGs are playing the crucial role to improve the limp condition. In this pious work MFIs are assisting their level best but at the present time, they also pervert and act like usury. Afterall Microfinance and Self Help Groups have brought the tremendous changes in rural domain. It enables the rural poor (especially women) to aim for economic empowerment, ponder to bring the dynamic development and right to live with dignity. It proves that rural poor are trustworthy and praiseworthy and not to be kept marginalised for ever.

Experiences of the different anti-poverty and other welfare programmes implemented throughout the world in general and India in particular have shown that the key to their success lies in the evolution and participation of community-based organizations at the grassroots level. People's participation in credit delivery and linking formal credit institution to borrowers through

intermediaries of Self-Help Groups (SHGs) have been recognised as a supplementary mechanism for providing credit support to the rural poor. The Self-Help Groups thus became a regular component of the Indian financial system since 1992 more particularly since 1996.

Case Studies

In order to provide the up-to-date information about women empowerment through SHGs and Microfinance several cases are cited in the book,viz. Self Help Group of Kohima (Nagaland) and Sabour block of Bhagalpur (Bihar), SGSY in East Champaran District of Bihar, Bihar-Rural Livelihood Promotion Project of Bihar. The purpose of these cases are to provide the readers a kind of applied material which will enable them to understand the context properly. Statistical Method is also applied in the book as Time series data on number of SHGs Linkage (exponential trend equation of type Y = ab x , Regional disparity in the distribution of bank offices and population has been studied with the help of Gennie's Coefficient, The Student's T-distribution, etc.)

Mithilesh Kumar Jha

Acknowledgements

At the very outset I would like to express my venerate, profound gratitude and heart-felt reverence to my distinguished, versatile Ph.D. Guide Dr. Hemchandra Lal Das, University Professor, P.G. Department of Economics, M.S. College, Motihari, for his expedite and valuable guidance right from the selection of the topic till the completion of this arduous and absorbing study untiringly without that it was impossible to complete the book.

I would like to express my deepest gratitude to all of those who have assisted and inspired me through their cooperation. Though I cannot requite my gratitude to all and sundry individually. But few names I would like to quote here as Prof. C.K.P. Sahi, BRA Bihar University, Muzaffarpur, Bihar, Late Prof. K. Borgohain, Retd. Joint Director, HTE, Kohima and former Principal, Yingli College, Longleng. Dr. Alempa Ao, Principal, and Shri B. Henshet Phom, Vice Principal. Dr. Mahabir Jha, Head Dept. of Pol.Sc., Dr. S. Kumar, Head, Deptt. of English, Yingli Govt. College, Longleng, Nagaland. My elder brother Prof. Narendra Nath Jha, Deptt. of Hindi, K.V.S. College, Uchaitha, Benipati (Bihar). My nephews Shiv Kumar Jha and Durganand Jha, niece Annu Kumari, sister Smt. Bina Devi and my mother-in-law Smt. Vidya Mishra.

I would like to express my deepest gratitude and heart-felt reverence to my father Late Shankar Jha and mother Smt. Godavari Devi who always appreciated and encouraged me to write the book with their firm aspiration. So, this book is dedicated to my beloved father.

I am thankful to Shri A.K. Mittal and staff of the Concept Publishing Company Pvt. Ltd., New Delhi for their kind and favourable support to shape the book.

It will be injustice if I do not express my deep sense of heart-felt gratitude to my wife Anupma, who sacrificed her comforts and played

a crucial role till the completion of this book from her intellectual inspiration, creative and artistic talents. She assisted and expedited me not only at home but in expedition to collect the data especially at Guwahati and in New Delhi. Her heart-warming and benevolent attitude always inspired me. Due to her benign support, aspire, love, keen desire and active cooperation in so many ways I could complete this work.

Further, I am utmostly thankful to my kids—Setu [Swapnil] and Rishu [Snehil] as they were utterly bereft of paternal love and affection during the writing of the book.

As the world changes at very fast rate of knots so do the facts and figures. It would be an endeavour to constantly modify the book to keep it as update as possible. I am sanguine that the readers will appreciate the book and any comments/suggestions in the direction of the development of the book, would be highly solicited.

Mithilesh Kumar Jha
Asstt. Prof. and Head
Department of Economics
Yingli Government College
Longleng, Nagaland

Contents

List of Tables

List of Figures

Abbreviations

AAY	Antyodaya Anna Yojana
ACP	Annual Credit Plans
AEZs	Agro Ecological Zones
APL	Above Poverty Line
APRACA	Asia-Pacific Regional Agricultural Credit Association
ARI	Acute Respiratory Infection
ASA	Activists for Social Action/Alternatives
ASSEFA	Association for Sarva Seva Farms (NGO Based in Chennai)
BC	Business Correspondence
BF	Business Facilitators
BDO	Block Development Officer
BMI	Body Mass Index
BPO	Business Process Outsourcing
BRAC	Bangladesh Rural Advancement Committee
BRLP	Bihar Rural Livelihood Promotion Project
BRLPS	Bihar Rural Livelihood Promotion Society
CDF	Credit Development Forum
CDS	Community Development Society
CEFP	Cooperative Education Field Project
CGAP	Consultative Group to Assist the Poorest (Consortium of Donors on Microfinance, Based at the World Bank)
CLCC	Central Level Coordination Committee
CPIAL	Consumer Price Index of Agricultural Labour
CPIIW	Consumer Price Index for Industrial Workers
CRWR	Capital Risk Weighted Ratio

CSO	Civil Society Organisation/Central Statistical Organisation
CYSD	Centre for Youth and Social Development
DCCBs	District Central Cooperative Banks
DDC	District Consultative Committee
DDM	District Development Manager
DDOs	District Development Officers
DRDAs	District Rural Development Agencies
DRI	Differential Rate of Interest
DWCRA	Development of Women and Children in Rural Areas (Indian Government Programme)
EAS	Employment Assurance Scheme
FDI	Foreign Direct Investment
FIF	Financial Inclusion Fund
FITF	Financial Inclusion Technology Fund
FSS	Farmer's Service Societies
FWWB	Friends of Women's World Banking, India (Based in Ahmedabad)
GB	Grameen Bank (Bangladesh)
GCC	Generalpurpose Credit Card
GIA	Grants-in-Aid
GISA	General Insurers' Association of India
GKY	Ganga Kalyan Yojana
GNP	Gross National Product
GoI	Government of India
HDI	Human Development Index
HDR	Human Development Report
HUDCO	Housing and Urban Development Corporation
IADP	Intensive Agricultural District Programmes
HYVP	High Yielding Varieties Programme
IAY	Indira Awas Yojana
IADP	Intensive Agricultural District Programme
ICT	Information and Communication Technology
JLGs	Joint Liability Groups
ICDP	Integrated Child Development Programme
IRDP	Integrated Rural Development Programme
IT	Information Technology
ITES	Information Technology Enable Service.

JRY	Jawahar Rojgar Yojana
KCC	Kisan Credit Card
KYC	Know Your Customer
LAB	Local Area Bank (Operating up to three contiguous district in India)
LPG	Liquefied Petroleum Gas
MACS	Mutually-Aided Cooperative Society
MAVIM	Mahila Arthik Vikas Mahamandal
MEDP	Micro Enterprises Development Programme
MFI	Micro Finance Institutions
MFDF	Micro Finance Development Fund
MIS	Management Information System
MIX	Microfinance Information Exchange
MPCE	Monthly Per Capita Consumption Expenditure
MRCP	Maharashtra Rural Credit Project
MRP	Mixed Recall Period
MST	Million Shallow Tube Wells
MYRADA	Mysore Rehabilitation & Development Agency
NABARD	National Bank for Agriculture and Rural Development.
NBFC	Non-Banking Financial Company
NBFI	Non-Banking Financial Intermediary
NCAER	National Council of Applied Economic Research
NCARDBF	National Confederation of Agriculture and Rural Development.
NCDP	National Community Development Programme
NCUI	National Cooperative Union of India
NDP	National Domestic Product
NES	National Extension Service
NFHS	National Family Health Survey
NGO	Non-Governmental Organisation
NMIB	National Microfinance Information Bureau
NPAs	Non-Performing Assets
NREGS	National Rural Employment Guarantee Scheme
NSSO	National Sample Survey Organization
OBC	Oriental Bank of Commerce, India
OCB	Overseas Corporate Bodies
OBGP	Overseas Corporate Grameen Project

OGs	Outgrowths
OSCB	Orissa State Cooperative Bank
OTS	One Time Settlement
PACS / PAX	Primary Agricultural Cooperative Societies
PADA	Professional Assistance Development
PCABs	Primary Cooperative Agricultural Banks
PDS	Public Distribution System
PLCPs	Potential Linked Credit Plans
PMGSY	Pradhan Mantri Gram Sadak Yojana
PMGY	Pradhan Mantri Gramoday Yojana
PMRY	Prime Minister Rozgar Yojana
POTD	Post Office Time Deposit
PRIs	Panchayati Raj Institutions
PURA	Providing Urban Amenities in Rural Areas
PWDP	Participatory Watershed Development Programme
RAC	Rural Advancement Committee
RB	Rashtriya Banijy
RBI	Reserve Bank of India (India's Central Bank)
RESCA	Regular Saving and Credit Association
RFI	Rural Financing Institution/Rural Financial Institution
RGVN	Rashtriya Gramin Vikas Nidhi (Foundation for the North-Eastern States in India)
RIDF	Rural Infrastructure Development Fund
RMGs	Rythu Mitra Groups
RMK	Rashtriya Mahila Kosh (National Credit Fund Women, India)
ROSCA	Rotating Savings and Credit Association
RRBs	Regional Rural Banks
Rs.	Indian Rupees
RTBI	Rural Technology Business Incubator
SAC	Service Area Credit
SACP	Special Agricultural Credit Plans
SAY	Samagra Awas Yojana
SC/ST	Scheduled Castes/Scheduled Tribes
SCARDBs	State Cooperative Agricultural and Rural Development Banks

SCBs	State Cooperative Banks
SCC	Swarozgar Credit Card
SEWA	Self Employed Women's Association, Ahmedabad
SGRY	Sampoorn Gramin Rozgar Yojana
SGSY	Swarnjayanti Gram Swarozgar Yojana
SHARE	Society for Helping Awakening Rural Poor Through Education (NGO Based in Hyderabad)
SHG	Self Help Group (Saving and Credit Group in India)
SHPI	Self-Help Promotion Institution
SIDBI	Small Industries Development Bank of India
SITRA	Supply of Improved Toolkits to Rural Artisans
SLCC	State Level Coordination Committee
SSIs	Small Scale Industries
STPs	Software Technology Parks
TADP	Tribal Area Development Programme
TRDEP	Thana Resources and Development Programme
TRYSEM	Training of Youth for Self-Employment
TSC	Total Sanitation Campaign
UNDP	United Nation Development Programme
UNICEF	United Nations International Children's Emergency Fund
UNIFEM	United Nations Fund for Women
URP	Uniform Recall Period
USAID	United States Agency for International Development
VC	Village Council
VDBs	Village Development Boards
VLWs	Village Level Workers
VRS	Voluntary Retirement Scheme
WCED	World Commission on Environment

1

Introduction

"Self-help is the best help and self-employment is the best employment". This is the central point of the philosophy of the self-help group. The approach towards poverty alleviation should be self-help. Others should help the poor to help themselves, because poverty and unemployment are danger to peace and prosperity everywhere. It is felt that individual effort is too inadequate to improve their fate. This brings about the necessity for organizing them in a group by which they get the benefit of collective perception, collective decision making and collective implementation of programmes for common benefits; the organization holds power and provides strength; it can be an antidote to the helplessness of the poor.

Individually, a poor trend to be rather tentative, uncertain in the behaviour but group membership smoothens the rough edges of his behaviour pattern, making him more reliable as a borrower. A poor person feels exposed to all kinds of hazards, he requires guidance and advice from people he knows and can trust. Membership of a group gives him a feeling of protection. Thus formation of a group would insure the best participation of the poor in a certain programme.

The multiplier effect of investment can be vividly demonstrated in a credit programme for the rural poor through the continuous expansion of their economic base. Incomes also rise with additional investment through borrowing. The vicious cycle of low

cycle of low income → low savings → low investment → low income can be broken by injection of credit in the cycle. More credit → more investment → more income → more saving → more investment → more income is the result.

Self-Help Groups (SHGs)

Experiences of the different anti-poverty and other welfare programmes implemented throughout the world in general and India in particular have shown that the key to their success lies in the evolution and participation of community-based organizations at the grassroots level. People's participation in credit delivery and linking formal credit institution to borrowers through intermediaries of Self-Help Groups (SHGs) have been recognised as a supplementary mechanism for providing credit support to the rural poor. The structure of rural financial market in developing economy, particularly in India, is dualistic with both formal and informal financial intermediaries. A consensus is growing among researchers that the formal financial sector is not effectively serving the rural population in the Third World countries.[1] This is mainly attributed to the failure of financial intermediaries in fulfilling their basic functions, viz. production credit to finance income generating activities, consumption credit to maintain and expand human productive capacity, and quality saving schemes for increasing risk-bearing capacity of the rural households. Moreover, these institutions have failed to promote any of its objectives.[2] To reach the poor, institutional innovations are needed that enable services to be expanded, while substantially reducing transaction costs for both financial institutions and clients.[3] In many countries in the world micro credit programmes have succeeded in generating self-employment by providing access to small capital to people living in poverty.[4]

The performance of formal financial institutions particularly in their lending to the poor has been unsatisfactory. They face a number of constraints in broadening their services to the poor. A large number of rural households are with limited land resources and small economic activity accompanied with poor technology.

But their demand for credit has been rising due to growing family size, increased consumption requirements, social obligations and so on. But the institutional agencies not only lacked the required mechanism to assess their credit needs but often overlooked their demand for credit on the ground that their needs are for non-productive purposes. Besides, perceived high risks, transaction costs to small scale rural lending and absence of collateral securities kept the poor away from the fold of formal financial intermediaries.[5]

The information, resources, skills and technology of the poor are very weak and the scales of their operation, irrespective of the economic activity pursued by them are, therefore, small. Their credit needs arise due to growing family size and social obligations, such as expenses on marriages and deaths, medical treatment and to bear market and climatic uncertainties.[6] The needs to expand or diversify operations places tremendous strain on the existing family income which is barely adequate to meet routine production and consumption requirements. Such additional demands are, however, rarely out of proportion, the line dividing production requirements from the conveniently termed consumption, requirements, seems to be rather thin as the latter has as vital an impact on economic activity as the seemingly direct 'productive' requirement.

In times of such emergencies, there is no credit institution to fall back upon and they are forced to rely on credit supplied by bigger landlords, traders and money lenders at high rates of interest. This is notwithstanding the threat of losing their means of production, indebtedness, and sometimes even bondedness an indication of their struggle to survive against all odds. The fact that they are generally able to repay their high interest loan only exemplifies their tremendous risk bearing capacity, exceptional ability to optimize on their frugal resources, the 'real' potential of their meagre income generation and the possibilities of mobilising tiny savings.

Formal and Informal Income Systems

Finance is one of the most critical inputs for economic activity,

growth and development. If finance through own accumulated resource or equity is neither available nor sufficient, debt assumes a major significance. Financial institutions play an important role in this regard by channelising funds from surplus sector (savers) to deficit sector (investors).[7] However, these institutions do not show much enthusiasm to put their resources in rural and backward areas for the benefit of the poorer people as these are commercial organizations and are basically interested in profitability and sustainability for two reasons: (i) incentive for functioning, and (ii) for safeguarding the interest of stack holders. Besides, the transaction in credit market is different from the transaction in goods market.[8] Unlike in the latter where transaction ends with the sale of goods and receipt of payment, which are more or less instantaneous, in the former what is important is the future endowment of the borrower which depends upon the purpose of the loan, viability of the project and creditworthiness and the strategic skill of the borrower. As these rural backward areas lack infrastructure, entrepreneurship, opportunities and people are victims of exploitations and ignorance, the transaction cost of investment by the borrowing investors is not attractive.

Besides, rural economic agents find the formal urban institutions alien and inaccessible; the attributes, characteristics and personal circumstances of the rural agents are not very much acceptable to the formal financial institutions for both an information gap exists. This accentuates the problem for the formal financial institution to locate both a good borrower and a good project. Borrowers know themselves better than the formal financial institutions, but do not desire to fully disclose all relevant personal and project information.[9] The information transfer is hampered by serious moral hazard and incentive problems.[10] Verification of true credentials by an outside may prove to be costly, if not impossible.[11] When market imperfections persist, lenders face the problem of managing the risk of loan default.[12] Raising the interest rate does not resolve the problems either.[13] On the other hand, the rural borrower and informal lender literally know each other quite well. The information wedge is easily eliminated, because both transactors operate within the same or

familiar socio-cultural and economic milieu. At the same time both the parties are able to draw up a very flexible and easily comprehensible loan contact. And the informal financial market continues to function in the same local environment. In the process both the formal financial institutions and the rural borrowers continue to be the losers. Whereas the formal loses a new credit market and potential surplus sector, the latter loses access to much larger and cheaper resource. As a result capital formation and, hence, development process takes a back seat in the rural areas. Besides, if land, labour and money market are interlocked, there arises a vested interest among the powerful class to thwart the development process and perpetuate indebtedness and poverty.[14,15]

The failure of formal institutions to serve the rural poor effectively led to a review and a look at the informal financial systems and lending groups.[16-18] "The traditional assessment of the informal sector has been that it is exploitative, usurious and dysfunctional and newly established institutional credit is thus often aimed at dismantling the informal sector. Such an approach may result in policies which displace informal lenders without offering alternate sources of institutional credit. In these circumstances rather than substitute for these informal arrangements, supplement and strengthen informal credit sources, and compete with informal lenders. Moreover, newly introduced systems could also learn from the informal sector."[19] "The informal sector as the oldest centre of enterprise preceding the arrival of formal institutions, is a natural and legitimate part of rural financial markets and it is better policy to acknowledge than to deplore the fact."[20]

It thus seems clear that informal financial system and informal lender are not on the same footing. Whereas the latter may be exploitative charging usurious rate of interest, the formal minimizing information gap and offering flexibility may be appropriate and efficient for the rural sector. There was thus a need to study the informal systems rather than informal lenders. What has thereafter been discovered are informal financial groups.

Tontines or Hui with 10-15 members involved in financial activities in cash or in kind have been in existence in Vietnam for

generations.[21] Bishi which is the short form of Bishimandal' or 'Chit fund', is an old institution of India in which members made periodic contributions that are pooled into a fund from which money is given to members.[22] Credit unions, fisherman groups, village based bank like institutions, irrigation groups, etc. were in existence in Indonesia.

In the international lexicon these informal groups have been termed as Rotating Savings and Credit Associations (ROSCA) and Regular Savings and Credit Associations (RESCA). In both regular savings are made by a fixed set of members for an agreed period. In ROSCA the total fund is given to each of the members in rotation until everyone has had a turn. Only one loan is made each time. After everyone has had a turn, the old cycle ends, and a new cycle may begin with the same or new members. In RESCA which is a non-rotating ROSCA, several loans are made from pool of savings. Whereas in ROSCA the funds does not grow during the life cycle, in RESCA the fund grows because of periodic contribution and repayment of loan. At the end of the period, there is nothing to be distributed at ROSCA. Accumulated fund is distributed among the members at RESCA. In ROSCA, generally three methods viz.: (i) lottery type, (ii) lottery with discount, and (iii) auction, are used to distribute the fund. In the latter two, there is incentive for saving and late winners earn a higher rate of interest.[23]

Whereas the encouraging feature of ROSCA/RESCA is that there is negligible information gap between the lender and the borrower and little transaction cost involved for both the parties, the problem is that they lack access to banks and external credit sources as well as consultancy services and most other modern inputs which just maintain a *status quo* by encouraging a near stationary economy going rather than expanding or modernizing it.[24]

To bridge the gap between formal and informal system, Professor Mohammad Yunus started a research project in Bangladesh in 1979 and established the Grameen Bank in 1983.[25] The lending programme of the Grameen Bank depends basically on external fund, although the member's savings fund has increased substantially over the time.

In 1984, the main conclusion in the international symposium

on the mobilization of personal savings in developing countries organized by the United Nations was that "the main means of improving the performance of the non-institutional sector were policies directed to enhancing its links with the institutional financial sector.[26] In the final resolution the participants agreed that (i) internal savings must provide the basic for credit programmes, (ii) state control of interest rates must be relaxed in favour of market or near market rates, (iii) the effective service, financial services need to be more decentralised, (iv) both formal and informal financial institutions are necessary for the financing of development, and (v) linkages between formal and informal financial institutions seem to be more promising than separate development.

In 1984, the Federal Ministry of Economic Corporation and the Agency for Technical Cooperation of the Federal Republic of Germany undertook a series of studies and workshops on rural finance in developing countries resulting in a new policy for promoting Self-Help Groups (SHGs), different from Grameen Bank model and Self-Help Promotional Institution (SHPI) as a financial intermediaries between the rural poor and the micro-enterprises in the informal sector, on the one hand and formal financial institutions on the other.[27]

At the Asia Pacific Regional Agricultural Credit Association (APRACA), regional workshop of May 1986 in Nanjing, the participants decided on a coordinate programme for "the Promotion of Linkages between Banks and SHGs for rural savings mobilization and credit delivery to the poor".

The project "Linking Banks and SHGs" (PHBK) in Indonesia started in 1988 as a pilot project of the Central Bank of Indonesia through the involvement of SHPI which would provide either training and consultancy services to the SHGs and in some cases additionally act as financial intermediaries.[28]

Linking Formal and Informal Systems in India

First official interest in informal group lending in India took shape during 1986-87 when the NABARD supported and funded an

action research project on "Savings and Credit Management of Self-Help Groups"[29] of Mysore Resettlement and Development Agency (MYRADA). In 1988-89, NABARD undertook a survey of 43 Non-Governmental Organizations (NGOs) spread over 11 States in India to study the functioning of SHGs and possibilities of collaboration between the banks and SHGs in the mobilization of rural savings and improving the delivery of credit to the poor.

Encouraged by the survey results, the NABARD impressed upon the Reserve Bank of India (RBI) to come out with a circular on July 24, 1991 advising the commercial banks (later Regional Rural Banks and Cooperative Banks also) to extend credit to SHGs under the pilot project of the NABARD. During the project period, the Association of Sarva Seva Farms (ASSEFA), Madras, promoted 214 groups, mobilized Rs. 1.4 million of thrift and disbursed credit of Rs. 2.3 million; Professional Assistance for Development Action (PRADAN), Madurai, promoted 313 groups, mobilized Rs. 1.3 million of thrift and disbursed credit of Rs. 3.9 million; People's Rural Education Movement (PREM), Behrampur promoted 829 groups, mobilized Rs. 1.9 million of thrift and disbursed credit of Rs. 1.9 million, Community Development Society (CDS), Alappuza promoted 150 groups mobilized Rs. 2 million of thrift and disbursed credit of Rs. 4.7 million. The results were thus quite encouraging.[30]

To formulate the mechanism further, the RBI constituted a working group in November 1994 to review the functioning of NGOs and SHGs and make suitable recommendations in April 1996. The RBI advised the banks that lending to the SHGs should be considered as an additional segment under priority sector advances and integrated with the mainstream credit operation.

The Self-Help Groups thus became a regular component of the Indian financial system since 1992 more particularly since 1996. The SHGs are small informal and homogeneous groups of not more than 20 members each. When financial transaction starts, there is no subsidy if the groups are identical.[31] The repayment rate tends to be lower in large groups,[32-33] as the magnitude of free-rider problem is high in large groups and the propensity to

default is high among heterogeneous groups.[34] These are the features which distinguish small, homogeneous and informal SHGs from large heterogeneous and formal cooperatives although both are found on the same principle of cooperation. Because of the heterogeneity and bureaucratic interference, the cooperatives in so many poor countries have been hijacked by the less poor, the land owners and by allied political interest.[35] Several countries including India have had problems with credit cooperative although it has succeeded in some other countries.[36]

The SHGs after being formed (generally by an external agency) start collecting a fixed amount (rarely variable amount) of thrift from each member regularly (mostly monthly). For about six months it only collects thrift, no loan is given to any member. Firstly, the working fund generated out of small thrift is negligible in the initial period, secondly, it tests the patience and tries to instill mutual trust among the members. During this period the groups are expected to open a savings account with financial institution which like to extend credit. After accumulating reasonable amount of resource, the group starts lending to its members for petty consumption needs. Claimants may be large but resource is small. This forces them to take appropriate decision to identify the most needy person with regard to endowment level and the purpose of the loan. A free and fair discussion removes the element of subjectivity from the decision making process, makes the borrowers understand the value of the credit and the importance of repayment and accountability to the group. The repayment of the loan along with interest and regular thrift enlarge the working fund and increase the scope of lending. Notwithstanding this, the working fund generated by the group may not be adequate to meet all types of credit needs of all the members. The group then approaches the financial institutions where it had opened the savings account. If the bank is satisfied with the group in terms of (i) genuineness of demand for credit, (ii) credit handling capacity of the members, (iii) repayment behaviour within the group, and (iv) the accounting system and maintenance of the records, it extends a term loan of smaller amount to the group. The group in turn continues to take decision

as in the past, the only difference being it has now higher amount of resource. In addition, the group is jointly liable to the bank for repayment. The group's responsibility in monitoring the members, therefore, increases. This joint liability, however, provides incentives or compels the group to undertake the burden of selection, monitoring and enforcement which would otherwise fall on the lender.[37]

This joint liability, decision making process and pressure at the group level are the most important aspects for the banks to do business with the poor, illiterate and informal groups. There is a huge demand for credit in small amounts for consumption health, education, marriage, petty production, petty trade etc. for very short to long durations which does not match with the supply menu of banks which consists of large amounts of loan for production purposes but not for very short periods. It is not the rigidity of the banks but their constraints due to high transaction costs and risk because of asymmetric information that they cannot extend such credit to individual borrowers. Individual borrowers, on the other hand face the problems of absorbing large amounts of credit for some unwanted purpose. Loan contract, therefore, does not take place between an individual small borrower and a formal lender basically because of mismatch of demand and supply of credit structures. Instead, when the financial institution extends credit to the SHG, (i) the transaction cost for the financial institution is minimized, because the group takes the decision to borrow on behalf of the members and also the responsibility to pay, (ii) the transaction cost of the individual members is reduced, because the members transact at the group level only, (iii) the mismatch between demand and supply is reduced, because the bank extends credit in lump sum amount and the group uses the amount according to its own needs, also repayment pattern of the members to the group and of the group to the bank need not be the same. When both the lender (financial institution) and the borrower (SHG) grow in mutual trust and the borrowers honour the previous contracts, the lender expresses its willingness to extend higher amount of credit and even provides cash credit facility implying more

flexibility and lesser interest burden for the borrower, the SHG in turn increases its capacity to manage higher amount of finance, develop entrepreneurial and communication skills, and logical ability, cooperative sense and finally, income and employment generating confidence. A sustainable financial relationship between the financial institution and the poor (SHG) people develops for their mutual benefit.

This is not confined to a single group of about 20 people. Either because of the efforts of the SHPI or demonstration effects, more groups start forming and functioning. A linkage among the groups also evolves. Some of the old leaders themselves take the role of facilitators for promoting other groups. The role of SHPI worker in a particular area then declines. He/She is now available for promotion of groups in other villages/areas. In some cases a number of nearby groups are federated. The federation is nothing but a coordinating mechanism and is not expected to assume any hierarchical role. Crucial decision making process for sanctioning loan to individual members remains with the SHG. The federation is basically supposed to (i) channelise funds from surplus to the deficit SHGs, (ii) promote more SHGs and act as facilitator for weak SHGs, and (iii) perform entrepreneurial jobs like helping the grassroots SHGs for backward and forward linkage and liaisoning with external agencies for the benefit of groups. The SHGs pay some membership fee for the sustenance of federation. Banks may sometimes find it more convenient and economical to deal with the federation rather than individual SHGs. It is, however, far better if the banks have direct links with the SHGs individually so that they can monitor their portfolios more closely. The federation may have stronghold over the SHGs, if the latter surrender substantial amount of management rights over their resources to the former which is against the principle of SHG promotion — a concept different from the existing cooperative structure. The peer pressure which is inversely proportional to the distance is much less at the federation level than at the village or group level. Nevertheless, the federation has an important role in the SHG framework, more as a development rather than a financial intermediator for the financial institutions.

The Grameen Bank Groups

Alternative to the SHGs, the other type of the group lending although in smaller number is through groups of Grameen Bank Group (GBG) model of Bangladesh. The groups are much smaller, i.e. of five members to start with thrift. However, unlike in the SHGs, the GBG does not manage its resources. The individual savings are deposited in the bank, and the members get loan directly from the bank. The GBG only helps the bank in screening the borrower and assuring repayment. Although the bank gets benefits, the GBG does not develop much skill in financial management. In fact, it does not have much financial resource to manage. Although 0.5 per cent of loan amount is deducted to develop a group fund, it is negligible in comparison to at least two per cent per month of rate of interest. As propensity to save (voluntary) for the poor people is much less than the compulsion to pay interest (involuntary), the forced saving in the GBG is much less than in the SHGs. The interest earned in the group after all belongs to its members. The GBG groups permanently remain dependent on the banks or promoter NGOs. But so many SHGs have been found to become independent banks for their credit requirement.[38]

A majority of the NGOs in India promote SHGs only, and the commercial Banks lend to the SHGs or to the NGOs or federation for 'on-lending' to the SHGs. Very few NGOs like ADITHI in Bihar, Activists for Social Alternatives (ASA) in Tamil Nadu, Loylam Bank of Rural Development and Organization (RDO) in Manipur and Society for Helping and Awakening Rural Poor through Education (SHARE) in Andhra Pradesh follow the Grameen Bank model for group lending.[39]

Besides these NGOs, one public sector bank, viz. Oriental Bank of Commerce (OBC) is experimenting with GBG model in Dehradun in Uttaranchal (now Uttarakhand) and Hanumangarh in Rajasthan which is called Oriental Bank Grameen Project (OBGP). Eight to ten groups in a village have been federated as a centre. To start with a completely dedicated branch in Rudrapur is transacting with such groups only. Interestingly, this branch

has started showing profit from the second year of existence, despite heavy expenditure on group formation in the initial period, it has been found to be more efficient than similar branches in that area; it has been found to be not only viable but also sustainable considering the business growth. Besides, a culture of subsidy-less credit has taken root in these villages.[40]

These SHPIs along with others who promote the SHGs, get reference from different national financial institutions like NABARD, Small Industries Development Bank of India (SIDBI), Friends of Women World Banking (FWWB), Housing and Urban Development Corporation (HUDCO), Rashtriya Mahila Kosh (RMK), Housing Development Finance Corporation (HDFC) and a host of other international institutions. Most of the above mentioned institutions except RMK and commercial banks, do not fix a ceiling on interest rates on the loan amount for lending to the members of the group. The groups are the best judges to determine the rate of interest. It should be as close to the market rate as possible. This excludes the possibility of moral hazard as an influential heterogeneous element in the group does not have any incentive to borrow from the group to lend at higher (market) rate of interest outside the group. Secondly, this interest amount goes back to the group fund which is owned by the members themselves. So this interest amount can be considered as deferred incomes which is forced saving in the current period. This acts as insurance substitute; increases the resiliency of food insecure households and also the risk bearing capacity which facilitates adoption of new technology.[41] New interest paid by the members varies between zero and bank rate of interest depending upon the composition of the working fund: (i) group saving, and (ii) bank credit.

Role of NGOs and SHPIs

The major factor behind the satisfactory growth of SHGs is the role of NGOs and SHPIs, and the Development Manager in the case of OBGP. These SHGs have not cropped up overnight. Whatever gain the SHG members have got or the benefits banks have received is because of hard work of fieldworkers (FWs) who

are generally women. These FWs require 5-6 visits to the village in a span of 3-4 months to form a group. Subsequent groups in the same village, however, take much less time for formation, if the earlier groups were successful. The FWs face lot of problems from different quarters while promoting these groups. The first problem while entering the village is the resistance they generally face. The second problem is related to work hazard which include: (i) inadequacy of training, (ii) attracting unhealthy alteration from the male world, (iii) need to work late in the night, and (iv) travelling through isolated areas in infrastructurally backward places. The NGOs which can support their FWs under these hazards can succeed in linking their SHGs to banks.

All these, however, are not free. The costs include: (i) salary of fieldworkers, (ii) travel cost of FWs from one village to another, (iii) training cost for FWs and other staff members and SHG members, and (iv) monitoring, controlling and supervision. For the village level framework only the first item is most important; training cost is required for the long term growth; travel cost is important for the operation in a cluster of villages; and supervision costs become significant when operational area is spread over more than one block or more than one district. For operation in one district, the district level monitoring is enough. Another tier of supervision is required if the SHG network covers a large number of districts or States.

Based on the data available from Mahila Arthik Vikas Mahamandal (MAVIM), a parastatal organization and the most SHPI in Maharashtra Rural Credit Project (MRCP), the average cost per SHG per annum in the first year ranges between Rs. 620 to Rs. 3,513 depending upon the items included in the cost calculated. The cost, however, declines over time as the SHG members themselves take up some of the responsibilities. In the fifth year the above cost on the basis of current price ranges between Rs. 555 and Rs. 2,868. This decline depends on the strategy of concentrating on a fewer villages, establishing a large number of groups there and then moving on to other villages.[42]

Microfinance

Microfinance refers to the entire range of financial and non-financial services, including skill upgradation and entrepreneurship development rendered to the poor for enabling them to overcome poverty. In the context of designing programme for the poor, micro-finance is recognized and accepted as one of the new development paradigms for alleviating poverty through social and economic empowerment of the poor with special emphasis on empowering women. The operational framework of microfinance, therefore, essentially rests on the premise that (a) formation of a self-employment enterprise is a viable alternate means of alleviating poverty, (b) lack of access to capital assets/credit acts as a constraint on the existing and potential micro enterprises, and (c) the poor are capable of saving despite their poor income level. In essence, therefore, microfinance may be referred to as an institutional mechanism of providing credit support in small amount and usually limited with small groups along with other complementary support such as training and other related service to the people with poor resources and skills for enabling them to take up economic activities.

Viewed purely from a historical perspective the origin of microfinance could be treated back to the beginning of the cooperative movement in Germany, where the movement was started in 1944 in the field of cooperative based system by the Raiffeeisen Societies as well as Rochdale Pioneers in England. Similarly, the enactment of Cooperative Credit Societies Act 1904 could be considered as the beginning of microfinance in India.

Attempts to formally define micro-credit or micro finance programmers usually refer to the objective of such programmes, viz., reaching small amounts of credit and other microfinancial services to the poor so as to promote income generating activities. The declaration of the Micro-Credit Summit held in Washington, D.C. in 1997 defined micro-credit programmes as those that "extend small loans to poor people for self-employment projects that generate income, allowing them to care for themselves and their families."[43] The Task Force on Microfinance established by

NABARD defines microfinance as the "provision of thrift, credit and other financial services and products of very small amounts to the poor in rural, semi-urban or urban areas for enabling them to raise their income levels and living standards."[44] while these definitions essentially seek to foreground the purpose of microfinance programmes ("income generation through self-employment"), the size of the financial services offered ("very small amounts") and the target clientele of such programmes ("the poor"), the terms microfinance and micro-credit have in the course of popular usage, come to signify not only the goal of reaching financial assistance to a designated target population, but, also to encompass a particular set of lending methodologies and transactional technologies, that set them apart from an earlier generation of credit programmes for the development of the agricultural sector. Tara Nair notes that microfinance actually refers to a system of decentralized credit delivery marked by the substitution of individual banking by social intermediation where peoples organizations are financial intermediaries.[45] According to the Microfinance Handbook, produced by the World Bank's sustainable Banking with the Poor Project, while the term microfinance refers to the provision of financial services to low income clients, many Microfinance Institutions (MFIs) provide social intermediation, training in financial literacy and management capabilities and, therefore, the definition of microfinance encompasses both financial and social intermediation.[46]

The current consensus aggressively propagated by some of the leading development organizations including the World Bank, the USAID and the DFID, which hold that microfinance-based programmes constitute the single most effective development intervention that can be universally adapted, may be attributed to the close association of microfinance with lending technologies that reduce transaction costs to the borrower and the lending institutions by lending to neighbourhood based 'primary groups', 'self-help groups' or 'solidaristic groups' (as they are variously called in different contexts). It is important to note that organizational structure of the peer groups based channel of

delivery of microfinancial service is remarkably heterogeneous, assumes diverse forms across the globe and ranges across a spectrum including the Grameen type groups of Bangladesh, the Indian Self-Help Groups, the village banking model prominent in Latin America etc. as the Microfinance Handbook of the World Bank points out, the MFIs in turn could be non-governmental organizations, credit unions, savings and loan cooperatives, government banks, commercial banks and non-bank financial institutions.[47] Although the term microfinance and micro credit are often used as interchangeable terms in the literature, it is generally agreed that micro credit or small loans for income generation or consumption purposes refers to one component of a larger array of microfinance services which could include savings, insurance and other related business development services as well.

Pros and Cons of Microfinance

An estimated 400-500 million people worldwide do not have access to financial services other than informal money lenders. This lack of access constraints private sector development and economic growth, and has distributional consequences since the poor and those living in rural areas are disproportionately affected. Microfinance has been touted as a promising means to reach the financially undeserved.[48]

The concept of microfinance is now several decade old. Its institutions provide small credits and other financial services to low income households and very small informal business. With constant innovation to meet the specific needs of the people they serve, microfinance institutions offer a menu of option. Through group lending, for example, they are able to provide credit, with minimal reliance on collateral, to group members who take turns borrowing and are jointly responsible for loan repayment.

Many microfinance institutions are owned and operated by non-governmental organizations which receive grants, and sometimes loans from multilateral development agencies, private charities, governments and similar institutions. In parts of the world, they follow the model of financial cooperatives, funding their lendings

from members deposits and capital contributions. While some have grown into formal, self-sustaining financial institutions, most remain informal and dependent upon donors funds.

But after years of experience with microfinance, surprisingly little is known about it. There are no comprehensive and authoritative data, for example, on the size of the industry or the populations served. Stylized facts, however, can be drawn from studies at the country and regional levels. These suggest that while the industry comprises a very large number of institutors — in the tens of thousands by some estimates — the number of people served and amounts of money involved are small. The studies also indicate that most microfinance activity is concentrated in a handful of countries and that only a few large institutions carry out a significant portion of the transactions.

The proponents advance many arguments in favour of microfinance. Although these loans carry a higher risk and, therefore, have a higher cost than traditional loans industry supporters and practitioners see benefits for poor families. There are numerous success stories to support their claims, and beyond the anecdotal evidence, their public policy argument in favour of microfinance. Economists have long recognized the existence of informational failure in financial markets that could prevent the realization of otherwise efficient transactions. Besides, access to financial services may help improve that living condition of the poor and empower them, ameliorating the "aid dependence syndrome" associated with other redistributive mechanisms.

But others point to concentrate arguments and note a number of caveats and risks. To them, it is not entirely clear whether microfinance techniques are effective in circumventing imperfections in financial markets or whether microfinance institution have an intrinsic advantages over traditional financial institutions. If they have an intrinsic advantage, it should perhaps materialize in better access to private funding, possibly various forms of cooperation and vertical integration within the financial industry. But to date, most external funding for the microfinance industry continues to come from donor sources, with very limited integration with traditional private financial integrations.

The excess reliance of the microfinance industry on donor funding prompts a second concern. Such subsidization comes at in the microfinance industry and creating unfair competitions with traditional financial institutions preventing them from expanding their outreach. Should microfinance institutions aim to be profitable and financially self-sufficient, perhaps after an initial phase of subsidization to help cover start up costs? Proponents of commercialization consider profitability as proof that microfinance is fulfilling its goals and see self-sufficiency as essential if the industry is to grow in the future.

They also voice concern that, as non-profit organizations, microfinance institutions may lack the appropriate ownership structure, staff, operational system and incentives to improve operating efficiency. On the other hand, those who see microfinance chiefly as a poverty alleviation tool, stress the importance of keeping the costs of financial services as low as possible while reaching the most destitute. In their view, the merits of subsidization should be decided on the basis of a cost-benefit analysis with other anti-poverty programmes.

A related open question is whether microfinance institutions are a cost-effective tool for redistributing scarce resources. How do they compare with the alternatives? While these institutions are presumed to have some advantages over more traditional redistributive mechanisms (notably through empowerment of the poor and recycling of funds through loan repayments), there is, in reality, too little data to compare their relative costs and benefits. Since providing financial services to the very poor is costly relative to the volume of resources in administrative and operational expenses. Besides, the increasing popularity of microfinance among donors combined with the lack of hard evidence on its cost effectiveness, also risks diverting scarce resources from other basic redistributive mechanism such as healthcare and education.

If it is to realize its potential, the microfinance industry will need to tackle a number of important challenges which lie ahead. One of the most important of these is achieving financial sustainability and integrating the microfinance industry into the formal financial sector. Studies indicate that only one per cent of

existing microfinance institutions worldwide are financially stable. Despite apparently high loan recovery rates, the small scale of microfinance operations, combined with the costs of reaching out to clients, pushes up operating costs and absorbs most of the interest margins. The new financially self-sustainable microfinance institutions tend to be longer, spreading fixed costs and achieving greater efficiency. But those striving to become commercially viable do not tend to target the very poor.

A related challenge entails the interaction, While there are success stories of microfinance institutions growing into formal financial institutions, as well as banks entering the microfinance niche and business relationships developing between banks and microfinance institutions, no clear trends have yet emerged.

There is also the matter of whether and how the microfinance industry should be regulated. So far, the industry has evolved largely outside the regulatory framework which applies to formal financial institutions. Prudential regulation of microfinance institutions would typically be predicted on whether they pose a threat to financial stability or engage in deposit intermediation. The weak approach applied to date in most countries thus seems justified, considering the small size of the industry and its frequent reliance on deposit funding.

As microfinance institutions become large and eventually move into traditional financial intermediation, however, regulatory and supervisory approaches would need to be considered. The optional approach would have to weigh the specific circumstances of individual countries and avoid diverting scarce supervisory resources from more systematically important financial institutions or over boarding microfinance institutions with information and compliance requirements. In some cases, a higher regulatory approach may be warranted, but it would have to minimize discrimination against traditional financial institutions and guard against establishing legal loopholes and opportunities for regulatory arbitrage.

Having the necessary information at hand is critical to addressing these challenges. While the information gap has been increasingly filled by independent data sets of varying quality and

coverage, the lack of generating more systematic information is complicated by a lack of consensus on the data needed, and the absence of clear cut definitions of the products and service that qualify as microfinance. An ongoing World Bank initiative is seeking to assess existing data sets, determine current and anticipated data needs, and formulate the best strategy for closing these gaps. But information gathering is further complicated by informality and dispersion of the industry, while the costs of data collection may prove excessively burdensome for microfinance institutions.

Ultimately, the path to developing a sound and sustainable microfinance industry and deepening financial services will provide the answers to these questions.

Microfinance for All

Microfinance is increasingly being touted as a miracle cure for poverty. Although microfinance has been around in various forms for thousands of years, its modern incarnation is most closely tied to Mohammad Yunus, the founder of the Grameen Bank in Bangladesh. In his autobiography he described, how as a professor in Bangladesh he came to understand the importance of finance for the poor. Horrified by the consequences of the recent famine, he left the sheltered walls of the University to find how the poor made a living.

In a neighbouring village, he strikes up a conversation with a young mother making bamboo stools. He learned that she needed 22 cents to buy the raw material for the stools. Because the young mother did not have money, she borrowed it from an intermediary to whom she was forced to sell the stools as repayment. She made a profit of only 2 cents. Yunus was appalled; finance would enable her to sell directly to the customers. But the intermediary would not offer her finance, for he would lose his hold over her. For want of 22 cents, the women's labour was captive.

In this vignette, many see the worst evil of capitalism; exploitation of labour by capital. But this situation could not be further form the essence of free market capitalism; free access to

a competitive financial market or to a friendly financial institution where the poor can borrow at a reasonable rate which keeps their labour captive.[49]

The poor have no access to finance—loans, savings accounts, cash withdrawals, and insurance. Let us dispense with one explanation of this phenomenon immediately: active discrimination against the poor. In a world hungry for profits, it is hard to imagine financial firms forgoing only customers. But passive discrimination may be one explanation: when a financial institution caters to the middle class, it may exclude the poor. The poor feel uncomfortable entering a bank, they are awed by the better educated and better dressed bank clerk.

Social distance may matter. Study by the Federal Reserve Bank of Chicago found that minority households, alike in all ways but rare were turned down for credit more often than others. A more detailed investigation revealed that loan officers were less likely to help minority applicants overcome problems with their applications, without intending to discriminate the loan officers ended up doing just that.

There are other forms of distance. The poor may have no one in their social network (and thus no one they trust who know the various financial transactions available). As a result, they may not know enough to choose wisely. Given the small volume of transactions, the poor are likely to undertake, the financial providers may not think it worthwhile to educate them even if the gulf of distrust that initially separate the two parties could be narrowed.

Finally, to the extent that bricks and mortar are involved, it makes far more sense for a profit minded bank to set up shop in richer neighbourhood, where there is more business, than in a poorer one. Given the physical distance between where the poor live and where the bank is located, the poor may simply not have access to financial service. This is a chicken-and-egg problem. If bank branches were more welcoming, more poor people would use them, the branch could profitably be located nearer the poor, and the presence of poor customers in the branches would encourage other poor people to use them.

As for lack of access to credit, common explanations are that the poor are not creditworthy, because they are untrustworthy, they do not have business opportunities or steady jobs, they have little collateral, and given the small size of transactions they are likely to make, the transaction costs are too high. On closer examination, some of these explanations are questionable. There is no reason why the poor should be intrinsically more untrustworthy than their richer brethren and studies show that the poor are more likely to be charitable than the rich.

Also the poor's lack of access to services means that, at the very least, these are profitable opportunities for those who can get loans and establish themselves as intermediaries. Many have heard of the Bangladesh villager who borrows money to buy a cell phone and then pays off loan by charging other villagers to use it. Besides intermediaries, all manners of self-employment; sewing, delivering small items, making handicrafts could be facilitated with a small amount of capital for a sewing machine, a bicycle or tools. The poor are not different from other small entrepreneurs in that managerial advice and access to business networks can make the difference between success and failures.

But one cannot minimize two problems. First, the poor have little legal collateral. But a lack of collateral does not seem to be a binding constraints for the middle class in many developing countries, who can borrow against their future salaries or the asset they are buying, such as a car or a house. The greater problems is that it is harder to keep track of the income the poor generate (unlike middle class salaries, which are typically paid by established organization) or the small assets they seek to buy, such as a bicycle.

Second, it is costly for financial institutions to deal with the poor. Accepting a rupee one deposit costs as much as accepting one of Rs. 1,000. It thus makes sense to allow financial institutions to charge the poor higher rates. But government often impose 'usury' ceilings on the rates financial institutions can charge, shutting out the very people these laws are ostensibly meant to help.

The microfinance revolution recognizes many of these problems and attempts to overcome them in innovative ways.

Distance is overcome, typically by the financier's going to the poor instead of obliging the poor to come to the financiers. Loan officers often are not far removed in social status and wealth from their customers. Also, the micro credit process is as much about education as about finance. For instance, one way to enable the poor to build a support network while giving them social collateral is to involve them in group lending schemes. The first member of a group gets a loan, but the second member must wait until a substantial portion of the first member's loan is repaid. Peer pressure ensures that the loan is repaid, and many micro-credit organizations demonstrate extraordinary repayment rates.

Has the micro-credit revolution succeeded in its goal? Clearly more poor people have access to finance. What is less clear is the extent of subsidy involved in extending this access to them. Group lending is very cost intensive and involves the time of both the loan officer and the group. If group lending involves subsidies, is that the best way to suspend those subsidies? Also, non-traditional microfinance tends to distance participants from the more formal financial system. This is not a problem unless the microfinance system does not grow fast enough and cannot transfer successfully participants to the formal system.

How can microfinance be made more viable? Asking this question relegates financial services for the poor to a separate and unequal existence. Instead one should ask how one can make financial services available to all. If one focuses just on finance for the poor, the thinking immediately shifts to subsidies and charities, which hurts the quality of service. Not only do the poor lack the collective voice to demand better services, but government money can spoil the credit culture. As one participant in the women's cooperative said, "We do not default now, because we would be defaulting on our sisters' money. If we took money from the government, default rates would go up because would all feel we were defaulting only on the government."

In truth, in many poor countries, the middle class also has limited access to finance. The same mechanisms that will expand their access will often expand access for the very poor as well. By defining the problem more broadly to include the middle class,

one can enlist a powerful supporter in the common fight for access. In the process, the links between the formal and informal financial systems will strengthen, allowing the poor to migrate upward.

What needs to be done? For one, the government should encourage the creation of infrastructure that can allow technology to bring down transaction costs. Giving every individual a national identification number and creating credit registers where lenders share information about their clients, repayment records can be enormously valuable. All borrowers would then have an asset—their future access to credit—that they implicitly offer as collateral when they obtain a loan. The government should also reduce the costs of registering or reprocessing collateral, as well as eliminate usury laws. Recognizing, through that the poor people can fall prey to unscrupulous operators, the government should improve consumer protection laws and services.

Perhaps most important, the government should encourage competition in the financial sector. As private sector banks find their traditional business coming under fierce competition, they will seek out non-traditional business, including providing services to the very poor. Given the right environment, the private sector banks have the ability, the incentives, and the resources to develop innovation services for the poor. A number of banks around the world, including City Bank, ICICI Bank and ING have started doing perniciously the same.

In sum, let us not kill the microfinance movement with kindness. If we want to become more than a fad, a temporary cause for the glitter, it has to follow the clear and unsentimental path of adding value and making money. On that path lies the possibility of a true, and large scale, escape from poverty.

Banking for the Poor

Microfinance is the banking for the poor. It has given millions of poor people with no credit history, collateral or steady income an access to financial services. Half of the world's population, nearly three billion poor people, lack such access. Most mainstream banks have considered the poor high-risk and hard to serve, because

they often live scattered across remote areas and because the small loans they need are costly to make and maintain. But microfinance which specializes in providing small loans and other financial services even to the world's most destitute, challenges those traditional assumptions.[50]

In the past three decades microfinance has mushroomed from acting non-profit experiment of Grameen Bank in Bangladesh to a global industry. Grameen Bank and its founder Professor Muhammad Yunus won the 2006 Nobel Peace Prize for pioneering efforts to provide financial services to the poorest of the poor. Many enthusiasts believe that microfinance is an important tool in the effort to end world poverty. Whether they are right is still open to question.

Today, microfinance players include government, philanthropists, social investors and commercial banks, which are attracted by the potential for profit and corporate social responsibility. Customers can still go to a Grameen Bank type institutions, but they can also go to microfinance credit unions, public sectors and commercial banks. Besides tiny business loans, MFIs offer deposits, savings and insurance products. Microfinance is growing, because need to insure assets such as farming equipment that they purchase with micro credit. In fact, MFIs are as important in providing savings, vehicles and transportation services as they are in lending.

Microfinance customers live in both rural and urban areas—the rural poor borrow for cattle fattening, dairy farming, bamboo making or weaving, whereas the urban poor borrow to become street vendors, rickshaw drivers or seamstresses. Moreover, microfinance has moved well beyond its roots in developing countries—some MFIs now serve poor people in industrial countries.

Still, reliable data are hard to come by. The number of MFIs operating today is estimated to range anywhere from 300 to 25,000 depending on the definition. The Microfinance Information Exchange (MIX) known as the 'Bloomberg' of microfinance reports on 1,000 microfinance institutions worldwide, nearly half of which are self-sustainable. The number of borrowers is hard to pin down, with estimates ranging from 30 million to 500 million.

The Washington based advocacy group Microcredit Summit Campaign verified more than 64 million worldwide in 2006 up from more than 9 million borrowers in 2000 (Table 1.1). Many more millions of poor people have their savings in MFIs.

Table 1.1 : Global Shot up in Microfinance Business (2000-2006)

Year	*No. of institutions verified*	*Number of poorest clients verified*
2000	78	9274175
2001	138	12752645
2002	211	21771448
2003	234	35837356
2004	286	47458191
2005	330	58450926
2006	420	64062221

Source : *State of the Microcredit Summit Campaign Report* (2006).

MFIs assume that their clients are clever enough to handle their own affairs, but do not assume that all the poor will be reliable borrowers. They have adopted two basic approaches: group lending and individual lending.

Group Lending

The Grameen Bank of Bangladesh is considered the pioneer of the group lending model which has now been adopted in many countries. Individual borrowers are required to form a group and take responsibility for each other's loans. Grameen Bank depends primarily of peer pressure to guarantee repayment. Moreover, it limits risks by targeting female borrowers, who are considered more reliable because of family-based community ties. In early 2007, the Grameen Bank reported almost of million borrowers—96 per cent of them poor, illiterate women from remote villages. And since 1970, $ 6 billion has been lent, with a repayment rate of 98 per cent.

Individual Lending

These loans are bigger and are made to individuals without a collective guarantee and on more flexible terms. Typical borrowers

are not the very poor seeking to start business; but the self-employed poor who are skilled business people. In some cases the borrower has a small amount of collateral. Action—leading MFI operating in Latin America and the Caribbean, Africa, and Asia, has adopted individual lending in the form of small, short term loans of $ 100 to $ 500 at interest rates which reflect the cost of lending. Loan officers look not only at a borrower's financial wherewithal but also at references from customers and neighbours. Incentives such as the possibility of borrowing progressively larger amounts and the opportunity to get business and vocational training encourage repayment. In countries like Bolvia, credit bureaus have been set up to enforce repayment.

Although microfinance appears to be a promising way to provide financial services to the poor, there is a considerable debate about it.

If microfinance can achieve commercial success, it can move beyond relying on subsidies, which today total hundreds of crores of rupees. MFIs are expected to increase their reach among the urban poor—who, because they are concentrated, are easier to serve. But it will be challenging to achieve sustainability while reaching the remote rural poor especially those at the bottom of the income ladder because of the high costs and risks involved.

A microfinance movement that becomes mainly commercial, might shift its focus from the poorest borrowers to relatively better off, more conventionally safe customers. Thus MFIs may evolve into direct competitions with commercial banks, and the special benefits for the poorest may be lost in the search for commercial sustainability. Yet in some locations heavily subsidized MFIs may be crowding out sustainable MFIs and the subsidies may, therefore, be of little additional benefit. One may also ask whether MFIs should concentrate on the poorest borrowers, or are other mechanisms better, given the constraints on aid budgets.

The interest rates on microfinance range from 20 per cent to 35 per cent (even after adjusting for inflation). MFIs are subject to significantly higher costs than commercial banks because of lending and administrative costs (for example, identifying and screening clients). For some MFIs, interest rates cover the cost of doing

business whereas others add a premium for risk. Some say that despite the high interest rates, the loans will provide positive welfare benefits for borrowers and that costs will fall as the infrastructure of the industry grows. There is a broad consensus that increased compensation is the key to driving down interest rates.

The regulatory and legal approach used for large scale commercial financial institutions may not be appropriate for microfinance. Countries such as Morocco and Kenya have developed legal frameworks to regulate MFIs. Key challenges are how best to protect depositors and borrowers while promoting the MFI sector, how to limit the costs of MFI supervision and how to prevent regulation from restricting innovation and competition, what, for example, is the balance between consumer protection, the regulatory burdens, and sustainability and development.

Technology may provide some answers. Today 'branchless banking' is active in the Philippines, South Africa and Colombia, commercial players are using point of sale devices and mobile phones to connect with rural poor, licensing local merchants and shop owners to make cash transactions on their behalf. The availability of such transfer services is especially important is areas where families rely on remittances from relatives working in economic centres or abroad. Technology will likely reduce transaction costs, allowing MFIs to grow and reach more customers.

Rural Development

Rural development has been drawing increasing attention of the government across the world. In the Indian context rural development assumes special significance for two important reasons: First, about two-thirds of the population still live in villages and there cannot be any progress so long as rural areas remain backward. Second, the backwardness of the rural sector would be major impediment to the overall progress of the economy. The industrial sector cannot think of sufficient demand for its products so long as the rural income are low.[51]

Rural development does not imply setting up of major industries in rural areas. Rural development on a sustainable basis is possible only when the rural resources are put to optimum use enhancing a steady growth in rural output and generating surplus income. This strategy would ensure self-reliance, self-competence, resourcefulness, problem solving capability, the ability to discern and wisdom to use knowledge.

Rural development remains an uphill task due to the complexity of problems existing in the rural sector. The rural sector requires a multidimensional approach to reach cost-effective solutions to these problems.

Rural development is a unique experience in India's attempts towards development planning in order to overcome economic and social backwardness in its vast widespread village society by inducing growth in agriculture and industry, and checking demographic profligacy through appropriate measures within an open democratic framework.[52] The rural society in the process is being lifted to join the stream of urbanization and modernization, While one must say that India has demonstrated certain notable achievements alongside of certain deficiencies in planning the immutable fact is that a large segment of our society especially in the rural areas, still lives in poverty. The different approaches to rural development and the programme and projects thereon target group oriented and location specific and their ultimate impact in enabling the affluent to become more affluent are common knowledge today. Various factors go into the formulation of their approaches, planning and implementation to remove poverty. The government agencies take their programmes to the villages at the implementation level and several problems and difficulties arise thereafter.

The rural areas suffer from poor infrastructural facilities. The villages are yet to emerge as the main centres of production activity. The proclivity is to produce goods in urban areas, even to meet the basic needs of rural consumers. This apart, the rural population requires not one but a few inputs and services. These have to be provided at the right time in the right sequence. This demands the right kind of coordination amongst agencies extending help to the rural sector.

It has been rightly pointed out that a purely agricultural country remains backward even in respect of agriculture. Much of the labour force in India depends on agriculture, not because it is remunerative, but because there is no alternative employment opportunities. This is a major cause for the backwardness reportedly seen in the Indian agricultural sector. We must opt for a type of rural industrialization which extend full support to the agricultural sector. A part of the labour force now engaged in agriculture needs to be shifted to non-agricultural occupations.

The new agricultural technology should be credited for the present comfortable foodgrain position. But the Green Revolution too has created some problems. Moreover, the first phase of the Revolution is said to have reached the saturation point. Agricultural scientists are laying stress on its second phase which alone can give the real boost needed by India's agricultural sector. Irrigation has emerged as the crucial input contributing to the success of the revolution. The farmers no doubt require price incentives, but their problems can be solved only when there is a steady increase in agricultural productivity. Technology should be cost effective and give good financial returns to the farming community.

Given the unfavourable power structure in rural India, the benefits of the revolution or even the anti-poverty programmes do not reach to benefit the rural population. The workers and small producers in India cannot put in their best in an inequities atmosphere. Therefore, production suffers. Also the rural sector cannot take advantage of opportunities available so long as the institutions are dominated by the risk.

For various regions, for lack of political will, land reforms have been neglected. The rural population requires support in terms of assets like land to improve their income levels and social status. Diversification of agriculture is needed to improve the plight of the agricultural labours. The rural artisans and other sections would benefit only when the rural economy is diversified with stress on non-farming activities Of course, organization of the rural sector is needed to put an end of all kinds of exploitations continuing in the rural sector for a long time.

The government has been implementing special schemes for the benefit of the rural sector since the early 1970s—worth mentioning are those for wage employment generations; others for asset distribution. However, these schemes have been implemented in a perfunctory manner. The 'income generating capacity' has failed to register an increase and thus remains limited. The situation worsened subsequently because of the absence of cost effective groundwork to implement these schemes.

However, if these resources do not exist, strategies should be worked out to generate the same to meet the needs and demands of the rural sector. Studies relating to the special schemes show irregularities in the identification of beneficiaries and programmes. The schemes should be based on available resources and needs. The industries being set up in rural areas must have forward and backward linkages which alone can ensure their steady progress. Above all, the special schemes must form an integral part of micro level planning. The stress should be on economically viable schemes which alone can strengthen rural economy. The implementation, monitoring and evaluation stages are crucial for the success and financial sustainability of the rural sector.

The rural sector also requires institutional credit to take up economically viable projects. But it needs to be noted that credit alone cannot deliver the goods. There is what is called 'credit absorption capacity' of the region. This depends on the implementation of economically viable schemes. Hence, the formulation of economic plans should precede the preparation of credit plans. There are certain agencies like the cooperatives, regional rural banks and farmer's service societies which are most appropriate to serve the rural population, but their performance needs to be 'toned up'. Of course, cheap credit needs to be discouraged.

The rural sector can derive due benefits from development schemes only with the help of the administration which needs to be strengthened. The Panchayati Raj Institution (PRI) should assume their new responsibilities in the development sphere. Of course, they should enjoy both functional and financial autonomy.

The rural people should take active part in all stages of the

planning process. At present, they look up to the government for each and everything. This dependency syndrome needs to be dispelled. People's participation in the development sphere is crucial. The people must be made fully aware of the opportunities available and how to take advantage of them.

In a vast sphere like rural development, voluntary agencies play an important role in providing infrastructure, in educating the public on development issues and opportunities available and in curbing leakages. They see to it that the government machinery becomes more responsive to the growing needs of the rural sector. They can tone up the rural delivery system by improving the performance of public agencies like the public distribution system. In short, the voluntary agencies are expected to provide the missing links in the long chain of rural reconstruction.

Concerted efforts are needed to bridge the widening gap between rhetoric and reality in the rural sphere. Untrammelled flow of credit into the rural sector is not the answer to unemployment and poverty problems. Successes on the rural front depends on the optimum utilization of the available local resources. Economic development ought to be based on individual and group initiatives.

Concept of Rural Development

The term 'Rural Development' is a sub-set of the broader term 'Development'. However, it is defined, development is a universally cherished goal of individuals, families, communities and nations all over the world. Development is also natural in the sense that all forms of life on the earth have an inherent urge to survive and develop. Given these two attributes, i.e. its universal supremacy as a goal and its natural occurrences, development deserves a scientific study and analysis. Hence it is not surprising that the subject of development has been studied by scholars of all faiths, ideologies and disciplines.[53]

Development is a subjective and value-loaded concept and hence, there cannot be a consensus as to its meaning. The term is used differently in diverse contexts. It basically means 'unfolding',

'revealing' or 'opening up' something which is latent. When applied to human being, it therefore, means 'unfolding' or 'opening up' their potential power. Generally speaking, the term development implies a change which is desirable. Since what is desirable at a particular time, place and in a particular culture may not be desirable at other places, or at other times at the same place and in the same cultural milieu, it is impossible to think of a universally acceptable definition of development. At best development in the context of society could be conceptualized as a set of desirable societal objectives which society seeks to achieve. Thus defined, development is cherished by all individuals, communities and nations, irrespective of their culture, religion and spatial location.

These days, sustainable development has become a buzzword. According to the World Commission on Environment and Development (WCED),[54] "Sustainable development is development that meets the needs of the present without compromising the ability of future generations to meet their own needs". In simple words, sustainable development is a process in which the set of desirable societal objectives, or the development index, does not decrease over time. Constancy of natural capital stock, including natural resources and the environment, is a necessary condition for sustainable development. The set of 'sufficient conditions' includes an appropriate institutional framework and governance system for implementation of sustainable development policy.

The term 'rural development' connotes overall development of rural areas with a view to improve the quality of life of rural people. In this sense, it is a comprehensive and multidimensional concept, and encompasses the development of agriculture and allied activities, village and cottage industries and crafts, socio-economic infrastructure, community services and facilities, and above all, the human resources in rural areas. As a phenomenon, rural development is the end result of interactions between various physical, technological, economic, socio-cultural and institutional factors. As a strategy, it is designed to improve the economic and social well-being of a specific group of people—the rural poor. As a discipline, it is multi-disciplinary in nature, representing an

intersection of agricultural, social behavioural, engineering and management sciences. In the words of Robert Chambers:

> "Rural Development is a strategy to enable a specific group of people, poor rural women and men, to gain for themselves and their children more of what they want and need. It involves helping the poorest among those who seek a livelihood in the rural areas to demand and control more of the benefits of rural development. The group includes small scale farmers, tenants and the landless."[55]

Thus the term rural development may be used to imply anyone of the above mentioned conditions. To avoid ineffective floundering among the myriad connotations, one should define rural development as a 'process leading to sustainable improvement in the quality of life of rural people especially the poor'.

In addition to economic growth, this process typically involves changes in popular attitudes, and in many cases even in customs and beliefs. In a nutshell, the process of rural development must represent the entire gamut of change by which a social system moves away from a state of life perceived as 'unsatisfactory' towards a materially and spiritually better condition of life. The process of rural development may be compared with a train in which each coach pushes the one ahead of it, and is in turn pushed by the one behind, but it takes a powerful engine to make the whole train move. The secret of success in rural development lies in identifying, and if needed, developing a suitable engine to attach to the train. There is no universally valid guidelines to identify appropriate engines of rural development, if at all they exist. It is a choice that is influenced by time, space and culture.

Elements of Rural Development

Whatever the geographic location, culture and historical stage of development of a society, there are at least three basic elements

which are considered to constitute the true meaning of rural development. They are as follows :

1. *Basic Necessities of Life :* People have certain basic needs, without which it would be impossible or very difficult for them to survive. The basic necessities include food, clothes, shelter, basic literacy, primary health care and security of life and property. When anyone or all of them are absent or in critically short supply, we may state that a condition of 'absolute underdevelopment' exists. Provision of the basic necessities of life to everybody is the primary responsibility of all economies, whether they are capitalist, socialist or mixed. In this sense 'we may claim that economic growth (increased per capita availability of basic necessities) is a necessary condition for improvement of the quality of life' of rural people, which is rural development.
2. *Self-Respect :* Every person/nation seeks some sort of self-respect, dignity or honour. Absence or denied of self-respect indicates lack of development.
3. *Freedom :* In this context freedom refers to political or ideological freedom economic freedom and freedom from social servitude. As long as a society is bound by the servitude of men to nature, ignorance, other men, institutions and dogmatic beliefs, it cannot claim to have achieved the goal of development. Servitude in any form reflects a state of underdevelopment.

The new economic view of development considers reduction or elimination of poverty, inequality and unemployment as an index of development. Seers[56] succinctly tackled the basic questions of the meaning of development when he wrote :

> "The question to ask about country's development are therefore : What has been happening to poverty? What has been happening to unemployment? What has been happening to inequality. If all three of these have declared from high levels, then, beyond doubt, this has been a period

> of development of the country, concerned. If one or two of these central problems have been growing worse, especially if all three have, it would be strange to call the result 'development' even if per capita income doubles."

Why Rural Development?

Since time immemorial, India has been, still continues to be and will remain in the foreseeable future, a land of village communities. As a matter of fact, the village was the basic unit of administration as far back as the Vedic age; there is a reference to 'graminic' (village leader) in the *Rig Veda*. The predominantly rural character of India's national economy is reflected in the very high proportion of its population living in rural areas: It was 89 per cent in 1901, 83 per cent in 1951, 80 per cent in 1971, 74 per cent in 1991 and 72.22 per cent in 2001. With more than 740 million of its population living in rural areas, and with the rural sector contributing about 30 per cent of the gross domestic product, no strategy of socio-economic development for India which neglects the rural people and rural areas can be successful. The rural character of the economy, and the need for regeneration of rural life was stressed by Mahatma Gandhi.[57] He wrote in the *Harijan*:[58]

> "India is to be found not in its few cities but in its 7,00,000 villages. But the town dwellers have believed that India is to be found in its towns and the villages were created to minister to our needs. We have hardly paused to enquire if those poor folk get sufficient to eat and clothe themselves with and whether they have a roof to shelter themselves from sun and rain."

He further wrote in *Harijan* (29 August, 1936) :

> "I would say that if the village perishes, India would perish too. It will be no more India. Her own mission in the world will get lost. The revival of village life is possible only when it is no more exploited"

Rural development is, therefore, an absolute and urgent necessity in India now and will continue to be so in the future. It is the *sine qua non* of the development of India.

Dimensions of Development

Literature on development abounds in a variety of dilemmas and dogmas such as rural *vs.* urban development, agricultural *vs.* industrial development, primacy of capital *vs.* labour and natural/autonomous *vs.* induced/planned. A brief critique of these dilemmas seems in order to clarify some of the issues.

Rural *vs.* Urban Development

Economic development in western countries/economies has been associated with growing urbanization as reflected in the increasing proportion of the urban population. Hence, there is a tendency among economists to consider urbanization as an index of development. Growing urbanization is obviously the consequence of the growing concentration of infrastructural networks and capital incentive industrial enterprises in urban centres. This type of concentration has resulted in the existence of what is known in the literature on the economics of development as 'dualism' or co-existence of two separate economic sub-systems in an economy in many developing countries. On the one hand, there exists in the economy a small but highly modern and developed urban sub-sector which absorbs most of the material, financial and educated and talented manpower resource. On the other hand, a very large but traditional and underdeveloped rural sub-sector characterized by widespread poverty, unemployment and low productivity, which forms the majority of the population. In many developing countries both the sub-sectors co-exist, but without those linkages between them that were once the main factors which contributed to the development of today's developed countries.

At the other extreme, there is another dogma rapidly emerging in many developing countries that rural development is prerequisite for overall development and, hence, it deserves the highest priority in terms of allocation of resources. In their

enthusiasm to promote the cause of rural development, the proponents of this school of thought usually tend to either disregard or underplay the linkages between the rural and the urban sub-sectors of the economy. What is needed is a new approach to development which explicitly recognizes the interlinkages and complementarily between the rural and the urban sub-sectors, and provides for integrating them completely.

Agricultural *vs.* Industrial Development

Closely analogous to rural *vs.* urban development dilemma, is the dogma that industrialization alone can modernize agriculture and thereby raise agricultural productivity, wage rates and provide employment to labour displaced by mechanization of agriculture. This has led many developed economists to associate development with industrialization. Following this dogma many developing countries have established highly capital-intensive and sophisticated industrial enterprises, similar to those in development countries. Such efforts, however, have often led to bitter disappointment when the desired results failed to materialise. Such projects are more showcases whose contribution to development is negligible and sometimes even negative, because they are built at the expense of enterprises which meet the basic needs of people. Nations with high agricultural potential spend enormous resources on agricultural imports and depend heavily on imported technology, capital and management. At the same time, local agriculture stagnates and nutritional standards remain far lower than those in the advanced countries. Distribution of income is tilted in favour of industrialists against farmers, workers and consumers.

At the other extreme is agricultural fundamentalism which holds that in the initial stages of development when per capita incomes are low, agriculture alone can serve as an instrument of development and that increased agricultural productivity is a prerequisite to increased income and industrialization. The proponents of this dogma argue for allocation of more resources and attention to agriculture; rather than to industry. They do not, however, realize that agriculture cannot develop alone, and that

concomitant development of industry and supporting infrastructure is essential not only for the growth of the national economy, but also for the advancement of agriculture itself. The non-agricultural sector with new farm inputs and services vital to its development, as also to absorb the manpower rendered surplus as a result increased labour productivity in agriculture.

Agricultural fundamentalism has generally resulted in growth without development, mainly because of lack of linkages between the agricultural and non-agricultural sectors, and partly because of distribution of income being skewed in favour of big landlords.

The establishment of small and less capital intensive industrial enterprise in rural areas, along with introduction of new technology in agriculture is likely to establish linkages between agriculture and industry. The Israeli strategy of integrating agricultural and industrial sectors is worth emulating. In Israel, industrial enterprises were set up in rural areas, along with the introduction of more efficient methods of agricultural production. Initially, the industrial enterprises included mostly services and industries connected with agriculture, such as feed mix plants, factories for processing agricultural produce and for production of tools and various accessories. Most of these enterprises are owned either fully or in part by the farmers themselves. In course of time, the scope of industrial enterprise was widened to include activities completely unconnected with agriculture such as jewellery, manufacture and ceramics.[59]

Capital *vs.* Labour Dogma

This is a legacy inherited by today's development economists from their predecessors in the developed countries, who considered capital to be the key instruments of development. The Harrod-Domar model represents a typical example of this dogma. In this model, the rate of growth is expressed as the product of the savings rate and the output capital ratio. Under the assumptions that 'capital and labour cannot be substituted of each other, and that labour is in surplus supply, capital becomes the overriding constraints on economic growth. This dogma received a further

fillip from those techno-economists who held that all new technology is embodied in capital.

Capital fundamentalism has been blindly accepted by development economists and planners in the developing countries. This has led to the promulgation of a number of policies in these countries, all aimed at increasing savings, redistributing income from the workers to the capitalists, granting monopoly rights to national and multinational corporations, transferring resources from the private to the public sector, increasing dependence on foreign aid and loans, and underpricing capital, particularly foreign exchange for capital goods. This has resulted in a number of adverse effects on the economies of these nations. For example, underpricing foreign exchange for capital goods has killed the incentive to develop labour-intensive technologies adapted to the domestic needs and circumstances, and has led to premature and excessive mechanization in a number of sector, resulting in unemployment of labour and underutilisation of other domestic resources.

Capital fundamentalism has extended to cover human capital formation as well. Higher education is highly subsidized in most of the developing countries, with the result that millions of college and university graduates are added annually to the pool of the unemployed white-collar proletariat. In India, enormous investment has been made in the institutes of higher learning, particularly in the fields of engineering, technology, agriculture, medicine and management. Many of the graduates of these institutes usually do not like the work environment and compensation rates prevailing in the country, and seek jobs abroad. Thus the scarce resource invested in their education and training are lost to the country. It seems that at this stage of India's economic and technological development, one needs more institutes to train barefoot agricultural and other technicians, engineers, doctors and rural managers, rather than institutes for highly advanced training. Similarly, one wonders why we should produce more college and university graduates in disciplines like arts, science, commerce, agriculture and veterinary science than we need. The demand for higher education could be brought down

to match the availability of jobs, by pricing it at its real resources cost which is nakedly higher than the present cost. In the USA and other Western countries, most students terminate their studies at the high school level and become self-employed but their training is broad-based and highly practical and relevant to their context, with the result that high school graduates are able and confident to set up and manage their own small business or take up wage paid jobs. One should learn from this experience, and make education less capital intensive and more relevant to requirements. It is needed to thoroughly overhaul the present education policy which has become outdated and irrelevant in the context of the changed environment. More emphasis needs to be placed on vocationalisation of education.

Autonomous *vs.* Induced Development

In every country, some development takes place naturally or autonomously over time but its level and pace may not be adequate to maintain a reasonably satisfactory standard of living. In such situations, some sort of intervention is needed to speed up the pace of natural development. Development planning is one of the forms of interventions that has become a fad in many developing countries of the world, and is considered a magic door to development. In fact, even the advanced countries have come to realize the need for some sort of planning or government intervention in the economic process. It seems that there is a growing consensus around the statement that any planning is better than no planning at all, and decentralized planning is better than centralized planning.

However, it should be realized that planning can make a positive contribution only if it facilitates the achievement of development objectives more rapidly and more efficiently than if development followed natural forces. It is becoming increasingly apparent that the development effort cannot be left to the government alone, it must be shared by private cooperative, corporate and other non-governmental organization and agencies, and above all by the people themselves. Planning by the

government should complement and supplement the efforts of individuals and non-governmental organizations.

Credit is a crucial input helping the rural poor in raising their incomes. As most farmers are small, they tend to borrow substantial finance from different sources to improve their agricultural output. The problem of rural indebtedness worsens when the loans are not put to productive uses. Providing adequate credit to the rural poor has become a problem because of the complex nature of the rural society. Moreover, it is not the borrowing that affects productivity, but indebtedness which lowers productivity by eliminating the will to change and by creating a despondent outlook.[60]

Credit is an important input in the development process. Gunnar Myrdal has termed credit as an accelerator of development. Ensuring the provision of timely and sufficient credit to as large a segment of rural population as possible has been one of the major policy initiatives which have guided the formulation of public policy in India. The rural credit system in India has evolved through different phases as a result of these initiatives there has been a substantial broadening of the infrastructure for credit delivery resulting in increased outreach and reduction in the influence of informal agencies as evidenced by the increase in the share of institutional sources of the cash debts of rural households from 7.3 per cent in the early 1950s to 64 per cent in 1991 as per the All India Debt and Investment Survey.

Policy measures were taken by the Reserve Bank of India following the nationalization of the commercial banks in 1969, aimed at increasing the spread of banking network in the rural areas and giving a new developmental thrust and orientation to the policies pursued by them. The primary emphasis at this juncture was on making banking facilities available in a large number of unbanked centres in rural and semi-urban areas both from the point of view of resource mobilization and extension of credit facilities. At this point the cooperatives were not able to meet the need for credit which had increased considerably with the Green Revolution and the boost which it had provided to agricultural production and productivity. The nationalization of

banks enabled them to supplement the efforts of the cooperatives. As there were still spatial gaps in rural lending, the Regional Rural Banks were introduced in 1975 and the Local Area Banks in 1996 to give a further fillip to the country's developmental efforts.

Summary

The key to the success of the different anti-poverty and other welfare programmes lies in the evolution and participation of community-based organization at the grassroots level. People's participations in credit delivery and linking formal credit institutions to borrowers through intermediaries of Self-Help Groups (SHGs) have been recognized as a supplementary mechanism for providing credit support to the rural poor.

The first official interest in informal group lending in India took shape during 1986-87 when the National Bank for Agriculture and Rural Development (NABARD) supported and funded an action research project on "Savings and Credit Management of Self-Help Groups of Mysore Resettlement and Development Agency (MYRADA). In 1988-89, the NABARD undertook a survey of 43 Non-Governmental Organizations (NGOs) spread over 11 States in India to study the functioning of SHGs and possibilities of collaboration between the banks and SHGs in the mobilization of rural savings and improving the delivery of credit to the poor.

Alternative to the SHGs, the other type of the group lending, although in smaller number, is through groups of Grameen Bank Group (GBG) model of Bangladesh. The Groups are much smaller, i.e. of five members to start with thrift. However, unlike in the SHGs, the GBG does not manage its resources. The individual savings are deposited in the bank and the members get loan directly from the bank. The GBG only helps the bank in screening the borrowers and assuring repayment. Although the bank gets benefits, the GBG does not develop much skill in financial management. In fact, it does not have much financial resources to manage. Although 0.5 per cent of loan amount is deducted to develop a group fund, it is negligible in comparison to at least 2 per cent per month of rate of interest. As propensity

to save (voluntary) for the poor people is much less than the compulsion to pay interest (involuntary), the forced saving in the GBG is much less than in the SHGs. The interest earned in the group after all belongs to its members. The GBG groups permanently remain dependent on the banks or the promoter NGOs. But so many SHGs have been found to become independent of banks for their credit requirements.

A majority of the NGOs in India promote SHGs only and the commercial banks lend to the SHGs or to the NGOs or federation for 'on lending' to the SHGs. Very few NGOs like Adithi in Bihar, Activities for Social Alternatives (ASA) in Tamil Nadu, Loylam Bank of Rural Development and Organization (RDO) in Manipur and Society for Helping and Awakening Rural Poor Through Education (SHARE) in Andhra Pradesh follow the Grameen Bank model for group lending.

Microfinance refers to the entire range of financial and non-financial services, including skill upgradation and entrepreneurship development, rendered to the poor for enabling them to overcome poverty. In the context of designing programmer for the poor, microfinance is recognised and accepted as one of the new development paradigms for alleviating poverty through social and economic empowerment of the poor with special emphasis on empowering women. The operational framework of microfinance, therefore, essentially rests on the premise that (a) formation of a self-employment enterprise is a viable alternative means of alleviating poverty, (b) lack of access to capital assets or credit acts as a constraint on existing and potential micro-enterprises, and (c) the poor are capable of saving despite their poor income level. In essence, therefore, micro-finance may be referred to 'as an institutional mechanism of providing credit support in small amount and usually limited with small groups along with other complementary support such as training and other related services to the people with poor resources and skills for enabling them to take up economic activities.

The concept of microfinance is now several decades old. Its institutions provide small credits and other financial services to low income households and very small informal businesses. With

constant innovation to meet the specific needs of the people they serve, microfinance institutions offer a menu of options. Through group lending, they are able to provide credit, with minimal reliance on collateral to group members who take terms borrowing and are jointly responsible for loan repayment.

Many microfinance institutions are owned and operated by non-governmental organizations which review grants and sometimes loans, from multilateral development agencies, private charities, governments and similar institutions. In parts of the world, they follow the model of financial cooperatives funding their lending from member's deposits and capital contributions. While some have grown into formal self-sustaining financial institutions, most remain informal and dependent upon donor funds.

But after years of experience with microfinance, surprisingly little is known about it. There are no comprehensive and authoritative data on the size of the industry or the populations served. Stylized facts, however, can be drawn from studies at the country and regional levels. These suggest that while the industry comprises a very large number of institutions—in tens of thousands by some estimates—the number of people served and amounts of money involved are small. Mostly microfinance activity is concentrated in a handful of countries and only a few large institutions carry out a significant portion of the transactions.

Rural development has been receiving increasing attention of the governments across the world. In the Indian context rural development assumes special significance for two important reasons. First, about two-thirds of the population still lives in villages and there cannot be any progress so long as rural areas remain backward. Second, the backwardness of the rural sector would be a major impediment to the overall progress of the economy. The industrial sector cannot think of sufficient demand for its products so long as the rural income is low.

The term rural development connotes overall development of rural areas with a view to improve the quality of life of rural people. In this sense, it is a comprehensive and multidimensional concept and encompasses the development of agriculture and

allied activities, village and cottage industries and crafts, socio-economic infrastructure, community services and facilities, and above all, the human resources in rural areas. As a phenomenon, rural development is the end result of interactions between various physical, technological economic, socio-cultural and institutional factors. As a strategy, it is designed to improve the economic and social well-being of a specific group of people—the rural poor. As a discipline, it is multi-disciplinary in nature representing an intersection of agricultural, social behavioural engineering and management sciences.

Precisely, rural development may be defined as a process leading to sustainable improvement in the quality of life of the rural people especially the poor.

Rural sector requires institutional credit to take up economically viable projects. But it needs to be noted that the credit alone cannot deliver the goods. There is what is called the credit absorption capacity of region. This depends on the implementation of economically viable schemes. Hence the formulation of economic plans should precede the preparation of credit plans. There are certain agencies like the cooperatives, regional rural banks and farmer's service societies which are most appropriate to serve the rural population, but their performance needs to be toned up. Of course, cheap credit needs to be discouraged.

Credit is an important input in the development process. It is an accelerator of development. Ensuring the provision of timely and sufficient credit to as large a segment of rural population as possible has been one of the major policy initiatives which have guided the formulation of public policy in India. The rural credit system in India has evolved through different phases as a result of these initiatives and there has been a substantial broadening of the infrastructure for credit delivery resulting in increased outreach and reduction in the influence of informal agencies as evidenced by the increase in the share of institutional sources of the cash debts of rural households from 7.3 per cent in the early 1950s to 64 per cent in 1991 as per the All India Debt and Investment Survey.

REFERENCES

1. Bouman, F.J.A., (1984), "Informal Savings and Credit Arrangements in Developing Countries: Observation from Sri Lanka", in Dale W. Adams, G.H. Graham and J.D. Von Pischke (eds.), *Undermining Rural Development with Cheap Credit*, Westview Press, London.
2. Desai, Bhupat M. and N.V. Namboodiri, (1996), "Whither Financial Institutions", *Economic and Political Weekly*, Vol. 31, No. 31, August 3.
3. Zellor, Manfred and Manohar Sharma, (1998) *Rural Finance and Poverty Alleviation*, (Food Policy Report), International Food Policy Research Institute, Washington, D.C., U.S.A.
4. United Nations, (1998), "United Nations General Assembly Resolution 52/194 passed in December 1997 (1998)", in Countdown 2005, *Newsletter of the Micro Credit Summit Campaign*, Vol. I, No. 3, February-March.
5. Namboodiri, N.V. and R.L. Shiyani, (2001), "Potential Role of Self-Help-Groups in Rural Financial Deepening", *Indian Journal of Agricultural Economics*, Vol. 56, No. 3, July-September, p. 401.
6. Karmakar, K.G., (1999), *Rural Credit and Self-Help Groups*, Sage Publications, New Delhi, p. 209.
7. Dasgupta, Rajaram, (2001), "An Informal Journey through Self-Help Groups", *Indian Journal of Agriculutural Economics*, Vol. 56, No. 3, July-September, p. 370.
8. Llanto, Gilberto, (1990), "Asymmetric Information on Rural Financial Markets and Interlinking of Transactions through the Self-Help Groups", *Savings and Development*, Vol. 14, No. 2.
9. Leland, H. and D. Pyle, (1977), "Information Asymmetric, Financial Structure and Financial Intermediation", *The Journal of Finance*, Vol. 32, No. 2.
10. Llanto, Gilberto, (1990), *op. cit.*
11. Leland, H. and D. Pyle, (1977), *op. cit.*
12. Von Pischke, J.D., (1992), *Finance at the Frontier—Debt Capacity and the Role of Credit in the Private Economy*, The World Bank, Washington D.C., USA, (EDI Seminar Series).
13. Stiglitz, J.E. and A. Weiss, (1981), "Credit Rationing in Markets with Imperfect Information", *American Economic Review*, Vol. 71, No. 3.
14. Basu, Kaushik, (1984), *The Less Developed Economy—A Critique of Contemporary Theory.*, Oxford University Press, Delhi.

15. Bhaduri, Amit, (1973), "A Study in Agricultural Backwardness under Semi Feudalism", *The Economic Journal*, Vol. 83, No. 329.
16. World Bank, (1983), *Indonesia Rural Credit Study*, Washington D.C., USA.
17. Huppi, M. and G. Fedder, "The Role of Groups and Credit Cooperatives in Rural Lending", *The World Bank Research Observer*, Vol. 5, No. 2, July.
18. Holt, S.I. and H. Ribe, (1991), "Developing Financial Institutions for the Poor and Reducing Barriers in Access for Women", *World Bank Discussion Paper*, 117, The World Bank, Washington D.C., USA.
19. World Bank, (1983), *op. cit.*
20. Boumen, F.J.A., (1989), *Small, Short and Unsecured Rural Finance in India*, Oxford University Press, Delhi.
21. Abiad, V.G., (1995), *Grassroots Financial Systems Development*, Asia Pacific Regional Agricultural Credit Association, Bangkok.
22. Bouman, F.J., (1989), *op. cit.*
23. *Ibid.*
24. Kropp, E.; M.T. Mars, B. Pramod, B.R. Quinions and H.D. Seibel, (1989), *Linking Self-Help Groups after Three Developing Countries*, Asia Pacific Regional Agricultural Credit Association, Bangkok.
25. Khandker, S.R., B. Khalily and Z. Khan, (1995), "Grameen Bank Performance and Sustainability", *World Bank Discussion Paper 306*, The World Bank, Washington D.C., USA.
26. United Nations, (1985), *Savings for Development: Report on the Third International Symposium on the Mobilization of Personal Savings in Developing Countries*, New York.
27. Kropp, E.; M.T. Mars, B. Pramod, B.R. Quinenes and H.D. Siebel, (1989), *op. cit.*
28. Koch, E. and S.M. Soetjipto, (1991), "Target Groups at a Glance: Linking Banks and Self-Help Groups after Three Years", *Savings and Development*, Vol. 17, No. 4.
29. NABARD. (1995), *Report of the Working Group on Non-Governmental Organisations and Self-Help Groups*, Mumbai.
30. *Ibid.*
31. Stiglitz, J.F., (1990), "Peer Monitoring Credit Markets", *The World Bank Economic Review*, Vol. 4, No. 3.
32. Mosley, P. and R.P. Dahal, (1985), "Lending to the Poorest: Early

Lessons from the Small Farmers Development Programme, Nepal", *Development Policy Review*, Vol. 3, No. 2.

33. Owusu, K. Opuku and William Tetteh, (1982), "An Experiment in Agricultural Credit: The Small Farmer Group Lending in Ghana", *Savings and Development*, Vol. 6, No. 1.
34. Rajasekhar, D., (1996), "Problems and Prospects of Group Lending in NGO Credit Programme in India", *Savings and Development*, Vol. 20, No. 1.
35. Harper, M., (1998), *Profit for the Poor*, Oxford & IBH, Publishing Co., Delhi.
36. Yaron, J., (1992), "Successful Rural Finance Institutions", World Bank Discussion Paper 150, Washington, D.C. USA.
37. Hoff, K. and J.E. Stigtiz, (1990), "Introduction: Imperfect Information and Perspectives", *The World Bank Economic Review*, Vol. 4, No. 3.
38. Dasgupta, R., N.B. Shete, K.D. Rao, and D.P. Khankhoji, (2001), *Maharashtra Rural Credit Project: Ongoing Evaluation IX*, National Institute of Bank Management, Pune (Unpublished Report).
39. HDFC, (1997), *Source Book on Reputed Indian Practices of Microfinance*, Housing Development Finance Corporation Ltd., Mumbai.
40. Rao, K.D.; R. Dasgupta, and D.P. Khankhoje, (2001), *OBC in the New Millennium—Banking with the Poor*, (*Unpublished Report*) National Institute of Bank Management, Pune.
41. Zeller, M.G.; G. Shrieder, J. Von Braun, and F. Hiedhves, (1997), *Rural Finance for Food Security for the Poor: Implications for Research and Policy*, Food Policy Review 4, International Food Policy Research Institute, Washington D.C., USA.
42. Dasgupta, R., N.B. Shete, K.D. Rao, and D.P. Khankhoji. (2001), *op. cit.*
43. Microcredit Summit, (1997), "Declaration and Plan Action", February 2-4, 1997 at *http://www.microcreditsummit.org/declaration.html.* Last accessed October 2003.
44. NABARD, (1999), *Task Force on Supportive Policy and Regulatory Framework for Microfinance: Report*, NABARD, Mumbai.
45. Nair, Tara S., (2001), "Institutionalising Microfinance in India", *Economic and Political Weekly*, Vol. 36, No. 4, January 27.
46. Ledgerwood, Joanna, (1999), "Microfinance Handbook: An

Institutional and Financial Perspectives, Sustainable Banking with the Poor", The World Bank, Washington, D.C., USA.

47. *Ibid.*
48. Vazquez, Francisco, (2005), "Pros and Cons of Microfinance", *IMF Survey.*, Vol. 34, No. 5, March 21, p. 72.
49. Rajan, Raghuram, (2006), "Separate and Unequal", *Finance and Development*, Vol. 43, No. 1, March, p. 56.
50. Kota, Ina, (2007), "Microfinance: Banking for the Poor", *Finance & Development*, Vol. 44, No. 2, June, p. 44.
51. Sundaram, I. Satya, (2002), *Rural Development*, Himalaya Publishing House, Delhi, p. v.
52. Subramanian, R., (ed) (1988). *Rural Development (An Inside Look at Problems and Prospects)*, Yatan Publications, New Delhi, p. ix.
53. Singh, Katar, (1999). *Rural Development*, Sage Publications, New Delhi, p. 19.
54. Chambers, Robert, (1983), *Rural Development: Putting the Last First*, Longman Press, London.
55. Todaro, Michal P., (1977), *Economic Development in the Third World*, Longman Press, London, pp. 16-18.
56. Seers, Deedley, (1969), "The Meaning of Development", paper presented at the Eleventh *World Conference of the Society of International Development*, New Delhi.
57. Anonymous, (1978), "Mahatma Gandhi on Rural Development", in *Indian Farming*, October-November.
58. Gandhi, M.K., (1936), "Rural Development", *Harijan*, April 4.
59. Wietz, Rannan., (1971), *From Peasant to Farmer*, Columbia University Press, New York, Chap. 9.
60. International Cooperative Alliance, (1966), *The Role of Cooperation in Social and Economic Development*, (Collection of papers, p. 27).

2

Rural Development : Concept and Dimensions

Rural development involves raising the socio-economic status of the rural population on a sustainable basis through optimum utilisation of local resources, both natural and human. While external help is necessary and appreciated, rural development can be achieved only when the rural people actively participate in the developmental process.

The essence of development is not in 'providing' but in pioneering the rural sector. The rural population should know how to sustain itself financially and gain economic independence. Therefore, the stress of rural development should be on self-reliance. Also, rural development should result in greater access to the rural population to goods and services.[1]

The soul of India lives in villages and India's salvation lies in rural reconstruction. Since time immemorial, India has been, still continues to be and will remain in the foreseeable future a land of villages. As per 2001 census, the total rural population was 741.9 million out of 1020 million population. The percentage of rural population in total population was 72.22 in 2001. The rural population lives in miserable conditions. Disease, hunger, abject poverty, illiteracy are their lifelong partners.

The development of a national economy does not merely rest on its capability to generate and sustain rapid gains in the growth of its Gross National Product (GNP), including per capita income.

This only constitutes prime elements in the development mix in developing societies and the growth process needs to be tilted in favour of the poor who should be enabled to participate and share benefits of development which is now part of the new cumulative view in growth and development. The problem of the development of the Indian economy in spite of growth of GNP, is mainly the problem of development of the rural economy. It is said that Indian economy is backward because the rural economy is underdeveloped. It is realised that unless the living conditions of the majority of the rural poor who live below subsistence level, are improved, there cannot be development in its true sense.[2]

Philosophy of Rural Development

The term 'rural development' is of focal interest and is widely acclaimed in both the developed and developing countries of the world. Rural development as a concept connotes overall development of rural areas with a view to improve the quality of life of rural people. In this sense, it is a comprehensive and multidimensional concept and encompasses the development of agriculture and allied activities, village and cottage industries and crafts, socio-economic infrastructure, community services and facilities, and above all, the human resources in rural areas.[3] To safeguard the human resource is the global task of today. If man is safe and abundance of human needs are fulfilled, the human resource is safeguarded. This can be possible only by rural development. Robert Chambers has defined rural development as a strategy to enable a specific group of people, poor rural women and men, to gain for themselves and their children more of what they want and need. It involves helping the poorest among those who seek a livelihood in the rural areas to demand and control more of the farmers, tenants and the landless.[4] Rural development implies priority production and investment attention to the commodities primarily produced in rural areas such as agricultural crops consisting of food and commercial ones, animal husbandry products, forestry, constructions in rural areas, rural crafts and village industry products etc. in rural areas and so on. The concept

of priority commodity development in rural areas also implies caring of provision for population and labour habitats in rural areas. It follows that priority commodity development biased for rural areas also has a human and employment angle.[5] The economic philosophy of rural development has to permeate in (a) capital allocation, (b) credit allocation, (c) wage differential policy, (d) pattern of institutional development, (e) infrastructure location and direction, (f) relative prices fixation, and (g) education, health, public utility supply and so on.[6]

Rural development as a concept is not a new one. It had received the attention of French Physiocrats, Ricardo, Marx, Gandhi, Tagore and many others in the past. In Indian context, Mahatma Gandhi felt absolute and urgent necessity of rural development in India. He wrote: "I would say that if the village perishes, India will perish too. It will be no more India. Her own mission in the world will get lost. The revival of village life is possible only when it is no more exploration."[7] Rural Development is a *sine qua non* of the development of India. The soul of India as Gandhiji said with agony and anguish, lies in villages and India's salvation lies in rural reconstruction. The driving force behind such a philosophy was a firm belief in the humanistic ideology of Gandhiji.[8] Gandhiji was more practical and attempted a purely indigenous solution to the socio-economic problems of rural India. He was determined not only to change their economic lot but to include certain values as well. Thus rural development is a broader concept and is concerned with the total development of the rural economy as a whole.

It was believed that overall growth of the economy will improve the lot of rural people also. But the experience of the earlier plans showed dismal picture of the rural areas. The conditions of rural mass became explosive on several fronts. So it was realised that rural development should be treated as a significant component of economic development. So the idea of rural development has recently received great deal of attention from social scientists and policy makers. The reasons for this may be political academic or even human considerations. In fact, the problem of improving the lot of 72 per cent of the country's population that lives in the rural

areas, has assumed greater significance because of its explosive nature which is threatening our very existence. A large number of people in rural areas live below the poverty line. They include landless labourers, small farmers, rural artisans, and other weaker sections of the society. They have been subjected to economic deprivation, exploitation, discrimination and oppression of the worst kind of all types. Their abject poverty and subhuman living conditions were standing monuments and living expression that demand a new policy framework which gives priority to the amelioration of the lot of our village population.[9] The government was committed to the philosophy of social justice and socio-economic development of the rural areas. Rural development meant developing the necessary infrastructure, cottage and small scale industries as well as secondary and tertiary sectors such as marketing which are vital for the process of economic development.[10]

Rural area means underdeveloped area of population. It covers the maximum area and maximum people. Due to irrational distribution of wealth, and property heritage, rich people are becoming richer and poor people are becoming poorer. Now the question is vital one. How the people of rural belt be uplifted? How plans of the government be implemented? Government is determined to eradicate the gap between the rich and the poor. But the principle is the ultimate bonus. This can be achieved through proper utilisation of government fund and proper distribution of resources and proper development of rural areas. In fact, the rural development has a socio-political aspect as well.

For rural development the knowledge of the poor about policy making and about the programmes of their upliftment is essential. This is because with knowledge would come power. Better educated men and women, free from the bonds of social subservience would see more clearly the society in which they wished to live and guide more firmly the conduct of democratic policy by which alone their hopes can slowly be established in the practice of the nation.[11] The economic ideology of the government should be the all-round development of the people of the rural areas. Welfare of the state should be the most important issue of

the government. Rural development is a prerequisite for overall development and, hence, it deserves the highest priority in terms of economic development.

Thus rural development is a dynamic concept which assumes significance in the context of socio-political and economic situation of India. Efforts should be made by the government to lift the rural mass from poverty and deprivation. It also gains relevance due to the multitude of government socio-economic programmes for rural development in India has been to lift the standard of living of rural poor. The main objective of rural poor above the poverty line. In India rural development is a unique experience in order to overcome economic and social backwardness in its vast widespread village society, the immutable fact is that a large segment of the Indian society, especially in the rural areas, still lives in poverty.

India is a land of villages and India's development depends on the development of its innumerable villages. Rural development in India constitutes the most significant part of the national development programme.

Ever since the planning era dawned in India, a number of development plans and programmes have been formulated and executed in the rural areas to bring about changes in the rural areas. Today on the beginning of the Eleventh Five Year Plan, the planners are placing still greater emphasis on development of the rural communities with more massive investment, unprecedented in the history of Indian planning. The Government of India is evolving a strategy which would ameliorate the lot of the poor living in villages. This has one of the more formidable and fundamental aspect to India's development efforts.

Rural Development

The new trend of populace involvement in social preference had transformed the world from 'Police State' to 'Welfare State', where the concept of development has demeaned the old notion of development, which was centralised in the central places only. The new paradigm of development is concentrating fiercely on its rural

development, especially the precedent of the developing countries, which by all predictions would make a world power (developed countries) in the next stipulated time period, because all the nations have traced out that under-development of any area will retard the growth of prosperity: 'poverty anywhere is a threat to prosperity everywhere'.[12] As Meir and Baldwin said, "A Study of the poverty of nations has even more urgency than a study of the wealth of nations."[13] At the present moment, rural development has become the *sine qua non* for all the nations and organisations. Adam Smith, the father of Economics, had composed the same as, "What improves the circumstances of the greater part can never be regarded as an inconvenience to the whole. No society can surely be flourishing and happy of which the far greater part of the members are poor and miserable."[14]

To improve the miserable condition of the destitutes, rural development has become the panacea. Rural development is a complex phenomenon covering a wide spectrum of activities. To understand the contextual framework of rural development, let us discuss as to what is meant by the term, 'Urban', 'Rural', 'Rurban' and 'Development'.

Concept of Urban

The word 'urban' has originated from the Latin word *urbanus*, from *urbcity*. The word urban is related to a town or city.[15] Thus 'town' signifies urban areas.[16] In the Census of India 2001, the definition of urban areas adopted is as follows:[17]

(a) All statutory places with a municipality, corporation, cantonment board or notified town area committees, etc.

(b) A place satisfying the following three criteria simultaneously :

  (i) a minimum population of 5,000;

  (ii) at least 75 per cent of male working population engaged in non-agricultural pursuits; and

  (iii) a density of population of at least 400 per sq. km. (1,000 per sq. mile).

To recognise the other areas as urban, Census of India 2001, has clarified as, for identification of places which would qualify to be classified as 'urban' all villages, which, as per the 1991 had a population of 4,000 and above, a population density of 400 persons per sq.km. and having at least 75 per cent of male working population engaged in non-agricultural activities were considered.

Apart from these, the outgrowths (OGs) of cities and towns have also been treated as urban under 'Urban Agglomerations': Examples of outgrowth are railway colonies, university campuses, port areas, military camps etc. that may have come up near a statutory town or city but within the revenue limits of a village or villages contiguous to the town or city. Each such individual area by itself may not satisfy the demographic criteria laid down at (b) above to qualify it to be treated as an independent urban unit but may deserve to be clubbed with the towns as a contiguous urban spread. Thus, the town level data wherever presented, includes the data for outgrowths separately of such towns and also town plus outgrowth(s) population (Census of India 2001).[18]

Concept of Rural

The word, 'Rural' which has been derived from the Latin word *ruralis*, from *rus* or *rur* which means country.[19] The etymon, rural meant the area which is not included in urban domain and signifies the poor infrastructure: infrastructure like roads, transport, power-house, insurance and banking, health, education, cottage industries, communication and modern equipments of development. Rural has become the acronym of agriculture and farming. It is pertaining to the country of distinguished from the city or the town,[20] and in relation to or characteristic of the countryside rather than the town.[21] Hence, the terms of reference is clear that the area related to agriculture purpose and not coming under the notified area of town, semi-town, and forest, wherein populace are engaged in agriculture and allied activities, where there is lack of industrial units and manufacturing units, opportunities of placement, where life commences with nature

and ends with nature's mercy is called rural area. Rural area means underdeveloped area of population. It covers the maximum area and maximum people.[22] Rural means village.[23] The census definition of rural area is as follows: "In India, the smallest area of rural habitation is the village. It generally follows the limits of a revenue village that is recognised by the district administration. The revenue village need not necessarily be a single agglomeration of habitations. It may have one or more hamlets. But the revenue village has a definite surveyed boundary and each village is a separate administrative unit with separate village accounts."[24]

Concept of Rurban

Rurban represents the intermediate scenario, where people lives in small groups and perform the allied activities of businesses. Karalay defines, "Rurban which represents the intermediate scenario like those: Living in farms or places nearby the towns where they carry on dairy, poultry or such businesses."[25]

Concept of Development

The meaning of the term 'develop' is to unfold itself or to grow into a fuller or mature condition. 'Ment' stands for instrument of action, an act or process. So, in simple words development is to discover or unfold any hidden field.[26] Development, in the contemporary context means well-being of the population. It is a multidimensional concept. It signifies the present status plus addition of more through growth (change). It is taken to mean growth plus change.[27] As,

$$D = G + \Delta G$$

Where, D = Development, G = Growth; and Δ = addition.

It is taken to mean growth plus progressive change in certain crucial variables which determine the well-being of people.[28] It is connected to qualitative moves in economic wants, commodities, incentives, institutions, working capacity, productivity, technical know-how and firm determination to pursue the goals of

upliftment with proper dignity and sustainable process or 'upward movement of the entire social system` [Myrdal].[29] It is an event constituting a new stage in a changing situation[30] to acquire better placement as derelict to hoi pollai and hoi pollai to an affluent. It is a process of strength. It has to proceed further position in which the kingdom of misery will eliminate and the robust society will take place. It is the way, which leads to perfection. It concerns not only man's material needs but the improvement of social conditions of life too. Development must represent the whole gamut of change by which an entire social system, turned to the basic needs and desires of individuals and social groups within that system, moves away from a condition of life widely perceived as unsatisfactory and towards a situation or condition of life regarded as materially and spiritually "better".[31]

Development is a gradual evolution or completion, also, the result of such an evolution or completion.[32] This gradual evolution provides the progressive attitude to reduce the deplorable condition of the weaker sections of the society. Development goals must be defined in terms of progressive reduction and eventual elimination of malnutrition, disease, illiteracy, squalor, unemployment and inequalities.[33] It is process of policy to accomplish on the aforesaid dire straits. It boosts the economy, in the way of apotheosis, which improves the quality of all human lives. It is embodying not just income and its growth but also achievements on other fronts: reductions in infant mortality, higher life expectancy, advances in literacy rates, widespread access to medical and health services, and so on.[34]

There are three equally important aspects of development:[35]

(1) Raising peoples liking levels—either incomes and consumption levels of food, medical services, education etc., through relevant economic growth process.
(2) Creating conditions conducive to the growth of people's self-esteem through the establishment of social, political and economic system and institutions that promote human dignity and respect.

(3) Increasing people's freedom by enlarging the range of their choice variables, as by increasing varieties of consumer goods and services.

The concept of development has been taken as the pragmatic shift from the very outset. Adam Smith, the first 'development economist' and his *magnum opus 'Wealth of Nations'* (1776), the first treatise on economic development along with other traditional economist accepted that development meant the capacity of a national economy, whose initial economic condition has been more or less static for a long time, to generate and sustain on annual increase in its gross national product [GNP] or gross domestic product [GDP] at rates of 5 per cent to 7 per cent or more.[36] Second approach to define the economic development is based on the use of rates of growth of income per capita or per capita GNP or per capita real income to take into account the capacity of a country to dilate its product at a rate faster than the growth rate of its population. Meir[37] defines economic development "as the process whereby the real per capita income of a country increases over a long period of time—subject to the stipulations that the number of people below an "absolute poverty line" does not increase, and that the distribution of income does not become more unequal." It occupied widest approval to measure the overall economic well-being of a population. Its gestation period is longer than GNP/GDP approach. Higgins clarifies development as "a discernible rise in total and in per capita income, widely diffused through occupational and income groups, continuing for at least two generations, and becoming cumulative."[38]

Development economist started to emphasize the meaning of development as 'industrialisation and growth' in lieu of GNP/GDP per capita approach. Development strategies have, therefore, usually focused on rapid industrialization. This concept of development was surpassed by welfare approach, as a process whereby there is an increase in consumption of goods and services of individuals. "Economic development is a sustained, secular improvement in material well-being, which we may consider to be reflected in an increasing flow of goods and services."[39] These principal economic measures of development have been

supplemented by the concept of social indicators: Some are 'inputs' such as nutritional standards or number of hospital beds or doctors per head of population. While others may be 'outputs' corresponding to these inputs such as improvements in health in terms of infant mortality rates, sickness rates etc.[40] Social indicators are focusing on some basic needs as gains in literacy, schooling, health conditions and services, food, water supply, sanitation and provision of housing. At the present moment, two indicators of human development are in vogue. First, physical quality of life index [PQLI], developed by M.D. Morris in 1979 after the comparison of 23 countries. It is based on three component indicators: infant mortality, life expectancy at age one and basic literacy at age 15. Each indicator of the three components is placed on a scale of zero to 100, where zero indicates 'worse' performance and hundred (100) shows 'best' performance.

Second, Human Development Index (HDI) developed by Lord Meghnad Desai and Nobel Laureate Amartya Sen in 1990, on the basis of this HDI, UNDP has been presenting annually, the Human Development Report [HDR] since 1990. HDI is a combination of three Social Indicators: Life expectancy, adult literacy alongwith years of schooling and per capita income. HDI value of a country is calculated by taking three indicators:[41]

(1) Longevity, as measured by life expectancy at birth.
(2) Educational attainment, as measured by a combination of adult literacy (two-thirds weight) and combined primary, secondary and tertiary enrolment (one-third weight).
(3) Standard of living, as measured by real GDP per capita based on purchasing power parity in terms of dollar (ppp$).

During this period of liberalisation, globalisation, privatisation and adjustment attitude, Prof. Amartya Sen stressed on the concept of promoting 'human capabilities.' He argues that the "capability to function" is what really matters for status as a poor or non-poor person.[42] He defines development as a state of freedom for people to live their lives as they want.[43] He clarifies it as, at the

core of human well-being is freedom of choice by enhancing people's capabilities for attaining higher standards of health, knowledge, self-respect and the ability to participate actively in community life. The status of a society should be evaluated by people's capabilities. The relevant capabilities are: being free from starvation, from hunger, from undernourishment; participation in communal life; being adequately sheltered and so on. The expansion of these capabilities implies freedom of choices—political, social, economic and cultural freedom.[44]

The concept of development once again is defined on the basis of sustainability as, 'Sustainable Development'. It was first used by the World Conservation Strategy in 1980. It defined, "development as meeting the needs of the present generation without compromising the needs of future generations" [Brundtland Report, 1987].[45] It means that development should be a continuous process, which should keep going on. We define it as a situation in which the development vector D does not decrease over time meanwhile maintaining the capital stock constant or increased.[46] It gives the more importance for the generation of sustainable enhancements in the quality of life of the human being through increases in per capita real income, developments in education, health and other improvements in quality of natural environmental resources.

The movement launched by Paul Streeten and his associates to measure the concept of development through 'basic needs' approach and UNDP's initiative to measure it through 'Human Development Index' have the main focus on human well-being. At the present outset, UNDP has mooted the Millennium Development Goals (MDGs), that are firmly embedded in human development outcomes. The international development community has now adopted specific and measurable MDGs performance targets to be accomplished by 2015. The broadening of goals of development from mere GDP growth to this wider range of Millennium Development Goals.[47] It is paradigmatic shift in the concept of development.

Development needs concrete guidelines to further enhancements. It requires and involves some sort of directions,

regulations, and guidance to generate the forces of expansion and maintain them [Bonne].[48] When the above mentioned requirements faster the development, it becomes the continuous process. It is a continuous and spontaneous change in the stationary state which for ever alters and displaces the equilibrium state previously existing.[49] It is connected with the excellent model of an institutional reform, technical improvement, findings of resources and regional disparities and to eliminate the regionalism. In brief, development must, therefore, be conceived of as a multidimensional process involving major changes in social structures, popular attitudes, and national institutions, as well as the acceleration of economic growth, the reduction of inequality, and the eradication of poverty. Development, in its essence, must represent the whole gamut of change by which an entire social group within that system, moves away from a condition of life widely perceived as unsatisfactory towards a situation or condition of life regarded as materially and spiritually better. This betterment makes the human being free from unfreedoms as undernourishment, morbidity and premature mortality, illiteracy, and the lack of political freedom and freedom of expression.

Development requires growth in all the factors, which can be achieved through proper strategy to development strategy. Any development strategy should lead to following ends :

(i) A higher rate of growth of GDP;
(ii) An enlargement of the employment potential leading to full employment;
(iii) Reduction of population living below poverty line;
(iv) Promotion of equality leading to better opportunities of development for the poor and less well-off section of the society by providing education, training in skill formation and better health facilities; and
(v) Reduction of regional disparities.[50]

Concept of Rural Development

When the world 'rural' is placed before a subjective and value-

loaded conceptual word 'development', it forms the term, 'Rural Development'. The new anemogram, rural development is almost synonym for modernization, advancement and proper placement in the developing world. Rural development is the subset of the broader term development.

The spread of the present mode of development brings the new light of change, which provides a contribution to the ill-furnished in the domain of remote and bucolic areas through the process of rural development. The term, rural development, connotes overall development of sylvan areas with a view to improve the quality of life of rural populace in social, cultural and institutional as well as economic condition in an efficient manner. It essentially means desired social and economic change in the rural area both quantitatively and qualitatively.[51] It affords the opportunity to the rural masses to break the vicious circle of poverty and come over the bleakness of insufficiency, in order to lead a successful life in this worldwide cut-throat competitive age without prejudice to the development of urban areas. Rural development is generally accepted to be an "holistic concept which recognises the complexity and inter-relatedness of the many variables which influence the quality of life in rural areas."[52]

The term 'rural development' is of focal interest and is widely acclaimed in both the developed and the developing countries of the world. Rural development is a strategy designed to improve the economic and social life of a particular group of a people—the rural poor. It involves extending the benefits of development to the poorest among those who seek a livelihood in the rural areas. The group includes small scale farmers, tenants and the landless [World Bank, 1975].[53]

At present, the world has come to an agreement to boost the all-round dynamic development in rural sector for faster economic development and welfare of common masses. There has been considerable discussion of the need for and the nature of shifts in emphasis and approach called for in rural development in keeping with the objective of overall development policy for speedy elimination of backwardness in rural areas and economic incentives to reduce the disparities between the "haves" and the "have-nots"

in rural sector. Today, not only government machineries and functionaries formulate the strategy of rural development, private institutions, Non-Governmental Organisations (NGOs), Multi-National Companies (MNCs) and others, also do the same. But their concepts of rural development differ.

Rural development means developing the necessary infrastructure, cottage and small industries as well as secondary and tertiary sectors such as marketing which are vital for the process of economic development.[54] Rural development is not merely development of rural areas but also the development of rural people into self-reliant and self-sustaining modern communities. Furthermore, rural development means structural change in the socio-economic situation in order that human welfare which is the prime goal of all development, is secured at the earliest and that the society would assimilate such changes in the realm of man-environment relationship, population growth, distribution and appropriate self-reliant technology and so on.[55] Rural development is defined as, "...improving living standards of the mass of low income population residing in rural areas and making the process of their development self-sustaining".[56] Rural development is, therefore, the development of rural areas in such a way that each component of rural life changes in a designed, direction and in sympathy with the other components. Besides these, rural development also encompasses structural changes in the socio-economic environment in the remote and bucolic domain in order that the welfare of human being which is the primary manifest goal of all development, secured at the earliest. It embraces all levels of human living, e.g. agriculture and related matters, irrigation, communication, education, health, supplementary employment, housing, training and social welfare.[57] Rural development, thus, should embrace all the objectives of enrichment and betterment of the overall quality of rural life through appropriate development of manpower, resources, infrastructural facilities and provision of minimum needs and livelihood.[58] It is building of robust physical infrastructure as well as dynamic human beings for the purpose of the upliftment of the living condition of the downtrodden sylvan society. At the present

circumstances, it is obvious, the process of development has surpassed or contiguous to the hunky-dory statement of the noted scholar, Chanakya, regarding the residence in rural areas,—

> "धनिकः, श्रोत्रियो, राजा, नदी, वैद्यस्तु पंचमः।
> पंच यत्र न विद्यन्ते न तत्रं दिवसं वसेत्।।
> [Dhanikah, Shrotriyo, Raja, Nadi, Vaidystu Panchmah.
> Panch Yatr Na Vidyante, Na Tatram Divsam Vashet]

i.e. People should not stay even for a day where the following five are not existing—affluent for the rainy days, scholar to spread the light of knowledge, king to protect and for justice, river for irrigation and safe drinking water and doctor for treatment.

The evidence would appear to suggest that rural development has approved the aforesaid factors and appended the sustainable development, communication, employment and three basic needs of the human being: food, apparel and shelter, poverty free world, boost the global technology to grab and make the world as a 'global village', benefits of basic infrastructure, fair distribution, electrification of the houses and corruption free social services etc. under the umbrella of rural development strategy. Whatever the strategies are adopted by the rural development functionaries, the main motive is to assist the needy, extremely poor to break through the web of inadequacy, vicious circle of poverty, monster of impoverishment, etc.

There is a consensus among the functionalism that rural development is a comprehensive and multi-dimensional, elastic and holistic concept and encompasses the development of agriculture and allied activities, village and cottage industries and crafts, socio-economic infrastructure, community services and facilities and above all the human resources in rural areas.[59] It is a process aimed at improving the well-being and self-realisation of people living outside the urbanised areas through collective effort to widen people's range of choices.[60] Efforts should be made towards preservation and improvement of the rural environment, and rural development planning may be conceived of as identifying the complex factors, which contribute to the creation, change or

development of rural areas or community.[61] Its process varies from region to region or from one village to another as it depends on factors such as the levels of development attained by the region or the village.[62] So, they came to an agreement that it can be reshaped the entire gamut of change by which all the factors reshuffle and desired development comes in existence. Katar Singh said, "As a phenomenon, rural development is the end-result of interactions between various physical, technological, economic, socio-cultural and institutional factors. As a strategy, it is designed to improve the economic and social well-being of a specific group of people—the rural poor. As a discipline multi-diplomacy in nature, representing an intersection of agricultural, social, behavioural, engineering and management sciences."[63]

Thus the main target of the rural development is to bring the destitute in the mainstream, as the best follower of Gandhian thought/way of life and renowned social worker, Late Vinoba Bhave dreamt and proclaimed 'Sarvodaya' meant all should rise. Ending poverty has been one of the most persistent economic challenges for governments across the developing world. Generally abject poverty prevails in rural areas in comparison of the urban areas. So, rural areas need proper development. Robert Chambers defines, "Rural development is a strategy to enable a specific group of people, poor rural women and men, to gain for themselves and their children more of what they want and need. It involves helping the poorest among those who seek a livelihood in the rural areas to demand and control more of the benefits of rural development. The group includes small scale farmers, tenants, and the landless."[64]

Development process enforces each factor to improve the quality of life. It happens through the synergy of each factor especially human beings active participation in each and every step of development planning and its implementation. Path to economic development lies entirely through determined hard work of the people.[65] Katar Singh said, "The process of development may be compared with train in which each coach pushes the one ahead of it, and is in turn pushed by the one behind, but it takes a powerful engine to make the whole train move. The secret of

success in rural development lies in identifying and if needed, developing a suitable engine to attach the train. There are no universally valid guidelines to identify appropriate engines of rural development, if at all they exist." [66] It is very difficult to find out the proper factor to enhance the desired well-shaped development in rural areas. Without the accurate and proper prognosis, *ad rem* accompaniment cannot be zoomed and accomplishment seems to be day-dream.

Why is Rural Development *sine qua non* for India?

India, a rural in character, is a country of villages. Since time immemorial, India has been, still continues to be and will remain in the foreseeable future a land of village communities.[67] Bulk of the people are living in rural areas. According to 2001 census out of the total population 1,028,610,328 of India 742,490,639 persons are residing in rural areas.[68] There are 638,588 villages and 5,161 towns in our country.[69] In percentage basis, according to 2001 census 72.22 per cent of the total population in the country have been living in the rural areas as compared to 74.3 per cent in 1991, 76.7 per cent in 1981, 80 per cent in 1971, 83 per cent in 1951 and 86 per cent in 1901. Rural sector contributes about 29 per cent of its gross domestic product, no strategy of socio-economic development for India that neglects rural people and rural areas can be successful.[70] M.K. Gandhi wrote in the *Harijan* (4 April, 1936): "India is to be found not in its few cities but in its 7,00,000 villages. But we town dwellers have believed that India is to be found in its towns and the villages were created to minister to our needs. We have hardly paused to enquire if those poor folk get sufficient to eat and clothe themselves with and whether they have a roof to shelter themselves from sun and rain." He further wrote in *Harijan* [August 29, 1936], "I would say that if the village perishes, India would perish too. It will be no more India. Her own mission in the world will get lost. The revival of village life is possible only when it is no more exploited." Rural development is, therefore, an absolute and urgent necessity in India now, and will continue to be so in future. It is the *sine qua non* of development of India.[71]

In global context, it is required for four main reasons: [David, A.M., *et al.*, 1983][72] First, about two-thirds of the population of developing countries live in rural areas and there is a higher proportion of rural dwellers in the poor countries. The number and proportions of poor people in the rural areas are variously estimated at 750-1,000 million people, consisting approximately 33.50 per cent of the rural population in developing countries. If these people are to have raised 'levels of life sustenance, human dignity and freedom' when there is an absence of any rapid expansion in the urban and industrial sectors, income and employment opportunities have to be generated in rural areas to exploit labour, to generate development, and to check rural-urban migration.

Second, the accelerated population growth had helped to create serious social and economic problems as open unemployment and underemployment. This is more pronounced in land and resource-scarce situations where the proportion of underemployed rural landless labourers has been increasing. The International Labour Office, in recognition of these symptoms carried out a number of research studies around the globe as a part of their world employment programme.

Third, despite substantial and impressive increases in growth of agricultural and food output in some regions of a number of developing countries, the plight of the landless labourers and small farmers have not been improved significantly. This is mainly because the increases in output productivity have been achieved by provision and use of yield raising inputs and technology by those with the ability, information and political power to demand these things. Thus, unavoidably, in the absence of any significant land reform, poverty for those without land is intimately related to the concentration of land in the hands of large farmers and land owners. These producers can achieve higher yields and output through greater use of machines and other inputs rather than by significantly increasing the use of local labour. The responsibility for this socially inappropriate agricultural growth lies with the international aid-donors and the national development strategies. Recent shifts in the attitudes of aid

agencies and the national development policy-makers, at least in their writings, is a recognition of the plight of landless labourers and marginal farmers who did not get a share in the fruits of recent growth of output.

Finally, the success of some of the developing countries in eliminating destitution and unemployment through a system of communes attracted the attention (and sometimes concern) of policy-makers around the world. Governments and international agencies started a search for alternatives to collectivist models; this led to many 'reformist' experiments in rural development.

Expectations of the people vary from person to person and from region to region, but the expectation of a marked improvement in material conditions of life is general throughout the world. People want to have nutritious food, decent dress, comfortable houses, better education, a secure life and freedom from servitude.

How it happens? Katar Singh clarifies it.[73] First, the demonstration effect of the rural elite, urban rich and foreign tourists engaging in ostentatious consumption of exotic and luxurious goods has distorted the consumption and utility functions of the poor. Second, films, radio, television and advertisements have exposed the masses to modern gadgets and lifestyles and have assured the rural poor of the modern amenities of life, if they would vote for them. Third, the Central Government has declared time and again that the eradication of poverty is the major policy goal. Through the media, the common man has first learned about the new products, gadgets and services, then comes the want for him, and the demand for him.

No economy or government can afford an opportunity to fulfil these expectations forthwith in future, but these expectations can be fulfilled, if government implements the rural development process programmes rapidly. In India the functionaries are committed to execute and implement programmes which enable the people satisfy their grievances through rural development. Here, rural development is not only a process, a method, a programme, but also a movement in our country.[74]

Importance of Rural Development

The emphasis on rural development in most of the developing countries is understandable. The majority of the population lives in the rural areas. As such, their backwardness would be retarding growth in other sectors and in the economy as a whole. The growth of towns and cities (urbanised) will be possible if it is backed by prosperity in rural areas. Rural backwardness is the major cause for the falling demand (recession) for most products.[75]

The stress on rural development is also due to many considerable constraints facing the rural areas which generally suffer from inadequate infrastructural facilities and technological advancements. The rural areas are not well placed in terms of even minimum needs like safe drinking water, primary health and road transport. This apart, the rural population suffers from indigence, ignorance and illiteracy. Their traditional outlook towards development has been preventing them from taking full advantage of the incentives offered by the government. But with substantial exposure to media, both electronic and print media, the rural sector is moving towards self-reliance and economic independence. Also, the ownership of land and other assets has been heavily concentrated in the hands of a few. It is precisely for the reason that the benefits of rural development programmes failed to reach the rural population targeted for these benefits to the extent expected.

It is true that the process of economic development involves a shift from agricultural and allied activities to non-agricultural activities. It is, however, erroneous to believe that the increase in non-agricultural activity should be confined to towns and cities. After all, villages with growing non-agricultural activity will, without doubt, become towns in course of time. What needs to be done is that non-agricultural activities in the rural areas need to be focused upon and strengthened on priority basis.

The rural areas remain impoverished with remuneration economic activities initiated to be carried out only in towns and cities. Thus even an essential commodity like soap is being

produced in urban areas. The agreement generally advanced for this is that rural areas lack the basic infrastructural facilities for setting up industrial units. But it is conveniently forgotten that such facilities would be available in rural areas only when these areas become centres of growing economic activity. It is not for nothing that Gandhiji laid stress on village development.

So long as rural areas are deprived of minimum facilities, there will be rural exodus. Migration of rural people to urban areas has serious implication proving to be of burden of on the available resources and facilities in urban areas. It is estimated that urban population is growing at 4 per cent per year and 2 per cent of the increase in urban population per year is reportedly caused by migration from rural areas.

The administration in the urban areas has been finding it difficult to provide employment to the rural labour force migrating to towns and cities. According to Michael Jadaro "Migration in excess of jobs opportunities is both a symptom and a contributing factor to Third World underdevelopment.[76] The social consequences of rural exodus like growing slums are too serious to be ignored by the urban administrative authorities.

Another disturbing trend in the rural sector is that the surpluses generated in the rural areas are being invested in urban areas for various reasons. While the government has stepped up its investment in rural areas, the rural surpluses are diverted to urban areas. When rural services are heavily subsidised by the government, the rural rich or affluent society have an obligation to step up their investment in rural areas.

Dimension of Rural Development

The concept of rural development is multi-dimensional. It connotes all round qualitative improvement in the life of the people residing in rural areas. It embraces such things as agricultural development, growth in income, better and expanded employment opportunities, reduction in poverty, more equitable distribution of income and wealth, improved human development index and environmental protection in rural areas.

Agricultural Development in India

India is primarily an agrarian society even today with almost 65 per cent of the population depending on agriculture for their livelihood. The progress of India's agricultural sector during the last five decades has been summarised in Table 2.1.

Table 2.1 : Some Key Indicators of Agricultural Progress

Items	*1950-51*	*1964-65*	*2003-04*	*Percentage increase between 1950-51 and 2003-04*
1	2	3	4	5
1. Food grains (million tonnes)	51	89	212	316
(a) Rice (million tonnes)	21	39	87	338
(b) Wheat (million tonnes)	6	12	72	1100
2. Oilseeds (million tonnes)	5	9	25	400
3. Sugarcane (million tonnes)	57	122	238	412
4. Cotton (million bales)	3	6	14	366
5. Jute (million bales)	3	4	1.1	268
6. Potato (million tonnes)	2	–	23	1050

Source : Economic Survey (2003-04).

Table 2.1 brings out the tremendous progress the country has achieved since the first plan, even though, the targets fixed in each plan might not have been fully met. Between 1951 and 2004, production of foodgrains had increased by 316 per cent, production of oilseeds by 400 per cent, that of sugarcane by 412 per cent and of cotton by 366 per cent. The increase in production of wheat has been really spectacular by over 1100 per cent.

Table 2.2 gives the annual compound growth rate since planning was initiated in 1951. During the first decade of planning (1951-1961) when the First and Second Five Year Plans were implemented the annual rate of growth in agriculture was 3.3 per cent. During the next two decades of planning (1961-1981), despite spectacular progress achieved under the new agricultural strategy and Intensive Area Development Programme (IADP) and High Yielding Verieties Programme (HYVP), the overall progress in agriculture was dismal. The average annual rate of growth declined to 2.2 per cent and 1.7

per cent respectively during 1961-1971 and 1971-1981 mainly because of the weather and poor monsoon conditions.

Table 2.2 : Growth of Agricultural Sector since 1950-51

Period	*Annual Compound Growth Rate (%)*	
	Agricultural & Allied Sector	*GDP*
1951-1961	3.3	3.8
1961-1971	2.2	3.5
1971-1981	1.7	3.3
1981-1991	1.9	5.7
1991-2001	2.8	6.7

Source : Economic Survey (2003-04).

But condition improved during the fourth decade of planning (1981-1991). The growth rate in the 1980s was highly respectable (3.9%). The compound growth rate for the period 1991-2001 was 2.8 per cent.

During 2002-03 the annual compound growth rate of agricultural production declined deeply to –7.2. per cent. The Tenth Plan had fixed a target growth rate of 4 per cent in agriculture to achieve 8 per cent growth in GDP. But the actual growth rate in agriculture and allied sector was only 2.3 per cent, while the actual growth rate in GDP was 7.6 per cent.

Table 2.3 : Annual Average Growth Rate (1985-90 to 2006-07)

Period	*Annual Compound Growth Rate (%)*	
	Agricultural & Allied Sector	*GDP*
1	2	3
Seventh Plan (1985-1990)	3.2	8.0
Annual Plan (1990-1992)	1.3	3.4
Eighth Plan (1992-1997)	4.7	6.7
Ninth Plan (1997-2002)	2.1	5.5
Tenth Plan (2002-2007)	2.3	7.6
2002-03	–7.2	3.8
2003-04	10.0	8.5
2004-05	0.0	7.5
2005-06	6.0	9.0
2006-07	2.7	9.2

Source: Economic Survey (2006-07).

With the introduction of planning in 1950-51, there was rapid extension of irrigation and application of intensive methods of agricultural practices including the adoption of hybrid seeds since 1964-65, there has been a steady and continuous increase in yield per hectare of almost all crops. Table 2.4 illustrates the growth of yield of principal crops in India.

Table 2.4 : Growth in Yield of Principal Crops in India since 1950-51

Items	*Yield per hectare*		
	1950-51	*1964-65*	*2004-05*
1	2	3	4
1. All foodgrains of which			
Rice (quintals)	7.1	10.8	20.5
Wheat (quintals)	6.6	9.1	27.6
Coarse Cereals (quintals)	4.3	5.1	11.5
Pulses (quintals)	4.0	5.2	6.2
2. All non-food crops of which			
Oilseeds (quintals)	5.2	5.6	10.7
Sugarcane (tonnes)	34.2	47.0	59.0
Cotton (kgs)	95.0	122.0	307.0
Potato (quintals)	66.0	84.0	200.0

Source : Economic Survey (2003-04).

As it is not feasible to lump together yield per hectare of different crops under the group of 'non-foodgrains', hence the yield per hectare in selected years for some selected crops has been shown. Monsoon and weather conditions affect average yield per hectare and, therefore, the variations in the yield per hectare reflect not only the effects of improved agricultural techniques but also that of natural factors, such as monsoon and weather conditions.

During the pre-green revolution period, rice recorded most impressive growth rate in yield—from 7 quintals per hectare in 1950-51 to nearly 11 quintals per hectare in 1964-65, a modest annual rate of growth of 1.3 per cent. Among non-foodgrains, cotton and sugarcane recorded low growth rates during this period.

Table 2.5 presents the trends in production of some selected crops in India from 2000-01 to 2006-07. It is evident from the

table that the production of foodgrains increased from 196.8 million tonnes in 2000-01 to 216.1 million tonnes in 2006-07. The production of cereals increased from 185.7 million tonnes in 2006-07. Rice witnessed the production of 69.7 million tonnes in 2006-07. Pulse recorded the production of 11.1 million tonnes in 2000-01 to 14.2 million tonnes in 2006-07. Oilseeds recorded the production of 18.4 million tonnes in 2000-01 to 345.3 million tonnes in 2006-07.

Table 2.5 : Agricultural Production in India (2000-01 to 2006-07)

Items	*Units*	*2000-01*	*2001-02*	*2002-03*	*2003-04*	*2004-05*	*2005-06*	*2006-07*
1	2	3	4	5	6	7	8	9
1. Foodgrains	Million Tonnes	196.8	212.9	174.8	213.9	198.4	208.6	216.1
2. Cereals	-do-	185.7	199.5	163.7	198.3	185.2	195.2	201.9
3. Rice	-do-	85.0	93.3	71.8	88.5	83.1	91.8	92.8
4. Wheat	-do-	69.7	72.8	65.8	72.2	68.6	69.4	74.9
5. Pulses	-do-	11.1	13.4	11.1	14.9	13.1	13.4	14.2
6. Oilseeds	-do-	18.4	20.7	14.8	25.2	24.4	28.0	23.9
7. Sugarcane	-do-	206.0	297.2	287.4	233.9	237.1	281.2	345.3

Source : Yojana, November 2007, p. 4.

During the post-green revolution period, however, the most spectacular growth rate was recorded by wheat (3.2% per annum). Potato recorded an impressive growth rate of 3.1% per annum. Pulses recorded a growth rate of 0.1 per cent per annum. This shows that the new biochemical technology was particularly suited to wheat production but was not effective in the case of other crops.[77]

Land Reforms in India: In the post-Independence period, the attempts of the Union as well as the State governments in the field of institutional change or land reforms have been found concentrated on the following four aspects:

1. Abolition of the Zamindari System;
2. Ceiling on land holdings;
3. Consolidation of holdings; and
4. Tenancy reforms.

After Independence, high priority was accorded to the abolition of intermediary tenures (zamindars). Accordingly, every State enacted its own legislation to abolish this tenure system on the payment of compensation. Basically, the law provided for the State takeover of the estates of the zamindars on payment of compensations and offering their ownership to cultivators on their payment of fixed sums. The process of legislative action commenced in 1948 and was completed in 1954, by which time most States had adopted necessary legislations. During the interim period of six years, the Abolition Acts were challenged in the High Courts and later taken to the Supreme Court for adjudication. The Supreme Court while upholding the rights of the legislature to takeover lands for public purpose, ruled that the question of the adequacy of compensation was justiciable issue. A constitutional amendment to meet the ruling of the Supreme Court was effected and the laws were revised. "However, during the six-year period of confusion, the zamindars not only extracted more compensation for the expropriated rights, they also resorted to several steps such as litigations, resuming personal cultivation, eviction of tenants by force or social pressure and parcelling of the estates to obviate the law."[78]

On the progress of the abolition of the intermediaries, the Draft Fifth Plan repeats the claim made 13 years ago in the Third Plan document that necessary legislation for the abolition of inter- mediary tenures or payment of compensation was adopted in almost all the States by 1954. Implementation of the enacted laws has since been practically all over the country and only a few minor intermediary tenures still remain to be abolished. But the periodical government, nobody is sure about the extent of the effected reforms. However, a comparison with the State-wise review done by the Task Force reveals that a number of intermediary tenures affecting sizeable sections of the poor peasantry still remain to be abolished in most of the States. Even in Kerala which is far ahead of the Indian States on the enactment and implementation of land reforms, even though several legislations for the abolition of intermediaries were enacted after 1954, there are several intermediary rights yet to

be abolished which cover a sizeable area affecting a large number of tenants.

Moreover, by asserting repeatedly in the Third, Fourth, Fifth and Sixth Plan documents that 20 million tenants are estimated to have come into direct contact with the State as a result of the abolition of intermediary tenures and resumption of large areas of privately owned forest land, grazing land and cultivable waste land by the State, one begins to wonder whether there had been any progress at all during the last 25 years between the Third and the Fifth Plans, because ever since the launching of the Third Plan in 1961, the number of persons who benefited from the land reform measures has remained constant, while there are claims about several measures implemented during this period. While it has to be accepted that some progress has been made in this regard, whatever has been done in this sphere to effect socio-economic justice to the weaker sections, has been negated by the payment of huge compensation to the zamindars (landlords) amounting to Rs. 670 crores, that is, Rs. 520 crores as compensation and Rs. 150 crore for interest charges. Curiously enough, the planners of the Fifth Plan complained that implementation of these reforms imposed a heavy administrative and financial burden on some of the State governments, while at the same time they themselves had earmarked the expenditure on compensation for the 5 years of the Fifth Plan. But in 1974, the planners were worried about the delay in making the payment of compensation to the landlords. It was emphasised in the Fourth Plan that "Progress made in the payment of compensation to ex-intermediaries in some States have been slow. Therefore, they wanted the assessment and payment of compensation to be expedited, particularly in Bihar, Orissa, Uttar Pradesh and West Bengal."[79]

Discussing the overall effect of the abolition of the zamindari system, Veil remarks: "Even though this brought the government into closer contact with a great many tillers of the soil, the devolution of wealth did not proceed very far. The losses were borne by a tiny number of landlords, who through various loopholes, continued to hold large estates. The benefits accrued to a large but still very limited number of farmers. On the balance, the lowest echelons of

society such as sharecroppers and day labourers neither gained nor lost from these rounds of land reforms.[80]

An important part of land reforms relates to the fixation of a ceiling or an upper limit on landholdings, and also by implication defining a 'floor' level or lower limit on landholding. There are two elements: One is related to fixation of ceiling above which nobody can hold land, and is applicable to future holders as well; and the second, surplus land from the holding above the ceiling for distribution among farmers and landless labourers to bring them up to the ceiling level. The object is two-fold: to reduce the size of landholdings of the big landowners on the one hand and to increase the size of holdings of small cultivators on the other.

Although the Union Government paid up sympathy to the question of land ceiling, it was only during the Third Plan that some attempts were made to enact ceiling laws. Legislation in some form or the other now exists in almost all the States providing for a ceiling on landholdings. But these laws are so full of loopholes and exemptions in favour of big land owners that they in collusion with bureaucracy, have reduced ceiling legislation to a mere mockery.

The class nature of the ceiling legislation becomes more pertinent by analysis of the figures on the size of the ceiling fixed in different States or regions, and the area declared surplus, and its distribution. The laws enacted by the State Legislature presupposes a ceiling on existing holdings that would preserve middle land holders and rich peasants. With more than 60 per cent of the total households on average owing only up to 2 acres each and together holding as little as 7 per cent of the total land, and 5 per cent of the upper group holds significance. The ceiling fixed by the principal States has been presented in the Table 2.6.

Land reforms in India had envisaged that beyond a certain specified limit, all lands belonging to the landlords would be taken over by the State and allotted to small proprietors to make their holdings economic or to landless labourers to meet their demand for land. Justifying an absolute limit to the amount of land to be held by an individual, the Report of the Committee of Panel on Land Reforms observed: "Among all resources, the supply of land

Table 2.6 : Ceiling Limits on Landholdings in India

(In hectares)

State	*Irrigated with two crops*	*Irrigated with one crop*	*Dry Land*
1	2	3	4
A. *Suggested in National Guidelines of 1972*	4.05 to 7.28	10.93	21.85
B. *Actual Ceiling*			
1. Andhra Pradesh	4.05 to 7.28	6.07 to 10.93	14.16 to 21.85
2. Assam	6.74	6.74	6.74
3. Bihar	6.02 to 7.28	10.12	12.14 to 18.21
4. Gujarat	4.05 to 7.28	6.07 to 10.93	8.09 to 21.85
5. Haryana	7.25	10.9	21.8
6. Himachal Pradesh	4.05	6.07	12.14 to 28.33
7. Jammu & Kashmir	3.6 to 5.06	–	5.95 to 9.20
8. Karnataka	4.05 to 8.10	10.12 to 12.14	21.85
9. Kerala	4.86 to 6.07	4.86 to 6.07	4.86 to 6.07
10. Madhya Pradesh	7.28	10.93	21.85
11. Maharashtra	7.28	10.93	21.85
12. Manipur	5.00	5.00	6.00
13. Orissa	4.05	6.07	12.14 to 18.21
14. Punjab	7.00	11.00	20.50
15. Rajasthan	7.28	10.93	21.85 to 70.82
16. Tamil Nadu	4.86	12.14	24.28
17. Sikkim	5.06	–	20.23
18. Tripura	4.00	4.00	4.00
19. Uttar Pradesh	7.30	40.95	18.25
20. West Bengal	5.00	5.00	7.00

Source: Government of India (2002), *Agricultural Statistics at a Glance (2002)*, Ministry of Agriculture, New Delhi, p. 250.

is the most limited and the claimants for its possession are extremely numerous. It is, therefore, obviously unjust to allow the exploitation of any large surface of land by single individual unless other overwhelming reasons make this highly desirable. Moreover, in the context of the current socio-political climate, redistribution of land would rather appear to be imperative."[81] Thus the case for pursuing a policy of imposition of land ceiling rests on the following grounds :

(i) In the rural sector, land is the principal source of income. If land, the fountainhead of income, benefits only a minor

fraction of the rural population, the whole structure of land ownership fails to meet the ends of social justice. The best course of bringing a reduction in inequalities of income is to bring about a reduction in inequalities of land ownership.

(ii) A policy of application of capital intensive methods in Indian agriculture would lead to unemployment on a massive scale. Consequently, the Government of India would like to create a large number of small peasant proprietors. Fears have been expressed by critics that the policy of breaking big estates will transfer land from the resourceful landlords to the resourceless peasants of tenants. It is alleged that such a policy may although enlarge employment, but will adversely affect production.

The whole argument of large-scale economies and maximising production is theoretical. Farm management studies reveal that gross output per area is greater on small farms than that on large farms. Historical evidence supports the imposition of ceiling because such a policy can enlarge employment and while meeting the ends of social justice does not in any way act as a hindrance to achieve maximum production.

Legislation for ceiling on existing holdings and units of application has been enacted in two phases. During the first phase which lasted up to 1972, ceiling legislation largely treated land holders as the unit of application. After 1972, it was decided to have family as the basis of holding. Further, the ceiling limit was also reduced to bring about a more equitable distribution of this scarce asset (Table 2.6).

The position of implementation of ceiling laws in India up to March 2002 has been presented in Table 2.7. Table 2.7 reveals that since the inception of ceiling laws on agricultural holdings, up to 31st March, 2003, total quantum of land declared surplus in the entire country was 73.73 lakh acres out of which 65.0 lakh acres have been taken in possession, and a total area of 53.93 lakh acres has been distributed among 54.47 lakh beneficiaries.

Table 2.7 : Implementation of Ceiling Laws in Different States in India (2002-03)

State	*Area Declared Surplus (acres)*	*Area taken in possession (acres)*	*Area distributed (acres)*	*No. of beneficiaries (lakh)*
1	2	3	4	5
1. Andhra Pradesh	799663	641655	582319	540344
2. Assam	613400	575377	545870	445848
3. Bihar	415447	390752	306964	379528
4. Gujarat	227404	160801	139853	32308
5. Haryana	107487	103017	102123	29228
6. Himachal Pradesh	316556	304895	6167	6259
7. Jammu & Kashmir	455575	450000	450000	450000
8. Karnataka	268478	161834	123204	33610
9. Kerala	141427	96891	68745	166814
10. Madhya Pradesh	298763	260323	186942	74705
11. Maharashtra	740002	670449	642835	140850
12. Manipur	1823	1685	1682	1258
13. Orissa	179176	167253	156948	139595
14. Punjab	223115	105834	104232	28574
15. Rajasthan	611096	569211	461147	81808
16. Tamil Nadu	200920	191628	181295	143683
17. Tripura	1995	1944	1598	1424
18. Uttar Pradesh	374125	341464	258698	294062
19. West Bengal	1383852	1294739	1064044	2651619
20. Dadra & N.H.	9406	9305	6851	3353
21. Delhi	1132	394	394	654
22. Pondicherry	2326	1209	1070	1464
All India	7373175	6500620	5393681	5646988

Source : Government of India (2003), *Annual Report (2002-03)*, Ministry of Rural Development, New Delhi.

In India, the fragmentation and subdivision of land has proved detrimental to increased agricultural production and other commodities. Consolidation of holdings, on the other hand, increases the operational and productive efficiency of cultivators by making land more compact. It stands for the substitution by exchange of fields among the farmers in an area in such a way as to make the holding held by each of them more compact. On consolidation, the number of fragments in the holdings is reduced. The fields are made contiguous with each other.

The legislation pertaining to the consolidation exist at present in most of the States. The main provision of the legislation refers

to (i) introduction of schemes; (ii) reservation of new areas for common purposes in the consolidation schemes; (iii) payment of compensation to those who have been allotted holdings of less market value than their original holdings; (iv) prescription of the rights of persons in the new holdings; (v) administrative machinery for carrying out the scheme; and (vi) filing of objections, appeals, penalties etc. No much progress was made in consolidation during the First Plan. In the Second Plan, this work was treated as an integral part of agricultural production programme. The Third Plan and the Annual Plans carried forward the programme of consolidation of holdings in the country. By 1968-69, 29.572 million hectares had been consolidated. During the Fourth Plan another 9.424 million hectares were expected to consolidate and a sum of Rs. 28,358 crore was provided in the States for this purpose.[82]

While the States like Punjab and Haryana had already completed the work of consolidation by 1968-69, the States like West Bengal, Bihar, Orissa and Assam were far lagging behind. Further, the States like Karnataka, Maharashtra, Gujarat, Madhya Pradesh and Rajasthan are the States where appreciable progress in regard to consolidation of holdings has been made. The poor performance of the States like Assam, Bihar, Orissa and West Bengal in the sphere of the consolidation of holdings shows the lack of political will and commitment in the government of these States to complete the work.

Thus, a significant feature of the consolidation work is the uneven progress in the different States, the bulk of the consolidated area being accommodated for Punjab, Haryana and Madhya Pradesh.[83]

By 1972, nearly 32.6 million hectares of land had been consolidated. Regarding the progress of consolidation of holdings by 1980, the Sixth Five Year Plan (1980-85) states :

> "It is estimated that by now, nearly 45 million hectares of land, i.e. about one-fourth of the consolidable land has been consolidated all over the country. However, the implementation has been extremely patchy and sporadic.

> Only in Punjab, Haryana and Western Uttar Pradesh, the work is complete. Even a beginning has not been made in the southern States and Rajasthan. In the eastern States, some work has begun only in Orissa and Bihar."[84]

Similarly, the Seventh Five Year Plan states :

> "Upto the year 1979-80, the consolidated area was 46.2 million hectares. The total area consolidated during the Sixth Plan was 5.6 million hectares. Thus the total area consolidated so far is 51.5 million hectares which is only 33 per cent of the total cropped area in the country."[85]

The consolidation operations have not made much headway in many States. Consolidation of landholdings is especially important in the States like Assam, Bihar, Orissa and West Bengal. Some of the factors working against consolidation are (a) fear of displacement among tenants and share-croppers, (b) advantage of having land in fragmented parcels in the event of floods and other natural calamities, and (c) apprehensions that the bigger farmers would get a better deal. These factors would have borne in mind while considering a policy for consolidation in future. As far as possible, the holdings of small and marginal farmers need to be consolidated in such a way that they form contiguous block of land so that the exploitation of ground water for them as well as provision of various agricultural services and inputs become economical.

Dr. Minhas observes : "However, the consolidation programme is defective. Firstly, it is not compulsory in all areas and its progress has been extremely slow. Secondly, the process of consolidation is not at all explicitly related to rational land development. Thirdly, the procedure is such that even after consolidation, farmers are left with not one but three or four disjointed parcels.[86]

It is true that most States (but not all) have passed Land Consolidation Acts. Only a few of them have achieved a measure of success in implementing them. A study by the Programme

Evaluation Organisation of the Planning Commission observes that except for Punjab, Haryana and Uttar Pradesh, the programme of consolidation has gone at snail's pace and that unless a high priority is accorded to the work, it may take another 50 years to complete it.

The sad social and economic plight of tenants and also their sheer number call for serious attention and concerted efforts for the improvement of their lot. Broadly speaking, tenants can be divided into (a) tenants-at-will, (b) sub-tenants, and (c) occupancy or permanent tenants. While the occupancy tenants enjoy fixation and security of rent and can get reimbursement of improvement made on the land, the other categories, especially tenants-at-will continue to suffer from serious disabilities. They are subject to ruthless exploitation, periodic enhancement of rents and eviction on any pretext. A high proportion of these tenants belong to the lower caste and backward social classes. They are thus in extremely vulnerable condition in dealing with land owners who are in a comparatively stronger position. In number tenants constitute 12.7 per cent of the total agricultural population and tenant households constitute 23.6 per cent of the total cultivating households in India. The percentage of area leased out forms 20 per cent of the total cultivation area though this ratio varies from 27 per cent in Punjab to 6.7 per cent in Madhya Pradesh.

The basic function of tenancy is to allow two parties—land owners and tenants—to combine their inputs into a single production unit. Economic theory tells that for maximising net revenue an owner-operator will carry production to the point where the value of marginal product is equal to the price of the inputs. In the tenant-landowners arrangements each party utilises inputs belonging to the other. If each party considers the inputs contributed by the other party to have a zero price (as is generally the case), there will be a tendency to use the other party's inputs upto the point where the value of marginal product is zero. The landowner would tend to push the use of the tenant's labour to the point of zero marginal product. The tenant, on the other hand, considers the price of land to be zero while for the landowner it is his investment. The tenant in that case will have

an incentive to use the additional land as product is greater than zero. The tenancy arrangement, thus creates a conflict of interests. Another case of conflicting interest is the degree of certainty of tenure for tenants. Insecurity of tenure is frequently pointed out as a major problem in tenancy arrangements. Uncertainty is said to prevent cultivating tenants for making long-term improvement on land and method of cultivation. Recent legislation has been aimed at protecting the tenants. In some countries especially in Europe, security of tenure has been increased to a degree which resembles ownership. Landowners have been reduced to little more than rent receivers, much as though they were holders of mortgage in the property. It is interesting to note that this type of feeling exists in India[87] in minds of landowners, with the resultant hesitancy. This high degree of security for tenants can be criticised as favouring misallocation of resources. If the landowner is to fulfil his role in the agricultural economy as an active partner, he should enjoy security of his investment in land and other fixed investments. This in turn would require less security for tenants. These conflicts in interests should be resolved by carefully weighing the relative priority accorded to the objectives such as equity and efficiency. There are several important considerations affecting tenant- landowners arrangement such as fixed rent *versus* rent varying output, length of tenure and the question of compensating tenants for capital improvement.[88] Khusro has provided a theoretical basis for the empirical findings in India that "where there is no cost-sharing by the landlord acre for acre, the tenant farmers invest less per acre than owner farmers and hence produce less per acre too."[89] It can be shown by equating marginal revenue curve and marginal cost curve for a one-half share rental arrangement, that, if the landlord and the tenant share variable costs in the same proportion as they share the returns from the farm, optimum use of the inputs is the same as for another operated farm.

The various States in India have enacted tenancy reforms legislations to protect the poorer tenants of different categories as outlined above. These measures pertain to Regulation of Rent, Security of Tenures and Conferment of ownership on Tenants.

A recent statement from the Task Force on Agrarian Relations appointed by the Planning Commission sums up the general effectiveness of the land reforms "The overall assessment has to be that programmes of land reforms adopted since Independence have failed to bring about the required change in the agrarian structure."[90] Unfortunately, the achievements from various land reform measures have fallen far short of the target. Commenting on the implementation of various measures, the Task Force further remarks: "In no sphere of public policy in our country since Independence, hiatus between precept and practice, between policy pronouncement and actual execution has been as great as in the domain of land reforms."[91] The National Commission on Agriculture has also derived the same conclusion in the same words.[92]

From the mid-1980s when liberalisation started entering the Indian economy at first steadily and then with thunderous gale force from 1991, land reform went off the radar screen of the Indian polity. It became a forgotten agenda. Marketers in the government find it repugnant to talk about it, just as in the case of the operations in the market get frightened by any State intervention in the land or lease market. They are finding the existing land reform laws which were enacted on the basis of the central guidelines of 1972, not only unwanted road blocks, but also obnoxious to the free play of the capital in the land market. Hence, there is a strong lobby to enhance or to give up land ceiling to recognise tenancy and allow free market forces to determine terms and conditions of tenancy or lease to allow corporate houses to enter the agrarian sector to introduce capitalist farming, to move away from tradition of crop husbandry to export-oriented crop production and the like. The short question is: has land reforms became totally irrelevant in these days of liberalisation privatisation and globalisation?

As a general proposition, it may be said that land reforms should remain an essential element of national agricultural and rural development strategies not only because land-based agricultural occupation must continue to provide livelihood to a vast majority of rural population, but also because macro-economic growth in

most contexts has failed to create improved prospects, gainful employment or increase their income and quality of life. While one cannot seriously challenge the above proposition, the experience world over has been that government budgets for agricultural and rural development has been reduced, farmer's cooperatives have been disintegrated prior focus on tenancy reforms has been replaced by a focus on land markets and flexible labour conditions and land price has escalated due to speculative activities and general pressure on land. Under such circumstances, it has become extremely difficult for the rural poor to have access to new productive land and maintain secure tenure unless there is a significant policy change towards comprehensive land and tenancy reforms with the active participation of the intended beneficiaries.

Rural Poverty Eradication in India

Poverty and unemployment anywhere are danger to peace and prosperity everywhere. According to the World Bank Report on Rural Development from Vision to Action, more than 1.3 billion people are compelled to live on less than one dollar (US $) a day. More than 800 million people are hungry and the number may exceed one billion by the year 2020. The report has further envisaged that 72 per cent of them live in rural areas and a significant majority depends on agriculture for their meagre livelihood.[93] Similarly, the *Human Development Report 2005*, published by the UNDP has envisaged that "Fighting hunger and poverty and promoting development are the truly sustainable way to achieve world peace. There will be no peace without development and there will be neither peace nor development without social justice."[94]

The rate of poverty is higher in rural areas than that of the urban areas and is more pervasive among the landless labour class in rural areas as compared to landowning class. According to the *National Human Development Report-2001*, 26.5 per cent of people in rural areas are living below the poverty line.[95] Another *Report on Food Security in India* envisages that 3.3 per cent of families in rural areas are suffering from hunger. The percentage is high in West

Bengal, Orissa, Assam and Bihar (10.4, 8.0, 7.1 and 6.0 respectively) (see Table 2.8).[96] According to UNICEF statistics 13.4 per cent of population in India is living in food insecurity. It has been estimated that about 27.3 million people had to suffer some degree of hunger and as many as 23 per cent of the population remained undernourished as of late 1990s.

Table 2.8 : State-wise Distribution of Population Below Poverty Line and Hunger in Rural India

State	Rural population below poverty line (%)	Rural families suffering from hunger (%)
1	2	3
1. Andhra Pradesh	10.5	1.9
2. Assam	40.2	7.1
3. Bihar	44.0	6.0
4. Gujarat	12.4	0.5
5. Haryana	7.4	1.5
6. Himachal Pradesh	7.5	N.A.
7. Karnataka	16.9	0.9
8. Kerala	9.4	2.9
9. Madhya Pradesh	37.2	3.1
10. Maharashtra	23.3	1.9
11. Orissa	47.8	8.0
12. Punjab	6.0	0.2
13. Rajasthan	13.4	0.2
14. Tamil Nadu	20.1	0.7
15. Uttar Pradesh	31.0	2.1
16. West Bengal	31.7	10.4
India	26.5	3.3

Source: For col. 1, Planning Commission (2002), *National Human Development Report (2001)*, Government of India, New Delhi. For col. 3, Vyas, V.S. (2005), "Food Security in India", in Vyas, V.S. (ed) *Food Security in Asian Countries in the Context of Millennium Goals*, Academic Foundation, New Delhi.

The State-wise rural and urban poverty lines for the year 2004-05 has been given in Table 2.9. The poverty lines have been estimated using the original State-specific poverty lines identified by the Expert Group and updating them to 2004-05 prices using the Consumer Price Index of Agricultural Labourers (CPIAL) for

rural poverty lines and Consumer Price Index for Industrial Workers (CPIIW) for urban poverty lines.

Table 2.9 : State-Specific Poverty Lines (2004-05)

(Rs. Per Capita Per Month)

State/U.T.	Rural	Urban
1	2	3
1. Andhra Pradesh	292.95	542.89
2. Assam	387.00	378.84
3. Bihar	354.36	435.00
4. Chhattisgarh	322.41	507.00
5. Delhi	410.38	612.91
6. Goa	362.25	665.90
7. Gujarat	353.93	541.16
8. Haryanå	414.76	504.49
9. Himachal Pradesh	394.28	504.49
10. Jammu & Kashmir	391.26	553.77
11. Jharkhand	366.56	451.24
12. Karnataka	324.17	599.66
13. Kerala	430.12	559.39
14. Madhya Pradesh	327.78	570.15
15. Maharashtra	362.25	665.90
16. Orissa	325.79	528.49
17. Punjab	410.38	466.16
18. Rajasthan	374.57	559.63
19. Tamil Nadu	351.86	547.42
20. Uttar Pradesh	365.84	483.26
21 Utarakhand	478.02	637.67
22. West Bengal	382.82	449.32
23. Dadar & Nagar Haveli	362.25	665.90
All India	356.30	538.60

Note : The poverty line (implicit) at All India level is worked out from the expenditure class-wise distribution of persons based on uniform recall period (URP)-consumption, i.e. consumption data collected from 30-day recall period for all items) and the poverty ratio at all India is obtained as the weighted average of the State-wise poverty ratio.

Source : Kurukshetra, Vol. 55, No. 7, p. 44.

The National Sample Survey Organisation (NSSO) has now released the result of the latest large sample survey data on household consumer expenditure (NSS, 61st Round), covering the

period July 2004 to June 2005 [Report No. 508, 61/1.0/1]. From these data, two different consumption distributions for the year 2004-05 have been obtained. The first from the consumption data collected using 30-day recall period (also known as reference period) for all the items. The other distribution is obtained from the consumption expenditure data collected using 365-day recall period for five infrequently purchased non-food items, namely clothing, footwear, durable goods, education and institution medical expenses and 30-day recall period for the remaining items. These two consumption distributions have been termed as Uniform Recall Period (URP) consumption distribution, and Mixed Recall Period (MRP) consumption distribution respectively. The Planning Commission, using the Expert Methodology has estimated poverty ratio in 2004-05 using both the distributions.

The State-specific percentage and number of poor in rural and urban areas estimated from URP consumption distribution has been given in Table 2.10.

From Tables 2.10 and 2.11 it is evident that about 27 per cent of India's population live below the poverty line. The poverty estimate in 2004-05 based on URP consumption distribution (27.5%) is comparable with the poverty estimates of 1993-94 which was 36 per cent. The poverty estimate in 2004-05 based on MRP consumption distribution (21.8%) is roughly but not strictly comparable with the poverty estimates of 1999-2000 which was 26.1 per cent.

Primary sector plays a very important role in eradication of rural poverty. As a matter of fact, agriculture is the mainstay of rural population and more than 70 per cent of population depends on agriculture for their livelihood and still it is the main source of employment in rural India. In India almost everything begins with agriculture. Industry itself depends on the growth of agriculture. Out of agriculture grows industry. The Planning Commission has envisaged that India needs to sustain an agricultural growth rate of 4 to 4.5 per cent in order to reduce food insecurity and poverty. At this growth rate agricultural development could more rapidly diversify into horticulture, fishery, dairying, animal husbandry and other areas.[97] Therefore, it is urged that tapping the full potential

Table 2.10 : Number and Percentage of Population Below Poverty Line by States in India (2004-05)
[Based on URP Consumption]

State / U.T.	Rural		Urban		Combined	
	% of persons	No. of persons (lakhs)	% of persons	No. of persons (lakhs)	% of persons	No. of persons (lakhs)
1	2	3	4	5	6	7
1. Andhra Pradesh	11.2	64.70	28.0	61.40	15.8	126.10
2. Arunachal Pradesh	22.3	1.94	3.3	0.09	17.6	2.03
3. Assam	22.3	54.50	3.3	1.28	19.7	55.77
4. Bihar	42.1	336.72	34.6	32.42	41.4	369.15
5. Chhattisgarh	40.8	71.50	41.2	19.47	40.9	90.96
6. Delhi	6.9	0.63	15.2	22.30	14.7	22.93
7. Goa	5.4	0.36	21.3	1.64	13.8	2.01
8. Gujarat	19.1	63.49	13.0	27.19	16.8	90.69
9. Haryana	13.6	21.49	15.1	10.60	14.0	32.10
10. Himachal Pradesh	10.7	6.14	3.4	0.22	10.0	6.36
11. Jammu & Kashmir	4.6	3.66	7.9	2.19	5.4	5.85
12. Jharkhand	46.3	103.19	20.2	13.20	40.3	116.39
13. Karnataka	20.8	75.05	32.6	63.83	25.0	138.89
14. Kerala	13.2	32.43	20.2	17.17	15.0	49.60
15. Madhya Pradesh	36.9	175.65	42.1	74.03	38.3	249.88
16. Maharashtra	29.6	171.13	32.2	146.25	30.7	317.38
17. Manipur	22.3	3.76	3.3	0.20	17.3	3.95
18. Meghalaya	22.3	4.36	3.3	0.16	18.5	4.52
19. Mizoram	22.3	1.02	3.3	0.16	12.6	1.18
20. Nagaland	22.3	3.87	3.3	0.12	19.0	3.99

(Contd.)

Table 2.10 : (*Contd*)

State / U.T.	Rural		Urban		Combined	
	% of persons	No. of persons (lakhs)	% of persons	No. of persons (lakhs)	% of persons	No. of persons (lakhs)
1	2	3	4	5	6	7
21. Orissa	46.8	151.75	44.3	26.74	46.4	178.49
22. Punjab	9.1	15.12	7.1	6.50	8.4	21.63
23. Rajasthan	18.7	87.38	32.9	47.51	22.1	134.89
24. Sikkim	22.3	1.12	3.3	0.02	20.1	1.14
25. Tamil Nadu	22.8	76.50	22.2	69.13	22.5	145.62
26. Tripura	22.3	6.18	3.3	0.20	18.9	6.38
27. Uttar Pradesh	33.4	473.00	30.6	117.03	32.8	590.03
28. Utarakhand	40.8	27.11	36.5	8.85	39.6	35.96
29. West Bengal	28.6	173.22	14.8	35.14	24.7	208.36
30. A & N Islands	22.9	0.60	22.2	0.32	22.6	0.927
31. Chandigarh	7.1	0.08	7.1	0.67	7.1	0.74
32. D. & N. Haveli	39.8	0.68	19.1	0.15	33.2	0.84
33. Daman & Diu	5.4	0.07	21.2	0.14	10.5	0.21
34. Lakshadweep	13.3	0.06	20.2	0.06	16.0	0.11
35. Pondicherry	22.9	0.78	22.2	1.59	22.4	2.37
All India	28.3	2209.24	25.7	807.96	27.5	3017.20

Source : *Kurukshetra*, Vol. 55, No. 7, May 2007, p. 45.

Table 2.11 : Number and Percentage of Population Below Poverty Line by States in India (2004-05)
[Based on MRP Consumption]

State / U.T.	Rural		Urban		Combined	
	% of Persons	No. of Persons (lakhs)	% of Persons	No. of Persons (lakhs)	% of Persons	No. of Persons (lakhs)
1	2	3	4	5	6	7
1. Andhra Pradesh	7.5	43.21	20.7	45.50	11.1	88.71
2. Arunachal Pradesh	17.0	1.47	2.4	0.07	13.4	1.54
3. Assam	17.0	41.46	2.4	0.93	15.0	42.39
4. Bihar	32.9	262.92	28.9	27.09	32.5	290.01
5. Chhattisgarh	31.2	54.72	34.7	16.39	32.0	71.11
6. Delhi	0.1	0.01	10.8	15.83	10.2	15.83
7. Goa	1.9	0.13	20.9	1.62	12.0	1.74
8. Gujarat	13.9	46.25	10.1	21.18	12.5	67.43
9. Haryana	9.2	14.57	11.3	7.99	9.9	22.56
10. Himachal Pradesh	7.2	4.10	2.6	0.17	6.7	4.27
11. Jammu & Kashmir	2.7	2.20	8.5	2.34	4.2	4.54
12. Jharkhand	40.2	89.76	16.3	10.63	34.8	100.38
13. Karnataka	12.0	43.33	27.2	53.28	17.4	96.60
14. Kerala	9.6	23.59	16.4	13.92	11.4	37.51
15. Madhya Pradesh	29.8	141.99	39.3	68.97	32.4	210.97
16. Maharashtra	22.2	128.43	29.0	131.40	25.4	259.83
17. Manipur	17.0	2.86	2.4	0.14	13.2	3.00
18. Meghalaya	17.0	3.32	2.4	0.12	14.1	3.43
19. Mizoram	17.0	0.78	2.4	0.11	9.5	0.89
20. Nagaland	17.0	2.94	2.4	0.09	14.5	3.03

(Contd.)

Table 2.11 : (*Contd*)

State / U.T.	Rural		Urban		Combined	
	% of Persons	No. of Persons (lakhs)	% of Persons	No. of Persons (lakhs)	% of Persons	No. of Persons (lakhs)
1	2	3	4	5	6	7
21. Orissa	39.8	129.29	40.3	24.30	39.9	153.59
22. Punjab	5.9	9.78	3.8	3.52	5.2	13.30
23. Rajasthan	14.3	66.69	28.1	40.50	17.5	107.18
24. Sikkim	17.0	0.85	2.4	0.02	15.2	0.87
25. Tamil Nadu	16.9	56.51	18.8	58.59	17.8	115.10
26. Tripura	17.0	4.70	2.4	0.14	14.4	4.85
27. Uttar Pradesh	25.3	357.68	26.3	100.47	25.5	458.15
28. Uttrakhand	31.7	21.11	32.0	7.75	31.8	28.86
29. West Bengal	24.2	146.59	11.2	26.64	20.6	173.23
30. A & N Islands	16.9	0.44	18.8	0.27	17.6	0.71
31. Chandigarh	3.8	0.04	3.8	0.36	3.8	0.40
32. D & N Haveli	36.0	0.62	19.2	0.16	30.6	0.77
33. Daman & Diu	1.9	0.03	20.8	0.14	8.0	0.16
34. Lakshadweep	9.6	0.04	16.4	0.05	12.3	0.09
35. Pondicherry	16.9	0.58	18.8	1.34	18.2	1.92
All India	21.8	1702.99	21.7	682.00	21.8	2384.99

Source : *Kurukshetra*, Vol. 55, No. 7, May 2007, p. 46.

of Indian agriculture to as Punjab, Haryana, Andhra Pradesh and Tamil Nadu which have higher adoption rate of modern varieties meet the rising domestic demand and to take advantage of the liberalisation of international trade will require first and foremost the recognition of the vital role agriculture can continue to play in national development.[98] Poverty ratios are lower in States such as Punjab, Haryana, Andhra Pradesh and Tamil Nadu which have higher adoption rate of modern varieties of rice. Despite the structural changes, agriculture still remains a key sector, providing both employment and livelihood opportunities to more than 70 per cent of the country's population, who live in rural areas. However, as far as agricultural productivity is concerned, yield of major crops and livestock in India is much lower than that in the rest of the world.

The failure of agriculture deeply affects the life and livelihood of rural people. Crop failure, food shortage and farmer's indebtedness deeply affect the life and livelihood of the people. The farmer's suicides in Andhra Pradesh, Maharashtra, Karnataka, Punjab, etc., reveal the correlation between agriculture and livelihood in rural India. The large scale land holders in the irrigated and even in the dry land belt enjoy exuberant lifestyle while the landless labourers and small and marginal farmers lead a miserable life. Development of India in real sense means development and modernisation of its agricultural and rural sector. A study conducted on income distribution among rural households in Punjab revealed that the total annual farm income of the smallest farmer's household was Rs. 1,231 while that of the biggest one was Rs. 24,283 and the disparities in the two income groups was found to be in the ratio of 1 : 20.[99] While showing the income disparities in dryland and wetland, a study in Tamil Nadu has revealed that the income disparities was in the ratio of 4.2 : 1.0 which suggests that in the wet area a poor peasant household's agricultural income is more than four times the average income of a corresponding household from the dry land area.[100] The percentage of poverty and hunger is higher among the landless than those of landowning classes. In West Bengal agrarian reforms in the State through their contribution to the institution of

condition of the poorest and provided some of the most favourable conditions anywhere in India for overcoming traditional pattern of deprivation along the lines of class, caste and gender.[101]

Proliferation of irrigation facilities and equitable distribution of land are the two major issues in agricultural development in rural India. It is suggested that a more equitable distribution of land would lead to a much larger investment in the farm sector and here it would be a stupendous vise in productivity.[102] The Green Revolution is a great success in the irrigated areas as compared to dry land areas. It is a well-known fact that if the fruits of development continue to be denied to large sections of the rural community while prosperity accrues to some, the resulting tensions—social and economic—may not only upset the process of orderly and peaceful change in the rural economy that even frustrate the national effort to step up agricultural production.[103]

Next to agriculture, in rural areas the allied sector activities like fishery, dairy, piggery, poultry, sheep and goat rearing, horticulture, etc. play an important role in the alleviation of household poverty. According to the central statistical organisation (CSO), the value of output from livestock and fisheries sectors at current prices during 2002-03 were Rs. 1,56,080 crore and Rs. 30,014 crore respectively. These sectors contributed 6.5 per cent of total GDP (5.4 per cent from livestock and 1.1 per cent from fisheries) in 2002-03. As envisaged in the *Economic Survey 2004-05*, the fishery sector provides employment to over 11 million people engaged fully in the activities pertaining to this sector with an equally impressive segment of the population engaged in ancillary activities. The percentage of poverty is comparatively more pervasive among the households without livestock than those with livestock.

The importance of horticulture in improving the productivity of land, generating employment, improving economic conditions of the farmers and entrepreneurship, enhancing exports and above all providing nutrition security to the people is widely acknowledged. Horticulture sector which includes fruits, vegetables, spices, floriculture and coconut, etc. with production

of 156.1 million tonnes in 2003-04, the sector contributed 30 per cent of GDP from agriculture. In the economically developed States like Punjab and Haryana and Western Uttar Pradesh, household dairy plays significant role in assuaging poverty among landless households. Similarly, in Himachal Pradesh horticultural activities have raised the standard of living of rural hilly tribal population. Fishery and poultry activities through cooperative entrepreneurship, farming have immensely helped many people in rural areas to earn substantial income and improve their livelihood conditions. In Andhra Pradesh fishery plays important role in raising the household income of the rural population. In West Bengal and Gujarat banana orchards and in Himachal Pradesh apple orchards influence the household income of the rural families.

The rising prices of pulses posits that farmers can gain a lot, if they diversify their agriculture either away from the traditional paddy cultivation or intensify inter-cropping of pulses. Vegetable oils (edible) and pulses constituted two main agricultural imports during the years 2002-03 and 2003-04. The percentage for vegetable oils of total agricultural imports was 64.7 and 71.3 respectively for the years 2002-03 and 2003-04. The cultivation of pulse influences the household income and nutrition in Eastern Uttar Pradesh.

Agriculture is the livelihood of rural India and is fundamental to the alleviation of rural poverty and hunger. The Green Revolution launched way back in 1960s has become too old and what Indian agriculture needs is a 'Second Green Revolution' in the 'dryland' and 'hunger belt' of the country. Moreover, Green Revolution should go hand in hand for the alleviation of poverty from the rural India.

The culture of cooperative farming needs to be revived and the landless agricultural labourer should be made a stakeholder of produce by the way of contributing their labour and by forging the opportunity cost of their wage.

Irrigation is the backbone of agriculture. The second Green Revolution as emphasised by the agricultural scientists should think of Green Revolution in the dry land areas.

Diversification of agriculture in dry land belt is the need of the hour. In the single rice crop belts of Orissa, Bihar, West Bengal, Assam, Uttar Pradesh and other States, the alternative system of utilisation of land particularly social specific of horticulture must be developed. Mango, banana, citrus, orange, guava and coconut orchards had to be undertaken in the dry land areas. Moreover, seasonal vegetable cultivation would substantiate household income. Efforts need to be made as how to involve more and more number of small and marginal farmers in the process of diversification of agriculture. Local specific pulse cultivation based on their agro-climatic condition and land varieties need to be promoted.

The allied sector activities need to be promoted to substantiate the income from agriculture. The cooperative dairy and poultry farming and fishery must be undertaken at the village level. Moreover, goat, sheep and pig rearing have been playing vital role in alleviation of poverty and hunger in socio-economically backward section of the society. In Himachal Pradesh and Jammu & Kashmir the sheep and goat rearing families have higher per capita income as compared to their counterpart only pursuing agriculture.

Creation of employment opportunities during the lean season would check the outmigration of rural youth to cities for employment. Capacity building of youth and women in agriculture and allied activities would generate their interest in primary sector. The outmigration of youth from villages in the long run would have adverse impact on agricultural development.

The Panchayati Raj Institutions (PRIs) need to play an important role in the development of primary sector. The 73rd Constitutional Amendment has envisaged that development of agriculture is one of the responsibilities of Panchayat. The Panchayati Raj Acts of many States have assigned duties and responsibilities to PRIs for the promotion of agriculture. For example, Punjab Panchayati Raj Act (1994) has envisaged formation of standing committees called Village Production Committees for the development of agriculture. The Standing Committees on agriculture need to be activated in all States for enhancing the involvement of PRIs in agricultural developments.

The soft loan available to the farmers must be sanctioned for the holistic development of agriculture, i.e. purchase of land, agricultural implements including bullock, seeds and fertilizers, allied sector activities etc. The farmers should be free from the clutches of money lenders and private exploiters.

The agricultural universities must play a proactive role. The interface between the farmers and agricultural scientists and veterinarians working at the grassroots level must be enhanced. It is well remarked that "A strategy of fine tuning research programmes to the specific needs of the poor based on their socio-economic characteristics and the agro-ecological conditions of their location. It involves identification of projects and commodity programmes that maximises benefits to the poor so that they produce more."[104]

The involvement of corporate sector in the diversification of agriculture in dry land areas would strengthen the backbone of agriculture in these needy areas. The corporate sector, i.e. Mahindra & Mahindra, Pepsi, Reliance, Bharati Groups, etc. are playing important role in the diversification of agriculture in Punjab.

Information and Communication Technology (ICT) and Rural Development

Information Technology (IT) is nothing but a happy marriage of computers and telecommunications. In the last 50 years, it is one technology which has grown dramatically and affected practically every aspect of life, that is information technology. The significant leverage provided by information technology (IT) for economic growth is the result of an evolution, significantly guided by a conscious government planning process, towards an eventual self-guided market. Nucleated in the mid-1950s by H.J. Bhabha and P.C. Mahalanobis, nurtured in the 1960s by Vikram Sarabhai and M.G.K. Menon focused for growth of applications in the 1970s by the Electronics Commission, the 1980s and the early 1990s saw government-steered liberalisation, preparing the ground work for the boom of the 1990s, whose momentum has sustained unabated to the present day. The 1984 computer policy, the 1986

Software Expert and Training Policy, the 1991-1995 macroeconomic and financial liberalisation policies, the setting up of a chain of Software Technology Parks (STPs), the 1998 National IT Task Force and the National Telecom Policy created the liberalisation and globalisation ambience that nurtured the initiatives of thousands of IT enterprises, whose combined effort has put India at the vanguard of the global IT and ITES (Information Technology Enable Services) outsourcing. The industry is well to achieve the set target of US dollar 50 billion by the end of 2008.

Urban India has been on move over the last ten years and the growth has accelerated especially over the last five years. However, the same cannot be said about the rural India. Urban Indians are full of confidence. But the rural Indians do not see much of a future for themselves. The only change in lives of many rural people is availability of some televisions which in fact have created greater aspiration amongst them. They can now visibly see the difference between the lives in Urban India and Rural India and cannot understand why they are being left so far behind.[105]

In a democratic set-up where some form of election (at Central, State or local levels) takes place almost every year and half, the feeling of deprivation amongst the people plays havoc, especially as rural people constitute 72.22 per cent of India's population. Every politician would be forced to be populist. Yet, there are a few constructive programmes which can really change the lives in rural India. Governments would be overturned frequently as no populist measure would rectify the great divide that is getting accentuated with India's urban growth. In fact, the policies required to sustain even the urban growth would be under threat and would not be consistently pursued. The only answer is a quick and urgent focus on rural areas towards rural transformation.

Over the last couple of centuries, rapid growth in the world has taken place in some parts, leaving the other parts to wait in turns. Fortunately in a functioning democratic set-up, this is not viable. India, therefore, presents a very interesting situation, where growth has to be simultaneously pursued for all sections of people. Solution to rural stagnation is the key to stability.

Rural India consists of about 700 million people living in 6,38,000 villages. The villages are characterised by low income. About 85 per cent of the rural households has an income less than Rs. 3,000 per month (amounting to Rs. 600 per month per person, assuming a family of five). Rural India now has very little industry. Its people are mostly underemployed in agriculture. At the same time, agricultural growth in India has slowed down to one per cent over last decade, falling behind the population growth.

Fortunately, most of villages in India has some form of roads today (even though they are in bad state) and at least one bus would ply a day to every village. Railway station is not very far off. Highways connect towns which are rarely farther than 15 km. Also, significant number of villages have electrical grid. However, the grid has power only during the period when the demand for power in urban India is low. During peak demand period, urban India has the capability of sapping all the power produced and the rural India is pumped only whatever is leftover. So even when the power flows into the rural grid (0 hour to 18 hours a day, depending on the State), the voltage could be as low as 90V (reflecting higher demand) to 440V (during nights when no one is using power). Decentralised power generation in rural India may be the only answer to this problem in the short run.

Telecommunication technology has advanced very rapidly. Even though only a small percentage of villages today have reliable telecom connection, the situation is fast changing. With the rural thrust it is reasonable to believe that most villages in India would band internet connection within the next three to four years. One may even hope to four years. One may even hope to get a 256 kbps reliable internet connectivity in most villages.

Fortunately, the information and communication technology (ICT) has the potential of being leveraged for transforming rural areas. If, along with ICT connectivity, a solution to decentralised power generation (or storage during off-peak demand hours) can be found, the basic infrastructure for transformation would exist. It is now time to build experiments and programmes which can leverage these technologies so that the efforts can be scaled as soon as ICT and power are available. The experiments need to be

conducted today so that the stage is set up for scaling. But without deriving significant learning's from the experiments, scaling could be disastrous.

There have been a number of companies which are setting up the base infrastructure in the villages, over the last several years. Internet Kiosks, run by a village entrepreneur, is the precursor to set up a full-fledged business centre in a village, which connects urban and rural India. While it could be a trade centre taking rural goods to urban markets and *vice versa*, the most important outcome could be setting up rural production centres, supplying goods and services not just in nearby urban markets, but all over the world. Lower manpower costs will shift production centres to these areas and create wealth there, thereby enhancing the help of ICTs, significant amount of experimentation and hard work is required to convert the opportunities into scalable realities. There has been some reluctance to commercialise and to scale and these projects collapse as soon as the intervening agencies move out. Also hardly only attempt has been made to examine the scalability of these projects to a larger number of villages.

Yet some interesting experiments and initiatives exist. The most significant has been on the education front where several efforts have shown to benefit young children. The most common of these programmes have been training rural children to obtain computer skills, n-logue communications, Tarahaat, Drishtee have done this in hundreds of villages around the country, training large number of children who use these basic skills to get a job. But the more interesting initiatives have been providing the rural children an internet-based coaching programme to help them pass school examinations, particularly school leaving examinations. The initial results of experiments on this on TeNet group of IIT, Madras have been fascinating. There are other efforts focused on conceptual education. While the content developed has been attractive there is as of yet, no model for these.

In the area of health care especially with some inexpensive tele-medicine kits, some interesting experiments are being carried out. A company called Heurosyptics have developed a remote monitoring of heart beat, remote blood pressure and ECG

measurement. Coupled with video-conferencing, remote diagnostics become feasible. However, the delivery of medicines, interfacing with existing health care efforts and business model for delivering health care in the villages need to be still worked out. Results need to be watched over the next year or two.

Another significant difference has been in terms of Rural BPO where the early sign show this to be a difficult but doable task. One could think of ten to twenty people in each village being employed in rural BPO in coming years. One may initially see migration to urban BPO, once a person gains experience and with time reverse migration when the experienced people go back to rural areas to set up the next set of BPO themselves. The efforts of a company called Desi Crew—a company incubated by Rural Technology and Business Incubator (RTBI) at IIT, Madras, would be interesting to watch.

Some initial work on IT enabled outsourcing of production (contract production work done in rural areas for urban business), does seem promising; but a lot more needs to be done to make this viable and scalable. Migration of people and migration of work has played a great equalising role in the world over the last 100 years and one could see this happening to rural India once communication and power infrastructure is available. ICT may enrich poverty alleviation programmes in a manner which has not been possible so far, adding a new dimension to all the rural development efforts.

Yet it is in agriculture where the maximum difference needs to be made. Use of ICT can get one to approach the problem in a very different way. ITC e-chaupal and EID parry have used ICT for providing support to farmers and carry out their procurement for several years. n-logue communications and e-Sagoo project of IIT,Hyderabad have used video-conferencing and photographs to provide advisory to farmers. But these efforts have been far from comprehensive.

ICT based Rural Agricultural Support centres can be set-up in each village which could provide complete agricultural support to each farm in the village. This would start with creating a farm history record for every plot, including measurement of soil

parameters. It would further carry out weather monitoring, provide agricultural knowledge and advisory services, connecting farmers with exports on video-conferencing and market information. Linking farmers to commodity exchanges, finance and insurance companies would be another task.

One of the biggest issue facing agriculture in many parts of the country is the risk associated with agricultural business. Indian newspapers have been reporting everyday suicide committed by farmers when they lose everything in agriculture and cannot pay their debt. One of the newspapers recently wrote an editorial questioning whether farming in India is any more a viable venture.

One of the ways to look at the risk is to understand the factors which are not in control of the farmers, resulting into an unpredictable and risky situation. These factors are crop disease, weather (rainfall), especially in areas dependent on rains for agriculture and the third is the market prices. Disease can wipe out a crop when everything else has gone well. Lack of rainfall can destroy a farmer who chooses to invest significantly on inputs in the farms that year. Even when everything has worked well and the crop is plentiful and ready to be harvested, price collapse in the market could destroy the farmer. Most other variables are insignificant control of the farmers.

It is possible to use ICT creatively to mitigate these three risks to a great extent. Experiments have been conducted in using video-conferencing to connect farmers to agricultural experts. As soon as there is a sign of a disease, a farmer can consult an agricultural expert, show the crop and the leaves and diseased parts on a video. In almost 95 per cent of cases, suitable solutions which can be applied locally, are suggested. This needs to be systematised and scaled.

If one estimates the rainfall pattern in any area in the last 80 years, it is found that rain fails badly typically once in eight years. In other years either the farmer gets very good outputs or at least enough to take care of the costs of the inputs. This is an ideal case for ensurance—rainfall ensurance. The inputs for the agriculture could be covered by the insurance at a small premium. The problem is that rainfall patterns are quite a bit different from one village to

another. To accurately determine the rainfall in a village, it is possible to put an electronic rain gauge in the village connected to some data storage system on internet. Internet can also be used to manage this insurance. Department of Science & Technology, (Government of India) has initiated a project to install such low cost weather monitoring stations in 100 villages.

The third problem in associated with market price risk. Fortunately, commodity exchanges now exist in India where crops can be sold months in advance using FUTURES and even OPTIONS to sell certain amount of crop which can be taken at a price known in advance. In other words it is possible to peg the price of the crop at the time of sowing itself. Coupled with rainfall insurance, it can estimate all production risks so long as disease can be handled as discussed above. The key to make this available to a small farmer, ICT can play a great role in enabling this.

Risks aside, steps need to be taken to increase the crop output which has levelled off over the last decade. Yet the productivity is very low as compared to that of most other countries. One of the reasons is that very little is being done to understand the specific conditions of the farm and apply appropriate therapy. One hardly takes into account the soil conditions and moisture content of a specific farm, figure out what was grown in the last season and how much was the output. Here, a farm historian system could leverage ICT to provide a micro-level history of individual plots. Input parameters would include rainfall recorded, water irrigated, fertiliser applied, soil test results, etc. This then could provide a personalised advisory to help the farmer (especially marginal farmers) to manage their crop better. The idea is to know the history of the farm so as to decide the kind of crop to be grown and the amount of inputs to be put.

Yet another intervention required is in terms of water harvesting for the village as well as nearby village cluster. Once again a computer could be used to create topographical maps of the village. If the ground water information can also be added, it would help in planning the micro-irrigation works in the village so that most rains can be captured for the benefit of the villages.

Agro-industry and small rural industries can also leverage ICT to trade better as well as for knowledge and training. Rural supply chains are needed to transport goods from a village and financial services need to be developed so that finance is available in rural areas at 10 to 12 per cent interest rates (instead of 24 to 30 per cent interest rates at which most microfinance companies provide loans). Several interesting experiments are being done in this direction. Both State Bank of India as well as ICICI Bank are experimenting with the use of internet Kiosks as a banking output in the villages.

One can go on and on. The key is to build some great pilots quickly where ICT is preintegrated in rural development work. One must see clear benefits in two or three years. Rural India will not wait longer to scale. India cannot afford to let rural India languish.

Services are key to make a significant difference to lives in rural India through the internet. But this is also one of the misconstructed areas of this endeavour. Many have understood providing services to rural areas to be equivalent to web-development or some software development. Software development is at most a tool and not a service, constitutes a small part of the effort to build services. Any service must have as its end result, the intention to impact the lives of people in rural India.

A tool or web-development which allows the farmers to ask questions to some agricultural experts and get an answer, is not by itself a service which would help agriculture. The service would require identifying the right experts and getting them to participate in the process and provide answers that would make a material difference in a timely manner. Also, there is an assumption that such a service is required by the farmers on a continuous basis for which they are willing to pay sufficiently to cover the cost of running an internet kiosk, connectivity, cost to experts and cost of infrastructure required at the experts end. Without this framework where the complete money flow including the logistics worked out, it is not a scalable service.

IT and communication has lifted India out of the gloom in the last 15 years. It has not just created wealth for the country, but

far more importantly, it has created confidence in the country. Youngsters in India no longer consider themselves to be inferior to any one else in the world. Urban middle class youngsters no longer believe that one has to be born rich to be highly successful in the country and thus entrepreneurship is thriving. India is on the move. But this confidence permeates to rural areas. ICT can help in this, but it would require a lot of effort. One must not forget that ICT is at best a tool. One needs to use it to make difference.

Rural-Urban Disparities

Reduction of poverty, unemployment and economic disparities across regions, sectors, gender and social groups have always been the major objectives of the Five Year Plans in India. However, even after five and half decades of economic planning, their eradication is still the major challenge before the policy makers. Although in the post-economic reform period India has grown economically faster, her performance in these areas has remained dismal. The failure of the neo-liberal policy regime in tackling these issues has now become well established fact. The delinking of growth with employment has significantly reduced the employment elasticity in various economic activities. Joblessness is particularly acute in the rural areas because agriculture has been in crisis, over the last decade. The remedy of these maladies, therefore, lies not only in achieving faster growth but also in making the growth broadbased, prorural and more inclusive.[106]

Rural India comprises 72 per cent of the country's population, but its share in the total national income is currently about 45 per cent. Rural India is characterised by low income levels, poor quality of life and a weak base of human development. Rural-urban divide is quite apparent in all spheres of human life. What worries most the policy planners is that the magnitudes of disparity has accentuated during the post-reform period due to change in the income growth trajectories of rural and urban areas. The growing rural-urban divide may have far-reaching economic social and political ramifications. It is, therefore, essential to examine the

extent of this divide and draw inferences for policy interventions for its rectification.

The main problem of post-independence India was how to modernise and develop its economy. Therefore, efforts were made to create an effective economic structure for rapid development of the economy through the instruments of economic planning. At the dawn of the planning era in India, the main concern was to identify an appropriate model for economic development. There were two alternative development models. The first model was based on the Western economic concept (Nehru-Mahalanobis model) and the other was based on Gandhian Economic thought (Vakil-Brahmanand Model). The First Plan was prepared without any specific growth strategy but the priority was given to the agricultural development. From the Second Five Year Plan onwards Nehru-Mahalanobis model was adopted. In this model, the main emphasis was laid on the establishment of modern large scale industries. The 'big push' and 'trickle-down' approaches adopted as development strategy during the planning period have generated inequalities across regions, sectors and rural urban locations. While thinking about his dream-India, Gandhiji said that, spirit of India resides in villages. The development of India means the development of villages. But the bitter truth of India's economic development is that the country failed to consider the real spirit of villages.

The 'wage good model' of C.N. Vakil and P.R. Brahmanand[107] was greatly influenced by the economic ideas of Mahatma Gandhi. According to this model, in the initial stage of development of a nation, greater emphasis must be given on agriculture and small scale industries to produce wage goods for *aam aadami* (common mass) and generate gainful employment for the large number of workforce, especially living in the rural areas. When these sectors sufficiently develop and become capable of absorbing manpower and supplying surplus raw materials, savings, labour and capital to the rest of the economy, then gradually focus should be shifted towards the growth of big industries and service sector. The experience of other countries also tells that the growth of agriculture and human resources is essential in the initial stage of

development and gradually the development strategy should be shifted towards developing and strengthening other sectors. This model could not get place in the Indian Planning. It is difficult to predict about what the fact of rural India would be if the development strategy suggested in this model were implemented. But it seems to be quite clear that if in the initial stage of development, more stress were given on producing wage goods, there might not be as much disparity between 'Grameen Bharat' and 'Urban India' as is perceived today.

India has completed over half a century of planning. It would not be nice if one says that India has not achieved any success during this period. The country has a conquest over the famine. During this period foodgrains production has increased from 50 million tonnes in 1950-51 to 208.3 million tonnes in 2005-06, industrial production index from 7.9 to 221.5 (at 1993-94 prices), per capita income from Rs. 3,687 to Rs. 20,734, gross domestic saving rate from 8.9 per cent to 32.4 per cent, and gross domestic capital formation from 8.7 per cent to 33.8 per cent. Literacy rate has increased from 18.33 per cent in 1951 to 65 per cent in 2001 and life expectancy has doubled from 32.1 years to about 63 years. But these achievements show only one side of the coin. If one has a glance on the other side, he gets only disappointment. Hunger, unemployment, starvation, diseases and poverty are everywhere in rural India which can be seen in its 6 lakh villages. There is lack of basic amenities like clean and safe drinking water, basic education, transportation, shelter and electricity in the villages. Due to the poverty and unemployment, rural workforce is migrating to cities; the result is that population is growing rapidly in the cities.

The new economic policy initiated by the government in 1991 has also affected the government capacity to mobilise resource to finance the rural development activities. The tax reforms and structural adjustment programmes have reduced the developmental role of the government. Agriculture—the backbone of the rural economy—has been adversely affected by the sharp decline in the public investment. Although there was not any direct reform in the farm sector but the reforms made in the non-

agricultural sectors have indirectly affected the farm sector. After the commencement of the World Trade Organisation (WTO), some direct initiatives were adopted in the farm sector which have some implications for agriculture. If one looks at the figures of workforce dependent on agriculture and its contribution to the overall GDP of the country, it is found that the farm workers have been significantly marginalised during one and a half decade of reforms. Farm productivity, profitability and sustainability have been drastically affected and the agricultural distress has culminated into the suicidal death of thousands of farmers in different parts of the country, including the most developed State Punjab. On the other hand urban economy has grown rapidly during this period, providing adequate opportunities to the educated and skilled workforce, which has attracted a high level of influx of rural workers to the urban areas, adversely affecting the carrying capacity of the urban areas.

Although the percentage of workforce dependent on agriculture has declined in 2001, the absolute number has increased from 185 million in 1991 to 235 million in 2001. The share of agriculture in the GDP decelerated sharply from 34.93 per cent in 1990-91 to about 18.5 per cent in 2006-07. The widening gap between per worker GDP in agriculture and non-agricultural sectors provides a clear indication of marginalisation of agricultural workforce and widening gap between the rural and urban areas. The ratio of per worker NSDP from non-agricultural to agricultural at 1993-94 prices for the year 2002-03 is above in Madhya Pradesh. Gujarat, Maharashtra, Rajasthan and Tamil Nadu, Punjab, Kerala, West Bengal and Assam have relatively lower magnitudes of the ratios. In brief, the share of rural areas in national income is now falling faster than its share in population. This has led to widen the rural-urban per capita income gap in the 1990s.

Table 2.12 shows trends in rural-urban income disparity in India. The Central Statistical Organisation (CSO) does not compile rural-urban break-up of GDP on annual basis. But it makes periodical estimation. The latest data is available up to 1999-2000. It is significant to note that the share of rural areas in the NDP at factor cost has steeply declined from 62.95 per cent in 1970-71 to

48.09 per cent in 1999-2000, whereas the corresponding percentage for urban areas has remarkably increased, as is indicated by Table 2.12. Today the urban population may earn nearly about three-fifths of the national income. Thus, in terms of generation of GDP, the centre of gravity in the Indian economy has shifted from rural to urban areas, whereas the majority of people still earn their livelihood in rural areas.

Table 2.12 : Trends in Rural-Urban Income Disparity in India

Particulars	*1970-71*		*1980-81*		*1993-94*		*1999-2000*	
	Rural	*Urban*	*Rural*	*Urban*	*Rural*	*Urban*	*Rural*	*Urban*
1	2	3	4	5	6	7	8	9
1. Share in NDP at factor cost (%)	62.35	37.65	58.88	41.12	54.27	45.73	58.88	51.91
2. Share in population (%)	80.22	19.78	76.88	23.12	73.51	26.49	76.88	27.47
3. Per capita income at current prices (Rs.)	529	1294	1245	2888	5783	13525	1245	30217
4. Ratio of urban income to rural income	2.45	–	2.32	–	2.34	–	2.32	–

Source : Government of India (2007), *National Accounts Statistics* (2007), Central Statistical Organisation, New Delhi.

If one looks at the rural share in the total population, one finds that over 72 per cent of the Indian people live in rural areas while they get only 48 per cent of the national income. Table 2.12 also shows the per capita income differential between rural and urban sector. In 1999-2000, as against per capita income of Rs. 30,217 in urban location, it was only Rs. 10,606 in the rural location. Since 1980-81, the ratio of urban-rural per capita income has been increasing. In 1999-2000, the ratio was 2.85, indicating that the per capita income in urban location is almost three times that of rural location. The difference in the per capita income of urban and rural areas has steeply widened during the last two decades.

Rural-urban income disparity can also be assessed on the basis of difference in the level of household consumption expenditure which could serve as a proxy for household monthly income. Table 2.13 shows the trend in the monthly per capita consumption expenditure (MPCE) in rural and urban areas. To facilitate comparison at constant prices, consumer price indices (based on CPI for agricultural workers for rural areas and CPI for non-manual employees for urban areas with 1972-73 as base) are used to convert the MPCE at constant prices. At current prices, in 1973-74, MPCE in urban areas was about 43 per cent higher than that of rural areas, whereas in 2004-05, it was higher by 88 per cent.

Table 2.13 : Monthly Per Capita Consumption Expenditure in Rural and Urban Areas

Year	*Rural*			*Urban*			
	MPCE at Current Price	*CPI-AL (1972-73 = 100)*	*MPCE at Constant Price (1972-73)*	*MPCE at Current Price*	*CPI-UNME (1972-73 = 100)*	*MPCE at Constant Price*	*Urban-Rural Ratio*
1	2	3	4	5	6	7	8
1973-74	44.17	100	100	63.33	100	63.33	1.43
1977-78	68.89	144	144	96.15	160	60.09	1.36
1983-84	112.31	227	227	165.80	258	64.26	1.30
1987-88	158.10	289	289	249.	364	68.66	1.25
1993-94	286.10	520	520	464.30	618	75.13	1.37
1999-00	486.16	833	833	854.92	998	85.66	1.47
2004-05	558.78	922	922	1052.36	1230	85.56	1.41

Source : NSSO 61st Round Report on Level and Pattern of Consumer Expenditure, 2004-05.

The rural-urban disparity in the MPCE at current prices has been significantly increasing since 1987-88. However, if one compares the rural-urban differences in the MPCE at constant prices, it shows a moderate increase revealing that CPI for agricultural labour increased at a rate lower than the CPI of urban non-manual employees.

The 61st Round Survey of the NSSO estimated that in 2004-05, 5 per cent of rural households spent less than Rs. 235 person per month on consumption. Another 5 per cent spent in the range Rs. 235-270 whereas the poorest 5 per cent of urban households have MPCE less than Rs. 335 and another 5 per cent spent in the range of Rs. 335-395. The Lorentz ratio for total consumer expenditure, indicating concentration in total consumption expenditure among the population, was 0.30 for rural India and 0.35 for urban India in 2004-05. Rural households spent 55 per cent of total consumption expenditure on food while the corresponding percentage for the urban households was 43. In the case of other two vital items of expenditure—health and education—the survey finds that medical expenses constituted 7 per cent of the total MPCE in rural areas and 5 per cent in urban areas, while the corresponding percentages for education were 3 per cent and 5 per cent respectively for rural and urban areas. This indicates that rural households spent relatively more on medical and less on education, while urban households spent more on education and less on health. Urban-Rural gap in the MPCE demonstrates that the disparity has accentuated since 1987-88.

Two issues may be relevant to regard of the rural-urban economic disparity. First is related to the migration of rural poor workers to the urban area. Many of them live in the urban slums. This process of migration actually exports the poverty from rural areas to urban areas and thus reduces the average per capita income of the urban people, and consequently becomes instrumental in under-estimation of the rural-urban economic disparity. The second issue is related to the growth of urbanisation of rural areas. Urban economic activities are moving out of big cities to the surrounding rural areas, as land becomes more expensive in the urban areas and environmental regulations become more stringent. High prices of agricultural land and better rural-urban linkage due to improved transport and communication infrastructure have made the rural people living in the vicinity of cities economically better off than the average rural people. Therefore, if the households of rural migrant workers from the

urban areas and population of urbanised villages are excluded from the estimation of per capita income and MPCE, the rural-urban disparity would be much higher.

Apart from education, health, nutrition, water and sanitation, the concept of human development (HD) encompasses many other human capabilities in expanding human choices. The *National Human Development Report (2001)* provides detailed information on various components of human development. However, Rural-Urban break-up of human development index (HDI) is available only for 1981 and 1991. As per the report, rural-urban disparity in the HDI is quite high. As against 0.511 value of HDI in urban areas in 1991, the HDI in the rural areas was only 0.340. This implies that the level of human development in the urban India was about 50 per cent higher than that of rural India. Rural-urban disparities in terms of the components of human development are discussed below.

In India the rural areas are highly disadvantaged in all components of human development. For instance, mean year of schooling is much longer in urban areas than that in rural India, not to mention the difference in the quality of education imparted. Further, fees paid by the rural poor for education are an extremely high percentage of their cash income which not only severely limit children, but also exacerbates other inequalities, in particular leading to lower access for girls to over primary education. Moreover, as educational institutions of professional and higher learning are located in urban areas, rural people, already limited in terms of economic well-being, have to bear additional expenses for boarding and lodging to send their children to such institutions. Therefore, other things remaining the same, cost of education to students from rural areas is much higher than that of their counterparts in urban areas.

The difference in the level of education in rural and urban areas can be assessed on the basis of findings of the 61st Round of NSSO survey conducted during 2004-05. The survey finds that in rural India, 26 per cent of households did not have any member in the age group of 15 and above who could read and write a simple message with understanding, while the corresponding percentage

in urban India was only 8. It also finds the significant difference in the literacy rates among rural and urban population. As against above 64 per cent and 45 per cent literacy rates among rural males and females respectively, the literacy rates among their urban counterparts were much higher at 81 per cent and 69 per cent respectively. Further, among persons aged 15 years and above, 5 per cent in urban areas had technical degrees/diplomas/certificates, while the proportion in rural areas was only one. Education being one of the vital determinants of socio-economic development and occupational mobility of individuals and households, needs to be invested additional, physical and financial resources in creating the sound education infrastructure in the rural areas.

Although health indicators have continued to improve over time, villages are far behind the towns and cities in the case of healthcare facilities and their outcomes. This difference can be observed both qualitatively and quantitatively. The major part of the health care facilities in rural areas are provided by unqualified and untrained medical profession. Most of the public hospitals and dispensaries are located in urban areas and almost all private clinics and nursing homes are in the urban areas. If looked at the rural-urban differences in the level of health care infrastructure, one finds that villages are far behind the cities. For instance, in 2001, there were 0.54 hospital, 1.49 dispensaries and 15.05 hospital beds per lakh population in rural India, while the corresponding figure in urban India were 0.80, 102.90 and 6.30 respectively. These figures clearly indicate that there exists wide inequality in the distribution of health care infrastructure among rural and urban location. Due to the deficiency of proper medical aid, the death rate, infant mortality rate and fertility rate all are higher in the villages than those in the cities. Although these rates have been declining over the years, these are still high, especially in the rural India. Provision of public health services, such as access to basic and preventive health care, sanitation, clean water and raising awareness about the causes of illness and their treatment are necessary for improving human development in rural India.

National Family Health Survey (NFHS) provides vital information on the health status of rural and urban people of the country, so far three surveys (NFHS I, NFHS II and NFHS III) have been conducted. Table 2.14 provides information on some of the health indicators for the last two surveys. A perusal of Table 2.14 reveals that urban India has better outcome of almost all health indicators. Fertility rate, infant death rate, under 5 mortality rate, and crude death rate are much higher in rural areas than the urban areas. In the case of birth delivered in medical institutions, it has been observed that in 2005-06, as against 69.4 per cent deliveries made in medical institutions in urban areas, such deliveries in rural areas were only 31.1 per cent. Similarly, percentage of birth assisted by medical professionals in rural areas was just half that of urban areas. Percentage of total unmet need to family planning was also higher in the rural areas. Percentage of total unmet need to family planning was also higher in the rural areas than that of the urban areas.

It is relevant to note that overall status of women and children in rural India is much poorer than their urban counterparts. For example, the results of NFHS III (2005-06) reveal that percentage of rural women with Body Mass Index (BMI) below normal was 38.8 while the corresponding percentage in urban women was only 19.8. There were more anaemic women and children in rural areas than those in the urban areas, as is evident from the data given in Table 2.14. Percentage of fully immunised children aged 13-23 months were only 38.6 per cent in rural areas, while the corresponding percentage in urban areas was 57.5. Percentage of children with Acute Respiratory Infection (ARI) in the last two weeks who were taken to health facility, were 59.9 and 78.1 respectively for rural and urban areas. If one compares the results of the two surveys, it is found that there has been some improvement in the health status of both rural and urban people in 2005-06 over 1998-99. However, in the case of a few indicators, the condition has deteriorated. For instance, percentage of anaemic women have increased in both rural and urban areas in the NFHS III, as compared to those in the previous surveys. Similarly percentages of anaemic children aged 6-35 months have also increased in 2005-06.

Table 2.14 : Rural-Urban Disparity in Health Care Indicators

Sl. No.	Particulars	National Family Rural Health Survey II (1998-99)		National Family Rural Health Survey III (2005-06)	
		Rural	Urban	Rural	Urban
1	2	3	4	5	6
1.	Total fertility rate (%)	3.07	2.85	3.0	2.1
2.	Birth assisted by health professionals (%)	33.50	73.30	39.1	75.2
3.	Birth delivered in medical institutions	24.60	65.10	31.1	69.4
4.	Two doses of T.T. Vaccination during pregnancy	62.5	81.90	—	—
5.	Mothers had at least 3 antenatal care visits for their last birth (%)	22.4	54.7	42.8	73.8
6.	Total unmet need for family planning. (%)	16.7	13.4	14.6	10.0
7.	Women whose Body Mass Index is below normal (%)	40.6	22.6	38.8	19.8
8.	Ever-married age 15-44 who are anaemic (%)	53.9	45.7	58.2	51.5
9.	Children 12-23 months fully immunised (BCG, measles & 3 doses of each of polio & DPT) (%)	29.3	51.9	38.6	57.5
10.	Children 12-23 months who have received BCG (%)	67.1	86.8	75.1	86.9
11.	Children 12-23 months who received 3 doses of polio vaccine (%)	58.3	78.2	76.5	83.1
12.	Children 12-23 months who received 3 doses of DPT vaccine (%)	49.8	73.4	50.4	69.1
13.	Children with diarrhoea in the last two weeks who received ORS (%)	25.0	32.7	24.0	32.7
14.	Children with diarrhoea in the last weeks taken to a health facility (%)	59.9	75.2	55.6	65.3
15.	Children with acute respiratory infection or fever in the last 2 weeks taken to a health facility (%)	61.8	75.1	59.9	78.1
16.	Children aged 6-35 months who are anaemic (%)	75.3	70.8	81.2	72.7
17.	Under-weight children below three years age (%)	49.6	38.4	49.0	36.4
18.	Infant mortality rate	73.0	68.0	62.0	57.0
19.	Under five mortalities (per 1000)	103.8	63.1	—	—
20.	Crude death rate (per 1000)	10.4	7.4	—	—

Source : Compiled from the *Reports of the National Family Health Survey II & III.*

In order to know the extent of disparity in rural and urban areas in the case of basic amenities, data on five amenities, namely pucca houses, piped drinking water, sanitary toilet, electricity and LPG cooking gas have been shown in Table 2.15.

Table 2.15 : Disparity in the Access to Basic Amenities

Sl. No.	*Particulars*	*1998*		*2004*	
		Rural	*Urban*	*Rural*	*Urban*
1	2	3	4	5	6
1.	Pucca House (%)	19.0	66.0	25.5	74.1
2.	Drinking Water through tap (%)	18.7	70.0	27.9	71.0
3.	Toilet facility (%)	17.5	74.5	25.9	83.1
4.	Electricity (%)	48.4	89.1	55.7	93.1
5.	LPG Cooking gas (%)	–	–	5.7	48.0

Source : Government of India (2006), Selected Socio-economic Statistics (2006), Central Statistical Organisation, New Delhi.

Table 2.15 shows that in 2004, as against 74.1 per cent urban households lived in pucca houses, only 25.5 per cent households in rural areas had this facility. In the case of drinking water, it is observed that only about 28 per cent rural households had tap water facility, whereas 71 per cent of urban households had this facility. Against 93.1 per cent urban households having electricity, the corresponding percentage for rural households was only 55.7. Moreover, availability and reliability of electricity are higher in urban areas than in the rural areas. Access to sanitary toilet is one of the crucial factors for health of people. A large number of rural people do not have toilet facility in their houses. Table 2.15 shows that only 25.9 per cent rural households had toilet facility, while the corresponding percentage in the urban areas was 83.1. LPG, as a cooking gas, is most effective source of cooking energy. In the case of this facility also, the rural India is far behind the urban India in 2004. Only 5.7 per cent of rural households had this facility, whereas in urban areas 48 per cent households used LPG as a source of cooking energy. Thus, the urban population has much better access to these basic amenities than the rural population.

Disparity between rural and urban households also exists in the case of access to the durable consumer assets. Seven such assets

have been identified and percentage of households having access to these assets have been presented in Table 2.16.

Table 2.16 : Access of Rural-Urban Households to Some Durable Assets in India (2001)

(Percentage)

	Particulars	2001		2004-05	
		Rural	Urban	Rural	Urban
1.	Radio	31.5	44.5	–	–
2.	Television	18.9	65.3	–	–
3.	Bicycle	42.8	46.0	–	–
4.	Motorcycle / Scooters	6.7	24.7	–	–
5.	Car	1.3	6.6	–	–
6.	Banking services	30.1	49.5	–	–
7.	Telephones	–	–	1.73	26.88

Source : Singh, S.P. (2007), Growing Rural-Urban Disparity in India, *Kurukshetra*, November, p. 11.

Except telephone facility which is measured in terms of number of telephones per 100 people for the year 2004-05, data on all other assets are percentage of households having access to the assets in 2001. As the figures clearly exhibit, the percentages of rural households having access to these assets are much lower than their urban counterparts. In the case of even possession of radio and bicycle, percentages of rural households are lower than that of urban households. In the case of access to television, the figure shows that as against 64.1 per cent urban households having the assets, the corresponding percentage in rural area is only 18.9.

Motorcycle/scooter is the most flexible and convenient mode of private transport especially in the rural areas, where public transport system does not adequately connect all the villages. Although demand for motorcycle/scooter has been constantly rising in the rural areas too, the access is still much lower than that of urban areas, for instance, in 2001, only 5.3 per cent of rural households possessed this assets, while the corresponding percentage in urban areas was 24.7. In the case of the possession of the other assets too, there exists wide disparity between rural and urban areas. Tele-density, measured by number of telephone

per 100 people, was only 1.33 in the urban areas. Further, it has been observed that nearly 50 per cent of urban households availed in banking services, while the corresponding percentage in rural India was 30.1.

There is a need to adopt two types of policies to reduce rural-urban disparity, first the policy which helps to generate sustained income and employment and also abate the undesirable flow of rural workforce to the urban areas; and the second, which helps to raise the socio-economic status of rural populace and enlarge their capability to participate actively in the developmental activities. There is a need for both qualitative and quantitative changes in the rural areas. In quantitative form, it must be reflected in more production, more income and more employment. In qualitative form, it must be reflected in the form of institutional changes in the areas of health, education, environment, transport and social welfare. It may be pointed out here that economic growth is necessary yet not sufficient condition for economic development. what matters more is the broad-base of the growth and its equitable distribution. Economic growth would be more effective in eliminating rural poverty and deprivation when it works with the indicators of human development in the multiplicative form. The following policy measures could be initiated to reduce the growing rural-urban disparities in India.

During the last one decade, public investment in agriculture has declined. The low credit-deposit ratio of the rural banks also shows that the rural money is outflowing to cities. There is a need to reverse this trend to lessen the rural-urban disparity, which is possible only through raising agricultural investment. As public investment in agricultural R & D, extension, roads, electricity and irrigation has significant impact on the agricultural productivity, top priority should be accorded to step up investment in these areas. In order to enhance real investment in the agricultural sector, non-merit subsidies could be down-sized and the resources so generated should be ploughed back to agriculture.

Farmer needs to get the right market signals to obtain remunerative price of their product. They must have access to information not only on domestic market but also on global trade,

production, demand, prices, subsidies and quality standards. This calls for a significant improvement in their education, knowledge and skills are better able to respond to new technology, market opportunities and risks; illiterate farmers usually copy their adoption behaviour. It is suggested to create a training infrastructure at the block level with a view to improve human capital base of farmers. The farmers should be taught modern farm practice, input management and marketing of agricultural products.

To augment the farmer's income and to make efficient use of available resources, there is need to evolve a policy which properly integrates all agriculture and allied activities. Emerging high value fruits and vegetables crops are yet to get due place in the national agricultural policy and planning. These are the crops which generate more employment and income to the farmers. But these are risky crops and in the absence of adequate marketing infrastructure and institutional arrangement, growers of these crops can bear the brunt of price and output volatility. Therefore, the agricultural policy is required to lay greater emphasis on creating efficient marketing insurance credit infrastructure and enabling institutional framework for the growth of these crops.

Agriculture could also be the major energy producer. There is immense potential of generating energy from the agricultural wastes. Sugar industry alone has the potential to generate about 5,000 megawatt through co-generation plants fuelled by bio-gas. This industry also has the potential to produce about two billion litres ethanol from molasses which can be blended with petrol to run automobiles. Another source of energy production from agriculture is cultivation of bio-diesel plants, such as Jatropha. For producing energy from agriculture, the agricultural policy should be properly linked to the energy policy.

Isolated and economically backward regions need to be connected to the markets through rural-urban linkages. Apart from all-weather road connectivity and provision of other essential economic and social infrastructure, development of information technology (IT) infrastructure in rural areas can play a vital role in this regard. Such infrastructure provides an opportunity to rural

households to combine farm and non-farm activities. IT can promote small business development, generate additional income and employment, improve agricultural production and marketing and contribute to better health, education and social welfare.

Rural non-farm sectors must be promoted through appropriate policy supports. Basic elements of policy should include the development of rural infrastructure in terms of road, electricity and institutional credit. Education and skill possession is a key factor in the occupational mobility of workers and great facilitator of livelihood diversification. Generally rural people lack basic knowledge and skills required to participate in the emerging economy. Therefore, imparting necessary education and skills to the rural youths is likely to have a relatively large impact on their ability to participate in the more lucrative non-farm activities. As IT companies and BPOs have been decentralising their activities from mega cities to B and C class cities, due to cost advantages. In future, they may further shift their base to small towns and even villages. Therefore, in order to avail this opportunity, rural youths must be given training in areas of technical and communication skills.

Improvement in the income, employment and living conditions of the rural people is not only necessary for the rural India as it is vital to improve political stability, make the investment climate, more attractive, build social cohesion and indeed economic growth. It may be pointed out that elimination of poverty and deprivation among the rural masses would also benefit corporate sector, because demand for manufactured consumer goods will increase when the incomes of the poor people rise. On these grounds also, claim of the rural sector on higher public funds for investment in the socio-economic infrastructure, agriculture, irrigation, power, roads, electrification, wealth education, etc. are justified.

The rural development must be inclusive, participatory and community based. Inclusive development approach can improve the efficiency as well as equity of resource-use. Within the framework of inclusive development, resource management can be improved, service delivery can be made effective and a more

conclusive environment can be created for social resource mobilisation.

Policy interventions are also required to facilitate interactions between local administration and rural communities for removing impediments to community action and insuring greater collaboration between communities and rural local self-government institutions. The process of development initiated through 73rd Constitutional Amendment Act, 1993 can re-distribute the political power in the society so as to enable the local communities to have a voice, say, a role in the societies power structure. However, due to lack of supportive social institutions and capacity building measures, the constitutional provision is inadequate to ensure communities effective participation in the development process.

The lack of access of rural youths to education, skill, health care facilities and resources limits their role in the emerging non-agricultural sectors, while their counterparts in the urban areas have amenities, resources and participate productively in the development activities. Central and State Governments have launched a number of schemes targeting the rural people, however, emphasis of most of these schemes is more on livelihood protection, rather than on income and wealth generation on sustainable basis. Moreover, delivery mechanism of these schemes is poor and needs to be improved. For instance, due to inefficient delivery mechanism and corruption among the officials about 50 per cent foodgrains supplied under the public distribution system (PDS) do not reach the intended beneficiaries.

In developed countries, retired employees prefer to live in village because there they have all amenities like electricity, water, road, transport, telephones banks, post office etc. While in India even the residents of village do not want return to village because there they do not have the comforts and facilities which they have in the city. Effective implementation of providing urban amenities in rural areas (PURA), a concept given by the former President Dr. A.P.J. Abdul Kalam, could encourage the reverse migration and reduce the influx of rural people to urban areas.

Approaches to Rural Development

India had gained vast experience in the implementation of rural development programmes. The approaches to rural development and planning have also changed over a period of time. In the light of the experience gained by following a particular approach, a new approach has been evolved. The shift in emphasis is intended not only to accelerate the pace of growth in the rural sector but also to ensure social justice by minimising wastage and leakages. In the following sections the various approaches to rural development like Gandhian approach, Planning Commission's approach, PURA approach, Panchayat Raj Institutions approach and Village Development Board approach of Nagaland have been discussed.

Gandhian Approach

Mohandas Karamchand Gandhi or Mahatma Gandhi, as he is generally called, was not only a freedom fighter but also a great thinker of the twentieth century. Gandhiji's views on rural reconstruction are an integral part of his philosophy of life which is characterised by truth and non-violence, respect for human nature, dislike for all kinds of injustice and exploitation.

Influenced by the teachings of the *Gita*, the *Upnishads*, the *Bible* and the writings of the thinkers like Tolstoy, Ruskin, Thoreau and saints like Kabir and Nanak, Gandhiji appeared on the Indian political scene when the national movement for the freedom was gaining momentum and spiritualised the Indian politics and economics truly and fully during his life time.[108]

In this section an attempt has been made to give a brief description of the economic ideas of Mahatma Gandhi with particular reference to the regeneration of villages, decentralisation, machines and technology and trusteeship.

Regeneration of Villages

Villages in ancient India had developed as form of agriculture and

industry in which there was little scope for exploitation. Production was almost simultaneous with consumption and distribution, and such a social structure alone was conducive to non-violence and truth as Gandhiji understood them. Therefore,he advocated the revival of the ancient villages:

> "My ideal of a Village *Swaraj* is that it is a complete republic, independent of the neighbours for its own vital wants, and yet dependent for many others in which dependence is a necessity. Thus every village's first concern will be to grow its own food crops and cotton for its cloth. It should have areas reserved for its cattle, recreation and play grounds for adults and children. Then, if there is more land available, it will grow useful money crops, thus excluding *ganja*, tobacco, opium and the like. The village will maintain a village theatre, school and public hall. It will have its own water works ensuring clean water supply. This can be done through wells and tanks. Education will be compulsory upto the final basic course. As far as possible, every activity will be conducted on the cooperative basis. There will be no castes as we have today with their graded untouchability."[109]

Gandhiji had a comprehensive plan for regeneration of Indian villages and the main plank of this programme was the *charkha* movement. The slogan was: 'Swaraj through spinning'. A subjugated India could not depend upon foreign masters to initiate genuine plans for economic development and, therefore, Gandhiji clearly saw that the solution of mass poverty in the villages lay in teaching the villagers self-help. He wanted honest work to be provided for them, not relief and charity. To Gandhiji, *charkha* thus became a symbol of economic independence as well as political emancipation.

In 1922, Gandhiji stressed this aspect of the question in his letter to Hakim Ajmal Khan: "Nothing can possibly unify and revivify India as the acceptance by all India of the spinning wheel as a daily sacrament, and the *khaddar* wear as a privilege and a

duty."[110] "For every revolution of the wheel spins peace, goodwill and love. The loss of it brought India's slavery; its voluntary revival with all its implications must mean India's freedom,"[111] thought Gandhiji.

In a capital deficient country like India, he saw in *khaddar* and spinning wheel an industry which required only limited capital. Raw materials needed would be available at low cost and there existed an unlimited market in the vicinity of manufacturer. Sociologically speaking this industry, since it carried work to the individual households, acted as a countervailing force against family disintegration. Moreover, the employment potential of *khaddar* industry was considerable. Gandhiji analysed the production statistics of the year 1922-23 and found that the contribution of *khaddar* in respect of its capacity to save foreign exchange and addition to per capita national income was significant.[112] Considering the circumstances under which the *khaddar* movement took shape, Gandhiji's campaign for the development of home made cloth industry is no more fad of a romantic eager to revive the past but a practical attempt to relieve the poverty and uplift the standard of the living.[113] The impact of Gandhian ideas on contemporary thought was truly significant. As Jawaharlal Nehru said, "Gandhiji has done a great service to India by his emphasis on village industry. Before he did this, we were all, nearly all, thinking in a lopsided way and ignoring the human aspect of the question and the peculiar conditions prevailing in India."[114]

Decentralisation

Gandhiji conceived decentralisation as an integral part of the social and productive organisation. A highly mechanised factory was inconsistent with the non-violent structure of society, since centralisation cannot be sustained without adequate force. He favoured cottage industries from the point of decentralisation as well as distribution.

Granting for the moment that machinery may supply all the needs of humanity, still it would concentrate production in

particular areas so that you would have to go in a round about way to regulate distribution, whereas if there is production and distribution both in the respective areas where things are required, it is automatically regulated and there is less chance for fraud or for speculation.[115]

Gandhiji saw that the degree of effective localisation varies with the nature of the interest. Perhaps it was his intention that cultural organisation on the village level could be more fully localised than those which pursued urban interests for the reason that cultural interest must be directly or personally communicated. Gandhiji did not deny the fact that there were universal aspects of order and efficiency which were best provided by a centralised control. Such an agency, however, could never be a substitute for the direct activity of the participant members.

It was pointed out that a world of large-scale and centralised organisations was inevitably a mechanised impersonal world based on violence. Gandhiji thought of it as a peril to the realisation of the fuller life of man of his essential humanity. One might argue that socialism where there was no individual economic exploitation, was an adequate remedy to such a situation. Gandhiji had his doubts: "You want me to express opinion on state controlled industry, i.e. an economic order in which both production and distribution are controlled and regulated by the state as is being done in Soviet Russia. Well it is a new experiment. How far it will ultimately succeed, I do not know. If it were not based on force, I will dote on it. But today since it is based on force, I do not know how far and where it will take us."[116]

Instead of mass production on large scale he desired production by the masses on a small scale and decentralised basis. "It is mass production but mass production in the people's own homes," said Gandhiji. He further added :

> "If you multiply individual production to millions of times, would it not give you mass production on a tremendous scale? But I quite understand that your 'mass production' is a technical term for production by the fewest possible number through the aid of highly complicated machinery.

> I have said to myself that is wrong. My machinery must be of the most elementary type which I can put in the homes of the millions."[117]

Machines and Technology

Gandhiji's ideas on machines and technological civilisation grew out of a deep conviction that the modern machine civilisation was at the root of all tensions and frustrations which bring about aggression, violence, and war. He saw how technology always led to the multiplication of wants and 'a state of culture in which material wants are the king'.

"Gandhiji compared machinery to a snake hole which may contain from one to a hundred snakes. Where there is machinery, there are large cities; where there are large cities, there are tram, cars and railways. And there only does not see electric light. Honest physicians will tell that where means of artificial locomotion have increased the health of the people has suffered."[118]

Gandhiji would have no serious objection to machinery of a type which would remove the drudgery of handicrafts. "I would welcome every improvement in the cottage machine, but I know that it is criminal to displace hand labour by the introduction of power driven to spindles unless one is at the same time ready to give millions of farmers some other occupation in their houses."[119]

Gandhiji would have heavy machine as well, provided the state-owned it on behalf of the community. Since ownership by state would not amount to possession and expropriation of surplus value for individual gain, or profit on the part of anyone. Gandhiji felt no objection to the idea :

> "The heavy machinery for work of public utility which cannot be undertaken by human labour, has its inevitable place, but all that would be owned by the state and used entirely for the benefit of the people. I can have no consideration for machinery which is meant either to enrich the few at the expense of the many, or without cause to displace the useful labour of money."[120]

To this extent Gandhiji was a socialist or even a communist as he called himself before Louis Fischer but with this difference that his socialism did not grow out of industrial civilisation, technological values, class conflict or according to the operations of the laws of dialectics.

The state ownership of Gandhiji's conception would be to the public good and be a guarantee of non-exploitation through large-scale machinery owned by the rich. In such a state Gandhiji would prize every invention made for the benefit of all. In the conditions prevailing in India of his days, probably there was less need of mechanisation. As he said :

> "Mechanisation is good when the hands are too few for the work intended to be accomplished. It is an evil when there are more hands than required for the work as is the case in India. The problem with us is not how to find leisure for the teeming millions inhabiting our villages. The problem is how to utilise their idle hours equal to the working days of six months in the year."[121]

Gandhiji's contention in regard to machines and technology was logical if one accepted the moral postulates underlying that approach. Employment of large scale machinery in an acquisitive society, he believed, would give rise to greed and avarice.

Trusteeship

Gandhiji conceived an ideal society in which there would not be much scope for glaring inequalities of wealth and incomes. In so far as these existed in the present society, the rich were duty-bound to act as trustees. Writing in the *Harijan* (25th August, 1940), Gandhiji defined trusteeship thus: "The rich man will be left in possession of his wealth of which he will use what he personally requires for his personal needs and will act as a trustee for the remainder to be used for the rest of the society." Gandhiji's belief in non-violence ruled out expropriation of the wealthy by the use of force. He extolled the principal of voluntariness enjoined by non-violence:

"As soon as a man looks upon himself as a servant of society, earns for its sake, spends for its benefit, then purity enters into his earnings and there is *ahimsa* in his venture. Moreover, if men's minds turn towards this way of life, there will come about a peaceful revolution in society and that without any bitterness."[122]

The princess and landlords should show the way since the have-nots have nothing to share with anybody except their pauperism and abjectness. The trustee should use his talent not for himself only but for the social structure as a whole of which he is but a part and on whose sufferance he lives. Conversely, the handnotes must repose their faith in the good intention of the rich as their benefactors.

"The objective of such an economic programme in the Gandhian order is a higher standard of life but not a progressively higher standard. The attempt is to arrive at some kind of an optimum such as would, on the one hand, save men from sheer want and degradation and, on the other, from greed and luxury."[123]

The independent India inherited four problems which are inter-related with each other—poverty, unemployment and under employment, wide disparities in personal income and attitudes militating against hard work—born out of wrong philosophy of life on the one hand and a long spell of foreign or minority rule on the other. The attainment of independence has not helped solve any of these problems, on the contrary they have assumed more serious proportions. A fifth has been added, viz. corruption of every possible form in the highest reaches, both political and administrative.

If the country has to get rid of these problems, it will have to return to Gandhi for redemption. His thought has immense relevance not only to India today but to India 2020. India made a great mistake in 1947 in entirely abandoning the Gandhian path and in adopting a westernised centralised, trickle-down—from the top model which persists even today contrary to general impression. Gandhian thought does not preclude large-scale or machine enterprises from which modern society cannot altogether be divorced. It will prefer small units to big units wherever possible and would turn to big units only when necessary Gandhiji

visualised the growth of Indian economy on the basis of its own resource endowments and its own techniques or techniques evolved to suit the country's conditions of scarce capital and redundant labour. The choice of any appropriate growth strategy was to be conditioned and determined entirely by what the country possessed. He accorded the top priority to self-reliance and called for an organisation of economic production on a widely decentralised basis which could utilize the local endowments and talents to the maximum.

Planning Commission's Approach

Any pragmatic approach to rural development in the Indian context should concentrate on (a) removal of disabilities (lack of necessary skills, absence of access to crucial inputs, etc.) from which the rural population generally suffers and (b) programmes meant to enhance gainful employment opportunities and raise the productivity levels of the rural sector.

India launched the First Five Year Plan in 1951. It was rightly thought that planning would not be effective without substantial participation of the people, thus suggesting that planning ought to be a 'people's movement'. Surely development effort cannot be the sole responsibilities of the government. The government may create a climate conducive to development, but the pace of development depends on the initiative and dynamism exhibited by people who must be equipped with necessary skills and resources to take advantage of and benefit from the government sponsored programmes.

Community Development Programme

The National Community Development Programme (NCDP) was launched in 1952. Its aim was to bring about the overall development of the rural community with people's participation in the development process. The government on its part decided to provide technical and other services in a coordinated fashion. An institutional structure was provided in the form of Panchayati

Raj, cooperative and village schools. The approach to rural development was a holistic one.

An important objective of the NCDP was to develop local leadership and self-governing institutions by strengthening programmes of resource development, improving the effectiveness of farm inputs, supply system and by providing and extending agricultural services to farmers.[124]

Initially, the NCDP was launched only in some parts of the country, but sooner and later, the entire country had to be brought under the programme. Therefore, a new programme of National Extension Service (NES) was launched in 1953. The intention was to provide the essential staff and funds so as to speed up development in the rural sector.

The tasks entrusted to NCDP and NES were enormous involving an all-round development of rural areas. They had to cover a vast area for agricultural and related programmes, communications, education, health, welfare, supplementary employment and training and social housing.

These tasks cannot be successfully undertaken without organisational support at the national, state, district and block levels. At the national level, a central committee was formed. At the State level, a State Development Committee or similar body was constituted. At the district level, a District Development Officer was made responsible for the implementation of community development programmes. Of course, all the districts do not have the same organisational structure.

The Block level is especially important so far as the community development programmes are concerned. The Block Development Officer (BDO) is made responsible for the implementation of the programme within the Block. He is assisted by eight or nine extension officers specialising in fields like agriculture, animal husbandry, rural engineering, public health, cooperation, social education women's and children's programmes and rural industries.

The responsibility for successfully implementing community development programmes in a cluster of villages was entrusted to the Village Level Workers (VLWs) and Gram Sevaks and two Gram Sevikas. They work under the advice and control of the BDO.

The Community Development Programmes met with limited success since the environment required for its success was absent. The agriculture sector remained weak. The Block team did not exhibit the required unity and coordinated effort, nor did it secure the help of non-official leadership. The local level organisations like cooperative and panchayats remained weak. The quality of services provided at the Block level lacked essence. The social structure of the village society did not undergo much change. Too much stress on welfare at the expense of development is not feasible.[125]

The financial material and administrative resources of the community development programmes were spread too thinly. Therefore, the programme could not produce a lasting impact on any sector, particularly the agricultural sector. There are other problems too: while the success of the community development programmes largely depends upon people's cooperation, people remained passive and the extension workers lacked the necessary training. As such, the programme was carried out in a perfunctory manner. In the absence of functional responsibility, inter-departmental jealousies assumed ominous dimension.

The community development programme also suffered because of paucity of trained and managerial staff. There has been shortage of professional managers for local enterprises and agencies. As such, even well conceived programmes could not be successfully implemented.

An appropriate combination of popularistic and paternalistic approaches to development will, without doubt, ensure rural development on a sustainable basis.

Though community development programme met with limited success, the experience gained is worth recalling and implementing its future programmes. It has drawn attentions to the crucial role of agriculture in economic development and also the need for extending incentives to farmers. It also made it clear that resources are to be diverted to most responsible areas to ensure and realise maximum gains in the shortest time.

A mere bureaucrat approach to rural development is not enough. Local people and organisations (voluntary agencies

cooperatives etc.) are to play a positive and productive role in rural construction. The government has been working on strategies to implement and coordinate their community development programmes.

Intensive Agricultural District Programmes (IADP)

As the agricultural yields were very low, the government thought it wise to evolve a new strategy to boost foodgrains output. Whereas the community development programme is based on equity principle, the Intensive Agricultural District Programme (IADP) launched in 1960, aimed at concentrating resources in agriculturally better placed areas.

The essence of IADP strategy has been to attain foodgrain self-sufficiency in favourable areas with maximum irrigation facilities and minimum natural hazards, providing simultaneously all the requisite essential inputs and services which were needed. Thus a package approach to step up agricultural production was evolved.

Seven districts were selected for IADP. These were Thanjavur (Tamil Nadu), West Godavari (Andhra Pradesh), Shahabad (Bihar), Raipur (Madhya Pradesh, now Chhattisgarh). Aligarh (Uttar Pradesh), Ludhiana (Punjab) and Pali (Rajasthan). The Government of India declared these seven districts as IADP districts in June 1960, and suggested that one district in each State may be selected for IADP.

For the successful implementation of the IADP, appropriate infrastructure was made available at the national, State and district levels. At the Block level, the staff responsible for implementing the community development programme was strengthened with additional staff. The subject-matter specialists provided technical assistance and training to the Block level staff.

Credit must be given to the efficiency of IADP that it has achieved its major objective. It has created a new dynamism in the farming communities, popularised the high yielding varieties (HYV) programme, greatly enhanced the technical inputs at the district level and also contributed to the growth of marketing and storage facilities as well as supporting services.

However, the IADP strategy faced many problems. the administration at the district level failed to generate benefits for the rural sector because of inadequate staff and inadequate training. Crucial inputs like fertilizers, cooperative credit and supporting services were not given to the rural population for becoming self-reliant. A unified responsibility at the district level with full control over all interrelated disciplines was absent.

Growth Centre Strategy

It is argued that if investment activities are intensified in selected areas of a region, they will produce sufficient 'spread effect' leading to the all-round development of the region. A leading industry exerts its influence on the economy through inter-industrial linkages, itself playing a leading and innovative role through backward and forward linkages. When once inter-industry linkages are well established, the process of development becomes smooth.

The concept of 'growth pole' which was first introduced by Perroux in 1955, is based on one simple truth: human activities must cluster together to generate internal and external economies. This may, however, involve some social costs which can be minimised in due course through policy interventions.

The village is neither a homogeneous unit nor it is necessarily a viable unit. In order to avoid wastage of resources Prof. V.K.R.V. Rao had suggested formation of clusters of villages implying that it is necessary to determine the minimum size of rural settlements. Regrouping of a small cluster of census villages with a central village or a small town as its focus point with functional inter-linkages should be the ideal unit/area for planning.

After the formation of clusters of villages, it is necessary to identify the dynamic clusters among them and locate the growth focii within them. These growth focii have to be interlinked with one another in such a way that hierarchy is established with service centres at the local level, growth points at the sub-regional level, growth centres at the regional level and the growth pole at the national level.

In India, in the Fourth Five Year Plan (1969-74), a pilot

research project for growth centres was launched, establishing 20 centres in various states. Each growth centre consisted of about 20 Blocks (two million population). An attempt was made to intensify location-specific activities.

The Draft Five Year Plan (1978-1983) suggested setting up of rural growth centres. The selection of such centres was to be based on the availability of infrastructure including cooperative institutions, presence of progressive farmers and effective local participation.

Walter Stohar has observed that "growth centres have essentially led to a shift of disparities from the inter-regional to the intra-regional level, but rarely seem to have led to an overall reduction of spatial disparities in living levels".[126]

The policy of growth centres in India is concerned more with the development of areas rather than with their rates of growth. However, the growth pole theory is inapplicable to all developmental situations and is too rigidly linked to industrialisation.[127]

In the Indian context, two approaches have emerged towards integration of spatial units, that is, villages. These are (a) the growth centre approach as developed by Gadgil and Sen and (b) the village cluster approach as developed by V.K.R.V. Rao and V.M. Rao. The former suggests a vertical integration between the hierarchy of human settlements, i.e. villages and towns. It is assumed that such a link up would transmit to the lower point in the hierarchy growth impulses from the top growth centres. The latter, on the other hand, advocates a horizontal link up among the villages themselves so that they support each other functionally so as to make the cluster of villages an economically viable unit, of course, both approaches stress on linkages backward forward.[128]

Integrated Rural Development

It has been realised that development should be an integrated one. This is possible when sectoral development programmes, human resource development programmes, social welfare schemes and infrastructural development programmes are brought within the framework of a perspective plan for implementation, where each programme reinforces the other through their linkages.[129]

The 'integration' in the decentralised framework has three dimensions: (a) spatial balance which is to be achieved through location, accessibility, efficiency and viability, (b) sectoral balance to be achieved through national and State priorities, local relevance, economic efficiency and internal consistency, and (c) the operational balance which can be achieved through organisation, delegation of functions, management procedures and personal systems.[130]

The most important single reason for laxity in the performance of various rural development programmes has been the negligence of inter-sectoral linkages and lack of coordination among various functionaries. For instance, when programmes for agricultural development are planned, an assessment of the backward linkages which include supply of seed, fertilisers, water, credit facilities gain priority. The forward linkages include supply of raw materials, fodder and provision of storage, transport, marketing and agricultural processing facilities.

Spatial integration refers to 'spatial planning' which in turn, implies appropriate location of social and economic activities over a physical space for the development of a region. Proper spatial planning is necessary to provide adequate inputs and infrastructural facilities to various rural sectoral programmes. As inputs and infrastructure are scarce, they have to be put to the optimum use. A uniform spatial planning may not be appropriate to all regions, in a country like India, because of their diverse nature. However, appropriate methodologies for spatial planning have been evolved through identification of central places (growth centres, service centres and central villages).

It has been rightly observed by John P. Lewis : "A serviceable rural development programme in India must deal with the several aspects of the rural economy in an integrated fashion. An isolated agricultural development effort unrelated to, and unsupported by other kinds of rural policies would be doomed to failure almost surely".[131]

There is need for integrating objectives, namely more production, more employment and more equitable distribution of income. A particular growth model may be successful in

stepping up growth rates, but very often it fails to solve the more important problem of poverty and unemployment. While a high rate of growth is, no doubt, welcome in Indian context, how it has been achieved is also important. In other words, the economic and social costs of development cannot be ignored, particularly in a country suffering from inequalities in income and wealth and regional disparities in development. Hence, the increasing stress on rural development and local level planning is required.

The concept of integration is also viewed as integration of low income segments with the rest of the rural community by ensuring them a better participation in the production process and a more equitable share in the benefits of development.[132]

While dealing with approach, strategy and perspective of integrated rural development, Sharma and Malhotra defined integrated rural development as follows: "It is a synergistic approach aiming at total development of the area and the people by bringing about the necessary institutional attitudinal changes and by delivering a package of services through extension methods to encompass not only the economic field, i.e. development of agriculture, rural industries act, but also the establishment of the required special infrastructure and services in the area of health and nutrition, education and literacy, basic civic amenities, family planning etc., with an ultimate objective of improving quality of life in the rural areas."[133]

While expressing their views on some aspects of rural development, Mishra and Sundaram conceived it as a desired positive change in the rural areas—both in a quantitative as well as qualitative sense.[134] Thus rural development is an area concept. It is completed term which integrates a variety of human life and activities which can broadly be classified into the broad dimensions of social economic, technological and natural. Rural development means desired changes in all these dimensions.

However, in brief, it can be stated that rural development involves a complex process of change in rural subsystems and their interaction, leading to desired improvements in rural income, employment opportunities, income distribution, rural welfare and other aspects of rural life. An integrated rural development

programme, therefore, is viewed as a package of action which covers a series of mutually supporting projects and activities concerned with different sectors of rural communities.

An ideally formulated workable and consistent rural development plan would have many facts and be optimally balanced. Optimal balance implies that different goals and targets, in addition to being feasible and mutually supportive, should be achievable with minimum input of effort and resources, ensuring efficiency and economy of resource use.

Planning for rural development is a long-run on-going process with goals long-run plans and time-bound specific plans with targets dovetailing one another. Local grassroots participants in this process is essential. Such a process is feasible, if there is pressure for its success from above and below. Enlightened national leadership can and does provide such pressure from above, while grassroots local peasants and rural workers organisation can also provide such pressure from below, and rural workers organisation can also provide such pressure from below. Thus planning for rural development in this sense is rather sophisticated business and the role of the government in initiating and implementing programmes is crucial.

Micro Level Planning

In a vast country like India, problems of poverty and unemployment cannot be solved unless attention is paid to local level planning. Development programmes ought to be related to local resources and needs. This alone can make both quantitative and qualitative difference to the planning process. The quantum of output can be increased by better utilisation of resources both natural and human. It can also lead to a socially relevant production pattern.

One of the lessons learnt during the period of experimentation is that rural development must focus on manageable areas in which development activity can be responsive to the specificity natural endowment and social order.[135] But the planning at the micro level faces a number of problems. It cannot be effective unless attention is paid to production programmes for the target groups, manpower

planning and skill development, provision of minimum needs and a programme for institutional support.[136]

The tasks before Block level planning are many. It has to compile an integrated inventory, prepare draft action plans and undertake a malady remedy analysis and select appropriate programmes with the involvement of the local community.[137] The stress should be obviously on the generation of gainful employment.

Briefly, the methodology for block level planning may be envisaged in seven phases which are not necessarily sequential :

(a) the acquaintance phase,
(b) the resource inventory phase,
(c) project formulation phase,
(d) employment planning phase,
(e) spatial planning phase,
(f) credit planning phase, and
(g) the coordination and implementation phase.[138]

The most important information which the planning team should collect involves listing of the number of farmers living below the poverty line.[139]

Of course, there must be consistency between macro- and micro-planning. Macro-planning naturally gives importance to growth, while micro-planning lays stress on redistributive aspects of development. But resource cannot be wasted on projects of doubtful utility at the micro level in the name of social justice. Both macro-planning and micro-planning should strive to step up growth rates. This is possible only when there is consistency between both the levels of planning.

PURA Approach

Dr. A.P.J. Abdul Kalam, ever since he became the President of India in 2002 and even after his retirement from the chair of presidentship in 2007, has been advocating his Vision 2020, and to eradicate poverty from India he has been emphasising the adoption of PURA

(Provision of Urban Amenities in Rural Areas). In his address to the Food Security Summit on the 5th February, 2004 and also in his address to the fourth convocation of Rajendra Agricultural University, PUSA, Samastipur, Bihar on the 14th February, 2004, he outlined the concept of economic upliftment of the villages. India currently has 260 million people living below the poverty line. The GDP growth rate has been on the average 6 per cent during the last decade. It has to be gradually increased up to 10 per cent and to be sustained for several years. Then it is possible for India to get the status of a developed nation.[140] To achieve this, the roadmap involves integrated action on the following five areas :

(a) *Agriculture and food processing*: The country should target for 360 million tonnes of food and agricultural production by 2020. Other areas of agriculture and agro-food processing would bring prosperity to rural people and speed up economic growth.
(b) Reliable and quality electric power for all parts of the country.
(c) Education and health for all.
(d) Expansion of information and communication technology to rural areas to promote education and create national wealth.
(e) Development of strategic sectors growth in nuclear technology, space technology and defence technology.

All these areas have to be developed into mission such as: Networking of rivers; Availability of high quality uninterrupted power; Providing Urban Amenities in Rural Areas; Second Green Revolution; Information and Communication Technology; Transforming into knowledge products; and Tourism.

The country (India) is poised towards execution of PURA for bridging the rural-urban divide and achieving balanced economic development in 4,130 rural clusters across the country during the next five years (from 2004). The north-eastern States, other special category States and backward areas, identified by the Planning Commission would get priority under the scheme.

PURA model involves four connectivities: physical, electronic, knowledge and thereby leading to economic connectivity to enhance the prosperity of cluster of villages in the rural areas.

Under physical connectivity, a group of 15 to 25 villages will be linked to each other by road. These villages connected by roads will also have a ring road so that each one of them can make use of it. Besides roads, provision of electricity and transport facilities have also been included.

Second is digital connectivity which aims to link villages with modern telecommunication and information technology services, e.g. public call offices, cyber cafe, etc.

Thirdly, knowledge connectivity tries to establish with this group of villages good marketing facilities so that all the commodities and services of daily use can be procured and the several people can sell their products in these markets.

Depending upon the region and the state of present development, PURA can be classified into three different categories, namely Type A, Type B and Type C PURA clusters. The characteristics of these types are :

Type A cluster is situated closer to an urban area having minimal road connectivity, limited infrastructure, limited support —school, primary health centre.

Type B cluster is situated close to urban area but has sparsely spread infrastructure and no connectivity.

Type C cluster is located far interior with no infrastructure, no connectivity and no basic amenities.

Uniqueness of PURA

PURA differs from the conventional ideas of economic development of rural areas in six different ways :

(a) It aims at a comprehensive development of rural areas to generate urban-level and not mere 'poverty alleviation'.
(b) It plans for an investment at urban levels and not the much lower amount that prevails at present.
(c) It aims to generate employment for the educated, thereby, halt and even reverse rural urban migration.

(d) It treats quality infrastructure as the prerequisite and not the consequence of development.
(e) It seeks modern industry investment in social and commercial service instead of rural handicrafts and agro-based small industry.
(f) It relies on private initiative. It is a for-profit enterprise not dependent on subsidy from the government.

Conventional rural development schemes suffer from two basic flaws: firstly, jobs which are created pay subsistence wages only, not the substantial salaries the organised sector pays. Secondly, the products are aimed at the local market which is neither large nor assured. PURA removes these road blocks by starting with an entrepreneur who brings in an assured global market and creates jobs which pay the substantial wages of the organised sector. However, this kind of exercise needs experts staff who will insist on getting a choice of schools, nursing homes, shopping malls, recreation facilities and of course, physical, electronic, economic and knowledge connectivities. A minimum size of population for a habitate to offer an acceptable bouquet of services.

Government Action on PURA

The Union Cabinet in its meeting on 20th January, 2004, had accorded in principle approval for the execution of PURA within the existing gross budgetary support for bridging the rural-urban divide and achieving balanced socio-economic development. The government envisaged development of over 4,000 rural clusters located in backward regions. A sum of Rs. 3 crore for each cluster had been provided and thus Rs. 12,000 crore would be spent on the development of 4,000 PURAs.

Although PURA draws its inspiration from the Gandhian model of development which emphasises rural development as a fundamental postulate, yet in the prescription, it is neo-Gandhian in the sense that it intends to bring rural regeneration with the avowed objective of taking modern technology and modern amenities to the rural areas. In this session, it does not enter into

the controversy of labour intensive *versus* capital intensive measures. However, it does emphasise the enlargement of employment as the sole objective to make use of rural citizens and thus can become more acceptable to them. In other words, the PURA model attempts a reconciliation between employment and GDP growth objectives.

Panchayati Raj Institutions (PRIs) and Rural Development

The intention of the Panchayati Raj Institutions (PRIs) is to translate the Gandhian Dream of village self-governance (Gram Swarajya) and making them an effective tool of rural development and reconstruction. The Article 40 of the Constitution of India tells: "The States shall endow such powers and responsibilities to the Panchayat so as to make them institutions of self-governance." The new Panchayati Raj Institutions, however, have assured the vibrant grassroots democracy through the 73rd Constitutional Amendment. This Constitutional amendment clearly speaks of the meaning of the decentralised governance. Decentralisation of economic power to the grassroots level, therefore, becomes essential not only for the sake of ensuring people's democracy, but also for higher growth and equity. Decentralised planning and associated devolution of powers to the village panchayats are new institutional arrangement which can be effectively utilised to meet the needs of rural people in changing environment.[141]

The issue of empowering PRIs by transferring the 3-Fs (Funds, Functions and Functionaries) to them has the central point of discussion between the Centre and the States since last 15 years or more. The Planning Commission and the Ministry of Rural Development have repeatedly impressed upon the State Governments the need of transferring these 3-Fs in respect of 29 subjects listed in the Eleventh Schedule of the Constitution of India to the panchayats.[142] These subjects are:

1. Agriculture, including Agricultural Extension;
2. Minor irrigation, water management and watershed development;

3. Animal husbandry;
4. Fisheries;
5. Social forestry farm;
6. Minor forest produces;
7. Land improvement, implementation of land reforms, land consolidation and soil conservation;
8. Small scale industries including food processing industries;
9. Khadi, village and cottage industries;
10. Rural housing;
11. Drinking water;
12. Fuel and fodder;
13. Roads, culverts, bridges, ferries, waterways and other means of transport and communication;
14. Rural electrification including distribution of electricity;
15. Non-conventional energy sources;
16. Poverty alleviation programmes;
17. Education, including primary and secondary schools;
18. Technical training and vocational education;
19. Adult and non-formal education;
20. Libraries;
21. Cultural activities;
22. Markets and fairs;
23. Health and sanitation including hospitals, primary health centres and dispensaries;
24. Family welfare;
25. Women and child development;
26. Social welfare including welfare of the handicapped and mentally retarded;
27. Welfare of the weaker sections in particular welfare of the Scheduled Castes and Scheduled Tribes;
28. Public distribution system; and
29. Maintenance of community assets.

The 29 subjects listed in the Eleventh Schedule of the Constitution of India cover all key aspects of village life. But in spite of the 73rd Amendment, most of the States have transferred very little power and financial resources to the panchayats.

Poverty Alleviation and Rural Development through Panchayati Raj Institutions

Panchayati Raj Institutions are now in the realm of fulfilling the most cherished goal of development with social justice, bringing the aspirations of the Indian people for their participation in the development process of the country. Since 1959, almost all rural development departments have been executing their programmes through PRIs. But with the implementation of State Acts under the spirit of the 73rd Constitutional Amendment, a clear-cut role of PRIs in rural development has been envisaged, and the Government of India and the different State Governments are now increasingly seeking the assistance of the PRIs in implementation of various schemes as well as poverty alleviation programmes. Of these the following development programmes of the Government of India and State Governments have invariably sought a meaningful involvement of the PRIs and carved out a specific role for them in the context of the Eleventh Schedule and Five Year Plans. The following are the programmes which are being implemented through the PRIs :

1. Sampooran Garmeen Rozgar Yojana (SGRY).
2. Swarnajayanti Gram Swarozgar Yojana (SGSY).
3. Indira Awas Yojana (IAY).
4. Samagra Awas Yojana (SAY).
5. Tribal Area Development Programme (TADP).
6. Pradhan Mantri Gramodaya Yojana (PMGY).
7. Antyodaya Anna Yojana (AAY).
8. National Rural Employment Guarantee Scheme (NREGS) and many other works.

Thus the PRIs are involved in rural development through involvement in planning and execution at the village level. Efforts are being made by various States to empower the Gram Sahba to involve all the people in decentralised planning. Even though funds and sanctioning power may still be at different levels, but when the question comes for execution of programmes, there is no

alternative but to involve the PRIs at the village level. True democracy really means that the power to plan and execute the village development plans has ultimately to be exercised by the people at grassroot, level.

There is no substitute to local governance if felt needs of the local population have to be met. The 73rd and the 74th Constitutional Amendments recognised that necessity. The passing of laws, however, has not led to local self-governance owing to three distinct sets of factors: lack of capacity building; and poor involvement of women.

The lowest tier of the local government, namely the Gram Panchayat is directly in contact with the citizen and can be taken to task in the Gram Sabha and by other means. It is responsible for a number of functions ranging from simple civic functions to complex development planning. But it could carry out these functions only when adequate powers and resources are devolved on it. The States have been reluctant to place powers and resources with the PRIs but have no reluctance in thrusting responsibilities on them.

The elected members should understand the law well through training sessions, but controlling the officials is a problem. They are often able to use the archaic structure of rules and procedures to scuttle schemes unanimously approved by the elected bodies. One way to address the problem is to make the Panchayat and related link department officials attend the training sessions for elected members. At last some of the trainers should be effectively used by the elected members to address the problems created by the lower level officials.

As regards women's effective participation in local governance, literacy is a must. Without some level of education, understanding the laws and the changes in rules and procedures periodically brought out becomes difficult. In the absence of some education, they are dependent on secretaries, sons, husbands, father and so on, who in turn usurp the powers of the elected women.

Village Development Board Approach (Nagaland)

The Village Development Board (VDB) of Nagaland is a unique rural planning and development institution which is based on the

rich traditional heritage of the community life of the Nagas. The concept of VDB was first introduced in 1976 in Ketsapo village in Phek district of Nagaland in the form of a committee to manage the village funds generated from the common property resources, a task which was customarily performed by the Village Council (VC). It was, therefore, only a delegated power till 1980 when the concept of VDB was adopted and introduced in the entire State with the enactment of VDB rules. Today the VDB which was started in a remote village on an experimental basis as a developing agency of the Village Council, has grown into a massive board comprising 1,083 VDBs operating in the entire State covering 2,16,503 households, spread over 52 community development blocks.[143] This has pioneered the grassroots level organisation for decentralised planning and rural development in the State.

Taking advantage of the conducive socio-cultural situation in Naga society, the Government of Nagaland formally launched VDB in the State under Clause 12 of Section 12 of the Nagaland Village Area Council Act of 1978. The primary objective of the VDB is to effectively channelise development to the villages through grassroots level planning and implementation of the programmes and projects. It was done so with a view to achieve the ideals of removal of rural poverty through community asset building and employment generation. It also aims at ensuring the devolution of economic power to the rural mass with the noble intention of raising the standard of living and to bridge the emerging gap of social disparity through economic entitlement. And finally, it also aims at involving the village in the State developmental affairs through recognisation of the traditional system of governance in Nagaland.

With the inception of the concept of VDB and particularly after the institutionalisation of the same, the powers conferred on the Village Councils (VCs) through the Nagaland Village Area Act (1973 and further amendment in 1978) for the purpose of formulation of plans and implementation of developmental programmes, have been devolved to the VDBs in all the villages. However, VDBs are accountable to the village council.

Organisation and Functions of VDB

The VDBs are basically constituted through democratic election with some cases of selection or nomination through general consensus. Each village council has a VDB in which all the *bona fide* citizens of the village are members. From among the members, a management committee of the VDB is formed, comprising not less than 5 and not more than 25 members themselves, they select a member who is at least a matriculate to be the VDB secretary for a term period. The secretary is given a token of at least Rs. 1,000 in lieu of his/her service rendered to the VDB. Also another important feature of the VDB management committee is that it is mandatory that one-fourth of its members should be women. The Deputy Commissioner/Additional Deputy Commissioner of the district acts as the *ex-officio* Chairman of the VDB and the accounts of each VDB is jointly operated by these officials along with the secretary of the VDBs in their respective districts and independent sub-divisions.

The general body meets at least once a year and passes resolution for management of the affairs of the VDB. The village council retains the prerogative to consider and ratify all the resolutions and proposals formulated by the VDB. The Managing Board of the VDB is required to sit every month for selection of schemes and beneficiaries and also to monitor the progress of the on-going works.

All rural development programmes and schemes, both under the State sector and the centrally sponsored schemes are implemented and executed by the VDBs in their respective villages.

Different developmental programmes and schemes are selected on the basis of priority and need-based requirements by the VDBs with technical support from the Block Development Officers (BDOs). On the recommendations of the BDOs, the schemes are submitted to chairman of the VDBs (DCs/ADCs) through the Project Director of the District Rural Development Agency (DRDA) for approval. On receipt of the approval, the projects/ schemes are taken up for the implementation and only on

satisfactory completion report, the payments are released to the VDBs. The VDB thereby plays the crucial role of translating the policies and programmes of the government into reality at the grassroots level.

The VDBs are locally engaged with the State-sponsored schemes known as matching cash grants popularly known as VDB fixed deposit schemes, and Grant-in-Aid (GIA) on the basis of households allocation. Subsequently, other schemes like Jawahar Rozgar Yojana (JRY) and Employment Assurance Scheme (EAS) were introduced followed by Indira Awas Yojana (IAY), Sampooran Grameen Rozgar Yojana (SGRY), Pradhan Mantri Gramodaya Yojana (PMGY), Post Office Time Deposit (POTD), Total Sanitation Campaign (TSC) and Swarnajayanti Gram Swarozgar Yojana (SGSY).

Among these, the Jawahar Rozgar Yojana (JRY) was introduced with the intention of creating a sustainable development for the rural poor with the schemes such as rural housing, construction of village wells, tanks for drinking water, construction of marketing shed, school building, Anganwari Kendra, community hall, road construction and development, at the same time generating a regular source of income and employment at the village level through social forestry, fishing ponds, pisciculture etc. Under JRY, the scheme of rural housing in particular has brought in a complete change in the village housing pattern from a dull thatched roofing. This scheme gives preference to the people living below poverty line. This scheme has made it possible for many villages in Nagaland to attain 100 per cent housing coverage. Further 99 per cent of the villages in the State have attained road connectivity. This has further encouraged villages in Nagaland to have their own community buses, which in turn has revolutionised the entire transport and communication systems in rural areas.

Village Development Boards as Financial Intermediaries

The VDB are essentially the financial institutions as they were conceived and created with a view to manage the village common fund. One of the main functions of the VDBs as stipulated in the

Model Rules is to borrow money from the banks for the community as well as individual beneficiaries. The programme of Grant-in-Aid (GIA) to the VDBs is one of the most crucial and challenging schemes. This programme was introduced to induce self-initiative for developmental activities at the village level. In Nagaland, the customary laws and practices, as well as the land and its resources are protected under special constitutional provisions (Article 371-A of the Constitution of India). Existing social and customary practices deter Nagas from selling or mortgaging their lands in any form particularly to outsiders or any outside agencies with the exception of Dimapur Sadar. Since mortgaging of land or property is a prerequisite to avail loans or financial assistance in many banks/financial institutions as collateral, chances for the rural masses or the educated unemployed youths to avail loans remain very slim under the prevailing customary situation. The GIA programme serves as an alternative, whereby the VDB borrows money from the government, banks or financial institutions, which is channelled to individual borrowers, and at the same, enables the VDB to act as a security for the repayment of loan by the individual borrowers, and at the same, enables the VDB to act as a security for the repayment of loan by the individuals. The VDB serves as a link between the people of village and the financial agencies to facilitate the flow of credit to individuals.

The VDBs as the development agency of the village councils have their own funds in the form of five different accounts received from the Central and State Governments. Every village has three separate Saving Accounts under the GIA to VDBs as State-sponsored scheme, JRY and EAS. Besides this, the VDBs have a Fixed Deposit in the nationalised banks to the tune of Rs. 5 lakh including Rs. 2.50 lakh as matching grant from the State government. So far, the total deposited amount including the matching grant is about Rs. 1035.25 lakh. Recognising the revised GIA for VDBs from Rs. 12.51 crore to Rs. 19.58 crore. Likewise, household grant which was started with an allocation of Rs. 100 per tax paying household in 1980, was increased to Rs. 800 per household in the year 2004 in all the 1,083 recognised villages of the State. Apart from GIA, the VDB also mobilises free community

labour as contribution in kind. With this novel idea the rural fund mobilisation by VDBs have account as creditable of Rs. 47 crore and now most of the villages have the basic infrastructure requirements available at their disposal. All the funds under the different accounts are used only for the development schemes of the villages, including security for taking loans from the financial institutions. As consequence of this, VDB has been recognised as a Non-Banking Financial Intermediary (NBFI) and accordingly, it is now entitled to give loan and collect repayment from the beneficiaries by obtaining funds from commercial banks. The introduction of NBFI is to integrate the credit mechanism as part of the infrastructural development and to ensure the grassroots organisations have financial control for overall sustainable development of the villages.

Many developmental works directly leading to an improvement in the quality of life could be taken upto completion because the choice of schemes is strictly in accordance with the people's own perception of their problems and needs. However, despite the many success stories of the VDBs, there are still many grey areas and loopholes which need to be taken care of in order for this institution to achieve full success. In order to empower the people at the grassroots level, proper planning and strategy need to be evolved for sound and proper training and management of the quality of human resources. Some of the major problems that plague the VDB system in the State, are such as political interference in the selection and the implementation of the projects, bureaucratic delays in timely releasing of the funds which have negative ramification at all levels of development process. Improper selection of the VDB secretaries leading to failure of maintaining transparency due to lack of proper record maintenance is a major problem at present. This factor combined with lack of proper and timely verification of projects by implementing officials often leads to mis-handling of funds and mismanagement by officials and VDB members.

The VDB institution, despite the many problems and limitations, is still one of the most successful experiments of decentralisation of power and responsibility in the country today.

Strengthening the existing traditional social systems and empowering the people at the grassroots level through community participation has been the key to success of the VDBs in Nagaland. In North East India, a substantial percentage of the population are tribal, whose socio-economic fabric is characterised by strong traditional and community values and ethos. In view of this, there is the strong possibility that the institution of VDB may be evolved into a common strategy and policy for rural development in the entire region, keeping in perspective the variants in the local situation of each State.

Summary

Rural development involves raising the socio-economic status of the rural population on a sustainable basis through optimum utilisation of local resources, both natural and human.

The term 'rural development' is of focal interest and is widely acclaimed in both the developed and developing countries of the world. Rural development as a concept connotes overall development of rural areas with a view to improve the quality of life of rural people. In this sense it is a comprehensive and multi-dimensional concept and encompasses the development of agriculture and allied activities—village and cottage industries and crafts, socio-economic infrastructure, community services and facilities and over all, the human resources in rural areas.

Today, the term 'rural development' has come to an agreement to boost the all-round dynamic development in rural sector for faster economic development and welfare of common masses. There has been considerable discussion of the need for the nature of shifts in emphasis and approach called for in rural development in keeping with the objective of overall development policy for speedy elimination of backwardness to reduce the disparities between the haves and have-nots in rural sector.

The emphasis on rural development in most of the developing countries is understandable. The majority of the population lives in the rural areas. As such, their backwardness would be retarding growth in other sectors and in the economy as a whole. The growth

of towns and cities will be possible, if it is backed by prosperity in rural areas. Rural backwardness is the major cause for the falling demand for most products.

The administration in the urban areas has been finding it difficult to provide employment to the rural labour force migrating to towns and cities. The social consequences of rural exodus like growing slums are too serious to be ignored by the urban administrative authorities.

Another disturbing trend in the rural area is that the surpluses generated in the rural areas are being invested in urban areas for various reasons.

Rural development embraces such things as agricultural development, growth in income, better and expanded employment opportunities, reduction in poverty, more equitable distribution of income and wealth, improved human development index and environmental protections in rural areas.

India has achieved tremendous progress since the First Five Year Plan, even though the targets fixed in each Plan might not have been fully met. Between 1951 and 2004, production of foodgrains had increased by 316 per cent, production of oilseeds by 400 per cent, that of sugarcane by 412 per cent and of cotton by 366 per cent. The increase in the production of wheat has been really spectacular by over 1100 per cent.

During the first decade of planning (1951-1961) when the First and Second Five Year Plans were implemented, the annual rate of growth in agriculture was 3.5 per cent. During the next two decades of planning (1961-1981), despite spectacular progress made under the IADP and HYVP, the overall progress in agriculture was dismal. The average annual rate of growth declined to 2.2 per cent and 1.7 per cent respectively during 1961-1971 and 1971-1981, mainly because of the weather and poor monsoon conditions. But conditions improved during the fourth decade of planning (1981-1991). The growth rate in the 1980s was highly respectable (3.9%). The compound growth rate of agriculture for the period 1991-2001 was 2.8 per cent.

During 2002-03 the annual compound growth rate of agricultural production declined deeply to 7.2. The Tenth Plan

had fixed a target growth rate of 4 per cent in agriculture to achieve 8 per cent growth in GDP. But the actual growth rate in agriculture and allied sector was only 2.3 per cent, while the actual growth rate in GDP was 7.6 per cent.

During the pre-green revolution period, rice recorded most impressive growth rate in yield — from 7 quintals per hectare in 1950-51 to nearly 11 quintals per hectare in 1964-65. The annual rate of growth was 2.1 per cent. Yield per hectare in the cost of wheat improved from 6.6 quintals in 1950-51 to 9.1 quintals in 1964-65, a modest annual rate of growth of 1.3 per cent. Among non-foodgrains, cotton and sugarcane recorded low growth rates during this period.

The production of foodgrains increased from 196.8 million tonnes in 2000-01 to 216.1 million tonnes in 2006-07. The production of cereals increased from 185.7 million tonnes in 2000-01 to 201.9 million tonnes in 2006-07. Rice witnessed the production of 85 million tonnes in 2000-01 to 201.9 million tonnes in 2006-07. Rice witnessed the production of 85 million tonnes in 2000-01 to 92.8 million tonnes in 2006-07. Similarly, wheat witnessed the production of 69.7 million tonnes in 2000-01 to 74.9 million tonnes in 2006-07. Pulse recorded the production of 11.1 million tonnes in 2000-01 to 14.2 million tonnes in 2006-1907. Oilseeds recorded the production of 18.4 million tonnes in 2000-01 to 23.9 million tonnes in 2006-07. The production of sugarcane increased from 206 million tonnes in 2000-01 to 345.3 million tonnes in 2006-07.

During the post-green revolution period, however, the most spectacular growth rate was recorded by wheat (3.2 per cent per annum). Potato recorded an impressive growth rate of 3.1 per cent per annum. Pulses recorded a growth rate of 0.1 per cent per annum. This shows that the new bio-chemical technology was particularly suited to wheat production but was not effective in the case of other crops.

In the Post-Independence period, the attempts of the Union as well as State Governments in the field of institutional change or land reforms have been found concentrated on the following four aspects :

1. Abolition of Zamindari System,
2. Ceiling on land holdings,
3. Consolidation of holdings, and
4. Tenancy reforms.

After Independence, high priority was accorded to the abolition of intermediary tenures (zamindari). Accordingly, every State enacted its own legislation to abolish this tenure system on the payment of compensation and offering their ownership to cultivators on their payment of fixed sums. The process of legislation action commenced in 1948 and was completed in 1954, by which time most States had adopted necessary legislations.

An important part of land reforms relates to the fixation of a ceiling or an upper limit on land holdings, and also by implications, defining a floor level or lower limit on land holdings. The laws enacted by the State legislatures presuppose ceiling on existing holdings which would preserve middle land holders and rich peasants. With more than 60 per cent of the total households on average owing only upto 2 acres each and together holding as little as 7 per cent of the total land; and 5 per cent of the upper group holding 42 per cent of the land, the ceiling fixed by the principal States holds significance.

Legislations for ceiling on existing land holdings and unit of application has been enacted in two phases. During the first phase which tasted up to 1972, ceiling legislation largely treated land holder as the unit of application. After 1972, it was decided to have family as the basis of holdings. Further, the ceiling limit was also reduced to bring about a more equitable distribution of this scarce asset.

Since the inception of ceiling laws on land holdings, and up to 31st March, 2003, total quantum of land declared surplus in the entire country was 73.73 lakh acres, out of which 65.01 lakh acres have been taken in possession and a total area of 53.93 lakh acres has been distributed among 54.47 lakh beneficiaries.

Consolidation of holdings stands for the substitution by exchange of fields among the farmers in an area in such a way as to make the holding held by each of them more compact. On

consolidation, the number of fragments in the holdings is reduced. The fields are made contiguous with each other.

The legislations pertaining to the consolidation exist at present in most of the States. A significant feature of the consolidation work is the uneven progress made in the different States, the bulk of the consolidated area being accounted for Punjab, Haryana and Madhya Pradesh.

The consolidation operations have not made much headway in many States. Consolidation of land holdings is especially important in the States like Assam, Bihar and West Bengal. Some of the factors working against consolidation are: (a) fear of displacement among tenants and share croppers; (b) advantage of having land in fragmented parcels in the event of floods and other natural calamities; and (c) apprehension that the biggest farmers would get a better deal. As far as possible, the holdings of small and marginal farmers need to be consolidated in such a way that they form contiguous block of land so that the exploitation of ground water for them as well as provision of various agricultural services and inputs become economical.

The sad social and economic plight of tenants and also their sheer number call for serious attention and concerted efforts for the improvement of their lots. Broadly speaking, tenants can be divided into (a) tenants at will, (b) sub-tenants, and (c) occupancy or permanent tenants. While the occupancy tenants enjoy fixation and security of rent and can get reimbursement of improvement made on the land, the other categories, especially tenants-at-will continue to suffer from serious disabilities. In a number tenants constitute 12.7 per cent of the total agricultural population and tenant households constitute 23.6 per cent of the total cultivating households in India. The percentage of the area leased out forms 20 per cent of the total cultivated area though this ratio varies from 27 per cent in Punjab to 6.7 per cent in Madhya Pradesh.

The various States in India have enacted tenancy reform legislations to protect the poorer tenants of different categories. These measures pertain to Regulation of Rent, Security of Tenures and Conferment of Ownership on Tenants.

From the mid-1980s when liberalisation started entering the Indian economy at first steadily and then with thunderous gale force from 1991, land reform went off the radar screen of the Indian polity. As a general proposition, it may be said that land reforms should remain an essential element of national agricultural and rural development strategies not only because land-based agricultural occupation must continue to provide livelihood to a vast majority or rural population, but also because macro-economic growth in most contexts has failed to create improved prospects for the rural poor to acquire assets, gainful employment or increase their income and quality of life.

Poverty and unemployment anywhere are danger to peace and prosperity everywhere. In India the rate of poverty is higher in rural areas than that of the urban areas and is pervasive among the landless labour class in rural areas as compared to the land owning class. About 26.5 per cent of people in rural areas are living below the poverty line. About 3.3 per cent of families in rural areas are suffering from hunger. The percentage of hungry people is high in West Bengal (10.4%), Orissa (8%), Assam (7.1%) and Bihar (6%). In India 13.4 per cent of population is living in food insecurity. About 27.3 million people had to suffer some degree of hunger and as many as 23 per cent of the population remained undernourished as of late 1990s.

About 27 per cent of India's population live below poverty line. The poverty estimates in 2004-05 based on Uniform Recall Period (URP) consumption distribution (27.5%) is comparable with the poverty estimates of 1993-94 which was 36 per cent. The poverty estimate in 2004-05 based on Mixed Recall Period (MRP) consumption distribution (21.8%) is roughly but not strictly comparable with the poverty estimate of 1999-2000 which was 26.1 per cent.

The Panchayati Raj Institutions need to play an important role in the development of primary sector. The 73rd Constitutional Amendment has envisaged that development of agriculture is one of the responsibilities of the Panchayats. The Panchayati Raj Acts of many States have assigned duties and responsibilities to the Panchayati Raj Institutions for the promotion of agriculture.

Information and Communication Technology (ICT) has lifted India out of the gloom in the last 15 years. It has not just created wealth for the country, but far more importantly, it has created confidence in the country. Youngsters in India no longer believe that one has to born rich to be highly successful in the country and thus entrepreneurship is thriving. India is on the move. But this confidence permeates to rural areas. ICT can help in this area, but it would require a lot of effort. One must not forget that ICT is at best a tool. One needs to use it to make difference.

Rural India comprises 72 per cent of the countries population but its share in the total national income is currently about 45 per cent. Rural India is characterised by low income levels, poor quality of life and a weak base of human development. Rural urban divide is quite apparent in all spheres of human life. What worries most the policy planners is that the magnitudes of disparity has accentuated during the post-reform period due to change in the income growth trajectories of rural and urban areas.

The share of rural areas in NDP at factor cost has steeply declined from 62.95 per cent in 1970-71 to 48.09 per cent in 1999-2000, whereas the corresponding percentage for urban areas has remarkably increased. Today the urban population may earn nearly about three-fifths of the national income. Thus, in terms of generation of GDP, the centre of gravity has shifted from rural to urban areas, whereas in 2004-05, it was higher by 88 per cent.

Urban India has better outcome of almost all health indicators. Fertility rate, infant death rate, under 5 mortality rate and crude death rate are much higher in the rural areas than those in the urban areas. In the case of birth delivered in medical institutions, it has been observed that in 2005-06, as against 69.4 per cent deliveries made in medical institutions in urban areas, such deliveries in rural areas were only 31.1 per cent. Similarly, percentage of birth assisted by professionals in rural areas was just half that of urban areas. Percentage of total unmet need to family planning was also higher in the rural areas than that of the urban areas.

In 2004, as against 74.1 per cent urban households lived in pucca house, only 25.5 per cent households in rural areas had this

facility. In the case of drinking water, only about 28 per cent rural households had tap water facility whereas 71 per cent of urban households had tap water facility. Against 93.1 per cent urban households having electricity, the corresponding percentage for rural households was only 55.7. Moreover, availability and reliability of electricity are higher in urban areas than those in the rural areas. Only 25.9 per cent rural households had toilet facility, while the corresponding percentage in the urban areas was 83.7. In 2004, only 5.7 per cent of rural households had LPG cooking gas facility, whereas in urban areas 48 per cent of households used LPG as a source of cooking energy. Thus the urban population has much better access to these basic amenities than the rural population.

Disparity between rural and urban households also exists in the case of access to the durable consumer assets like radio, television, bicycle, motorcycle/scooter, car, banking services and telephones. In the case of even possession of radio and bicycle, the percentages of rural households are lower than those of urban households. In the case of access to television, as against 64.1 per cent urban households having the asset, the corresponding percentage in rural areas is only 18.9. In 2001, only 5.3 per cent of rural households possessed motorcycle/scooter, while the corresponding figure for the urban areas was 24.7 per cent. Tele-density measured by number of telephones per 100 people was only 1.33 in the rural areas against 26.88 in the urban areas. Further, it has been observed that about 50 per cent of urban households availed the banking services, while the corresponding figure for the rural areas was only 30.1 per cent.

There is a need to adopt two types of policies to reduce rural-urban disparity, first, the policy which helps to generate sustained income and employment and also abate the undesirable flow of rural workforce to the urban areas; and second which helps to raise the socio-economic status of rural populace and enlarge their capability to participate actively in the developmental activities. There is a need for both qualitative and quantitative changes in the rural areas. In the quantitative form, it must be reflected in more production, more income and more employment. In

quantitative form, it must be reflected in the form of institutional changes in the areas of health, education, environment, transport and social welfare. Economic growth per cent is necessary but not sufficient condition for economic development. What matters more is the broad-base of the growth and its equitable distribution. Economic growth would be more effective in eliminating rural poverty and deprivation when it works with the indicators of human development in the multiplicative form.

Mohandas Karamchand Gandhi or Mahatma Gandhi, as he is popularly known, appeared on the political scene when the national movement for the freedom was gaining momentum. He spiritualised the Indian politics and economics truly and fully during his life time.

Gandhiji had a comprehensive plan for the regeneration of Indian villages. The main plank of his programme was the *charkha* (spinning wheel) movement. The slogan was 'Swaraj through spinning'. Subjugated India could not depend upon foreign masters to initiate genuine plans for economic development, and, therefore, Gandhiji clearly saw that the solution of the mass poverty in the villages lay in teaching the villagers self-help. He wanted honest work to be provided for them, not relief or charity. To Gandhiji *charkha* thus became a symbol of economic independence as well as political emancipation.

Gandhiji conceived decentralisation as an integral part of the social and productive organisation. Highly mechanised factory was inconsistent with the non-violent structure of society since centralisation cannot be sustained without adequate force. He favoured cottage industries from the point of decentralisation as well as distribution.

Gandhiji's ideas on machines and technological civilisation grew out of deep conviction that the modern machine civilisation was at the root of all tensions and frustrations which bring about aggression, violence and war. He saw how technology always led to the multiplication of wants and as state of culture in which material wants are the king. His conviction in regard to machines and technology was logical if one accepted the moral postulates underlying that approach. Employment of large scale machinery

in an acquisitive society, he believed, would give rise to greed and avarice. Gandhiji conceived of an ideal society in which there would not be much scope for glaring inequalities of wealth and income. In so far as these existed in the present society, the rich were duty bound to act as the trustees. According to Mahatma Gandhi, "the rich man will be left in possession of his wealth of which he will use what he reasonably requires for his personal needs and will act as a trustee for the remainder to be used for the rest of the society." His belief in non-violence ruled out expropriation of the wealthy by the use of force. He extolled the principle of voluntariness enjoyed by non-violence.

If the modern India has to get rid of poverty, unemployment and underemployment, wide disparity in personal income, attitudes militating against hard work, and corruption in the highest riches—both political and administrative—it will have to return to Gandhiji for redemption. His thought has immense relevance to India of today and tomorrow. He visualised the growth of the Indian economy on the basis of its own resources endowment and its own technique or techniques evolved to suit the country's conditions of scarce capital and redundant labour. He accorded the first priority to self-reliance and called for an organisation of economic production on a widely decentralised basis which would utilise local endowment talents to the maximum.

The National Community Development Programme (NCDP) was launched in 1952. Its aim was to bring about the overall development of the rural community with people's participation in the development process. The Government on its part decided to provide technical and other services in a coordinated fashion. An institutional structure was provided in the form of Panchayati Raj, Cooperative and village schools. The approach to rural development was holistic one.

The Intensive Agricultural District Programme (IADP) launched in 1960, aimed at concentrating resources in agriculturally better placed areas. The essence of IADP strategy has been to attain foodgrains self-sufficiency in favourable areas with maximum irrigation facilities and minimum natural hazards,

providing simultaneously all the requisite essential inputs and services which were needed. Thus a package approach to step up agricultural production was evolved.

The policy of growth centres in India is concerned more with the development of areas rather than with their rates of growth. However, the growth pole theory is inapplicable to all developmental situations and is too rigidly linked to industrialisation.

Integrated Rural Development Approach (IRDA) is a synergistic approach aiming at total development of the area and the people by bringing about the necessary institutional attitudinal changes and by delivering a package of services through extension methods to encompass economic field as well as establishment of the required special infrastructure and services in the area of health and nutrition, education and literacy, basic civic amenities, family planning, etc. with an ultimate objective of improving quality of life in the rural areas.

One of the lesson learnt during the period of experimentation in India is the rural development must focus on manageable areas in development activity can be responsive to the specificity of natural endowment and social order. But planning at the micro level faces a number of problems. It cannot be effective unless attention is paid to production programmes for the target groups, manpower planning and skill development, provision of minimum needs and a programme for institutions support.

Providing Urban Amenities in Rural Areas (PURA) consists of four connectivities: physical, electronic, knowledge and thereby leads to economic connectivity to enhance the prosperity of clusters of villages in the rural areas. The economic connectivity would generate a market and the production establishments for servicing the market. The PURA has all the dimensions to become a business enterprise which has global dimensions but operating in every nook and corner of our country. The PURA entrepreneur has to have the skill for evolving a business plan with banks and also create infrastructural support such as educational institutions, health centres, and small scale industries, transportation services, tele-education, tele-medicine, e-governance services in the region

integrating with national and global markets to sell the products and services.

The intention of the Panchayati Raj Institutions (PRIs) is to translate the Gandhian Dream of Village Self-governance (Gram Swarajaya) and making them an effective tool of rural development and construction. The new PRIs, however, have assured the vibrant grassroots democracy through the 73rd Constitutional Amendment. This constitutional amendment clearly speaks of the meaning of the decentralised governance. Decentralisation of economic power to the grassroots level, therefore, becomes essential not only for the sake of ensuring people's democracy, but also for higher growth and equity. Decentralised planning and associated devolution of powers to the village panchayats are new institutional arrangement which can be effectively utilised to meet the needs of rural people in changing environment.

The Village Development Board (VDB) of Nagaland is a unique rural planning and development institution which is based on the rich traditional heritage of the community life of the Nagas. The concept of VDB was first introduced in 1976 in Ketsapo village in Phek district of Nagaland in the form of a committee to manage the village funds generated from the common property resources, a task which was customarily performed by the Village Council (VC). It was, therefore, only a delegated power till 1980 when the concept of VDB was adopted and introduced in the entire State with the enactment of the VDB Rules. Today, the VDB which was started in a remote village on an experimental basis as a developing agency of the Village Council, has grown into a massive board comprising 1,083 VDBs operating in the entire State covering 2,16,503 households, spread over 52 Community Development Blocks. This has pioneered the grassroots level organisation for decentralised planning and rural development.

REFERENCES

1. Singh, Katar, (1986) *Rural Development, Principles, Policies and Management*, Sage Publications, New Delhi, p. 165.

2. Vidyarthi, Chaman Ram, (1996) "The Philosophy of Rural Development" in Narendra Prasad (ed.), *Constraints on Rural Development*, Amar Prakashan, Delhi, p. 8.
3. Singh, Kartar, (1986) *Rural Development*, Sage Publication, New Delhi, p. 18.
4. Chambers, Robert, (1983) *Rural Development: Putting the Last First*, Longman Publication, London, p. 147.
5. Brahmanand, P.R., (1987) "Prelude towards an Economic Philosophy of Rural Development" in *Dimension of Rural Development in India*, Himalaya Publishing House, New Delhi, pp. XIII-XIV.
6. *Ibid.*, p. XVII.
7. Gandhi, M.K., (1936) *Harijan*, August 29.
8. Srivastava, A.K., (1986) *Integrated Rural Development Programme in India*, Deep & Deep Publications, New Delhi, p. 10.
9. George, Susan, (1977) *How the Other Half Dies?*, Harper Publications, New York, p. 10.
10. Azad, R.N., (1983) "Integrated Rural Development" in S.K. Sharma (ed.), *Dynamics of Development*, Concept Publishing Company, New Delhi, pp. 42-26.
11. Durban, E.F.M., (1963) *Problem of Economic Planning*, p. 24.
12. Jhingan, M.L., (2005) *The Economics of Development and Planning*, Vrinda Publications, New Delhi, p. 1.
13. Jhingan, M.L., (1988) (quoted by), *The Economics of Development and Planning*, Konark Publication, New Delhi.
14. Dhingra, I.C., (1992) (quoted by) *The Indian Economy: Resources, Planning, Development and Problems*, Sultan Chand & Co., New Delhi, p. 8.
15. Pearsall, Judy, (ed.), (2000) *Concise Oxford Dictionary*, Oxford University Press, London.
16. Registrar General & Census Commissioner of India, (2004) *Census of India 2001*, Series-1: India, Final Populations.
17. *Ibid.*
18. *Ibid.*
19. Pearsall, Judy, (2000) *op. cit.*, p. 1254.
20. Encyclopedic Edition, (2003) The New International Webster's Comprehensive Dictionary of the English Language, p. 1102.
21. Pearsall, Judy, (2000) *op. cit.*, p. 1254.
22. Vidyarthi, Chaman Ram, (1990) *op. cit.*, p. 10.
23. Registrar General and Census Commissioner of India, (2004) *op. cit.*
24. Rajneesh, Shalini, (2002) *Rural Development through Democratic Decentralization*. Deep & Deep Publications, New Delhi, pp. 33-34.
25. Karalay, G.N., (2005) *Integrated Approach to Rural Development: Policy Programmes and Strategies*, Concept Publishing Company, New Delhi, p. 3.

26. Rajneesh, Shalini, (2002) *op. cit.*, p. 34.
27. Jhingan, M.L., (2005) *op. cit.*, p. 5.
28. Mishra, S.K. and V.K. Puri, (2001) *Indian Economy*, Himalaya Publishing Co., Mumbai.
29. Jhingan, M.L., (2005) (quoted by), *op. cit.*
30. Pearsall, Judy, (Ed.), (2000) *op. cit.*, p. 392.
31. Mukerjee, Suman L., (2002) *Textbook of Economic Development*, Orient Longman, Private Limited, Kolkata, p. 3.
32. Encyclopedic Edition, (2003) *op. cit.*, p. 350.
33. Haq, Mahbub Ul, (1971), "Employment and Income Distribution in the 1970's: A New Perspective", *Pakistan Economic and Social Review*, June-December, p. 6.
34. Ray, Debraj, (2004) *Development Economics*, Oxford University Press, New Delhi.
35. Todaro, Michael P. *et al.*, (2003) *Economic Development*, Pearson Education, Washington, U.S.A. Edition 9th, p. 792.
36. Todaro, Michael. *et al.*, (2003) *op. cit.*, pp. 8 and 15.
37. Meir, G.M., (1991) *Leading Issues in Economic Development*, Oxford University Press, New Delhi, p. 6.
38. Higgins, Benjamin (1994) *Economic Development, Problems, Principles & Policies*, Universal Book Stall, New Delhi, p. 147.
39. Jhingan, M.L., (2005) (quoted by), *op. cit.*, p. 9.
40. Jhingan, M.L., (2005) *op. cit.*, pp. 10-11.
41. Jhingan, M.L., (2005) (quoted by), *op. cit.*, pp. 17-18.
42. Todaro, Michael, P. *et al.*, (2003) *op. cit.*, p. 17.
43. Mundle, Sudipto, (2005) "Ethics and Development", *Indian Economic Bulletin*, Asian Development Bank, January, Vol. 3, No. 1.
44. Jhingan, M.L., (2005) *op. cit.*, pp. 21-22.
45. Jhingan, M.L., (2005) *op. cit.*, pp. 22, ii.
46. Pearce, David. W, *et al.*, (1990) *Sustainable Development, Economic and Environment in Third World.*
47. Mundle, Sudipto, (2005) *op. cit.*, p. 20.
48. Jhingan, M.L., (1988) (quoted by), *op. cit.* p. 17.
49. Todaro, Michael, P. *et al.*, (2003) *op. cit.*, p. 17.
50. Datt, Ruddar, (ed.), (2002) "Second Generation Reforms Need for Changing Growth Strategy", in *Second Generation Economic Reforms in India*, Deep & Deep Publications, New Delhi, pp. 6-7.
51. Imnayongdang, (1990) *Levels of Rural Development in Nagaland : A Spatial Analysis*, A.S. Prakashan, Meerut, p. 1.
52. Imnayongdang, (1990) (quoted by), *op. cit.*, p. 1 in Tylor, D.R.F., *Spatial Aspects of Kenya's Rural Development Strategy: Spatial Aspect of Development*, (ed.), Hoyle, B.S. John Willey & Sons, New York, 1974, p. 167.
53. The World Bank, (1975) *Rural Development Sector, Policy Paper*, Washington D.C., February, p. 167.

54. Azad, R.N., (1990) "Integrated Rural Development" in *Dynamics of Development*, Sharma, S.K., (ed.), Concept Publishing Company, New Delhi, pp. 420-26.
55. Imnayongdang, (1990) *op. cit.*
56. Lele, Uma, *Design of Rural Development, Lessons from Africa*, Dhingra, I.C., (1992) (quoted by), *op. cit.*, p. 20.
57. Dhingra, I.C., (1992) *op. cit*, p. 8.
58. Singh, Roshan, *et al.*, (2001) "Rural Development and Cooperatives." *Yojana*, July.
59. Singh, Katar, (1999) *Rural Development, Principles, Policies and Management*, Sage Publications, New Delhi, p. 20.
60. Rajneesh, Shalini, (2002) (quoted by), *op. cit.* p. 36.
61. *Op. cit.*
62. Imnayongdang, (1990) *op. cit.*, p. 2.
63. Singh, Katar, (1999) *op. cit.*, p. 20.
64. Singh, Katar, (1999) (quoted by) *op. cit.*
65. Sharma, B.D., (1978) *Tribal Development: The Concept and Frame*, Prachi Prakashan, New Delhi, p. 44.
66. Singh, Katar, (1999) *op. cit.*, p. 21.
67. *Ibid.*, p. 23.
68. Registrar General & Census Commissioner of India, (2004), *op. cit.*, p. 1.
69. *Op. cit.*, p. IX.
70. Singh, Katar, (1999) (quoted by), *op. cit.*, p. 23.
71. Singh, Katar, (1999) *op. cit.*, p. 23.
72. Mital, Mukta (ed.), (1995) (quoted by) *Rural Development in India*, Anmol Publications, New Delhi, p. 8.
73. Singh Katar, (1999) *op. cit.*, p. 24.
74. Gandhi, P. Jagadish, (2005) (ed.), *Dr. Kalam's PURA Model and Social Transformation*, Deep and Deep Publications, New Delhi.
75. Sundaram, Satya, (2002), *Rural Development*, Himalaya Publishing, Mumbai.
76. Todaro, Michael P., (2003) *op.*cit.*
77. Datt, Ruddar and K.P.M. Sundharam, (2006) *Indian Economy* S. Chand & Co., New Delhi, p. 493.
78. Das, H.C.L., (1993) *Agricultural Efficiency in India*, Mittal Publications, New Delhi, p. 252.
79. Planning Commission, (1969) *Fourth Five Year Plan (1969-74): A Draft Outline*, pp. 88-89.
80. Veil, Laurance A. (1976) *India's Second Revolution*, McGraw-Hill Publishing Co., New York, p. 245.
81. Government of India, (1962) *Report of the Committee of Panel on Land Reforms*, Ministry of Agriculture, New Delhi.
82. Planning Commission, (1969) *Fourth Five Year Plan (1969-74): Draft Outline Government of India*, New Delhi, p. 140.

83. Planning Commission, (1970) *Fourth Five Year Plan (1970); Final*, Government of India, New Delhi, p. 181.
84. Planning Commission, (1985) *Sixth Five Year Plan (1980-85)*, Government of India, New Delhi, p. 115.
85. Planning Commission, (1985) *Seventh Five Year Plan (1985-90), Vol. II*, Government of India, New Delhi, p. 63.
86. Minhas, B.S., (1974) *Planning and the Poor*, Oxford University Press, New Delhi.
87. (a) Uppal, J.S., (1969) "Implementation of Land Reforms in India", *Asian Survey*, Vol. 9, No. 5, pp. 359-372.
    (b) Uppal, J.S., (1969) "Attitudes of Farm Families towards Land Reforms in Some Punjabs Villages ", *Journal of Developing Areas*, Vol. 4, No. 1, pp. 59-68.
88. Bishop, C.E. and W.D. Taussiant, (1970) *Agricultural Economic Analysis*, Chap. 14.
89. Khusro, A.M., (1973) *Economics of Land Reforms and Farm Size in India*, Allied Publisher, Calcutta, p. 27.
90. Planning Commission, (1973) *Report of the Task Force on Agrarian Relations in India*, Government of India, New Delhi, pp. 8-9.
91. *Ibid.*, p. 9
92. Government of India, (1976) *Report of the National Commission on Agriculture*, Ministry of Agriculture, New Delhi, p. 79.
93. Patnaik, B.K., (quoted by) (2007) "Rural Poverty and Need for Primary Sector Development", *Kurukshetra*, Vol. 55, No. 7, p. 38.
94. *Ibid.*, p. 39.
95. Planning Commission, (2002) *National Human Development Report (2001)*, Government of India, New Delhi.
96. Vyas, V.S., (2005) "Food Security in India", in Vyas, V.S. (ed.) *Food Security in Asian Countries in the Context of Millennium Goals*, Academic Foundation, New Delhi.
97. Planning Commission, (2003) *Vision 2020*, Government of India, (New Delhi).
98. Parikh, K.S. and Radhakrishna, (eds.) (2005) *India Development Report (2004-05)*, Oxford University Press, New Delhi.
99. Bhalla, G.S. and G.K. Chadha, (1983) *Green Revolution and the Small Peasants (A Study of Income Distribution among Punjab Cultivators)*, Concept Publishing Co., New Delhi.
100. Athreya, V. *et al.*, (1983) "Identification of Agrarian Classes—A Methodological Essay: Empirical Material from South India" *Arbejadspapir*, No. 21 (Mimeo) Sociology Institute, Copenhagan University.
101. Sengupta S. and H. Gazadr, (1977) "Agrarian Politics and Rural Development in West Bengal", in Jean Dreze and A. Sen (eds.), *India Development: Selected Regional Perspective*, Oxford University Press, New Delhi.

102. Deva, S., (1984) "Problems of Rural Development in Green Revolution Areas", *Social Scientist*, No. 130, March 1984.
103. Venkatappiah, B., (1962) "Small Farmers Development Agency", Address to the *29th Annual Conference of the Indian Society of Agricultural Economics*, December 30.
104. Srinivasan, P.V., (2002) "Poverty and Agricultural Research", *India Development Report 2002*, Oxford University Press, New Delhi.
105. Jhunjhunwala, Ashok and Roshni Menon, (2007) "ICT to Empower Rural India", *Yojana*, August, p. 77.
106. Singh, S.P., (2007) "Growing Rural Urban Disparities in India", *Kurukshetra*, November, Vol. 56, No. 1, p. 4.
107. Brahmanand, P.R. and C.N. Vakil, (1956) *Planning for an Expanding Economy*, Allied Publishers, Bombay.
108. Das, H.C.L. and S.K. Jha, (1985) "Economic Ideas of Mahatma Gandhi", paper presented in the *68th Conference of the Indian Economic Association*, Ahmedabad, December, 28-30.
109. Prabhu, R.K. and H.R. Rao, (1948) *The Mind of the Mahatma*, J.C. Cooper & Co., Bombay, p. 127.
110. Tendulkar, D.G., (quoted by) (1950) *"Mahatma: Life of Mohandas Karamchand Gandhi."*
111. M.K. Gandhi, (1942) *India of My Dreams.*
112. Unnithan, T.K.N., (1950) *Gandhi and Free India.*, pp. 100-02.
113. Cole, G.D.H., (1950) (quoted by) J.K.N. Unnithan, *op. cit.*, p. 103.
114. Nehru, Jawahar Lal, (1951) (quoted by Nym Wales, *China Builds for Democracy*, p. 6.
115. Gandhi, M.K., (1924) *Young India*, November, 13.
116. Gandhi, M.K., (1934) *Harijan*, November, 2.
117. *Ibid.*
118. Prabhu, R.K. and H.R. Rao, (1948) *op. cit.*, p. 123.
119. *Ibid.*, p. 120.
120. *Ibid.*
121. Gandhi, M.K., (1934) *Harijan*, November 16.
122. Gandhi, M.K., (1940) *Harijan*, August 25.
123. Anjaria, J.J., (1952) (quoted by) *An Essay on Gandhian Economics*, p. 9.
124. Singh, Katar, (1999) *Rural Development; Principles, Politics and Management*, Sage Publications, New Delhi, p. 165.
125. Misra, R.P., K.V. Sundaram and V.L.S. Rao, (1976) *Regional Development Planning in India*, Vikas Publishing House, New Delhi. pp. 143-44.
126. Stohar, Walter and Franz Stodtlins., (1980) "An Evaluation of Regional Policies—Experiences in Market and Mixed Economics", in V.M. Hansen, (ed.) *Human Settlement Process*, Ballinger Publishing Co., Cambridge.
127. Sharma, S.K. and S.L. Malhotra, (1980) *Integrated Rural Development: Approach Strategy and Perspectives*, Abinav Publications, New Delhi.

128. Aziz, Abdul, (1989) "Approaches to Micro Area Development Planning", in I.S. Sundaram (ed.) *Rural Poverty and Area Planning,* B.R. Publishing Corporations, New Delhi.
129. Mitra, S.K., (1992) "Rural Development: Need for Holistic Approach", *The Economic Times,* November 21.
130. Kumar, B. Das, (1988) *Spatial Framework for Rural Development and American Policy,* Asia Publishing House, Mumbai, p. 142.
131. Lewis, John P. (1970), *Quit Crisis in India: Economic Development and American Policy,* Asia Publishing House, Mumbai.
132. F.A.O., (1977) *Joint Report on the Expert Consultations, Policies and Institutions, for Integrated Rural Development, Colombo and Nairobi,* Rome.
133. Sharma, S.K. and S.L. Malhotra, (1980) *op. cit.*
134. Mishra, R.P., K.V. Sundaram and V.L.S. Prakash Rao, (1976) *op. cit.*
135. Sundaram, K.U., (1979) "Some Recent Trends in Rural Area Development Planning in India", in R.P. Mishra and K.V. Sundaram (ed.) *Rural Area Development Perspective and Approaches,* Sterling Publishers, New Delhi, p. 25.
136. Planning Commission, (1970) *Report of the Working Group on Block Level Planning,* Government of India, New Delhi, pp. 3-4.
137. Swaminathan, M.S., (1979) "Self-Replicating Process for Employment Generation", *Yojana,* March 1, p. 20.
138. Mishra, R.P. and K.V. Sundaram, (1980) *Multi-level Planning and Integrated Rural Development in India,* Heritage Publishers, New Delhi, p. 42.
139. Planning Commission, (1978) *op. cit.,* p. 16.
140. Datt, Ruddar, (2005) "PURA—A Neo Gandhian Approach to Development", in P. Jagdish Gandhi (Ed) *Dr. Kalam's PURA Model and Social Transformation,* Deep and Deep Publication, New Delhi.
141. Singh, S.N. and C.B. Kumar, (2007) "Rural Development and Poverty Alleviation through Decentralisation of Governance in India", *90th Conference Volume,* Indian Economic Association, University of Kashmir, Srinagar (J&K), October 25-27, p. 1412.
142. Sinha, Subodh Kumar and Rajesh Kumar, (2007) "Grass Root Democracy and Governance", *90th Conference Volume,* Indian Economic Association, University of Kashmir, Srinagar (J&K), October 25-27, p. 1259.
143. Lkr, Lanushashi and Toshimenla Jaamir, (2006) "Village Development Board—Quest for Revolution in Rural Development in Nagaland", *Proceedings of the Eighth Annual Conference of the North Eastern Economic Association,* Mizoram University, Aizawl, Mizoram, November 16-17, p. 106.

3

Microfinance and Rural Development

In the past decades, the world has realized that the poor are bankable and poor women are the most trustworthy in providing financial services. Overtime, the notation of micro credit has broadened into microfinance which includes not only savings and credit but also insurance and pension, and even housing. The challenge in future is that the low income people are inclusive to financial systems. Microfinance can be robustly sustainable. When the model is right, the growth of microfinance is fast. Worldwide microfinance institutions have grown 13 to 15 per cent a year in the last decade. Still two-third of population (in India) does not have a basic bank account. It is an entry point which allows the person/women to have the money outside the household when the empowerment process starts. This fact has captured the attention of governments, international financial institutions, philanthropists, social investors, mainstream bankers, even royalty and celebrities. The drive is strong, but not strong enough to grow further.

The factors of 'inclusive finance' are complex and difficult to predict. However, in coming years the client base will change for banks and microfinance institutions. The younger will be seeking financial services. More than half of India's population today are children and teenagers who will be more urban clients. By 2009, urban dwellers will be in majority in our country. Thirdly, these young clients will be more counted and informed as a result of communication technology. It also means that they will be more

easily influenced by outside forces, branding, etc. However, unemployment of youths is a problem which will be more acute, youths will seek different ways of earning. Self-employment will be more attractive. These clients will be the first time entrepreneurs, particularly so in the case of the youths from rural areas. The involvement of the governments in microfinance will increase. All these will depend on what happens in the mainstream financial sector, nor just in microfinance institution. When global financial markets thrive or diversify, the poor consumers would benefit. If the prior sneeze, the latter catch cold.[1] How can the public and private international community contribute to the increase in financial service access for underserved people, that is the challenge.

According to the United Nations (UN), in 2002, almost one-fifth of the world population (i.e. 1.3 billion people) was living in extreme poverty, earning less than one dollar a day. In recent public debates microfinance has been mentioned as an important instrument to combat poverty. Therefore, microfinance has received a lot of attention, both from policy makers as well as in academic circles. Especially, during the past 10 years, microfinance programmes have been introduced in many developing economies. Well known examples are the Grameen Bank in Bangladesh, Banco Sol in Bolivia and Bank Rakyat in Indonesia. The Grameen Bank system of group lending (established in 1976 by Prof. Mohammad Yunus, a Bangladesh banker and economist), in particular, has been copied in other developing countries.[2] Between December 1997 and December 2005, the number of microfinance institutions increased from 618 to 3,113 million (84 of them being women) during the same period.[3]

To support the view that microfinance can be an important instrument to fight poverty, UN declared 2005 to be the *International Year of Microcredit.*

> "The International Year of Microcredit 2005 underscores the importance of microfinance as an integral part of our collective effort to meet the millennium development goals. Sustainable access to microfinance helps alleviate

> poverty by generating income, creating jobs, allowing children to go to school, enabling families to obtain health care and empowering people to make the choices that best serve their needs. Together we can and must build inclusive financial sectors that help people improve their lives."
>
> —*Kofi Annan*, United Nations State Secretary General

Recently, the attention for microfinance and its role in reducing poverty was further increased when Mohammad Yunus received the Nobel Peace Prize. According to the Nobel Peace Committee, microfinance can help people to break out poverty, which in turn is seen as an important prerequisite to establish long lasting peace.[4] This has led to an almost euphoric attitude among policy-makers and aid organisations about potential poverty reducing effects of microcredit.

Concepts of Microfinance and Microcredit

Microfinance refers to the entire range of financial and non-financial services, including skill upgradation and entrepreneurship development, rendered to the poor for enabling them to overcome poverty. In the context of designing programme for the poor, microfinance is recognised and accepted as one of the new development paradigms for alleviating poverty through social and economic empowerment of the poor with special emphasis on empowering women. The operational framework of microfinance, therefore, rests on the premises that (a) formation of the self-employment enterprise is a viable alternate means of alleviating poverty, (b) lack of access to capital assets/credit acts as a constraint on the existing and potential microenterprises, and (c) the poor are capable of saving despite their poor income level. In essence, therefore, microfinance may be referred to as an institutional mechanism of providing credit support in small amount and usually limited with small groups along with other complementary support such as training and other related services to the people with poor resources and skills for enabling them to take up economic activities.

Attempts to formally define microfinance or microcredit programmes usually refer to the objective of such programmes, viz. reaching small amounts of credit and other microfinancial services to the poor so as to promote income generating activities. The Declaration of the Microcredit Summit held in Washington, D.C. in 1997, defined microcredit programmes as those that "extend small loans to poor people for self-employment project that generate income, allowing them to care for themselves and their families."[5]

The Task Force on Microfinance set up by NABARD defines microfinance as the "provision of thrift, credit and other financial services and products of very small amounts to the poor in rural, semi-urban or urban areas for enabling them to raise their income levels and living standards."[6]

While these definitions essentially seek to foreground the purpose of microfinance programmes ("income generation through self-employment"), the size of the financial services offered ("very small amounts"), and the target clientele of such programmes ("the poor"), the term 'microfinance' and 'microcredit' in the course of popular usage, come to signify not only the goal of reaching financial assistance to a designated target population, but also to encompass a particular set of lending methodologies and transactional technologies, that set them apart from an earlier generation of credit programmes for the development of the agricultural sector.

Tara Nair notes that microfinance actually refers to a system of decentralised credit delivery marked by the substitution of individual banking by social intermediation, where people's organisations are financial intermediaries.[7] According to the Microfinance Handbook, produced by the World Bank's Sustainable Banking with the Poor Project, while the term microfinance refers to the provision of financial services to low income clients many microfinance institutions (MFIs) provide social intermediation services comprising group formation, training in financial literacy and management capabilities, and, therefore, the definition of microfinance encompasses both financial and social intermediation.[8]

The current consensus aggressively propagated by some of the leading development organisations including the World Bank, the USAID and the DFID which hold that microfinance based programmes constitute the single most effective development intervention that can be universally adapted, may be attributed to the close association of microfinance with lending technologies that reduce transaction costs to the borrower and the lending institutions by lending to the neighbourhood based 'primary groups', 'self-help groups' or 'solidaristic groups' (as they are variously called in different contexts. It is important to note that organisational structure of the peer group based channel of delivery of microfinancial services are heterogeneous, assumes diverse forms across the globe and ranges across a spectrum including the Grameen Bank type groups of Bangladesh, Indian self-help groups, the village banking model prominent in Latin America, etc. As the Microfinance Handbook of the World Bank points out, the MFIs in turn could be non-governmental organisation, credit union savings and loan cooperatives, government banks, commercial banks and non-bank financial institutions.[9]

Although the terms microfinance and microcredit are often used interchangeably in the economic or financial literature, it is generally agreed that microcredit or small loans for income generation or consumption purposes refers to one component of a larger array of microfinance services which could include savings, insurance and other related business development services as well.

Microcredit is defined as provision of thrift, credit and other financial services and products of very small amount to the poor in rural, semi-urban and urban areas for enabling them to raise their income levels and improve living standards. Microcredit institutions are those which provide these facilities.

It is generally observed that the poor people do not have access to bank loans. Private money lenders charge a very high interests rates. This makes it difficult for the poor people to have access to funds for starting small income generation activities like sewing, buying buffalo, opening a tea stall or some other small shop. Microcredit caters the need of people for small loans. Microfinance

includes support services along with the loan component, in microcredit more emphasis is placed on loans. Microfinance, thereby, opens up channels for thrift, market assistance, technical assistance, capacity building, insurance, social and cultural programme. Thus microfinance has an element of 'credit plus' while microcredit is 'only credit'.

Under the financial reforms regime, banks have been given freedom to formulate their own lending norms keeping in view the ground realities. They have been asked to diverse appropriate loan and savings product and the related terms and conditions including size of the loan, unit cost, unit size, maturity period, grace period, margins, etc. Such credit covers not only consumption and production loans for various farm and non-farm activities of the poor, but also includes their other credit needs such as housing and shelter improvement.

Microcredit is delivered through self-help groups (SHGs). A self-help group is a registered/unregistered group of micro-entrepreneurs having homogeneous social and economic background, voluntarily coming together to save small amounts regularly. They mutually agree to contribute to a common fund and to meet their emergency needs on mutual help basis. The group members use collective wisdom and peer pressure to insure proper end use of credit and timely repayment thereof. In fact peer pressure has been recognised as an effective substitute for collaterals.

An economically poor individual gains strength as part of a group. Besides, financing through SHGs reduces transaction costs for both lenders and borrowers. While lenders have to handle a single SHG account instead of a large number of small-sized individual accounts, borrowers as part of an SHG cut down expenses on travel (to and fro the branch and other places) for completing paper work and on the loss of work days in canvassing for loans.

A non-governmental organisation (NGO) is an integral part of the microfinance system. An NGO is a voluntary organisation established to undertake social intermediation like organising SHGs of micro-entrepreneurs and entrusting them to banks for

credit linkage or financial intermediation like borrowing bulk funds from banks for on lending to SHGs.

The Government of India vide its notification dated August 29, 2000, has included microcredit/rural credit in the list of permitted Non-Banking Financial Company (NBFC) activities for being considered for Foreign Direct Investment (FDI)/Overseas Corporate Bodies (OCB)/Non-Resident Indian (NRI) investment to encourage foreign participation in microcredit projects. This covers credit facility at micro level for providing finance to small producers and small micro enterprises in rural and urban areas.

There is an urgent need for microcredit providers to shift from a minimalist approach—that is, offering financial intermediation—to an integrated approach to poverty alleviation taking a more holistic view of the client including provision of enterprise development services like marketing, infrastructure, introduction of technology and design development. In this context, the setting up of the microfinance development fund marks an important step.

The reforms of the interest rate regime has constituted an integral part of the financial sector reforms initiated in India in 1991. In consonance with this reform process, interest rates applicable to loans given by banks to microcredit organisation or by the microcredit organisation to self-help groups/member beneficiaries has been left to their discretion. The interest rate ceiling applicable to direct small loans given by banks to individual borrowers, however, continues to remain in force.

Microfinance providers in India can be classified under three broad categories: (a) formal, (b) semi-formal, and (c) informal. The formal banking sector constitutes the first category, while the semi-formal group consists of a variety of MFIs and SHGs. Informal providers, on the other hand, are not legal entities and include money-lenders and various social networks. Today, semi-formal and informal lenders dominate the scene.[10]

(a) Formal

Despite the large size of the formal financial sector, the outreach

to the poor remains rather limited. The banking sector consists 105 commercial banks, 196 regional rural banks and 12,128 cooperative banks primarily serve rural areas and are the first to provide financial services to the poor. Among the most prominent the Self-Employed Women's Association (SEWA) Bank which primarily serves urban women. In March 1999, the deposits held by cooperative banks totalled to Rs. 677 billion, while their loan properties stood at Rs. 708 billion. The regional rural banks provide credit for agriculture and micro-enterprises and generally target the poor. As on March 1999, their deposits stood at Rs. 368 billion while their advances totalled Rs. 113 billion. Within commercial banks' priority ending requirements 18 per cent is for agriculture and 10 per cent is for disadvantaged groups. Today, formal banks are increasingly using microfinance to meet these targets.

(b) Semi-formal

The majority of institutional microfinance providers in India are semi-formal organisations broadly referred to MFIs. Registered under a variety of legal acts, these organisation greatly differ in philosophy, size and capacity.[11]

The least regulated institutions include over 500 Non-Government Organisations (NGOs) registered as societies, public trusts or non-profit companies. While NGOs play a crucial role in the formation and bank linkage of SHGs microfinance is often but a subset of their activities. Nonetheless, many NGOs have emerged as successful financial intermediaries between banks and apex institutions on the one hand, and individuals, SHGs and other groups of borrowers on the other.

Other semi-formal providers can be further classified under two groups—mutual benefit institutions and for profit institutions, neither of which is constrained to serve only the poor. Mutual benefit institutions include State cooperatives and national credit cooperatives.

These institutions may not be able to access government funds, their greater accountability and relative freedom from government

intervention have prompted a majority of State credit cooperatives into Mutual Aid Cooperative Societies (MACS), leading to a total number of 92,000.

The largest and most profitable MFIs in India are registered as non-banking financial companies (NBFCs). While the vast majority of the 37,000 NBFCs target the rural and urban middle class, a few such as BASIX focus on providing microfinance services to the poor. Unlike NGOs, the NBFCs, with permission from the Reserve Bank of India, are able to mobilise savings and can thus provide a wider array of services.

(c) Informal

In addition to friends and families, money lenders, landlords and traders constitute the informal sector. While estimates of their importance vary significantly, it is undeniable that they continue to play a significant role in the financial lives of the poor. Data from the All India Debt Investment Survey 1992 reveals that households in the lowest asset ownership category owed 58 per cent of their outstanding debt to the informal sector. Other studies suggest that the informal sector accounts for as much as 84 per cent of poor households credit usage. While the informal sector charges the highest interest rates on loans, these are increasingly being driven down by competing from other microfinance providers.[12]

In India, the microfinance movement is gaining momentum over the past one and half decade with the active involvement of about 3,000 NGOs, with the support of apex institutions such as NABARD, Small Industry Development Board of India (SIDBI) Rashtriya Mahila Kosh, etc. Microfinance institutions through SHG-Bank Linkage programme has passed through various phases since 1992.

Importance of Microfinance

The multipliers theory occupies an important place in modern economic theory. The basic concept of multiplier says that the

effect of investment on income, output and/or employment is manifold than the original increase in investment. The same can be distinctly demonstrated in a credit programme for the rural poor through the continuous expansion of their economic base. Income also rises if borrowers from the banks are channelised for productive purposes, i.e. low savings → low investment → low income can be broken with the injection of credit in the cycle. "Credit intended for more investment → more income → more savings → more investment, more income" is the result which is sought through the credit investment. It is assumed that those who save and those who go to the bank and borrow, are two different groups of people. Savers put away deposits in banks while borrowers go to the banks and borrow the savings of other people at price (interest). However, a saver can himself be an investor as is the usual in the case of the poor. His investment is calibrated in very small amount and any time. The poor pressure subtle, at times not-so-subtle, keep the poor members in lines and contribute to the collective strength of the group.[13] The impact of microfinance on the different sectors of the economy can be well understood with the help of Figure 3.1.

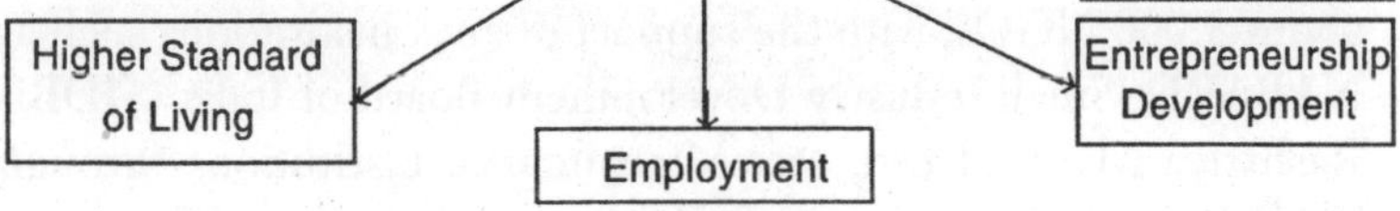

Fig. 3.1 : Impact of Microfinance

Experiences throughout the world have proven that microfinance can improve the livelihood of poor and low income people in a significant manner. This helps poor people to have access to savings, credit, insurance and other financial services so that they are able to cope up with everyday demands more

resiliently and confident.[14] Besides, with the help of microcredit, poor people can set up their own micro-enterprises. Thus it helps in eliminating poverty by providing a regular source of livelihood, creating jobs, allowing children to go to schools, enabling families to obtain health care and empowering people to make their choices which best serve their needs. Since more than 90 per cent of microfinance beneficiaries are women, empowering the lady of the house does more miracles in uplifting the standard of living of poor and enables them to be integrated with overall economic development of the nation and this will be one step forward in the direction of empowerment of women.

Microfinance initiatives are now recognised as a cost effective and sustainable way of expanding the banking system to the rural poor. The guiding spirit behind microfinance initiatives are :

(a) To offer cost-effective approach to formal institutions for expanding outreach to poor,
(b) To develop collateral substitutes,
(c) To focus on the rural and the urban poor, especially women,
(d) To pilot test other micro-credit delivery mechanism as alternative channels to the formal banks, and
(e) To effectively pursue the objectives of macro economic growth.

Microfinance and Rural Credit

Villages are the cells of a human body. When every cell is healthy, the body is healthy. Further credit is an important input in the development process. Gunnar Myrdal has termed credit as an accelerator of development. Ensuring the provision of timely and sufficient credit to as large a segment of rural population as possible has been one of the major policy initiatives which has guided the formulation of public policy in the developing countries.[15]

The rural credit system in India has evolved through different phases as a result of these initiatives and there has been a substantial broadening of the infrastructure for credit delivery resulting in

increased outreach and reduction in the influence of informal agencies as evidenced by the increase in the share of institutional sources of the cash debts of rural households from 7.3 per cent in the early 1950s to 64 per cent in 1991 as per the All India Debt and Investment Survey.

Policy measure were taken by the Reserve Bank of India following the nationalisation of the commercial banks in 1969 aimed at increasing the spread of banking network in the rural areas and giving new developmental thrust and orientation to the policies pursued by them. The primary emphasis at this juncture was on making banking facilities available in the large number of unbanked centres in rural and semi-urban areas both from the point of view of resource mobilisation and extension of credit facilities. At this point, the cooperatives were not able to meet the need for credit which had increased considerably with the green revolution and the boost it had provided to agricultural production and productivity. The nationalisation of commercial banks enable them to supplement the efforts of the cooperatives. As there were still spatial gaps in rural lending, the Regional Rural Banks were introduced in 1975, and the Local Area Banks in 1996 to give a further fillip to the developmental efforts.

Rural credit in India is purveyed through a multi-agency system comprising cooperatives, commercial banks and Regional Rural Banks. The major policy in the sphere of rural credit has been its progressive institutionalisation so as to ensure timely and increased credit support to the special programmes. Thus a rural network of formal financial institutions for channelising funds efficiently to sectors and target groups in the rural economy, in accordance with the national plans has been put in place. The organisational framework for provision of rural credit has been shown in Fig 3.2.

The cooperative credit structure in India has two main wings—the long-term credit structure and the short-term credit structure. Long term credit is provided generally by a two-tier structure comprising the State Cooperative Agricultural and Rural Development Banks (SCARDBs) and Primary Cooperative Agricultural Banks (PCABs). The main source of funds of these

institutions are debentures floated by them which are subscribed by NABARD. Short term credit, on the other hand, is provided by a three tier structure of State Cooperative Banks, District (Central) Cooperative Banks and Primary Agricultural Credit Societies (PACS/PAX). While the PACS operating at the grass-

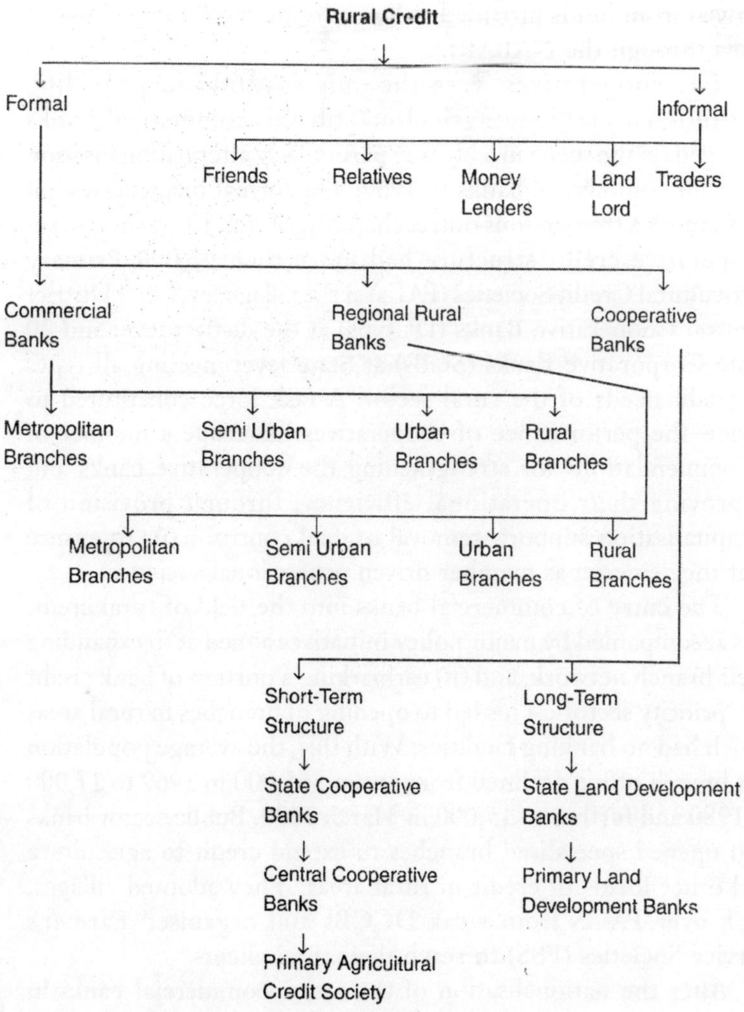

Fig. 3.2 : Organisational Framework for Provision of Agricultural and Rural Credit in India

roots levels are by and large, conduits for flow of funds from the higher level financing agency to the borrower and *vice versa*, with little resources of their own by means of public deposits, the institutions at the two higher tiers mobilise resources, *inter alia*, by way of deposits from the general public. Even so, the bulk of short-term credit requirements of the cooperative structure are derived from funds provided at low rates by the Reserve Bank of India through the NABARD.

The cooperatives were the only institutions providing institutional credit to agriculture till the commercial banks emerged on the scene in a big way particularly after nationalisation of major commercial banks in 1969. The formal financial system now enjoys a tremendous outreach. As on March 1999, short term cooperative credit structure had more than 92,000 Primary Agricultural Credit Societies (PACs) at the village level, 364 District Central Cooperative Banks (DCCBs) at the district level and 20 State Corporative Banks (SCBs) at State level meeting all types of credit needs of the rural sector. A task force constituted to review the performance of cooperatives has made a number of recommendations for strengthening the cooperative banks and improving their operational efficiency, through provision of recapitalisation support, removal of dual control so as to ensure that they emerge as member driven professional societies.

The entry of commercial banks into the field of rural credit was accompanied by major policy initiatives aimed at (i) expanding their branch network, and (ii) earmarking a portion of bank credit for 'priority sector'. This led to opening of branches in rural areas which had no banking facilities. With this, the average population per branch office declined from around 65,000 in 1969 to 17,000 in 1980 and further to 15,000 in March 2000. Public sector banks also opened specialised branches to extend credit to agriculture and other forms of credit in rural areas. They adopted villages, took over PACS from weak DCCBs and organised Farmer's Service Societies (FSS) to reach their rural clients.

After the nationalisation of the major commercial banks in 1969, the concept of priority sector lending was developed to ensure that credit was channelled to various sectors of the economy

in accordance with the national planning priorities. This, *inter alia*, implied flow of credit to the sector which were hitherto neglected. Banks were advised to ensure that they attained the prescribed level of advances to these sectors. In November 1974, the banks were nationalised to raise the share of these sectors in their aggregate advances to the level of 33.33 per cent by March 1979. At a meeting of Union Finance Minister with head of the public sector banks in March 1980, it was agreed that banks should aim at raising the proportion of their advances to priority sector to 40 per cent by 1985.

The economy of India is largely agrarian. Keeping in view the crucial importance of agriculture and in the context of the strategy adopted for increasing foodgrains production so as to ensure food security and the need for greater involvement of banks in supporting this effort, banks were asked to step up the direct finance extended to agriculture (including allied activities) so as to reach a level of at least 10 per cent of total outstanding credit by March 1990. This was done as credit support from banks was considered necessary for increasing agriculture production in the country. Later, this target was made inclusive of indirect lending to agriculture and it was stipulated that the agricultural lending under the indirect category should not exceed one-fourth of the sub-target of 18 per cent (i.e. 4.5% of net bank credit).

At present the priority sector comprises agriculture, small scale industry, small road and water transport operations, retail traders, small business, professional and self-employed persons, self-help groups (SHGs), housing, consumption loans for weaker sections, government poverty alleviation and employment generation programmes, etc. Within the priority sector 10 per cent of net bank credit is required to be channelised to the weaker sections which compromise small and marginal farmers, landless labourers, rural artisans beneficiaries of special poverty alleviation programmes and the socially underprivileged class. A target for lending to the priority sector is at 32 per cent of net credit in the case of foreign banks operating in India (which is inclusive of export credit).

With a view to improve the flow of credit to Agriculture, Public Sector Banks were advised in 1994 to formulate Special Agricultural Credit Plans (SACP) with self-set target for disbursement during the year. Banks have also been advised to fix these targets showing an increase of about 20 to 25 per cent over the disbursement made in the previous year. The flow of credit to agriculture from Rs. 8,255 crore in 1994-95 to Rs. 24,654.40 crore in 2000-01, at an annual compound growth rate of 20 per cent.

As an innovative measure of credit delivery, all the banks are implementing the Kisan Credit Card (KCC) scheme for the farmers to enable them to readily purchase agricultural inputs such as seeds, fertilizers, pesticides, etc. and draw cash for their production needs. KCC is a revolving cash credit facility which aims at providing adequate and timely credit to the farmer. In the budget speech for the year 1999-2000, the Union Finance Minister had advised the coverage of KCC to 20 lakh farmers during the year, and in the Budget Speech for the subsequent year 2000-01 he advised that all cooperative banks and commercial banks, regional rural banks and commercial banks together should issue additional 75 lakh Kisan Credit Cards during the year.

As per the Union Finance Minister's announcement in his Budget Speech for the year 2001-02, banks are required to provide personal insurance package to the KCC holders, as is often done with other credit cards, to cover them against accidental death or permanent disability upto maximum amount of Rs. 50,000 and Rs. 25,000 respectively. All eligible farmers are to be covered under the scheme. The premium burden will be shared by the issuing institutions.

Banks have also been extending finance to small scale industries (SSIs) including the tiny sector of rural artisans/cottage and village industries. In view of the importance of tiny industries in the rural economy of the country, banks are required to lend 60 per cent of their total SSI advances to the tiny sector within the small scale industries.

The domestic banks, which fail to achieve their target in lending to the priority sector, have to contribute in proportion to the extent of their shortfall in lending to the priority sector to

Rural Infrastructure Development Fund (RIDF) operationalised through NABARD with the purpose of assisting the State Governments in quick completion of projects relating to rural infrastructure such as medium and minor irrigation, soil conservation, watershed management, rural roads and bridges, etc. RIDF-I to RIDF-X have been set up in NABARD during the period 1995-96 to 2004-05 with an aggregate amount of Rs. 42,000 crore. With completion of projects assisted under the RIDF scheme, it is expected that credit absorption capacity of the rural areas will increase leading to increase in agriculture production and productivity.

The Lead Bank Scheme was devised as an area approach with the district as a unit for planning and dispensation of credit. The aim is to achieve the overall development of the district with the participation of banks. Under the scheme, a major public sector bank functioning in the district is designated as the Lead Bank for the district. It controls and coordinates the activities of banking and other developmental agencies through the various fora set up under the scheme at State, district and Block level. It envisages launching of Annual credit plans for the district for credit extension for various activities and monitoring the progress in implementation of the same through the various fora as the Block level bankers committee at the Block level, the district consultative committee and the district level review committee at the district level, and the State level bankers committee at the State level set up under the scheme.

By 1982, to consolidate the various arrangements made by the Reserve Bank of India to promote /supervise institutions and channelise credit to rural areas, the National Bank for Agriculture and Rural Development (NABARD) was established for greater focus on agricultural and rural development. Though several efforts were made to increase the flow of institutional credit for rural and agricultural lending, there were persistent mismatches in credit and production. Field studies conducted to determine the reason, revealed that it was due to absence of effective local level planning. It was felt that with the establishment of large network of branches, a system could be adopted to assign specific

areas to each bank branch in which it can concentrate on focused lending and contribute to the accelerated development of the area. With a view to implement this approach, the Reserve Bank of India introduced a scheme of Service Area approach for commercial banks in 1989.

With this the planning process was further decentralised. Each rural/semi-urban bank branch was allotted a specific area comprising 15 to 25 villages which is its allocated 'service area'. Each branch is required to prepare a Service Area Credit Plan (SACP) for all the villages in its service area based on the potential of the area and the needs of various priority sector activities in the service area. The service area credit plan of all the branches in the Block are aggregated to form the Block credit plan and further all Block credit plans are aggregated to form the annual credit plans (ACP) for the district.

The Regional Rural Banks which were expected to combine the expertise of the commercial banks with the local feel and familiarity of the cooperatives, were established in the year 1975 with participation of public sector banks, the Central and State Governments as a part of the multi-agency systems particularly for mopping up rural savings and providing credit to small and marginal farmers, rural artisans and other weaker sections of the rural society. The primary objective for setting up these banks was to remove the disabilities in the cooperatives such as low resource mobilisation, poor appraisal, inadequate credit supervision, low absorptive capacity, managerial weakness, etc., and the weakness of the commercial banking system such as high cost structure and attitudinal shortcomings of their staff which was largely urban oriented. There are 196 Regional Rural Banks with a network of over 14,300 branches covering 484 districts all over the country. Primarily due to an administered interest rate regime and the lack of leeway in the margins available to it (unlike the commercial bank the regional rural banks did not have any scope for cross subsidisation), many of the regional rural banks could not meet the test of viability. In order to make their operations viable, a number of steps have been taken in recent years which include recapitalisation, comprehensive financial and

managerial restructuring of these banks through widening the target group, etc. As a consequence, 166 of the regional rural banks have effected a turnaround.

In order to provide an institutional mechanism to the private sector for promoting rural savings as well as channelising adequate credit for promoting rural viable economic activities, setting up of Local Area Banks (LABs) in the private sector has been allowed with an area of operation restricted to two or three contiguous districts. Their activities will be focused on local consumers and it is expected that their lendings will be towards agriculture and allied activities, agro-industrial activities, and the small and micro enterprise sector. So far five local area banks have been established.

The main concern of the Government of India and the Reserve Bank of India relates to the provision of credit to the rural poor so that they are able to come out of the stranglehold of poverty through available employment opportunities leading to increased and sustained incomes. The important factors in this regard are cost-effectiveness of the delivery system, the ability to provide non-credit inputs to help self-employment activities, ability to generate enduring relationship with the client, etc. This has led to fostering linkages between the formal and the informal credit delivery systems and the role of the voluntary sector comprising Self-Help Groups (SHGs) and Non-Governmental Organisations (NGOs) assume importance in this context.

It has been observed that a sizeable section of the rural poor did not have access to the formal credit institutions and also the latter could not reach them individually. The poor need assistance in small doses at different times suitable to them and for a variety of purposes and the formal credit delivery system is not adequately equipped for the purpose. This has led to promotion of informal groups of the rural poor for pooling their small savings or thrift with a view to helping themselves in financing their emergent needs either with the help NGOs or otherwise. The self-help group is normally a response to a perceived need, besides being centred around specific productive activities.

Studies by various agencies have shown that the self-help savings and credit groups have the potential to bring together the

formal banking structure and the rural poor for mutual benefit. The benefit to the formal credit institution (banks) lies in externalisation of part of credit needs, approach, disbursal, supervision and repayment, reduction in the formal paper work involved and a consequent reduction in transaction costs and assured recovery of loans through peer pressure support. These groups utilise social collateral which the poor being assetless lack.

The NGOs have a critical role in organising the rural poor into SHGs and ensuring their proper functioning. Of late, they have emerged as important links between organised credit disbursing agencies and those who have the need and are eligible to obtain credit from such institutions. Based on the reports of the Microcredit Special Cell which was set up in the Reserve Bank of India and the Task Force on Supportive Policy and Regulatory Framework for Microfinance, set up by the NABARD during 1999-2000, two thousand branches of banks were instructed to pursue vigorously the action initiated for mainstreaming microcredit. Banks have been advised that micro-credit extended by them to individual borrowers either directly or through any intermediary would be reckoned as part of their priority sector lending. Banks have been given freedom to prescribe their own lending norms keeping in view the ground realities and devise appropriate loan and savings products in this regard. Priority should be accorded to this sector in preparation credit plans by banks. Banks have also been advised that micro-credit should form an integral part of their corporate credit plan and should be reviewed at the highest level every quarter.

In view of the effectiveness of routing financial assistance to the poor through the self-help groups, the Central Government has accorded priority to converge of SHGs by banks with the help from NABARD and the Small Industries Development Bank of India (SIDBI).

The Union Finance Minister in his Budget speech for the year 2001-02 had advised the NABARD to link one lakh additional SHGs under the SHG-Bank linkage programme during 2001-02 to provide access to credit to an additional 20 lakh families. All scheduled commercial banks have been instructed to form such linkage.

Banks, including regional rural banks and cooperative banks, extended microcredit to 1,49,050 new SHGs during the year 2000-01. Cumulatively, the number of SHGs which linked with banks as at the end of March 2001, stood at 2,63,825. In terms of volumes, microcredit extended by banks aggregated Rs. 287.9 crore during the year. The cumulative microcredit from banks to SHGs stood at Rs. 480.8 crore as at the end of March 2001.

For giving a boost to the microcredit movement, a Microfinance Development Fund with a start up contribution of Rs. 100 crore from the Reserve Bank of India, and select public sector banks has been set up in the NABARD which would broadly support (a) provision of training and exposure to SHG members, partner NGOs, banks and government agencies, (b) provision of start up funds to microfinance institution and meeting their initial operational deficiencies, (c) meeting the cost of formation and nurturing of SHGs, (d) designing new delivery mechanisms, and (e) information systems and dissemination of best practices in microfinance.

The role of credit institutions is important in poverty alleviation because of the relation between assetlessness and poverty. The main thrust of the poverty alleviation programmes has, therefore, been provision of assets to the poor with the help of bank credit and government subsidy. The Integrated Rural Development Programme (IRDP) was the major poverty alleviation programme for families below poverty lines in the rural areas of the country. Both individuals and groups were assisted with bank loans and governmental subsidy under the scheme. However, with effect from April 1, 1999, the IRDP and the allied schemes have been restructured into a single programme known as Swarnajayanti Gram Swarozgar Yojana (SGSY).

The Swarnajayanti Garm Swarozgar Yojana aims at establishing a large number of micro-enterprises in rural areas of the country. The objective of the scheme is to bring every assisted family above the poverty line in three years by providing them income generating assets through a mix of bank credit and government subsidy. It is a holistic programme covering all aspects of self-employment such as organisation of the poor into self-help

group, training credit technology infrastructure and marketing. There is no ceiling on the size of the loan amount and -group activities are given preference under the scheme.

The Prime Minister Rozgar Yojana (PMRY) was launched in October 1993 with the objective of providing self-employment opportunities to educated unemployed youth in the age group of 18 to 35 years. The Government of India has made certain changes in the parameters of PMRY with effect from April 1, 1999 to enable the scheme to cater to a larger ambit of activities and allowing acceptance of collateral for projects with higher cost.

Further, under the Differential Rate of Interest (DRI) scheme which was introduced in 1972, loans up to Rs. 6,500 are provided by banks at concessional rate of interest (4 per cent per annum) to select low income groups for productive endeavours.

The growth of financial intermediation through the expansion of banking services has been powerful agent for development. Still banks are facing difficulties due to declining recoveries and mounting overdue. Good progress has been made in provision of credit through institutional agencies in the rural sector. Still more needs to be done. As revealed from the All India Debt and Investment Survey, 1991, rural households with assets less than Rs. 20,000 could have access to institutional sources for their credit needs only to the extent of 35 to 37 per cent. The share of non-institutional agencies in their outstanding debts was as high as 52 to 62 per cent. On the other hand those having higher asset base had better access to institutional credit upto 70 per cent of their outstanding debts.

Financial markets contain a formal and an informal sectors. The formal sector is institutional and officially monitored and regulated. It comprises the commercial banks, regional rural banks, local area banks and cooperatives. This sector is characterises by large scale operations and offers a wide range of financial products and services over a large geographical expanse which in the case of the nationalised banks can exceed regional and national boundaries. The strength of this sector lies in that it is protected by legislation, controlled by the central bank of the country, supported by the State, national and international banking community.

The informal sector is difficult to categorise due to its heterogeneity. The term covers the activities of large number of intermediaries as the indigenous banker, professional and non-professional money lenders, shopkeepers, merchants, guilds, self-help groups rotating savings and credit associations, savings and loan associations.

Due to several problems involved in getting loans from financial institutions, rural households especially the poor ones often turn to informal sources such as money lenders, traders, landlords, etc. to finance consumption or working capital. Several factors induce the borrowers to take loans from informal/non-institutional sources. The transaction costs of informal borrowing are low as money lenders are located conveniently, loan procedures are minimal and cash is disbursed promptly, even at odd hours. But the interest rates are very high. The average rate of interest charged by money lenders turned out to be 36 per cent per annum in 1991-92 which further increased to 42 per cent in 2002-03. It is more than three times the interest charged by the institutional agencies.[16]

The interest rate charged by the money lenders varied across the States, but remain high in all the States compared to that charged by the institutional agencies. Further, it appeared that the poorer households were compelled to pay even a higher rate of interest. The effective monthly interest rates charged by money lenders were from about 5 per cent to more than 100 per cent.[17] The high variance in the interest rates charged by the money lenders may be attributed to the differences in the type of loan risks in money lending and bargaining power of the borrowers. High transaction costs of lending, low lending volumes, high opportunity cost of capital and the absence of legal course for loan recovery were amongst the factors which induce the money lenders to keep the interest rates high. These high rates of interest have significant economic and social costs. They in fact inhibit the growth of borrower's entrepreneurial ability and in some cases force them to become defaulters. The findings clearly exhibited that the interest charged by informal money lenders was exploitative and, therefore, a stable, reliable and reasonable credit

delivery system is a necessity to prevent the exploitation of rural households by the informal money lender.

Microfinance and Rural Development

Development of local resource-based economy provides additional employment to people living in rural areas. In this context Sumacher[18] observed that in order to bring work to the people not people to the work, it was absolutely necessary to establish millions and millions of small scale industries in rural areas.

Developing economies like India aim at maximum utilisation of their own national and manpower resources. Even such countries availing raw material in abundance and cheap labour resources, they cannot achieve their targeted growth rate without having sufficient financial resources. In a labour extensive economy it is necessary to liberalise and fluctuate the financial and monetary policy which are the tools to achieve the multidimensional life goal of the poor. To achieve these goals and to keep the rural poor away from the burden of heavy interest rates prescribed by the moneylenders; the government, the NGOs and voluntary organisations play a crucial multi-linked role in rotating microfinance. Now-a-days microcredit is worldwide scheme and it is broadly established as a tool to uplift the rural poor from the measurable and deplorable condition.

Lessons from the experiences of other developing countries like Bangladesh, Indonesia, Bolivia and Philippines, motivated India too to start experimenting with the scheme of microfinance and Self-Help Groups (SHGs) which are known as 'thrift and credit groups'. The microcredit/SHGs is a brainchild of Grameen Bank of Bangladesh which was established by Prof. Mohammad Yunus of Chittagong University in the year 1975. In India the NABARD initiated it in 1986-87, but the real effort was made after 1991-92 from the linkage of SHGs with the banks.

For sustainable development in rural areas in consonance with rural peoples wishes and aspirations, huge investments are being made by the Ministry of Rural Development, Government of India through the different programmes. A pro-poor policy in terms of

which the rural poor are treated as a net resource replete with their own ideas and experiences well in tune with the local conditions forms an integral part of strategy. In the process, the most disadvantaged section of the society receive high priority. A number of new initiatives have been introduced in the course of the last 7 years.[19]

The allocation for rural development have been increasing substantially. In the year 2001-02, the budgetary outlay for the programmes of the Ministry of Rural Development, Government of India, was Rs. 12,265 crore as against Rs. 9760 crore in 2000-01. This increase was the part of the government's commitment to set apart the major share of funding for rural development sector. Coupled with the State share as well as the bank credit (in respect of self-employment programmes, housing, etc.) the total outlay of the programmes of the Ministry was of the order of about Rs. 18,000 crore.

Programmes of the Ministry of Rural Development are all implemented by the State Governments mainly through the Panchayati Raj Institutions (PRIs). In order that the formulation and execution of the rural development programmes reflected the felt needs and aspirations of the rural areas, the PRIs must constitute the bedrock of all development programmes. Therefore, a predominant role has been assigned for the PRIs in the implementations of different programmes. The Government is also pursuing with State Government, devolution of requisite powers and funds to PRIs and holding of regular elections. As a result, elections have been held in a number of States in 2000 and 2001, and again 2006 and 2007. A national consensus was evolved in a conference of State Ministers in July 2001 to devolve by March 2002 the powers and funds to the Panchayati Raj Institutions, and also to hold regular election to these bodies. The institution of Gram Sabha is vital for efficient functioning of the PRIs. All Sarpanchs have been requested to hold Garm Sabha regularly and to utilise the Gram Sabha as an effective forum for increasing awareness as well as to monitor and review the progress of the different schemes.

In December 2000, the Government of India launched a major initiative—Pradhan Mantri Gram Sadak Yojana with the objective of providing connectivity to all unconnected habitations with a population of more than 1,000 persons by the year 2003 and similarly habitations with a population of 500 by 2007. The programme was likely to result in significant improvement in Gross Domestic Product (GDP) as well as in reducing poverty in the rural areas. An investment of Rs. 60,000 crore was envisaged for providing rural connectivity. A sum of Rs. 2,500 crore was allotted to States annually. Project proposals for Rs. 7,000 crore had been approved so far. Work had commenced in most of the States. As a result, all unconnected habitations with a population of over 1,000 have now been fully covered in eight States.

The Government of India has for the first time, set up a separate department for drinking water supply in 2005 to make potable drinking water available to all villages in five years. Through Accelerated Rural Water Supply Programme, the Ministry of Rural Development is endeavouring to accelerate the pace of coverage of drinking water supply in rural areas. Consequently, 14.04 lakh of the 14.23 lakh rural habitations in the country have now access to safe drinking water. The programme has been revamped to usher in reforms by institutionalising community participation in rural water supply sector with a view to gradually replace the government oriented, centralised, supply driven, and non-people participating rural water supply programme by people oriented, decentralised demand driven and community based rural water supply programme.

Shelter is a basic human requirement. To meet this requirement on priority basis, a comprehensive Action Plan for Rural Housing has been envisaging construction of 25 lakh houses annually in rural areas as also upgradation of unserviceable kutcha houses by 2007. The Action Plan is being implemented through various programmes such as Indira Awas Yojana (IAY), credit-cum-subsidy scheme for Rural Housing and Habital Development, Rural Building Centres, Equity Contribution by Ministry of Rural Development to HUDCO, Samagra Awas Yojana (SAY) and National Mission for Rural Housing and Habital Development.

About one crore houses have been constructed since inception. In the year 2000-01, a sum of Rs. 1,850 crore was released to the States/UTs under different programmes including Indira Awas Yojana and Pradhan Mantri Gramoday Yojana. During the year 2001-02 the allocation for rural housing was of the order of Rs. 2,000 crore.

Rural sanitation is another area in which initiatives have been taken. The Central Rural Sanitation Programme encompasses personal hygiene, home sanitation, safe water, garbage and waste water disposal. The component of the programme includes construction of individual sanitary toilets for households below the poverty line, construction of village sanitary complexes for women; setting up of sanitary marts, intensive campaign for creation of awareness and health education, etc. Total sanitation campaigns are being implemented in 200 districts of the country. There are definite indications of attitudinal changes and increasing demand. A sum of Rs. 150 crore was earmarked for sanitation for the year 2001-02.

Gainful employment, food security and strengthening of infrastructure in rural areas are must for national renewal for a resurgent India. The Sampoorna Grameen Rozgar Yojana has been launched to attain these objectives. The scheme envisages an annual expenditure of Rs. 10,000 crore. Under the scheme, 50 lakh tonnes of foodgrains (worth Rs. 5,000 crore) are provided every year to the States/UTs free, the balance of Rs. 5,000 crore is to be utilised to meet the wage and material costs. The programme is self-targeting in nature and available to all the rural poor (BPL APL) who are in need of wage employment and are willing to take up manual unskilled work. Five kilograms of foodgrains are to be distributed as part of wage per capita per day. All the wage employment schemes of the government are the part of the composite Sampoorna Grameen Rozgar Yojana (SGRY). Accordingly, Jawahar Gram Samridhi Yojana, and Employment Assurance Scheme of the Ministry of Rural Development stand fully integrated with SGRY from the financial year 2002-03.

The plethora of self-employment programmes for the rural poor have been emerged into a single holistic programme called

Swarna Jayanti Gram Swarozgar Yojana (SGSY). It is conceived as a holistic programme of micro enterprises covering all aspects of self-employment, viz., organisation of the rural poor into Self-Help Groups (SHGs) and their capacity building, planning of activity clusters, infrastructure build-up, technology, credit and marketing. The approach is to identify a few activities in each Block based on the resources, occupational skills and availability of markets, organise rural poor into self-help groups and provide the required back up support. So far 6.23 lakh SHGs had been organised by the end of December 2001. It was decided to raise the number of SHGs to 14 lakh by the end of 2004 so as to have one viable SHG in each habitation in the country.

Land is a critically important national resources among the natural resources, the efficient management of which is vital for economic growth and development of rural areas especially while addressing the concerns of poverty and backwardness. To meet the need, a separate department of Land Resources came into existence in April 1999 under the Ministry of Rural Development. All the land based programmes/schemes which were earlier with different departments of the Ministry, have now been located in Department of Land Resources. All the area development programmes are being implemented through the watershed development approach in accordance with the recommendations of the Hanumantha Rao Committee since April 1995. With a view to achieving comprehensive area development, instructions have also been issued for convergence of all rural development programmes in the areas where Watershed Development is taken up.

The Ministry of Rural Development, Government of India has been focusing on the four pronged strategy :

(a) Enhancing the level of awareness about the scheme,
(b) Promoting transparency in the implementation of the programmes,
(c) Encouraging people's partnership, and
(d) Ensuring accountability/social audit.

All the four elements of the above strategy are complementary to each other. For enhancing the level of awareness an intensive campaign through most of the available modes of communications is being undertaken by the Ministry. The Prasar Bharti has been entrusted with the task of production and telecast/broadcast of audio visual/audio software of the programmes of the Ministry. It is stressed that there should be total transparency in the implementation of the programmes right from the selection of beneficiaries. It is the specific direction of the Ministry that all the beneficiaries under different programmes would be selected by the Gram Sabha. The details of estimates regarding civil works should also be available to the public. In order to impart greater transparency, the Chief Ministers have been addressed advising arrangement of display boards at the district, Block and Gram Panchayat levels, indicating therein the funds available to the respective areas under different programmes of the Ministry of Rural Development and the work being taken up.

People's partnership particularly of target groups of various rural development programmes is sought to be promoted not only through institution of Gram Sabha, but also through execution of works by people themselves under different programmes of the Ministry of Rural Development. The participation of all the segments of society is a must for national resurgence. A series of dialogue has also been initiated with the corporate houses through ASSOCHAM and CII for establishing an effective public private partnership for rural development.

John E. Akoten[20] has indicated that microcredit and small enterprises play an important role in improving livelihood of rural and urban populace in developing countries. There is a significant difference in the mean values of men and women. Women getting higher proportion (90%) rather than men (10%), because poverty can be easily eradicated through the active participation of women in income generating and saving motivating activities. The most important goal of microcredit is to eradicate world poverty by 2015.

Shylendra[21] stated that through linkage programme the NABARD would like to realise the vision of empowering rural

poor by improving their access to the formal credit system in an effective and sustainable manner to reach the goal of 100 per cent poor through one million SHGs by 2008.

Rosalinda[22] evaluated that microcredit has integrated the scope for personal, social, and political empowerment. The experience of microcredit started in the early 1980s as a development initiative to alleviate rural poverty, has created positive impact on cash-starved poor women in rural areas to increase confidence, sense of self-worth, higher consciousness of their rights, greater awareness and exposure to the outside world greater decision making power with the household and outside and improvement in health and nutrition of family members.

Ravi Kumar[23] has stated that SHG is small economically homogeneous and affinity of rural/urban poor voluntarily formed to save and contribute a common fund to be lent to its members as per group decision and for working together for the socio-economic upliftment of their families and community. SHG is a medium group for the development of saving habit among women. These SHGs come to the rescue of women and enhance the quality of status of women as participants, decision-makers and beneficiaries in the democratic economic, social and cultural spheres of life.

Nagayaya[24] has reported that Action for Social Advancement (ASA) in Bangladesh, Society for Helping and Awakening Rural Poor through Education (SHARE) in India, Centre for Youth and Social Development (CYSD) in South Asia and Bangladesh, Rural Advancement Committee (RAC), Consultative Group to Assist the Poorest (CGAP), Professional Assistance Development (PADA), Self-Employed Women's Association (SEWA), and Credit Development Forum (CDF) are focusing their financial attention to the income and employment generation to the rural poor with livelihood support. Under the scheme of SHARE, 11 per cent of Andhra Pradesh and 44 per cent of Bihar respondents raised their employment opportunities in the year 2004. About 97 per cent of the PRADAN and about 97 per cent of the SHARE schemes belonged to *adivasis*, *dalits* and other backward castes in rural areas.

A federation of SHG members can function as coordinating and monitoring agency for a particular coverage area. The federation is a democratically elected body, and it can evaluate all the activities carried out by the groups of SHG under one Panchayat. The federation gives support, motivates and trains members apart from networking with other agencies for village development. The ultimate goal of the federation is to evaluate all the activities carried out by SHGs for the betterment of the group as well as society.

Narayansamy[25] has pointed out that out of 100 SHGs, 98 groups are composed of only women members, engaged with micro enterprises, because they are the main key to close the poverty. The basic principles of SHGs are group approach, mutual trust, organisation of small and marginal groups, group cohesiveness, spirit of thrift, demand based lending collateral-free women friendly loan, peer group pressure in repayment, skill training, capacity building and empowerment.

Reddy[26] extricates that non-farm activities undertaken by the women groups in rural areas are precious for the industrial sector, construction services, trading, etc., providing employment opportunities and entrepreneurial skill at the maximum level.

Pitt[27] mentioned that 90 per cent of SHGs clients were women in the Grameen Bank of Bangladesh. Their consumption expenditure increased by 18 taka for every 100 taka borrowed by women. Credit provided to women significantly improved the indices measures of health and nutrition along with the educational status of their children. The Grameen Bank of Bangladesh has earned name and fame as the pioneer of credit services for the rural poor throughout the country. Slowly but surely, more and more people can bring themselves out of poverty. The Grameen Bank achieved the repayment rate of 98 per cent from its borrowers, 94 per cent of whom were women.

The Union Budget 2007-08 (Government of India) focused on agriculture and rural development in line with the government's efforts to impart growth, equity and social justice. The highlight of budget was a 31 per cent hike in allocation towards the Bharat Nirman Programme for upgrading rural infrastructure from

Rs. 18,696 crore to Rs. 24,603 crore and substantial increase in farm credit.

The percentage share of agriculture in GDP has fallen sharply over the years and large portion of India's rural population still lives on agriculture. The percentage share of agriculture in GDP in 1990-91 was 32 per cent which has fallen to below 20 per cent in 2005-06. On the other hand, the share of service sector has increased from 41 per cent in 1990-91 to over 54 per cent in 2005-06. This lopsided development has powered large scale migration of rural poor towards the cities. Instead of people migrating from rural areas to urban areas for jobs, facilities should be created in rural areas for jobs.

The endeavour of the government to accelerate growth in the rural development is reflected in the Budget 2007-08 proposals. Though the service sector has improved in the 1990s, the agricultural sector would get the maximum attention by the government in the year to come. The Planning Commission has set a 10 per cent gross domestic product growth target by the end of the Eleventh Plan period.

The Government's plan for rural development now talks of inclusive growth and is not just confined to only anti-poverty programmes. The growth of agriculture, sustainable rural development along with social development expressed in terms of educational and health sectors in the main task on the road to future rural development of India.

The Plan outlay for agriculture and allied activities has been hiked by 15.8 per cent to Rs. 8,558 crore for 2007-08. Additional irrigation potential of 24 lakh hectares was to be created under Bharat Nirman Programme including 9 lakh hectares under AIBP with an allocation of Rs. 11,000 crore for 2007-08. It was proposed to create 7 million rain water harvesting structures and dug wells (including 2 million for SFs/MFs) with a view to improve ground water recharge.[27]

A financial mechanism similar to Special Purpose Tea Fund launched for replantation and rejuvenation of tea was to be put in place for coffee, rubber, spices, cashew and coconut. To enhance productions of pulses, focus was to be given on increasing the production of breeder, foundation and certified seeds.

Weather-Based Crop Insurance Scheme was to be implemented on pilot basis in two or three States by the Agricultural Insurance Corporation on an actuarial basis with an element of subsidy. A sum of Rs. 100 crore was allocated for 2007-08. A revamped Training and Visit (T&V) programme was to be introduced by MOA in consultation with State governments. Custom duties were to be reduced from 7.5 per cent to 5 per cent for sprinkler and drip irrigations systems used for agricultural and horticultural purposes.

To improve the resource base, the NABARD has been allowed to raise Rs. 5,000 crore by issuing 'Rural Bonds' which would be guaranteed by the government and eligible for suitable tax exemptions. The corpus of the RIDF-XIII has been raised to Rs. 12,000 crore for 2007-08 from Rs. 10,000 crore for 2006-07. A separate window for rural roads would continue under RIDF-XIII with a corpus of Rs. 4,000 crore.

Farm credit target for 2007-08 was fixed at Rs. 2,25,000 crore and 50 lakh new farmers were to be brought into the banking fold. Interest subvention for short-term crop loans of 2 per cent would continue for which a budgetary provision of Rs. 1,677 crore was made. Regional Rural Banks were to take up a branch expansion programme with at least one branch in 80 uncovered districts.

A Financial Inclusion Fund was to be set up with corpus of Rs. 500 crore for meeting the cost of developmental and promotional interventions. Further a Financial Inclusion Technology Fund was to be set up with corpus of Rs. 500 crore to meet the cost of technology adoption with NABARD.

Government's concept of rural development is limited to anti-poverty programmes implemented by the Ministry of Rural Development. However, in view of the inclusive growth one cannot think of rural development on sustained basis without consideration of agricultural development. It is the key to rural development leading to inclusive growth. But sustainable agricultural and rural development is not possible without social development expressed in terms of educational and health sectors.[28]

Facts sheet of the present status in rural development in India is stated to comprehend the challenges of India. One may understand the budget 2007-08 in the light of these facts keeping all the limitations of annual budgetary exercise.

Rural poverty in India has record of 27.1 per cent, i.e. 280 million rural poor make larger size than India had in 1947, constituting 13 Australia. The Rural unemployment growth was just 0.5 per cent per annum between 1993-2000, the daily status unemployment rate has increased from 5.63 per cent in 1993-94 to 7.21 per cent in 1999-2000. To meet the job needs of labour growth which is double than that of population, one needs 8 million jobs every year where it officially is.

In India 26 per cent people are suffering from income poverty and 56 per cent people are suffering from nutritional poverty. According to Dr. Swaminathan's Food Insecurity Atlas, India has largest absolute number of undernourished people in the world.

In the first year of the XI Five Year Plan (2007-12) the Approach Paper of the plan has claimed the new approach to direct XI plan towards faster and more inclusive growth. Inclusive growth is expected to be achieved by Rejuvenation of agriculture, education and health sector development.

The Government of India has reviewed the Bharat Nirman Programme and considered as 'impressive' as most of the targets are achieved. Additional irrigational potential of 2,40,000 hectares has been created. Facilities of drinking water has been provided in 55,512 of 73,000 villages. 12,198 km of rural roads have been constructed. 7,83,000 rural houses have been structured and 9,14,000 houses are under construction. Thus the target of 1,50,000 houses is likely to be exceeded. 19,578 villages have been electrified under the Rajiv Gandhi Vidyutikaran Yojana. 15,074 villages have been provided with telephones against the target of 20,000 villages.

Encouraged by this achievement, the Government has provided Rs. 24,603 crore in 2006-07 Budget leading to 31 per cent rise in total outlay. Infrastructure is being key to provide the facility for inclusive growth and rural development. This is the step in right directions, but in view of the huge resources

requirement, the targets of the Bharat Nirman by 2009 would not be possible without acceleration of the programmes for which some attractive provisions could have been made to encourage public-private partnership in this programme.

The National Rural Employment Guarantee Scheme (NREGS) is one of the major flagship programmes of the government, launched in February 2006. Though the scheme being demand driven, there is inter-State variation in its implementation. The government has expanded the NREGS from the current level of 200 districts to 330 districts. Thus 130 additional districts would be covered for which the government has provided Rs. 12,000 crore in the budget 2007-08.

However, the allocation for NREGS is perhaps not adequate. It is a matter of great concern that most of the States have not utilized the available funds. However, an addition expansion of NREGS in 130 districts will need at least Rs. 18,000 crore which would mean that 100 days work would not be possible to provide unless the government makes additional allocation. From April 01, 2008, the National Rural Employment Guarantee Scheme has extended to all the districts of the country.

Apart from the NREGS, the Sampoorna Garmeen Rozgar Yojana (SGRY) has been provided additional fund of Rs. 28,000 crore for these districts which are not covered by the NREGS. Thus the Government has used the NREGS as a substitute for almost half of the districts of India. The difficulty with the SGRY is that its guidelines are not honestly followed for political compulsion as well as inadequate understanding of the scheme.

Similarly, to encourage the innovation of self-employment, the Swarnajayanti Gram Swarozgar Yojana (SGSY) had been encouraged by additional allocation of Rs. 600 crore in 2006-07. However, for the SGSY programme, self-help groups are formulated in large scale but in proportion to that SHGs actually engaged in economic activities are very much limited, and out of them how many have helped the poor members to cross the poverty line is questionable. What is required is the implementation of all the components of the programme seriously, instead of just expanding the number of self-help groups only.

Potential of both the programmes have yet not been realised not due to lack of funds or the faulty programmes, but due to less than satisfactory implementation as reflected in recent current evaluation reports.

The Union Budget of 2007-08 makes a refreshingly bold departure from the traditional track by refocusing on rural development and agriculture, because if these crucial segments were cold-shouldered, the development and progress of the country would remain uneven and unpleasant. A country with large population has to be nearly self-sufficient in essential food items; otherwise supply constraints could upset macroeconomic stability and growth prospects. Hence, agriculture must top the agenda of the policy makers and must hold the first charge on resources of the country given the inescapable reality that inflation has reared its ugly head in recent months, the Union Budget 2007-08 has truly trained its gun on tackling inflation. The budget attempts to do it through creating salutary and stable environment for farm sector and rural regeneration so that supply constraints could be overcome and there is not binding constraint for India's growth trajectory.[29]

Summary

In the past decade the world has realised that the poor are bankable and poor women are the most trustworthy in providing financial services. Overtime, the notation of microcredit has broadened into microfinance which includes not only savings and credit, but also insurance and pension and even housing. The challenge of future is that the low income people are inclusive to financial systems. Microfinance can be robustly sustainable. When the model is right, the growth of microfinance is fast.

Recently, the attention for microfinance and its role in reducing poverty was further increased when Prof. Mohammad Yunus received the Nobel Peace Prize. According to the Nobel Peace Committee, microfinance can help people to break out of poverty, which in turn is seen as an important prerequisite to establish long lasting peace. This has led to an almost euphoric

attitude among policy makers and aid organisations about potential poverty reducing effects of microcredit.

Microfinance refers to the entire range of financial and non-financial services, including skill upgradation and entrepreneurship development, rendered to the poor for enabling them to overcome poverty. In the context of designing programme for the poor, microfinance is recognised and accepted as one of the new development paradigms for alleviating poverty through social and economic empowerment of the poor with special emphasis on empowering women. The operational framework of microfinance rests on the premises that formation of a self-employment enterprise is available alternate means of alleviating poverty, lack of access to capital assets credit acts as a constraint on the existing and potential micro enterprises and the poor are capable of saving despite their poor income level. In essence, therefore, microfinance may be referred to as an institutional mechanism of providing credit support in small amount and usually limited with small group along with other complementary supports such as training and other related services to the people with poor resources and skills for enabling them to take up economic activities.

Microcredit is delivered through self-help groups (SHGs). A self-help group is a registered/unregistered group of micro-entrepreneurs having homogeneous social and economic background voluntarily coming together to save small amounts regularly. They mutually agree to contribute to a common fund to meet their emergency needs on mutual help basis. The group members use collective wisdom and peer pressure to ensure proper end-use of credit and timely repayment thereof. In fact, pear pressure has been recognised as an effective substitute for collaterals.

Microfinance providers in India can be classified under three broad categories—formal, semi-formal and informal. The formal banking sector constitutes the first category, while the semi-formal group consists of a variety of microfinance institutions and self-help groups. Informal providers, on the other hand, are not legal entities and include money lenders and various social networks. Today semi-formal and informal lenders dominate the scene.

The growth of financial intermediation through the expansion

of banking services has been a powerful catalytic agent for development. Though good progress has been made in the provision of credit through institutional agencies in the rural sector, banks face difficulties due to declining services and mounting overdues.

In order to provide an institutional mechanism in the private sector for promoting rural savings as well as channellising adequate credit for promoting rural viable economic activities, setting up of Local Area Banks (LABs) in the private sector has been allowed with an area of operation restricted to two or three contiguous districts.

In view of the effectiveness of routing financial assistance to the poor through the self-help groups, the Union Government has accorded priority to coverage of SHGs by banks with the help from the NABARD and the Small Industries Development Bank of India (SIDBI).

The Swarnajayanti Gram Swarozgar Yojna (SGSY) aims at establishing a large number of micro-enterprises in rural areas of the country. The objective of the scheme is to bring every assisted family above poverty line in three years by providing them income generating assets through a mix of bank credit and government subsidy.

For sustainable development in rural areas in consonance with rural people's wishes and aspirations, huge investments are being made by the Ministry of Rural Development, Government of India, through different programmes. A pro-poor policy in terms of which the rural poor are treated as a net resource replete with their own ideas and experience well in tune with the local conditions, forms an integral part of development strategy. In the process, the most disadvantaged sections of the society receive high priority.

The plethora of self-employment programmes for the rural poor have been merged into a single holistic programme called Swarnajayanti Gram Swarozgar Yojana. It is conceived as a holistic programme of micro enterprises covering all aspects of self-employment.

Gainful employment, food security and strengthening of infrastructure in rural area is a must for national renewal for a resurgent India. The Sampoorna Grameen Rozgar Yojana (SGRY)

has been launched to attain these objectives. The scheme envisages an annual expenditure of Rs. 10,000 crore.

The people's partnership particularly of target groups of various rural development programmes is sought to be promoted not only through institution of Gram Sabha but also through execution of works by people themselves under different programmes of the Ministry of Rural Development.

The Union Budget 2007-08 of the Government of India focused on the agriculture and rural development in line with the government's efforts to impart growth, equity and social justice. The highlight of the budget was a 31 per cent hike in allocation towards the Bharat Nirman Programme for upgrading rural infrastructure from Rs. 18,696 crore to Rs. 24,603 crore and substantial increase in farm credit.

Farm credit target for 2007-08 was fixed at Rs. 2,25,000 crore and 50 lakh new farmers were to be brought into the banking fold. Interest subvention for short-term crop loans of 2 per cent would continue for which a budgetary provision of Rs. 1,677 crore was made Regional Rural Banks were to take up a branch expansion programme with at least one branch in 80 uncovered districts.

The National Rural Employment Guarantee Scheme (NREGS) is one of the major flagship programmes of the Government of India, launched in February 2006. Though the scheme being demand driven, there is inter-State variation in its implementation. The Government has provided Rs 12,000 crore in the 2007-08 Budget. From April 1, 2008 the NREG would be extended to all the districts of the country.

The Union Budget 2007-08 makes a refreshingly bold departure from the traditional track by refocusing on rural development and agriculture, because if these crucial segments were cold-shouldered, the development and progress of the country would remain uneven and unpleasant. A country with large population has to be nearly self-sufficient in essential food items; otherwise supply constraints could upset macro economic stability and growth prospects. Hence, agriculture must top the agenda of the policy makers and must hold the first charge on the resources of the country. Given the inescapable reality that inflation has reared its ugly head in recent

months, the Union Budget 2007-08 has truly trained its gun on trackling inflation. The budget attempts to do it through creating salutary and stable environment for farm sector and rural regeneration so that supply on constraints could be overcome and there is no binding constraint for India's growth trajectory.

REFERENCES

1. Bhatt, Ela R. (2008), "Forward", *Yojana*, January, p. 5.
2. Hermes, Niels and Robert Lensinsk (2007), "Impact of Microfinance: A Critical Survey", *Economic and Political Weekly*, Vol. 42, No. 6, February 10, p. 462.
3. Daley-Harries, S. (2006), *State of the Microcredit Summit Campaign Report 2006*, Microcredit Summit Campaign, Washington D.C.
4. Norwegian Peace Committee (2006), "The Nobel Peace Prize 2006", *Press Release*, Oslo, October.
5. Microcredit Summit (1997), "Declaration and Plan of Action", February 2-4, 1997, at *http://www.microcredit summit.org/declaration.htm.*, last accessed October 2003.
6. NABARD (1999), *Task Force on Supportive Policy and Regulatory Framework for Microfinance: Report.* National Bank for Agriculture and Rural Development, Mumbai.
7. Nair, Tara S. (2001), "Institutionalising Microfinance in India", *Economic and Political Weekly*, Vol. 36, No. 4, January 27.
8. Ledgerwood, Joanna (1999), "Microfinance Handbook: An Institutional and Financial Perspective, Sustainable Banking with the Poor", The World Bank, Washington D.C., U.S.A.
9. *Ibid.*
10. EPW (2004), "Microfinance: Productive Linkages", *Economic and Political Weekly*, March 6, 2004.
11. Planet Finance (2000), *Country Study: India*, July, http://www.planetfinance.org.
12. Mahajan, Vijay and Bharti Gupta Ramola (2004), "Microfinance in India: Banyan Tree and Bonsai" *BASIX Quarterly Review*, October.
13. Aurora, S.S. (2005), *Microfinance India Conference and A Look at the Expanding Market*, Financial Sector Team, Policy Dimension, DFID, United Nations Capital Development Funds (UNCDP) Issue 13, (June).
14. Reddy, Y.V. (2005). "Micro-Finance: Reserve Bank's Approach", Address to Reserve Bank of India at the *Microfinance Conference* Organised by the Indian School of Business, Hyderabad, August 6.

15. Joshi, Deepali Pant (2002), "Rural Credit", *Yojana*, January, p. 38.
16. Kumar, Anjali, D.K. Singh and P. Kumar (2007), "Performance of Rural Credit and Factors Affecting the Choice of Credit Sources", *Indian Journal of Agricultural Economics*, Vol. 62, No. 2, July-Sept., p. 303.
17. Robinson, M.R. (2001), *The Microfinance Revolution: Sustainable Finance for the Poor*, Open Society Institute and World Bank, Washington D.C., U.S.A.
18. Sumacher, E.F. (1974), *Small is Beautiful*, Sphere Book Limited, London, p. 147.
19. Naidu, M. Venkaiah (2002), "Rural Reconstruction", *Yojana*, January, p. 5.
20. Akoten, John E. (2006), "The Determinants of Credit Access and Impacts of Micro and Small Enterprises", *Economic and Cultural Change*, Vol. 54, No. 4, pp. 927-44.
21. Shylendra (2004), "The SHG-Bank Linkage Programme", *Journal of Rural Development*, Vol. 23, No. 4, pp. 131-35.
22. Rosalinda (2005), "Problematising Micro-Finance as an Empowerment Strategy for Women Living in Poverty", *Journal of Gender, Technology and Development.*
23. Ravi Kumar, Ratna (2006), "A Premier on Micro-Finance : The Paradox of Plenty in Poverty," *Journal of Chartered Accountant*, Vol. 54, No. 11, pp. 1631-33.
24. Nagayya (2000), "Microfinance for SHGs", *Kurukshetra*, Vol. 48, No. 11, pp. 10-15.
25. Narayansamy (2005), "Microcredit and Rural Enterprises", *Journal of Rural Development*, Vol. 4, No. 3, pp. 353-76.
26. Reddy, Sudhakar (2000), "Rural Non-Farm Employment", *Journal of Rural Development*, Vol. 19, No. 1, pp. 131-35.
27. Pitt, Mark M. (2003), "Empowering Women with Micro Finance", *Journal of Economic Development and Cultural Change*, Vol. 54, No. 4, pp. 759-831.
28. NABARD (2007), *Annual Report, (2006-2007)*, National Bank for Agricultural and Rural Development, Mumbai, p. 22.
29. Shah, Dilip (2007), "Central Budget 2007-08 and Rural Development in India", *Kurukshetra*, April, p. 3.

4

Self-Help Groups and Rural Development

One of the glaring and dominant outcomes of the development process in developing societies has been the general bypassing the poor in spreading the benefits of development. This has been so whether the societies have embraced left-of-centre socialist policies or right-of-centre liberal market oriented economic policies. A root cause for this has been the economic planning strategies adopted by almost all countries without significant redistribution of land and such other physical assets. The consequence has been the bulging of the incidence of poverty and galloping of the absolute number of the poor people socially and economically deprived.

It is the failure to make a dent into the problems of poverty, unemployment and social deprivations that has been at the centre of the heated debate in the development of economic literature since the beginning of the 1970s. The debate has taken varied forms, but generally amenable to a caricature descriptions of the two extremes—neoclassical framework of economic policies dethroning Keynesianism; government's failure leading to market as a sure recipe for all economic ills; and rapid economic growth and 'trickle down' effects as substitutes for any 'structuralist' design for direct attack on poverty. The economic literature has lively contributions seeking to buttress both the opposing themes of thought, but amazingly the all-pervasive influence that has been

brought about to bear on the economic policies of developing countries has been generally one-sided, one or the other aspect of what has come to be known as 'Washington Consensus' in the form of free markets and unfettered competition, free trade, monetarism and fiscal compressions, and minimal governmental intervention in economic management. Even the sincere efforts of the United Nations Development Programme (UNDP) to place people as both the means and the ends of economic development has generally attracted limited attention and resources on human development.

The initial performance of the above mainstream policy in action now for over a decade in many countries has been rather disappointing, and hence, it is contended that "the new theories of development imply new policy prescription and a need for policy makers to go beyond the 'Washington consensus'.[1] In that perspective, it is now agreed that there are limits to markets, with imperfect information and incomplete markets government intervention can improve overall efficiency. It is further perceived that a decentralised system of governance can be the answer to multiple issues of transparency, bureaucratic delays and indifference and widespread corruption. Above all, it is recognised that development economics must pay more attention to the promotion and nurturing of institutions. In other words, dependence on private markets remains the corner stone of the mainstream policy framework, but the dynamics of capitalism will unleash the forces of growth only if institutions are strengthened, appropriate laws and regulations are introduced and reforms are effected. This policy of liberalisation and privatisation with proper regulatory systems is now here more vigorously advocated than for the financial system of the developing countries so that they get integrated into the global financial system which is the prime-mover of the world economic system today. As it is recognised at the same time that in this new financial architecture too, the concerns of the assetless poor are unlikely to be accommodated, the system of microfinance has been viewed as a powerful tool for the upliftment of the economic conditions of the beneficiaries in programme implementation.

The concept of microfinance thus executed with the instrumentality of self-help groups (SHGs) provides a paradigm shift in the strategy for resolving the socio-economic deprivation of the poor. It is an intermediate strategy which combines myriad issues of development experiences. It is emerging at once as an answer to both the market failure and the government failure. In it the sector of non-governmental organisations (NGOs) has begun to occupy a pivotal 'third space' in the development process in developing societies. Bureaucracy is replaced by the NGOs as promotional agencies which serve the role of catalytic agents. Decentralisation and the bottom up system become the system of governance.

Self-help groups are participative in character, they embody cooperative principles of joint endeavour for fighting social ills as much as for thrift and mobilisation of financial assistance. Subsidies and targets which characterised the traditional government programmes and programmes of banks for poverty alleviation, are avoided as they led to misdirection of assistance, induced instincts of avoiding loan repayments and promoted a general sense of dependence psychology amongst the beneficiaries. Women get a way out of gender discrimination and inequality as well as for exploiting their entrepreneurial talents. Activities surrounding the organisation of microfinance also enable the participants to go beyond economic pursuits, they are empowered to fight against social evils and address social backwardness. Self-help groups confer an added strength for the poor to bind them together in their common endeavour to overcome poverty and social ostracism. It also imparts healthier behavioural attitudinal approaches to issues of common concerns.

Experiences of the different anti-poverty and other welfare programmes implemented throughout the world in general and India in particular have shown that the key to their success lies in the evolution and participation of community-based organisations at the grassroots level. People's participation in credit delivery and linking formal credit institutions to borrowers through intermediaries of Self-Help Groups (SHGs) have been recognised as a supplementary mechanism for providing credit support to

the rural people. The structure of rural financial market in developing economy, particularly in India, is dualistic with both formal and informal financial intermediaries. A consensus is growing among researchers that the formal financial sector is not effectively serving the rural population in the Third World countries.[2] This is mainly attributed to the failure of financial intermediaries in fulfilling their basic functions, viz. production credit to finance income generating activities, consumption credit to maintain and expand human productive capacity, and quality saving schemes for increasing risk-bearing capacity of the rural households. Moreover, these institutions have failed to promote any of its objectives.[3] To reach the poor, institutional innovations are needed that enable services to be expanded, while substantially reducing transaction costs for both financial institutions and clients.[4] In many countries in the world microcredit programmes have succeeded in generating self-employment by providing access to small capital to people living in poverty.[5]

The performance of formal financial institutions, particularly in their lending to the poor has been unsatisfactory. They face a number of constraints in broadening their services to the poor. A large number of rural households are with limited land resources and small economic activity accompanied with poor technology. But their demand for credit has been rising due to growing family size, increased consumption requirements, social obligation and so on. But the institutional agencies not only lacked the required mechanism to assess their credit needs but often overlooked their demand for credit on the ground that needs are for non-productive purposes. Besides, perceived high risks, transaction costs in small scale rural lending and absence of collateral securities kept the poor away from the fold of formal financial intermediaries.[6]

The information, resources, skills and technology of the poor are very weak and the scales of their operation, irrespective of the economic activity pursued by them are, therefore, small. Their credit needs arise due to growing family size and societal obligations, such as expenses on marriages and deaths, medical treatment and to bear market and climatic uncertainties.[7] The need to expand or diversify operations places tremendous strain on the

existing family income which is barely adequate to meet routine production and consumption requirements. Such additional demands are, however, rarely out of proportion, the line dividing production requirements from the conveniently termed 'consumption' requirements, seems to be rather thin as the latter has as vital an impact on economic activity as the seemingly direct 'production' requirement.

A SHG is defined as a voluntary group valuing personal interactions and mutual aid as a means of altering or ameliorating the problems perceived as alterable, pressing and personal by most of its participants.[8] These groups are voluntary associations of people formed to attain certain collective goals that could be economic, social or both. The policy planners and development planners cherish the myth that poor people do not have the spirit to thrift but recent reports from different parts of the globe challenge this.[9]

Self-Help Groups (SHGs) is an association or body of people which is homogeneous, has a common aim and whose members in one way or the other, help one another. It is a micro-cooperative. All or a majority of members of an SHG may be drawn from the low income strata, for instance SHGs have come to encompass a wide range of activities. These range from income generating activities to overcoming problems of addiction and ensuring safe sex. While the SHGs in the developing countries have been dealing with disabilities apart from other activities, the most important job it has taken up is the propagation of microfinance. It has been increasingly realised that lending to a SHG offers unique opportunities, since the recovery rate is between 90 and 100 per cent.

Micro-credit is delivered through self-help groups (SHGs). A SHG is a registered/unregistered group of micro entrepreneurs having homogeneous social and economic background, voluntarily coming together to save small amounts regularly. They mutually agree to contribute to a common fund and to meet their emergency needs on mutual help basis. The group members use collective wisdom and peer pressure to ensure proper use of credit and timely repayment thereof. In fact, peer pressure has been recognised as an effective substitute for collaterals.

An economically poor individual gains strength as part of a group. Besides, financing through SHGs reduces transaction costs for both lenders and borrowers. While lenders have to handle a single SHG account instead of a large number of small sized individual accounts, borrowers as part of a SHG cut down expenses on travel (to and fro from the branch and other places) for completing paper work and on the loss of work days in canvassing for loans.

Self-Help Groups (SHGs) are small groups of poor people. The members of a SHG face similar problems. They help other to solve their problems. SHGs promote small savings among their members. The savings are kept with the bank. This is the common fund in the name of the SHG. The SHG gives small loans to the members from its common fund. After six months, if the SHG satisfies the bank as per the check list for quality, bank can give loans to the SHG. Very poor people can save small amounts. Like the little drops of water making an ocean, such savings become lakhs of rupees.

The ideal size of a SHG is 10 to 20 members. The group need not be registered. From one family only one person can become a member of a SHG. The group normally consists of either only men or only women. Mixed groups are generally not preferred. Women's groups are generally found to perform better. Members should have the same social and financial background.

The group should meet regularly. Ideally, the meeting should be weekly or at least monthly. Full attendance in all the group meetings will make it easy for the SHG to stabilise and start working to the satisfaction of all. Membership register, minutes register, etc. are to be kept up-to-date by the group by making the entries regularly.

Due to the flexibility of the micro-credit programme, different SHG models can be experimented with. These different models are :

- Banks deal directly with the SHG, providing financial assistance for on lending to individual members.
- Banks give direct assistance to the SHG while the NGO

provides training and guidance to the SHG in effective functioning.

- The NGO can be a financial intermediary between the bank and a member of an SHG, with the NGO accepting the contractual ability for loan repayment to the banks and the linkage between the bank and the SHG is indirect.

Banks give loans directly to individual SHG members on recommendations of the SHG and the NGO. The NGO assists the bank in monitoring, supervising and recovery of loans.

A conservative banker will start with the third model depending on the NGO while a good banker-NGO relationship would start with model two or even model one. However, the general evolutionary process is to move from model three to model two, then to model one, and finally, model four wherein individuals have direct access to the bank.

Characteristics of SHG

SHGs are mostly informal groups where members pool savings and relend in the group on a rotational basis. The groups have a common perception of need and improvise towards collective action. Many such groups formed around specific production activities, promote savings among members and use the pooled resources to meet various credit needs of members (especially consumption needs). Where fund generation is low in the initial phases due to low saving capacities, this is supplemented by external resources loaned/donated by NGOs. Thus SHGs have been able to provide primitive banking services to its members which are cost-effective, flexible and without defaults. Based on local requirements, SHG have evolved their own characteristics of functioning :

- Group members usually create a common fund by contributing their small savings on a regular basis.
- Groups evolve flexible systems of working (sometimes with the help of NGOs) and manage pooled resources in a democratic way.

- Loan requests are considered by groups in periodic meetings and competing claims on limited resources are settled by consensus.
- Loans are given mainly on trust with minimum documentation and without any security.
- The loan amounts are small, frequent, for short duration and are mainly for unconventional purposes.
- The rates of interest vary from group to group and the purpose of loan. It is higher than that of banks but lower than that of money-lenders.
- At periodic meetings, besides collecting money, social and economic issues are also discussed.
- Defaults are rare due to group pressure and intimate knowledge of the end use of credit.

Functions of a SHG

- *Savings and Thrift* : All SHG members regularly save a small amount. The amount may be small but savings have to be regular and continuous habit with all the members. "Savings first-credit latter" should be the motto of every SHG member. SHG members take a step towards self-dependence when they start small savings. They learn financial discipline through savings and internal lending.
- *Internal Lending* : The SHG should use the savings amount for giving loans to members. The purpose, amount, rate of interest, schedule of repayment, etc. are to be decided by the group itself. Proper accounts are to be kept by the SHG.
- *Discussing Problems* : In every meeting, the SHG should be encouraged to discuss and try to find solutions to the problems faced by the members of the group. Individually the poor people are weak and lack resources to solve their problems. When the group tries to help its members, it becomes easier for them to face the difficulties and come up with solutions.
- *Taking Bank Loan* : The SHG takes loan from the bank

and gives it as loan to its members soon after a SHG is formed and one or two meetings are held where the savings are collected, a savings bank account can be opened in the name of the SHG. After saving for a minimum period of 2 to 3 months, the common savings fund should be used by the SHG for lending to its own members. The loan from a bank is always sanctioned and issued in the name of the individual members. The amount of loan to the SHG can be to the tune of 1 to 4 times of its savings. The SHG makes the repayment to the bank. NABARD/RBI rules stipulate that no collateral security should be taken from SHGs. Collateral security is not necessary for the loans sanctioned to SHGs.

Table 4.1 : Basic Features of SHGs Promoted by NGOs/Banks

	Feature		Description
1.	Organisation	:	Homogeneity in status of economic/socio-economic status, common identity of activities, etc.
2.	Nature of target group	:	Generally poor and weaker sections of the people in rural areas particularly women.
3.	Management	:	Selected/elected leader and duty generally rotated, holding meetings regularly.
4.	Financial Institutions	:	
	(a) Common Funds	:	Created out of savings, interest earned on loan, donations etc.
	(b) Savings mobilisations	:	While in certain cases no fixed rate of savings, in some cases regular and fixed rate of savings, and in some cases as per capacity of the member.
	(c) Loaning	:	Decided by the purpose, quantum and the resources available with the SHGs. Purpose of loans for individuals include consumption, cleaning outside debts, social, medical, education, business, agriculture, etc. and loans for common production activities.
	(d) Repayment Period	:	Generally lower than prescribed by banks.
	(e) Rate of Interest	:	Varies between 12 to 20 per cent. In a few cases the interest rates are determined by the NGOs.
4.	Financial Institutions	:	
5.	Linkage with banks	:	Banks treat SHGs as borrower.

Sources : Desai, Bhupat M. and N.V. Namboodari (2001), *Organisation and Management of Rural Financial Sector: Test, Cases, and Exercises*, Oxford & IBH Publishers Company Pvt. Ltd., New Delhi.

Some of the basic features of the SHGs promoted by NGOs and banks in various parts of India are given in the Table 4.1. A typical SHG Model is depicted in Fig. 4.1. One of the important features observed is the homogeneity of the group in terms of

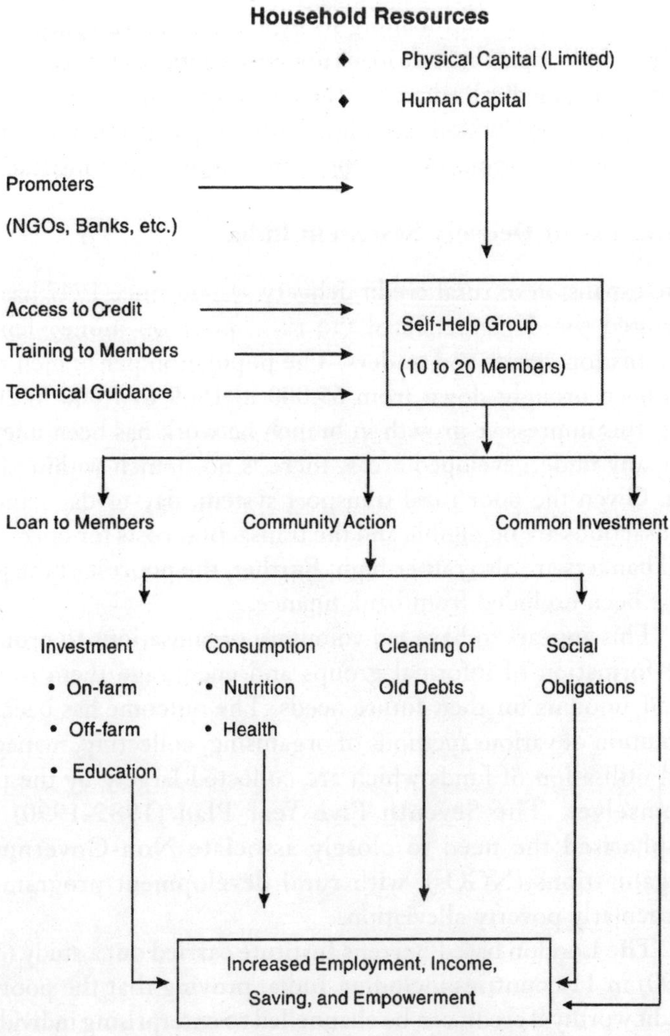

Fig. 4.1: A Typical SHG Model

social and economic status. The size of membership in each group is advocated between 10 and 20. While there is no gender specificity, majority of that formed are of women. The group is expected to function in a democratic manner and the leader may be elected or selected. The basic functions envisaged are saving mobilisation, creation of common fund out of saving, availing credit from banks and loaning to members. Various purposes of loans to individuals include loans for consumption, clearing outside debt, social, medical, education, business, agriculture, etc., besides for common production activities. Thus, the portfolio of the SHGs largely deviated from that of the formal refinancing institutions.

Rural Credit Delivery System in India

The expansion of rural credit delivery system since 1947 has not changed the dependence of the rural poor on money lender, commission agents and traders. The population per branch ratio has been brought down from 65,000 in 1969 to 7,000 in 2001. But this impressive growth in branch network has been uneven, in many underdeveloped areas, there is no branch within 10-20 km. Given the poor rural transport system, day-to-day banking transactions are negligible and the transaction costs for borrowers and bankers are also rather high. Further, the poorest of the poor have been excluded from bank finance.

This appears to have led voluntary organisations to promote the formation of informal groups and encourage them to save small amounts for their future needs. The outcome has been the evolution of various methods of organising, collecting, managing and utilisation of funds which are collected largely by the poor themselves. The Seventh Five Year Plan (1985-1990) had emphasised the need to closely associate Non-Government Organisations (NGOs), with rural development programmes particularly poverty alleviation.

The London based Barrens Institute carried out a study (May 1990) in 11 countries including India, proving that the poor are credit worthy if credit can be channelled to enterprising individuals and small groups through non-banking organisation. Credit

schemes are founded on the basis of solidarity and loans are given to individuals in a group (between 10 and 30 people) who are also borrowers and act as co-guarantees for loans. NGOs, besides facilitating the creation of SHGs, also discuss the whole range of rural problems, including social, political and personal. In several cases, after the success of the villagers own credit efforts, commercial banks give follow up loans without asking for any guarantees for the member of a credit group. This represents an attractive development effort.

The proportion of all rural households borrowing from formal credit agencies has been steadily increasing, as revealed in the All India Debt and Investment Survey Reports (1951, 1961, 1971 and 1981) set out in the Table 4.2 (from 7.2 per cent in 1951, to 17.3 per cent in 1961, to 29.2 per cent in 1971, and 61.2 per cent in 1981). Also the percentage of non-cultivator borrowers depending on non-formal sources of credit (agriculturist money lender, professional money lender, landlord and traders) contained to be above 50 per cent. The dependence of the rural poor on non-institutional sources of credit is one of the causes that perpetuate their poverty and restrict surplus generation to maintain their mega economic activities and households.

Table 4.3 shows a clear inverse relationship between the incidence of poverty reflected by assest-holding of the households and the need to incur debt for household expenditure. There is also a positive relationship between the wealth of the household and the debt contracted for productive purposes (crop loans, etc.) Credit has been an important element in linking the factor and commodity markets to rural areas, especially where the poor are concerned. Institutional rural credit agencies lack the required mechanism to assess credit needs of the poor and meet their specific requirements at specific points of time and hence are at a considerable disadvantage. The emergence of SHGs in partnership with the banks has been encouraging.

The main features of these SHGs are :

- The line dividing consumption and productive credit needs

Table 4.2 : Percentage Share of Debt of Rural Households in India

Source of Debt	1951		1961		1971		1981	
	Culti-vators	All Households	Culti-vators	All Households	Culti-vators	All Households	Culti-vators	All Households
A. Formal Sources:								
1. Government	3.9	3.7	6.7	6.6	7.1	6.7	3.9	4.0
2. Cooperative	3.7	3.5	11.4	10.4	22.0	20.1	29.8	28.6
3. Banks	---	---	0.5	0.3	2.6	2.4	29.5	28.6
Total	7.6	7.2	18.6	17.3	31.7	29.2	63.2	61.2
B. Informal Sources:								
4. Relations and Friends	11.4	11.5	5.2	5.8	13.1	13.8	8.7	9.0
5. Landlords	3.2	3.5	0.9	1.1	8.1	8.6	3.7	4.0
6. Agriculturalist Moneylenders	25.2	25.2	48.0	47.0	23.0	23.1	8.3	8.6
7. Professional Moneylender	46.8	46.4	13.8	13.8	13.1	13.8	7.8	8.3
8. Traders and Commission agents	4.7	5.1	7.0	7.5	8.4	8.7	3.1	3.4
9. Others	1.1	1.1	6.5	7.5	2.6	2.8	5.2	5.5
C. Total	92.4	92.8	81.4	82.7	68.3	70.8	36.8	38.8
D. Grand Total	100.0	100.0	100.0	100.0	100.0	100.0	100.0	100.0
E. Total Debt			3126.0	3610	3292	3754	2164	2336

Note : 1. Includes insurance and provident funds.
2. At 1970-71 prices.

Source : All India Rural Debt and Investment Survey Report (1981).

is blurred when economic operations are at a subsistence level.

- Consumption credit needs for the poor are very important and also determine productivity.
- The consumption/productive credit needs of the poor have to be met as and when they arise so as to prevent dependence on non-institutional credit sources.

Table 4.3 : Percentage Distribution of Cash Dues Outstanding by Asset Group and Major Purposes for Rural Households

Asset Group	*Capable Expenditure*	*Current Expenditure*	*Household Expenditure*
1	2	3	4
Upto Rs. 1,000	5.7	3.8	79.1
1,000 to 5,000	12.5	9.4	59.3
5,000 to 10,000	19.7	8.8	44.6
10,000 to 20,000	24.4	20.4	34.6
20,000 to 50,000	35.8	19.1	27.2
50,000 to 100,000	42.6	22.0	19.2
100,000 to 500,000	54.3	19.8	10.1
500,000 and Above	79.4	4.0	1.6
Total	42.4	17.6	22.4

Source : All India Debt and Investment Survey (1981).

A flexible credit strategy which meets the needs of the poor to rise above the subsistence level of living, needs to be implemented.

Since independence India increased wheat output from 6 million tonnes in 1947 to 72.5 million tonnes in 2007, per capita power consumption from 15.3 KWh to 606 KWh, telephones from 1.1 million to 218 million, national highways from 19,634 km to 65,569 km, exports from Rs. 403.4 crore, doctors from 0.5 lakh to 5.54 lakh and reduced infant mortality from 145.6 per 1000 live births to 58 per 1000 live births.[10]

As against these significant achievements, imports too have sharply increased from Rs. 408.7 crore to Rs. 8.20 lakh crore and government expenditure shot up from Rs. 200 crore to Rs. 5.64 lakh crore.

Rural areas have also witnessed varying rates of development,

growth and progress. More importantly, rural financial institutions (RFIs) during 60 years have touched the lives of millions and supported through efficient resource mobilisation and credit deployment, banks' own as well as government's programmes aimed at accelerating process of integrated rural development, stepping up farm output, creating self-employment opportunities, minimising incidence of poverty and regional imbalances. It is against this background that an attempt has been made here to appreciate the role and effectiveness of rural financial institutions in their efforts to disburse credit for the development of farm and allied sector, small scale industries, rural and cottage industries, including handloom and handicrafts and service and business sector, empowerment of women through forming self-help groups, and linking them with banks, development of scheduled castes and tribes and creating most essential rural infrastructure in villages.

A buoyant agricultural sector is necessary to ensure food security, provide livelihood to a large proportion of the workforce contribute to the growth of the economy by producing wage goods, raw material for industry, goods for export, generate surpluses and provide markets for non-agricultural goods. Comparative advantage in several agricultural products add to its significance as an important contributor to foreign exchange earning.

Rural Financial Institutions

Institutional rural credit in India was put in place during the 1970s, when the government began the practice of extending loans to farmers in drought year. Later it was decided to experiment with rural credit cooperatives on the lines of the Raiffeison models in Germany, (based on the principles of mutualism, solidarity, participation in management and one-person-one-vote democracy) and since beginning of the 1900s, when the first cooperative credit institution was established, which continued to be the primary lending institution, catering to the short term and long term needs of farmers for their agricultural operations. The system was subjected to a major

review in 1950 by the All India Rural Credit Survey Committee which observed that a large share of the credit requirements of rural households, particularly the poor came from traditional sources such as relatives, landlords, traders and money lenders.

India's rural credit system is unique in its reach and diversity. Besides, the basic role of financial intermediation, the rural financial institutions play a unique role in accelerating efforts to reduce poverty and regional imbalances. To make the rural credit delivery system vibrant and dynamic and the functioning of the rural financial institutions proactive, the RFIs have been under periodic examination over the years. The pioneering All India Rural Credit Survey (1954) was followed by the All India Rural Credit Review Committee (1979), the Committee to Review Arrangements for Institutional Credit for Agriculture and Rural Development (1981) and the Agricultural Credit Review Committee (1989), which had comprehensively investigated various emerging issues in rural credit and made recommendations. In addition, a number of issue-specific and institution-specific studies have also been made from time to time by various agencies. The recommendations of these committees/ studies and the actions thereon have brought about momentous changes in the rural credit scenario of the country.

Multi-Agency Approach

By the mid-1960s the credit requirements of agricultural sector grew multifold with the realisation that cooperatives alone would not be able to fulfil the burgeoning demand of rural credit. Therefore, the concepts of a multi-agency approach to rural credit and the social control measures were adopted. The major commercial banks which were privately owned, were brought under 'social control' and within a few years thereafter they were nationalised. The nationalised commercial banks were called upon to extend credit to rural areas on a priority basis, and they were directed to expand the network of their branches in rural areas to serve rural masses especially the poor.

In 1972, the Banking Commission observed in its report that

despite the massive expansion of network of commercial banks, there would still be the need and possibility of having specialised network of bank branches to cater to the needs of rural poor. Thus originated the concept of 'rural bank' by 1975 when the structure of rural moneylenders was regulated under the government's efforts to eradicate rural indebtedness as a part of the '20-point economic programme', an urgent need was felt for an alternative institutional mechanism to reach the rural poor particularly the small and marginal farmers, artisans and agricultural labourers. Consequently, the Government of India constituted the Working Group on Rural Banks in July 1975.

The Working Group recommended for the setting up of state-sponsored, region-based, rural oriented commercial banks which would blend the rural touch, local feel, the professional discipline, ability to mobilise deposits and access to central money markets and the modernised outlook of commercial banks. In a sense, it was an experiment to hybridise commercial banking culture with the rural ethos. The role as perceived for this new institution was to supplement and not supplant the existing financial institutions in the rural sector. It was envisaged that this new institution would help in reducing regional imbalances by mobilising and simultaneously deploying resources in the same region. It was asserted that these banks would cover primarily the small and marginal farmers, landless labourers, rural artisans, small traders and other weaker sections of rural society for their productive credit needs and to a limited extent, the consumption credit needs.

The institutional credit delivery system in rural India comprises the cooperative credit institutions, commercial banks and the regional rural banks. The cooperative credit delivery is a century old primary rural credit delivery system in the country and is organised into its short-term and long-term arms at primary/grassroots level, central level and flat/apex level which operate through more than one lakh windows covering about 4.5 crore borrowing members. There are 28 public sector commercial banks and 32 banks in the private sector operating in the villages through their more than 32,000 branches in rural and semi-urban areas.

Similarly 196 regional rural banks provide their financial services to rural masses through 14,311 branches.

It is discernible that the cooperative credit institutions were virtually the only institutions providing credit for agricultural activities till 1970-71, when the commercial banks made a beginning in this area. With the spread of their branches, the commercial banks moved fast by 1988-89, when they adopted the service area approach, they claimed more than 41 per cent of the share in disbursement of agricultural credit and about 54 per cent in outstanding agricultural credit. The market share of the regional rural banks in agricultural credit by this time was a mere 5 per cent but the credit had gone entirely to the rural poor. The demand for credit had risen fast from year to year and the figures of annual disbursements for agricultural purposes moved from Rs. 7,438 million in 1970-71 to Rs. 91,062 million in 1988-89 until the concept of service area approach was implemented. And now the disbursements have shot up to Rs. 1,574,800 millions in 2005-06. Tables 4.4 and 4.5 exhibit the phenomenal contributions made by the RFIs during the period from 1970-71 to 1999-2000 and the resultant impact on informal sources of credit from 1951 to 1991 respectively.

Disbursement of Farm Credit

With the induction of public sector and nationalised banks and regional rural banks, credit disbursement has increased significantly from year to year since 1970-71. Total disbursement rose from Rs. 7,438 million in 1970-71 to Rs. 3,005,182 million at the end of 1999-2000. Annual growth in the disbursement by all banks had not been progressively rising as it varied from 42 per cent to 131 per cent. Annual disbursement on an average was Rs. 49,688.2 million by cooperatives, followed by commercial banks at Rs. 42,911.6 million and regional rural banks at Rs. 6,826.8 million. The share of cooperatives was as high as 51.25 per cent followed by commercial banks at 42.84 per cent whereas it was 5.91 per cent in the case of the regional rural banks (Table 4.4).

Table 4.4 : Credit Disbursement by Banks in India during 1970-71 to 1999-2000

S. No.	Year	Cooperative	Commercial	Regional Rural	Total	Per annum
1	2	3	4	5	6	7
1.	1970-71	7,438	—	—	7,438	7,438
2.	1971-72 to 1974-75	36,428	5,829	—	42,257	10,564.2 (42%)
3.	1975-76 to 1979-80	75,037	32,567	1,622	109,226	21,845.2 (106%)
4.	1980-81 to 1984-85	133,077	83,023	9,628	225,728	41,145.6 (188%)
5.	1985-86 to 1989-90	223,653	176,831	24,292	424,776	84,955.2 (106%)
6.	1990-91 to 1994-95	353,691	272,491	34,636	662,818	132.,563.2 (56%)
7.	1995-96 to 1999-2000	711,010	716,609	107,320	1,534,939	306,987.8 (131%)
8.	Total	1,540,334 (49,688.2)	1,287,350 (42,911.6)	177,498 (6,827.8)	3,005,182	98941.3
9.	Per cent Share	51.25	42.84	5.91	100	

Notes : 1. Figures in brackets in col. 7 indicate per cent growth over previous year.

2. Figures in brackets in the row 8 indicate amount of credit per annum.

Source : Patil, Amit (2007), "Rural Financial Institutions in India: Touching the lives of millions", *Kurukshetra*, October, p. 6.

Table 4.5 : Access of Rural Households to Formal and Informal Sources of Credit (1951, 1961, 1971, 1981 and 1991)

Credit Agency	*1951*	*1961*	*1971*	*1981*	*1991*
1	2	3	4	5	6
A. *Institutional*	7.2	17.3	29.2	61.2	64.0
1. Government	3.7	6.6	6.7	4.0	6.1
2. Cooperatives	3.5	10.4	20.1	28.6	21.6
3. Commercial Banks	–	0.3	2.2	28.0	33.7
4. Insure Corporation	–	–	0.1	0.3	0.3
5. Provident Fund	–	–	0.1	0.3	0.76
6. Other Institution	–	–	–	–	1.6
B. *Non-institutional*	92.8	82.7	70.8	38.8	36.0
1. Zamindars	3.5	1.1	8.6	4.0	4.0
2. Agri. moneylenders	25.2	47.0	23.1	8.6	7.1
3. Prof. moneylenders	46.4	13.8	13.8	8.3	10.5
4. Businessmen/traders	5.1	7.3	8.7	3.4	2.5
5. Relatives/friends	11.5	5.8	13.8	9.0	5.5
6. Others	1.4	7.5	2.8	5.5	3.2
7. Unspecified	–	–	–	–	3.3
Total (A+B)	100.0	100.0	100.0	100.0	100.0

Source : Patel, Amit (2007), Rural Financial Institutions of India: Touching the lives of millions, *Kurukshetra*, p. 6.

Rural Indebtedness

Dependence of rural households on non-institutional sources of credit was as high as 92.8 per cent in the year 1951, just four years after India's independence, which declined to 82.7 per cent in 1961 and further to 70.8 per cent in 1971 when cooperative credit institutions made their presence felt on the rural scene after acceptance and implementation of recommendations of the All India Rural Credit Survey Committee in 1954 and entry of major private sector banks after their nationalisation in the year 1969. Access of rural households to formal credit institutions sharply increased to 61.2 per cent in 1981 partly because of enabling measures initiated by the Reserve Bank of India to direct public sector banks towards rural lending and partly because of the establishment of the Regional Rural Banks from the year 1975 onwards specifically to cater to the credit needs of rural poor households. However, in the year 1991, there was only marginal

increase in the institutional sources of credit from 61.2 per cent in 1981 to 64 per cent in 1991. While dependence of rural households on professional money-lenders in particular declined from 46.4 per cent in 1951 to 8.3 per cent in 1981, it again increased to 10.5 per cent in 1991. Role of agricultural moneylenders had also decreased progressively from 47 per cent in 1961 to 7.1 per cent in 1991. The performance of commercial banks was very spectacular between 1971 and 1981, but it showed little improvement in 1991. Cooperative had shown good performance from 1961 to 1981 but its performance declined in 1991.

Doubling Farm Credit

The goal of the Government of India as announced by the Finance Minister in the budget speech in 2004, to double the flow of farm credit in three years (2004-07) was achieved in two years. Actual flow of credit during the year 2006-07 exceeded the target of Rs. 1,750,000 million during April to December 2006, around 5,337,000 new farmers as against the target of 5 million, were linked with the institutional credit system. For the year 2007-08, the target of farm credit disbursement was fixed at Rs. 2,250,000 million (28.6 per cent over the target of 2006-07) and an addition of 5 million new farmer borrowers. Table 4.6 exhibits banks commitments, particularly of commercial banks and regional rural banks to respond to Finance Minister's call to double the credit disbursements during 2004-07.

Total disbursements progressively increased from Rs. 620,450 million in the year 2005-06, reflecting a rise by 153.8 per cent. Commercial banks and regional rural banks recorded phenomenal rise by 216 per cent and 189 per cent respectively as compared to 58 per cent by the cooperatives. While there has been progressive rise in each successive year in the case of cooperatives, commercial and regional rural banks, there has been secular increase during 2004-05 and 2005-06 in respect of commercial banks and regional rural banks. The share of cooperatives in the total disbursements of short-term and long-term credit progressively declined from 37.91 per cent in 2001-02 to 23.65 per cent in 2005-06 whereas

Table 4.6 : Farm Credit Disbursement by Cooperative, Commercial and Regional Rural Banks in India (2001-02 to 2005-06)

Year	*Cooperative Banks*	*Commercial Banks*	*Regional Rural Banks*	*Others*	*Total*
1	2	3	4	5	6
2001-02	235,240 (37.91)	335,870 (54.13)	48,540 (7.82)	800 (0.040)	620,450 (100)
2002-03	236,360 (34.00)	397,740 (57.18)	60,700 (8.72)	800 (0.14)	695,600 (100)
2003-04	268,750 (30.91)	524,410 (60.29)	75,810 (8.71)	840 (0.09)	869,810 (100)
2004-05	312,310 (24.92)	814,810 (65.02)	124,040 (9.91)	1,930 (0.15)	1,253,090 (100)
2005-06	372,520 (23.65)	1,061,520 (67.41)	140,760 (8.94)	N.A.	1,574,800 (100)
Total	1,425,180 (28.42)	3,134,350 (65.52)	4,49,850 (8.97)	4,370 (0.09)	5,013,800 (100)

Notes : 1. Figures in brackets shows percentage share to total.
2. N.A. = Not available.

Source : Patel, Amit (2007), "Rural Financial Institutions in India: Touching the Lives of Millions," *Kurukshetra* (October), p. 7.

that of commercial banks recorded progressive increase from 54.13 per cent to 67.41 per cent during the corresponding years. The regional rural banks accounted for 7.82 per cent in 2001-02 which progressively rose to 9.91 per cent in 2004-05 but declined by one percentage point in the following year. The flow of agricultural credit for the banking system as a whole during 2005-06 has surged to Rs. 1,804,860 million, reflecting 128 per cent of the target of Rs. 1,410,000 million which was set for that year (Table 4.7).

The data further revealed that proportion of short-term credit to enable farmers to conduct seasonal agricultural operations was around 63 per cent as against 37 per cent of long-term credit for investment purposes. Table 4.7 exhibits comparative performance among banks and within banks during nine months of 2005 and 2006.

Agricultural credit flow target for 2006-07 had been pegged at Rs. 1,750,000 million. However, for the fiscal year 2006-07,

Table 4.7 : Flow of Farm Credit during April to December 2005 and 2006

(in millions of rupees)

Period (April-Dec.)	Public Sector Banks	Private Sector Banks	Cooperative Banks	Regional Rural Banks	Total
1	2	3	4	5	6
2005	689,910 (57.92)	100,310 (8.42)	289,470 (24.30)	111,460 (9.36)	1,191,150 (100)
2006	868,650 (58.16)	141,340 (9.46)	331,740 (22.22)	151,700 (10.16)	1,493,430 (100)
Percent increase in 2006 over 2005	25.91	40.91	14.60	36.10	25.38

Note : Figure within brackets show per cent to total.

Source : Patel, Amit (2007), "Rural Financial Institutions in India: Touching the Lives of Millions", *Kurukshetra*, October, p. 7.

agricultural credit upto December 2006 stood at Rs. 1,493,430 million which represented an increase of 25.38 per cent over the achievement of Rs. 1,191,150 million record in the same 9 months period in the previous year. Agricultural credit flow during April to December 2006 from public sector banks grew by 25.91 per cent to Rs. 868,650 million from Rs. 689,910 million during the corresponding period in the previous year. In the case of the private sector banks, it increased by 40.90 per cent to Rs. 141,340 million from Rs. 100,310 million. While cooperative banks recorded an increase by 14.60 per cent from Rs. 288,470 million to Rs. 331,740 million during the period, the regional rural banks showed increase by 36.10 per cent from Rs. 111,480 million to Rs. 151,700 million. The share of public sector banks in the total disbursement of agricultural credit during April-December 2006 accounted for as high as 58 per cent followed by the cooperative banks at 22 per cent whereas the regional rural banks and private sector banks had almost equal share of 10 per cent and 9 per cent respectively.

Service Area Approach and Recovery of Credit

Rural and semi-urban branches of each of the public sector banks have been allotted service area comprising specified number of villages since April 1989. This has facilitated all villages (about 650,000) of the country easy and dependable access to banks to meet rural households financial services (savings, credit and remittances). Each branch is expected to formulate Service Area Credit Plan every year for the purpose of providing credit to the rural households. This micro-level credit planning exercise should help the bank to progressively bring within its fold all eligible households for receiving credit and related services. In the ultimate process this exercise should prove to improve the quality and productivity of lending. The Reserve Bank of India since the year 1994-95 has advised public sector banks to ensure 25 per cent annual growth rate in the matter of disbursement of credit in their service area. Accordingly, the data presented in Table 4.8 showed that annual growth was between 12.5 per cent and 24 per cent respectively during 2000-01 and 2003-04. The growth was spectacularly high at 54.5 per cent during 2004-05 which, however, declined to 44.6 per cent in the following year. Disbursements of credit as against targets ranged from 92.1 per cent to 117.3 per cent during the six years period. Achievements were higher than 100 per cent only in the last two years.

Public sector banks recovery to demand under direct agricultural advance were 69.3 per cent during the year 2000-01 which gradually increased during the following three years. It, however, phenomenally rose to 84.1 per cent in the year 2005. During the five years period, the demand (loan amount to be recovered) and percentage of recovery to demand have progressively increased in the successive years whereas overdue amount has increased until the year 2003-04 and then it steeply declined by Rs. 29,620 million in the following year. Table 4.8 exhibits the impact of formulating and implementing the service area credit plans by banks.

Table 4.8 : Targets and Achievements under Service Area Credit Plan and Recovery of Direct Agricultural Advance by Public Sector Banks during 2000-01 and 2005-06

Year	*Target*	*Achievement*	*Annual Growth (%)*	*Demand*	*Recovery*	*Overdue*
1	2	3	4	5	6	7
2000-01	258,930	246,540 (95.2)	12.5	224,290	155,400 (69.3)	68,890 (30.7)
2001-02	308,830	293,320 (95.0)	19.0	245,610	177,580 (72.3)	68,030 (27.7)
2002-03	368,380	339,210 (92.1)	15.6	289,400	210,110 (72.6)	79,300 (27.4)
2003-04	425,760	422,110 (99.1)	24.4	355,440	250,020 (74.5)	85,420 (25.5)
2004-05	556,160	652,180 (117.30)	54.5	351,920	296,120 (84.1)	55,800 (15.9)
2005-06	850,240 (110.9)	942,780	44.6	N.A.	N.A.	N.A.

Note : Figure within brackets in columns 3, 6 and 7 show percentage.

Source : Patel, Amit (2007), "Rural Financial Institutions in India: Touching the Lives of Millions," *Kurukshetra*, October, p. 8.

Priority Sector Lending

In India the commercial banks and the rural banks have been providing credit for small scale industries, rural and cottage industries, tiny sector, khadi and village industries, handloom, handicrafts, coir and silk units under secondary sector as well as for a wide variety of purposes under service and business sector. Thus, priority sector advances include agriculture, small scale industries and services and business sector. The credit support to priority sector not only stimulates increased farm and non-farm sector output, but also creates large scale self-employment opportunities. Table 4.9 exhibits commercial banks comparative performance on outstanding credit to agriculture as well as to priority sectors.

During the seven years period from 2000 to 2006 public sector banks outstanding credit to priority sectors increased by 221.9 per cent from Rs. 1,274,780 million as on 31st March, 2000 to Rs. 4,103,790 million as on 31st March, 2006, whereas that of

Table 4.9 : Priority Sector and Agricultural Outstanding Credit by Public and Private Sector Banks (31st March 2000 to 31st March, 2006)

Year	Public Sector Banks		Private Sector Banks	
	Priority Sector	Agriculture	Priority Sector	Agriculture
1	2	3	4	5
2000	1,274,780 (43.3)	452,960 (14.3)	183,680 (38)	40,230 (8.3)
2001	1,491,160 (43.7)	523,710 (15.7)	215,670 (36.7)	56,340 (9.6)
2002	1,714,840 (43.5)	581,420 (14.8)	241,840 (38.4)	65,810 (8.5)
2003	1,997,860 (41.2)	705,010 (14.5)	366,480 (44.1)	99,240 (10.9)
2004	2,444,560 (43.6)	844,356 (15.1)	489,200 (47.3)	147,300 (14.2)
2005	3,070,460 (42.8)	1,099,170 (15.3)	698,860 (43.6)	216,360 (12.3)
2006	4,103,790 (40.3)	1,549,000 (15.2)	1,065,660 (42.8)	361,850 (13.5)

Note : Figures within brackets show percentage to net bank credit.

Source : Patel, Amit (2007), "Rural Financial Institutions in India: Touching the Lives of Millions," *Kurukshetra*, October, p. 9.

private sector banks shot up by 480.2 per cent from Rs. 183,680 million to Rs. 1,065,660 million during the period under consideration. Priority sector advances of public sector banks as group accounted for over 43 per cent of net bank credit in four years as against the target of 40 per cent which, however, declined from 42.8 per cent to 40.3 per cent in the three years. In this respect private sector banks as a group had less than that of targeted 40 per cent during initial three years but they showed impressive performance (42.8% to 47.3%) in the following four years.

Agricultural advances by public sector banks during the period rose by 242 per cent from Rs. 452,960 million to Rs. 1,549,000 million whereas that of private sector banks increased significantly by 799 per cent from Rs. 40,230 million to Rs. 361,850 million

during the period under consideration. The share of agricultural advances in the net bank credit by public sector banks ranged between 14.3 per cent and 15.7 per cent, whereas that of private sector banks varied from 8.3 per cent to 14.2 per cent during the period under consideration. Neither public sector banks nor private sector banks as a group could achieve targeted agricultural credit of 18 per cent of net bank credit.

During 2005-06, all public sector banks (except State Bank of India and State Bank of Patiala) were able to meet the priority sector target for agriculture. None of the private sector banks could meet sub-target for lending to agriculture.

Kisan Credit Card

The Kisan Credit Card (KCC) scheme was introduced in August 1998 to facilitate farmer's easy and timely access to short term credit for purchasing farm inputs while conducting seasonal agricultural operations for raising crops. Now the scheme has been extended to cover tenant farmer, oral lessees, farmers to redeem debt from informal sources, besides providing long term as well as consumption credit. During the period from 2001-02 to 2005-06, banks provided 59,093,000 Kisan Credit Cards to farmers to facilitate them to purchase farms inputs and other requirements. Share of the commercial banks was 37 per cent as against cooperatives and regional rural banks at 51 per cent and 12 per cent respectively (Table 4.10).

Refinance Facilities

The NABARD has been providing refinance facilities at reduced interest rate (6-6.5%) to cooperative banks and regional rural banks for their short and long term credit and to commercial banks for long term credit in order to augment their loanable resources and enable them to on-lend to farmers at reduced interest rate. The refinance provided by NABARD to Banks has significantly increased from Rs. 45,210 million in 1998-99 to Rs. 86,223 million in 2005-06. Only commercial banks availed significantly increased amount

Table 4.10 : Number of Kisan Credit Cards issued during 2001-02 to 2005-06

Year	Commercial Banks	Regional Rural Banks	Cooperative Banks	Total
1	2	3	4	5
2001-02	3.071	0.834	5.436	9.341
2002-03	2.700	0.964	4.579	8.243
2003-04	3.094	1.274	4.878	9.246
2004-05	4.395	1.729	3.556	9.686
2005-06	4.165	1.249	2.598	8.012
Total	21.803 (37%)	6.878 (12%)	30.412 (51%)	59.093 (100%)

Source : Patel, Amit (2007), "Rural Financial Institutions in India: Touching the Lives of Millions," *Kurukshetra*, October, p. 10.

of refinance in successive years. Share of refinance in the total agricultural loans disbursed by cooperatives was as high as 50.3 per cent, followed by commercial banks at 31.4 per cent whereas regional rural banks accounted for 18 per cent (See Table 4.11).

Table 4.11 : Refinance Disbursement by NABARD to Banks (1998-99 to 2005-06)

Year	SCARDBS	SCBS	Commercial Banks	Regional Rural Banks	PUCBS/ ADFCS	Total
1	2	3	4	5	6	7
1998-99	21,680	4,300	12,060	7,140	30	45,210
1999-00	23,460	5,400	15,470	7,750	70	52,150
2000-01	23,400	7,230	22,010	8,680	260	61,580
2001-02	27,320	10,890	16,080	11,780	760	66,830
2002-03	N.A.	N.A.	N.A.	N.A.	N.A.	N.A.
2003-04	25,441.4	17,365	17,136	15,893.5	217	76,052.9
2004-05	27,099.8	12,439.2	25,695.6	20,491.1	48.9	85,774.6
2005-06	20,824.7	11,737.2	40,277.4	13,324	60.4	86,223.7
Total	169,225.9 (35.7)	69,414.4 (14.6)	148,729 (31.4)	850,586 (18.1)	14,46.3 (0.3)	473,821.2 (100)

Notes : 1. N.A. = Not available

2. Figures in the brackets in the last row show percentage.

Source : Patel, Amit, (2007), "Rural Financial Institutions in India: Touching the Lives of Millions," *Kurukshetra*, October, p. 10.

Self-Help Groups

The late 1980s and early 1990s witnessed the beginning of what was to usher in the Self-Help Group-Bank-Linkage movement in India, a movement which has been described as the largest microfinance intervention in the world. At present the major involvement of commercial banks in Indian microfinance is through SHGs. Self-Help affinity were started by NGOs which were doner-funded and established for a range of community purposes. With increasing skepticism about the ability of commercial banks and regional rural banks to lend directly to the rural poor, the NABARD proposed that if these SHGs could be linked to whole sale suppliers of credit, then this could be a way to channel institutional credit to the poor. This led to a pilot project in 1992 and subsequent mainstreaming of the approach. The SHG model is a financial delivery model which has as its objective reaching out to the unreached poor in conjunction with achieving cost-effectiveness for the participating financial institutions. It involves three partners : (1) SHGs, (2) the banks as wholesale suppliers of credit, and (3) NGOs, government agencies and individuals as agencies to organise the poor, build their capacity and facilitate empowerment. SHGs have been described as a unique form of community level financial system, sharing a number of characteristics with credit unions, though lacking even a minimal legal structure. SHGs as compared to Grameen Bank Groups pioneered by the Grameen Bank of Bangladesh, are more independent, flexible and democratic in character.

As on the 31st March, 2006, the number of SHGs linked with banks were as high as 2,238,565 as compared to 1,079,091 in 2004 and 1,618,456 in 2005. Credit disbursed to these SHGs was also as high as Rs. 113,975.5 million in 2006 as against Rs. 39,042 million in 2004 and Rs. 68,984.6 million in 2005. Share of commercial banks in respect of number of SHGs linked with banks and credit disbursed was the highest followed by the regional rural banks and cooperatives (Table 4.12).

Table 4.12 : Number of Self-Help Groups and Credit Disbursed by Banks during 2004-06

(Credit in Rs. millions)

	Banks			*2004*	*2005*	*2006*
	1			2	3	4
1.	Commercial Banks	(a)	No. of SHGs	538422	843473	118807
			(%)	50	52	53
		(b)	Credit	22548.3	41590.2	69877.0
			(%)	58	60	61
2.	Regional Rural Banks	(a)	No. of SHGs	405998	563846	740024
			(%)	38	35	32
		(b)	Credit	12782.5	20995.5	38221.5
3.	Cooperative Banks	(a)	No. of SHGs	134671	211137	310194
			(%)	12	13	14
		(b)	Credit	3711.2	6398	10871
			(%)	9	9	10
4.	Others	(a)	No. of SHGs	–	–	271.2
			(%)			
		(b)	Credit	–	–	5.2
			(%)			
	Total	(a)	No. of SHGs	1079091	1618456	2238585
			(%)	100	100	100
		(b)	Credit	39042.0	68984.6	113975.5
			(%)	100	100	100

Source : Patel, Amit (2007), "Rural Financial Institutions in India : Touching the Lives of Millions," *Kurukshetra*, October, p. 11.

As on the 31st March, 2006, the number of SHGs stood at just over two and quarter million of which over one and a half million had outstanding bank loans. Even with this huge number of SHGs, it is estimated by the committee on Financial Inclusion that the number of SHGs will have to be doubled to cover all the 50 million poor households in the country.

As reported under the NABARD-GTZ Rural Finance Programme, at above 98 per cent on time repayment to the SHGs is reported to be very high.

Commercial banks and regional rural banks have been actively involved in providing credit support to government sponsored programmes which have specified aims and objectives, viz. alleviating poverty, improving socio-economic status of the schedule castes, scheduled tribes and weaker sections of the society, etc.

Integrated Rural Development Programme was one of several programmes under which bank credit was linked with capital subsidy provided by the Government to the beneficiaries targeted as 'below poverty line' (BPL). Under the programme while data on the number of beneficiaries, amount of credit and subsidy provided during the period from 1980 to 1988 were not available, total amount of credit and capital subsidy provided to 25,906,000 beneficiaries was Rs. 153,166.5 million and Rs. 83,529.2 million respectively. Recovery percentage to demand varied from 29 per cent in 1990-91 to 4 per cent in 1994-95. As on 31st June, 1996, the overdue amount was as high as Rs. 12,100 million as compared to Rs. 5,310 million recovered out of demand of Rs. 17,140 million.

Under the differential interest rate scheme (at 4%) loan outstanding as on 31st March, 2005, was of the order of Rs. 4,900 million outstanding with 389,000 borrowers accounting for 0.07 per cent as of previous year's outstanding credit as against stipulation of one per cent.

As on the 31st March, 2006, credit outstanding with weaker sections of the society was as high as Rs. 1,045,768.9 million.

Outstanding credit to tribals increased from Rs. 14,851,330 million in 1993-94 to Rs. 39,620,390 million in 2000-01, reflecting the share of commercial banks as high as 57 per cent followed by 29 per cent of cooperative banks and 14 per cent of regional rural banks.

During the year 2005-06 banks have lent Rs. 6,440 million accompanied with government's subsidy of Rs. 2,380 million to 755,969 beneficiaries of Swarnajayanti Gram Swarozgar Yojana and under the Pradhan Mantri Rozgar Yojana a sum of Rs. 7,610 million was provided to 131,290 beneficiaries.

Commercial banks, regional rural banks and cooperative banks have disbursed a sum of Rs. 221.4 million, Rs. 22.2 million and Rs. 70.5 million to 5,173 farmers, 283 farmers and 2,826 farmers respectively to redeem their past debt with informal sources during the year 2005-06.

Rural Infrastructure Development Fund

Rural infrastructure (both physical and institutional) such as irrigation, watershed development, rural electrification, roads, markets, credit institutions, rural literacy, agricultural research and extension, etc. together play a key role in determining the agricultural output in India. For instance, irrigation infrastructure increases the land use intensity and cropping intensity, and provides incentives to farmers to use yield increasing inputs, thus results in higher agricultural output. Rural electrification increases the energisation of pump sets which helps to increase the irrigated area using ground water, the output of crops under ground water irrigation is always higher than those under canal irrigation, because of the better reliability and controllability. Rural road increases the diffusion of agricultural technology by improving access to markets, enhances more efficient allocation of resources, reduces the transaction costs as well as helps the farmers to realise better input and output prices. Improved road infrastructure also increases the transportation facility through which the rural farm households are able to get better health care, education, and credit facility. Rural-urban linkages are developed through road development which also helps strengthening the backward and forward linkages in agricultural sector.

A classic study shows that Indian States with highest rural infrastructure index (a composite measure for rural electrification, roads, transport, health, irrigation farm credit, fertilizer, agricultural marketing, research and extension) such as Punjab, Haryana and Tamil Nadu have the highest foodgrains productivity per hectare and the States with lowest index such as Rajasthan, Bihar and Madhya Pradesh have lowest foodgrains productivity per hectare; the rural infrastructure explains about 68 per cent of the variability in the yield in the different States and 10 per cent improvement in rural infrastructure index in States with lower score would increase their foodgrains productivity by about 470 kg per hectare on an average. This study established a strong relationship between the level of rural infrastructural development and the level of agricultural output.

Indian State level time series data for 1957 to 1991 show that States with better initial endowments of physical and human infrastructure (towards the early 1960s) achieved higher rates of agricultural output growth than poorly endowed States. Higher initial irrigation, higher initial literacy and lower initial infant mortality, all contributed to higher long term growth rates.

Using State level data for 1970-93 in India, researches studied the relationship between government expenditure on agricultural research and development, roads, irrigation, education, power, soil and water conservation, rural development spending on agricultural growth and rural poverty. The study concludes that improved rural infrastructure and technology have all contributed to agricultural growth, but their impacts have varied by settings. Government expenditure on roads and R & D have by far the largest impact on poverty reduction and growth in agricultural productivity. Government spending on education has the third largest impact on rural poverty and productivity growth. Irrigation investment has had only modest impacts on growth in agricultural productivity and rural poverty reduction even after allowing for trickledown benefits.

The linkages between the Green Revolution Technology package (irrigation, research and extension, improved varieties of seeds and fertilizers) and other rural infrastructure and agricultural output/growth are well established by several researches at all India level, State level, taluka/sub-divisional level and village level. Likewise, studies using Agro-Ecological Zones (AEZs) typology also provide further evidence on varied contribution of infrastructure to agricultural output growth in India.

A recent comprehensive study to better understand the linkages between rural infrastructure development and agricultural output using cross-sectional data for 256 districts in India drawn from 13 States at three points of time (1970-71, 1980-81 and 1990-91) shows that the districts having value of agricultural output above the average are better placed in terms of rural infrastructure development (irrigation, road, literacy, school facility, rural electrification and fertilizer) than the other districts.

NABARD in its annual exercise of preparing district-wise potential linked credit plans has been sharply focusing on the

immediate needs for creating rural infrastructure having direct impact on increasing farm output and the sustainable development of farm sector. In order to supplement the efforts of the State Governments, at NABARD level Union Government has established Rural Infrastructure Development Fund (RIDF) which has yielded rich dividends. The Tables 4.13 and 4.14 exhibit the use of the fund in creating rural infrastructure from 1995-96 to 2005-06.

Table 4.13 : Number of Projects and Amount Disbursed under RIDF in India during 1995-96 to 2005-06

Year	*Number of Projects*	*Amount (Rs. Millions)*
1	2	3
1995-96	4,168	17,608.7
1996-97	8,334	23,979.5
1997-98	14,346	24,535.0
1998-99	6,172	24,280.0
1999-00	12,254	30,326.6
2000-01	43,354	38,568.2
2001-02	24,987	37,568.2
2002-03	21,012	44,403.4
2003-04	19,605	33,874.8
2004-05	59,979	29,678.1
2005-06	30,440	18,070.8
Total	244,651	322,893.3

Source : Patel, Amit, (2007), "Rural Financial Institutions in India: Touching the Lives of Millions," *Kurukshetra*, October, p. 13.

Commercial banks falling short of achieving priority sector/ agricultural lending targets have since 1995-96 till 2005-06 deposited Rs. 287,499.5 million with NABARD under Rural Infrastructure Development Fund at very reduced interest rate. The NABARD has so far disbursed a sum of Rs. 322,893.3 million to support 244,651 projects in various parts of the country (Table 4.13).

Types of projects supported by the RIDF relate to irrigation development, construction of rural bridge and roads, social sector and power generation, etc. The share of irrigation development projects in terms of number was the highest at 38.7 per cent, followed by social sector and rural roads, whereas in terms of

amount disbursed, the irrigation development accounted for as high as 34.3 per cent share followed by rural roads, rural bridges and social sector (Table 4.14).

Table 4.14 : Types and Number of Projects and Amount Disbursed under RIDF in India during 2005-06

	Types of Project	*Number of Projects*	*Amount Disbursed (Rs. Millions)*
	1	2	3
1.	Irrigation	78,442 (36.7)	146,841.5 (34.3)
2.	Rural Bridge	9,285 (4.3)	47,608.4 (11.1)
3.	Rural Roads	43,857 (20.5)	144,935.7 (33.9)
4.	Social Sector	67,995 (31.7)	38,718.4 (9.1)
5.	Power Sector	717 (0.3)	12,943.7 (3.0)
6.	Others	13,915 (6.5)	36,639.1 (8.6)
	Total	214,211 (100)	427,686.8 (100)

Note : Figures within brackets show percentage to total.

Source : Patel, Amit, (2007), "Rural Financial Institutions in India: Touching the Lives of Millions", *Kurukshetra*, October, p. 13.

With the progressive institutionalisation of rural credit system through adoption of multi-agency approach, farmers dependence on informal sources of credit sharply declined from 92.8 per cent in 1951 to 36 per cent in 1991. More importantly the share of moneylenders (agricultural and professional) declined from 71.6 per cent to 17.1 per cent, and that of banks (cooperatives and commercial) increased from 3.5 per cent to 55.3 per cent during the period under consideration. According to All India Debt and Investment Survey, the share of institutional credit apparently declined from 64 per cent in 1991 to 57 per cent in 2001. Moreover, debt sourced from moneylenders (the very informal agents the institutionalisation of credit was designed to replace) sharply increased in overall share of rural debt from nearly 18 per cent in

1991 to nearly 30 per cent in 2001. According to the recent survey, formal institutional credit provision in India now accounts for just 27 per cent of total cultivator debt, and that this reduces to 20 per cent if data for the five States reporting the highest proportion of formal rural debt are removed. Moreover, nearly 90 per cent of households reporting no debt either formal or informal are headed as small and marginal farmers. Intriguingly, Andhra Pradesh, the State with the highest concentration of SHGs, MFIs and banks, reports the highest proportion of rural non-institutional debt (nearly 73%) and the highest proportion of rural moneylender debt (nearly 57%) for all the States in India.

Findings of NSSO

The findings of the National Sample Survey Organisation revealed the following :

- At the All India level the estimated number of rural households were 147.80 million of which 60.4 per cent (89.35 million) were farmer households.
- Of these farmer households, 48.60 per cent (43.3 million) were reported to be indebted to either formal or informal or both sources of credit.
- This implied that 51.4 per cent (45.93 million farmer households were not indebted at all, and 88 per cent of these excluded farmer households were either marginal farmers (less than one hectare) or small farmers (1-2 hectares).
- The incidence of indebtedness was 60 per cent in four States, viz. Andhra Pradesh (82%), Tamil Nadu (74.5%), Punjab (65.4%) and Kerala (64.4%). However, incidence of indebtedness was lower in the States of Meghalaya (4.1%), Arunachal Pradesh (5.9%), Uttarakhand (7.2%), Assam (18.1%), Jharkhand (20.9%), Mizoram (23.6%), Manipur (24.8%), and Jammu & Kashmir (31.8%).
- This indicated that incidence of indebtedness was relatively

higher in agriculturally advanced States than that in agriculturally less developed States.

- Out of 43.2 million indebted farmers 54 per cent (23.3 million) were indebted to formal sources.
- Of the total farmer households (89.35 million) coverage to formal sources (cooperatives, banks and government) was 28 per cent.
- More than 50 per cent of the indebted farmer households took loans for capital and current expenditure in farm business. Such loans accounted for 58.4 per cent of the outstanding loans.
- The extent of farmer households not indebted to formal or informal sources of credit was more in the case of farmers with landholding of less than one hectare (55%) than farmers with landholdings of four hectares and more (33%).

The findings of the World Bank and National Council of Applied Economic Research (NCAER)[11] conducted in Andhra Pradesh and Uttar Pradesh in 2003 also paints a very disheartening picture. The data reveal that :

- Only 21 per cent rural households had access to formal credit.
- Small and marginal farmers were at a relatively disadvantaged position as only 11.8 per cent of marginal farmers in Andhra Pradesh and 13.5 per cent in Uttar Pradesh secured loans from banks.
- The time taken for loan clearance ranged from 24 to 33 weeks and loans were generally collateralised.

According to NSSO, the rural poverty declined from 27.1 per cent in 1993-94 to 21.1 per cent. This shows that rural areas have still very large number of households below poverty line.

While these shocking findings are engaging the attentions of the Union and State Governments and the Reserve Bank of India and further need immediate comprehensive research, broadly the factors contributing to this development are :

(a) The percentage share of agriculture and allied sectors in the total plan outlay of the annual budgets has sharply declined from 16.4 per cent in the Fourth Five Year Plan to 11.3 in the Fifth Five Year Plan and to 6 per cent in Sixth Five Year Plan.
(b) While total investment in agriculture has been continuously declining from 2.2 per cent to 1.3 per cent of the GDP, the share of public sector investment has also declined from 33 per cent to 17.8 per cent during the period from 1993-94 to 2004-05.
(c) Rural infrastructure as pointed out in Annual District Plans prepared by NABARD has grossly been inadequate.
(d) While commercial banks have financial resources which they have been deploying and their share has significantly increased in the total credit, they have their own limitations.
(e) Cooperative banks being leaders in the field of rural lending are very weak in all respects and are in the process of restructuring and being recapitalised.

Even today approximately 72 per cent of the total population in India lives in rural areas. Lack of access to financial services for the vast majority of Indian population is the biggest hurdle in realising the full growth potential of the economy in this non-urban part of the country. Credit is a kind of key, a passport to explore the potential of a person. Credit was the missing link between people and their creative potential. It was required to make credit available to more and more poor people to give them the chance of better future. Therefore, rural credit has to play a critical role in the socio-economic development of the country.

Despite all the noble efforts on the part of the government and non-government agencies, access to financial services for all at affordable rates remains a distant dream. Remoteness of the rural areas and poor infrastructure lead to market inefficiencies and a huge gap between demand and supply of credit. Problem is compounded by the fact that the rural population is still largely illiterate and not so technology driven (technology itself comes at

cost). For the overall development of the country these problems related to rural credit should be addressed in a proper way. Steps are required at both policy level and organisational level to solve these problems.

Summary

Self-help group (SHG) is an association of body of people which is homogeneous, has a common aim and whose members in one way or the other help one another. It is a micro-cooperative. All or a majority of members of an SHG may be drawn from the low income strata, for instance SHGs have come to encompass a wide range of activities, to overcoming problems of addiction and ensuring safe sex. While the SHG in the developing countries have been dealing with disabilities apart from other activities, the most important job it has taken up is the propagation of microfinance. It has been increasingly realised that lending to an SHG offers unique opportunities, since the recovery rate is between 90 and 100 per cent.

The proportion of all rural households borrowing from formal credit agencies has been steadily increasing, as revealed in the All India Debt Investment Survey Reports (1951, 1961, 1971 and 1981) from 7.2 per cent in 1951 to 17.3 per cent in 1961, to 29.2 per cent in 1971 and 61.2 per cent in 1981. Also the percentage of non-cultivator borrowers depending on non-formal sources of credit (agriculturist money lender, professional money lenders, landlord and trader) continued to be above 50 per cent. The dependence of the rural poor on non-institutional sources of credit is one of the causes that perpetuate their poverty and restrict surplus generation to maintain their meagre economic activities and households.

There is a clear inverse relationship between incidence of poverty reflected by asset holding of the household expenditure. There is also a positive relationship between the wealth of the household and the debt contracted for productive purposes (crop loan, etc.).

It is discernible that the cooperative credit institutions were

virtually the only institutions providing credit for agricultural activities till 1970-71, when the commercial banks made a beginning in this area. With the spread of their branches the commercial bank moved fast by 1988-89 when they adopted Service Area Approach, they claimed more than 41 per cent of the share in disbursement of agricultural credit and about 54 per cent in outstanding agricultural credit. The market share of the regional rural banks in agricultural credit by this time was a mere 5 per cent but the credit had gone entirely to rural poor. The demand for credit had risen fast from year to year and figures of annual disbursements for agricultural purposes moved from Rs. 7,438 million in 1970-71 to Rs. 91,062 million in 1988-89 untill the concept of Service Area Approach was implemented. And now the disbursements have shot up to Rs. 1,574,800 million in 2005-06.

Dependence of rural households on non-institutional sources of credit was as high as 92.8 per cent in the 1951, just four years after India's independence, which declined to 82.7 per cent in 1961 and further to 70.8 per cent in 1971 when cooperative credit institutions made their presence felt on the rural scene after acceptance and implementation of recommendations of the All India Rural Credit Survey Committee in 1954 and entry of major private sector banks after their nationalisation in the year 1969. Access of rural households to formal credit institutions sharply increased to 61.2 per cent in 1981, partly because of enabling measures initiated by the Reserve Bank of India to direct public sector banks towards rural lending and partly because of the establishment of the Regional Rural Banks from the year 1975 onwards specifically to cater to the credit needs of rural poor households. However, in the year 1991, there was only marginal increase in the institutional sources of credit from 61.2 per cent in 1981 to 64 per cent in 1991. While dependence of rural households on professional moneylenders in particular declined from 46.4 per cent in 1951 to 8.3 per cent in 1991. Role of agricultural money-lenders had also decreased progressively from 47 per cent in 1961 to 7.1 per cent in 1991. The performance of commercial banks was very spectacular between 1971 and 1981

but it showed little improvement in 1991. Cooperative had shown good performance from 1961 to 1981 but its performance declined in 1991.

The goal of the Government of India as announced by the Finance Minister in the budget speech in 2004, to double the flow of farm-credit in three years (2004-05 to 2006-07) was achieved in two years. Actual flow of credit during the year 2006-07 exceeded the target of Rs. 1,750,000 million set for the year by Rs. 150,000 million. During April to December 2006, about 5,337,000 new farmers, as against the target of 5 million, were linked with the institutional credit system. For the year 2007-08, the target of farm credit disbursement was fixed at Rs. 2,250,000 million (28.6 per cent over the target of 2006-07) and an addition of 5 million new farmer-borrowers.

Total disbursements progressively increased from Rs. 620,450 million in 2001-02 to Rs. 574,800 million in the year 2005-06, reflecting a rise by 153.8 per cent. Commercial banks and regional rural banks recorded phenomenal rise by 216 per cent and 189 per cent respectively as compared to 58 per cent by cooperatives. While there has been progressive rise in each successive year in the case of cooperatives, commercial banks and regional rural banks, there has been spectacular increase during 2004-05 and 2005-06 in respect of commercial banks and regional rural banks. The share of cooperatives in the total disbursements of short-term and long-term credit progressively declined from 37.91 per cent in 2001-02 to 23.65 per cent in 2005-06 whereas that of the commercial banks recorded progressive increase from 54.13 per cent to 67.41 per cent during the corresponding years. The regional rural banks accounted for 7.82 per cent in 2001-02 which progressively rose to 9.91 per cent in 2004-05 but declined by one percentage point in the following year. The flow of agricultural credit for the banking system as a whole during 2005-06 has surged to Rs. 1,804,860 million, reflecting 128 per cent of the target of Rs. 1,410,000 million which was set for the year.

The proportion of short-term credit to enable farmers to conduct seasonal agricultural operation was around 63 per cent as against 37 per cent of long term credit for investment purposes.

Under the service area approach to rural financial services the annual growth of target was between 12.5 per cent and 24 per cent respectively during 2000-01 and 2003-04. The growth was spectacularly high at 54.5 per cent during 2004-05 which, however, declined to 44.6 per cent in the following year. Disbursements of credit as against targets ranged for the six years period. Achievements were higher than 100 per cent only in the last two years.

Public sector banks recovery to demand under direct agricultural advance were 69.3 per cent during the year 2000-01 which gradually increased during the following three years. It, however, phenomenally rose to 84.1 per cent in the year 2004-05. During the five years period, the demand (loan amount to be recovered) and percentage of recovery to demand have progressively increased in the successive years whereas overdue amount has increased until the year 2003-04 and then it steeply declined by Rs. 29,620 million in the following years.

During the seven-year period from 2000 to 2006, the public sector bank's outstanding credit to priority sectors increased by 221.9 per cent from Rs. 1,274,780 million as on 31st March, 2000 to Rs. 4,103,790 million as on 31st March, 2006, whereas that of the private sector banks shot up by 480.2 per cent from Rs. 183,680 million to Rs. 1,065,660 million during the period under consideration. Priority sector advances of public sector banks as group accounted for over 43 per cent of net bank credit in four years as against the target of 40 per cent which, however declined from 42.8 per cent to 40.3 per cent in three years. In this respect, private sector banks as a group had less than that of targeted 40 per cent during initial three years, but they showed impressive performance (42.8% to 47.3%) in the following four years.

Agricultural advances by the public sector banks during the period rose by 242 per cent from Rs. 452,960 million to Rs. 1,549,000 million whereas that of the private sector banks increased significantly by 799 per cent from Rs. 40,230 million to Rs. 361,850 million during the period under consideration. The share of agricultural advances in the net bank credit by the public sector banks ranged between 14.3 per cent and 15.7 per cent,

whereas that of the private sector banks varied from 8.3 per cent to 14.2 per cent during the period under consideration. Neither public sector banks, nor private sector banks as a group could achieve targeted agricultural credit of 18 per cent of net bank credit.

During 2005-06, all public sector banks (except State Bank of India and State Bank of Patiala) were able to meet the priority sector target for agriculture. None of the private sector banks could meet sub-target for lending to agriculture.

During the period from 2001-02 to 2005-06, banks provided 59,093,000 Kisan Credit Cards to farmers to facilitate them to purchase farm inputs and other requirements. Share of the commercial banks was 37 per cent as against the shares of cooperatives and regional rural banks at 51 per cent and 12 per cent respectively.

The refinance provided by NABARD to banks has significantly increased from Rs. 45,210 million in 1998-99 to Rs. 86,223.7 million in 2005-06. Only the commercial banks availed significantly increased of refinance in successive years. Share of refinance in the total agricultural loans disbursed by cooperatives was as high as 50.3 per cent, followed by commercial banks at 31.4 per cent whereas regional rural banks accounted for 18 per cent.

As on the 31st March, 2006, the number of SHGs linked with banks were as high as 2,238,565 as compared to 1,079,091 in 2004 and 1,618,456 in 2005. Credit disbursed to these SHGs was also as high as Rs. 113,975.3 million in 2005. Share of commercial banks in respect of number of SHGs linked with banks and credit disbursed was the highest followed by the regional rural banks and cooperatives.

The commercial banks falling short of achieving priority sector/agricultural lending targets have since 1995-96 till 2005-06 deposited Rs. 287,499.5 million with NABARD under Rural Infrastructure Development Fund at very reduced interest rate. The NABARD has so far disbursed a sum of Rs. 322,893.3 million to support 244,651 projects in various parts of the country.

The share of irrigation development projects in terms of

number was the highest at 38.7 per cent, followed by social sector and rural roads, whereas in terms of amount disbursed, the irrigation development accounted for as high as 34.3 per cent share followed by rural roads, rural bridges and social sector.

Despite all the noble efforts on the part of the governmental agencies, access to financial services for all at affordable rates remains a distant dream. Remoteness of the rural areas and poor infrastructure leads to market inefficiencies and a huge gap between demand and supply of credit. Problem is compounded by the fact that the rural population is still largely illiterate and not so technology driven (technology itself comes at cost). For the overall development of the country these problems related to rural credit should be addressed in a proper way. Step are required at both policy level and organisational level to solve these problems.

REFERENCES

1. World Bank (1997), "Emerging Issues in Development Economies", *World Bank Policy and Research Bulletin*, October-December.
2. Brouman, F.J.A. (1984), "Informal Savings and Credit Arrangements in Developing Countries: Observations from Sri Lanka" in Dale W. Adams, G.H. Graham and J.D. Von Pischke, (eds.), Undermining Rural Development with Cheap Credit, Westview Press, London.
3. Desai, Bhupat M. and N.K. Namboodiri (1996), "Whither Financial Institutions", *Economic and Political Weekly*, Vol. 31, No. 31, August 03.
4. Zellor, Manfred and Manohar Sharma (1998), Rural Finance and Poverty Alleviation, (Food Policy Report), International Food Policy Research Institute, Washington D.C., USA.
5. United Nations (1998), "United Nations General Assembly Resolution 52/194 passed in December 1997 (1998)", in count down 2005, *Newsletter of the Micro Credit Summit Campaign*, Vol. I, No. 3, February-March.
6. Namboodiri, N.V. and R.L. Sayani (2001), "Potential Role of Self-Help Groups in Rural Financial Deepening", *Indian Journal of Agricultural Economies*, Vol. 56, No. 3, July-September, p. 401.

7. Karmakar, K.G. (1999), *Rural Credit and Self-Help Groups*, Sage Publications, New Delhi, p. 207.
8. Smith, D.H. and K. Pillhiemer (1983), "Self-Help Groups as Social Movement Organisations: Social Structure and Social Change", *Research in Social Movements, Conflicts and Change*, Vol. 5, No. 2.
9. Brouman, F.J.A. (1984), *op. cit.*
10. Patel, Amit (2007), "Rural Financial Institutions in India: Touching the Lives of Millions", *Kurukshetra*, Vol. 55, No. 12, October, p. 4.
11. World Bank and NCAER (2005), *Rural Financial Access Survey* (2003), New Delhi.

5

Self-Help Groups, Microfinance and Rural Development in India

Self-Help Groups

"Behold what is rapidly becoming the largest self-help undertaking in human history, bringing hope, dignity and empowerment to tens of millions of low income families worldwide. Behold a movement with global outreach, which has penetrated beyond city slum and market towns to even the most isolated villages. Behold an industry that embraces thousands of NGOs, credit unions, public and private banks, and hundreds of thousands of community-based self-help groups, which are enabling many of the planet's poorest households to generate the additional income and savings they need to keep their children alive, nourished, healthy and able to attend school. Behold a profession which appears simple in concept but is extremely difficult to practice, because it involves myriad adjustments to highly different cultural settings, methodologies, and institutional structures, while simultaneously facing complex challenges involving client outreach, financing, evaluation, governance, training, government regulation, economic instability, civil disturbances and natural disasters."

"NABARD/India : Of all the innovations reported in this paper, the one which has achieved the largest scale to the world's

poorest families is clearly the savings-led self-help group programme of the National Bank for Agricultural and Rural Development (NABARD). Building on an infrastructure of 1,42,000 rural and semi-urban branches whom NABARD refinances (one for every four villages in India), NABARD has enrolled the participation of 750 NGOs as facilitators of 3,64,000 client-managed self-help groups (SHGs), averaging 16 members each, to serve 5.8 million rural saver-borrowers of whom 85 per cent are women. These SHGs mobilise their own savings, transforming them into loans to members (average loan size less than $22), and plow their earnings from interest income back in to equity. After a year or so, the experienced SHG is allowed to supplement their member loan portfolio by borrowing from their nearest NABARD supported bank branch office. The programme's on-time payment rate is 95 per cent. NABARD is currently negotiating with international donors for loan funding in excess of $1 billion to further expand its hybrid public-private-SHG methodology to tens of millions of additional rural clients both within India as well as throughout the Asian region." ["Innovations from the Field : A Daringly Brief Summary of a Huge Phenomenon" by John K. Hutch with Sara R. Levine and Amanda Penn, (June 2002).][1]

Ever since the first bout of nationalisation of commercial banks in July 1969, credit planning has become an integral part of overall national development planning. Since the soul of India lives in its villages, and agriculture is the mainstay for majority of its populace, credit planning for agricultural and rural development received a priority status. The features of a typical loan product evolved as equal to that were: (i) a large per unit cost with or without state subsidy, (ii) concessional or market rate of interest, (iii) a longer repayment period, and (iv) backed by physical collateral as security.

With the above loan-products, the credit needs of the poorest of the poor—those surviving on a day-to-day basis without ensured food, shelter, health-care, education and so on—requiring small sums with shorter repayment periods and not able to provide physical collaterals but are quite prepared to pay an interest rate somewhat higher than the one prevailing in formal sector, could

not be institutionalised. And in a typical Third World country like India, they constitute one-third of population. Financial products are considered as the building-blocks of a country's economy. With one-third lacking these building-blocks, one cannot usher in an all-inclusive nation building process.

Experiences of the different anti-poverty and other welfare programmes implemented throughout the world in general and India in particular have shown that the key to their success lies in the evolution and participation of community based organisations at the grassroots level. People's participation in credit delivery and linking formal credit institutions to borrowers through intermediaries of self-help groups (SHGs) have been recognised as supplementary to the rural poor. The National Bank for Agricultural and Rural Development (NABARD) is a pioneer in conceptualising and implementing the concept of SHGs-Bank linkage programme since 1992.

The SHGs are small informal and homogeneous groups of not more than 20 members each. The group has been recommended to be informal to keep them away from bureaucracy and corruption, unnecessary expenditure and profit constraints. The size of 20 members has been made mandatory, because any group larger than this would need to be registered under the Indian legal system. There is, however, something beyond this. These groups are expected to foster true (direct) democratic culture where all the members participate actively by taking part in debate and decision making process which is possible in small groups, otherwise when the group becomes larger, direct democracy tends towards indirect democracy—a coterie of decision making and formation of vested interest within the group. Groups are expected to be homogeneous so that the members do not have conflicting interest and all the members can participate freely without any fear and adverse consequence.

The exponential trend equation of the type $y = ab^x$ has been fitted into the time-series data on the number of SHGs linkage, amount of bank loan to SHGs, amount of refinance assistance to SHGs from NABARD, and the amount of bank loan per SHG. On the basis of this trend equation, the compound growth rate per annum of all the

4 variables have been estimated. The students t-distribution has been applied to test the level of significance of the estimates of the growth rates.[2] The following formulae have been used :

Exponential trend equation: $Y = ab^x$

Logarithmic form of the equation :

$$\text{Log } Y = \log a + x \cdot \log b$$

Corresponding normal equations :

$$\Sigma \log y = N \cdot \log a + \log bx$$

$$\Sigma x \cdot \log y = \log a \cdot \Sigma x + \log b \cdot \Sigma x^2$$

Compound growth rate : $GR = 100 \cdot (b - 1)$

$$Syx = \sqrt{\frac{\Sigma \log y^2 - \log a \cdot \Sigma \log y - \log b \cdot \Sigma x \cdot \log y}{N - K}}$$

$$Sb = \frac{Syx}{\Sigma (x - \bar{x})^2}$$

$$t = \frac{\log b - 0}{sb}$$

Where

y = Number of SHGs-linkage,
Amount of bank loans to SHGs,
Amount of refinance assistance to SHGs from NABARD,
and Amount of bank loan per SHG.

x = Number of years = 14 (from 1992-93 to 2005-06)

a = Intercept (parameter)

b = Trend value (parameter)

GR = Compound Growth Rate per cent per annum.

Syx = Standard errors of estimates.

N = Number of years = 14

K = Number of constraints in the equation = 2

Sb = Standard deviation of b

t = Student's t-statistics.

Analysis

Table 5.1 presents the picture of commulative progress in respect of SHG-bank linkage, amount of bank loan, and amount of refinance assistance to the SHGs from the NABARD during the period 1992-93 to 2005-06. It is very much clear from the table that the number of SHGs linked with banks increased cumulatively from 255 in 1992-93 to 2,238,565 in 2005-06. The amount of bank loans to the SHGs during the period under consideration increased from Rs. 2.9 million to Rs. 113,975 million. Similarly, the amount of refinance assistance to the SHGs from NABARD increased from Rs. 2.7 million in 1992-93 to Rs. 41,597 million in 2005-06.

Table 5.1 : Cumulative Progress in Self-Help Groups-Linkage Programme in India (1992-93 to 2005-06)

Year	*SHG-Linkage (Number)*	*Bank Loan (Rs. Millions)*	*Refinance Assistance (Rs. Millions)*
1	2	3	4
1992-93	255	2.9	2.7
1993-94	620	6.5	4.6
1994-95	2122	24.4	23
1995-96	4757	60.6	51.6
1996-97	8598	118.4	106.5
1997-98	14317	273.6	213.9
1998-99	32995	570.7	520.6
1999-00	94645	1929.7	1501.3
2000-01	234873	4808.7	4007.2
2001-02	461478	10203.0	7965.0
2002-03	717360	20487.0	14188.0
2003-04	1079091	39042.0	21242.0
2004-05	1618456	68985.0	30920.0
2005-06	2238565	113975.0	41597.0

Sources :

1. NABARD (2001), NABARD and Micro Finance, NABARD, Mumbai.
2. NABARD (2002), NABARD and Micro Finance, NABARD, Mumbai.
3. NABARD (2004), Progress of SHG-Bank Linkage, NABARD, Mumbai.
4. NABARD (2005), Progress of SHG-Bank Linkage, NABARD, Mumbai.
5. NABARD (2006), Progress of SHG-Bank Linkage, NABARD, Mumbai.

The year-wise progress of SHG-bank linkage from 1992-93 to 2005-06 has been produced in Table 5.2. Table 5.2 reveals that

the number of SHGs linked with banks increased from 255 in 1992-93 to 6,20,109 in 2005-06 on the year-after-year basis. The amount of bank loan to SHGs increased from Rs. 2.9 million in 1992-93 to Rs. 49,090 million in 2005-06. Similarly, the amount of refinance assistance from NABARD increased from Rs. 2.7 million in 1992-93 to Rs. 10,677 million in 2005-06. Finally, the average amount of loan per SHG increased from Rs. 11,373 in 1992-93 to Rs. 79,164 in 2005-06.

Table 5.2 : Yearly Progress of SHG-Bank Linkage in India (1992-93 to 2005-06)

Year	*SHG-Linkage (Number)*	*Bank Loan (Rs. Millions)*	*Refinance Assistance (Rs. Millions)*	*Bank Loan SHG*
1	2	3	4	5
1992-93	255	2.9	2.7	11373
1993-94	365	3.6	1.9	9863
1994-95	1502	17.9	18.4	11917
1995-96	2635	36.2	28.8	13730
1996-97	3841	57.8	54.9	15048
1997-98	5719	119.2	107.4	20843
1998-99	18678	333.1	306.7	17834
1999-00	61650	1350	980.7	22044
2000-01	140198	2879	2505.9	20535
2001-02	226635	5454.3	3957.8	24066
2002-03	255882	10224	6223	39956
2003-04	361731	18555	7034	51295
2004-05	539365	29943	9698	55515
2005-06	620109	49090	10677	79164

Sources:
1. NABARD (2001), NABARD and Micro Finance, NABARD, Mumbai.
2. NABARD (2002), NABARD and Micro Finance, NABARD, Mumbai.
3. NABARD (2004), Progress of SHG-Bank Linkage, NABARD, Mumbai.
4. NABARD (2005), Progress of SHG-Bank Linkage, NABARD, Mumbai.
5. NABARD (2006), Progress of SHG-Bank Linkage, NABARD, Mumbai.

The growth trends in SHG- bank linkage have been presented in Table 5.3. The table makes it very much clear that the SHG-bank linkage has increased at the rate of 90.90 per cent per annum during the period 1992-93 to 2005-06. While the bank loan increased at the rate of 121.37 per cent per annum, the amount of refinance assistance to SHGs from NABARD increased at the rate

of 104.16 per cent per annum during the period under consideration. Finally, the amount of bank loan per SHG increased at the rate of 15.96 per cent per annum during the period under consideration. All these growth rates have been found statistically highly significant.

Table 5.3: Trends in SHG-Bank Linkage Programme in India (1992-93 to 2005-06)

Items	*Geometric Mean*	*Growth Rate (1% per annum)*	*t-value*	*Level of Significance*
1	2	3	4	5
1. SHG-Bank Linkage	22617.25	+90.9	9.808	0.001
2. Bank Loan	Rs. 15.03 million	+121.37	9.561	0.001
3. Refinance Assistance	Rs. 334.21 million	+104.16	8.913	0.001
4. Average Bank Loan per SHG	Rs. 22,771.36	+15.96	6.087	0.001

Source : Estimated on the basis of Table 5.2.

Grameen Bank and Group Lending in Bangladesh

Bangladesh with per capita annual income at around US$ 254 only is one of the poorest and least developed countries in the world. Among the rural population the incidence of poverty was as high at around 58 per cent. It was equally high at around 42 per cent among the urban population. Significantly, both among rural and urban poor around one-third was the hard-core poor, under such policy imperatives, the Government of Bangladesh evolved multipronged strategies and programmes to address the problem of poverty in the country. The essential features of the government sponsored poverty elevation programmes included recognition of traditional top-to-down approach based on the trickle down strategy, channelling large government resources to the poor through provisions of sufficient services, emphasising on redistribution of income and assets, promoting programmes of income generating activities and ensuring transfer of income to the poor, including provision of social safety nets. However, it is

well-recognised that the efforts of the government could not succeed to break the shackles of poverty.

The absence of institutional credit further restricted the efficacy of the planned efforts in tackling the problem of poverty in the country. Formal banking sector of the country comprising 4 nationalised banks, 4 government sponsored specialised banks, 18 private sector banks, 14 foreign banks and 14 non-banking financial institutions, all of them together having a rural network of 2,700 branches could hardly make their presence felt in the poverty eradication measures.

The microfinance institutions (MFIs) in Bangladesh have been in operation for a sufficiently long period of time. The important microfinance institutions in Bangladesh are the Grameen Bank itself, micro-credit programmes organised by internationally acclaimed Bangladesh non-government organisations (NGOs), such as Bangladesh Rural Advancement Committee (BRAC), Association for Social Action (ASA), and Proshika, and the Bangladesh Government's microcredit programme—Rural Development Project-12 (RD-12) and the Thana Resources Development and Employment Programme (TRDEP). Some of the largest and best known microfinance institutions of Bangladesh have modelled the organisational structure of their micro-lending programmes on the Grameen Bank, so that one may speak of a 'Grameen System' as Harper[3] puts it, that is used not only by more than million clients but also by each of Proshika and BRAC. Furthermore, it has been estimated that over 10 million clients in Bangladesh use the *grameen* system through 30 micro-finance institutions with more than 10,000 clients and hundreds of other organisations which are following the *grameen* model in Bangladesh.[4] In their study of the BRAC and the governments Thana Resource Development and Employment Programme, Montgomery and others[5] note that the lending players in microfinance in Bangladesh have designed programmes which are practically indistinguishable from each other and offer little by way of alternative programme design to clients.

The Grameen Bank owes its origin to the concern felt by its founder Professor Mohammad Yunus at the pitiable conditions of landless women labourers who were exploited both by their masters and in their own families. Professor Yunus felt that if these women could work for themselves instead of working for others, they could retain much of the surplus generated by their labour, currently appropriated by other and benefit their families. Professor Yunus first himself gave loan to women during famine in 1974. The first loan he gave was to the tune of $27 from his own pocket. He lent it to 42 women basket weavers in the village Jobra. After sometime he discovered that they could repay the amount quickly. He set up the Grameen Bank in 1976, and started giving loans to the poor. In 1983 he officially and legally formed the Grameen Bank on the principle of 'trust and solidarity'.

The Grameen Bank method of lending is very simple. Five poor rural women are made to form a group. Eight groups form a centre/kendra, normally in the same village. They meet once in a week and discuss and deal only in microfinance. They seek loan for productive income purposes or for education and housing. The loans are approved on the basis of satisfactory credit history and purpose. All the members save regularly and repay weekly and share responsibility.

Table 5.4 presents the picture of the progress of the Grameen Bank project of rural development. It is evident from the table that the number of villages covered by the Grameen Bank project increased from 363 in December 1980 to 1,88,125 in August 1990. The number of branches of the bank increased from 25 to 741 during the same period. The number of members of the bank increased from 0.05 lakh in December 1980 to 7.90 lakh in August 1990. The number of males and females of the bank increased from 0.59 lakh and 1.13 lakh in December 1985 to 0.75 lakh and 7.15 lakh respectively in August 1990. The number of groups of the bank increased from 2,935 in 1980 to 98,073 in 1988. The number of borrowers of the bank was 0.15 lakh in 1980 which rose to 4.72 lakh in 1988.

Table 5.4 : Progress of Grameen Bank of Bangladesh (1980 to 1990)

	Items	*As at 1980*	*The end of 1985*	*December 1980*	*August 1990*
1	2	3	4	5	6
1.	Number of villages covered	365	3,666	10,522	1,88,125
2.	Number of branches	25	266	501	741
3.	Number of members (lakh)	0.15	1.72	4	7.9
	Males	N.A.	0.59	0.69	0.75
	Females	N.A.	1.13	4.21	7.15
4.	Number of groups	2,935	3,43,244	98,073	N.A.
5.	Number of borrowers (lakh)	0.12	1.52	4.72	N.A.
6.	Loan distributed (taka crore)	1.71	42.84	128.04	N.A.
7.	Cumulative position of loans since inception and upto the end of the year (taka crore	2.01	92.77	155.94	681.07
8.	Saving in Group Fund (taka crore)	0.15	7.14	298.74	57.45
9.	Savings in Emergency Fund	N.A.	1.26	5.45	11.16
10.	Loan from Group Fund (cumulative disbursement since inception) (taka crore)	N.A.	2.23	13.19	30.91

Source : Karmakar, K.G. (1999), *Rural Credit and Self-Help Groups: Micro Finance Needs and Concepts*, Sage Publications, Delhi, pp. 275-76.

In 1980, the bank had disbursed the loan of 1.71 taka crore. The corresponding figure for 1988 was Taka 128.04 crore. The cumulative amount of loan disbursed increased from Taka 2.01 crore in 1980 to Taka 681.07 crore in August 1990. The savings in group fund increased from Taka 0.15 crore in December 1980 to Taka 57.45 crore in August 1990. The savings in emergency fund of the bank increased from Taka 1.6 crore in 1985 to 11.16 taka crore in August 1990. The loans from group fund (cumulative disbursement since inception) increased from Taka 2.23 crore in 1985 to Taka 30.91 crore in 1990.

As of July 2004, the Grameen Bank of Bangladesh has 3.7 million borrowers, 96 per cent of whom are women. With 1,267 branches the Grameen Bank provides services in 46,000 villages covering more than 68 per cent of the total village in Bangladesh.

The Bangladesh Grameen Bank has a unique approach to provide credit to the rural poor. It imposes a strict discipline on the borrowers as well as the bank staff. The management also services the poorest of the poor in the rural areas who would otherwise have not been eligible for credit from other institutions. By virtue of peer pressure among its borrowers and loan supervision, the Grameen Bank has achieved a repayment recorded in an area which other credit schemes fail. An elaborate system of discipline and supervision incorporated into loan procedures and characterises its credit operations as well as related social development activities. Individually the procedures may not be significant but together, constitute a formidable system.[6]

The study of Abdullah and others[7] makes an attempt to determine the extent to which empowerment factors affect women's decision making of the loan use. The results indicate that the minimalist credit programme of the Grameen Bank has better empowering impact on clients than the integrated approach of the BRAC. The study conceptualises empowerment as a function of the decision process and constructs a composite index on the basis of other empowerment of individual woman. On the basis of these two indicators, it was found that the Grameen Bank's minimalist approach is more empowering for the woman than the BRAC's integrated approach.

Researchers have pointed to the low levels of institutional innovation within the microfinance sector on account of the propensity to produce clones of the Grameen Bank model and have agreed that the propagation of the 'Grameen Model' has assumed hegemonic dimension within the microfinance industry, not only within Bangladesh, but globally as well, due to the active promotion of the Grameen model, especially by the Consultative Group to Assist the Poorest (CGAP), as the ideal model for emulation by microcredit NGOs focusing their services on the rural poor.[8] Prominent global institutions such as the International

Fund for Agricultural Development (IFAD) and the Asian Development Bank have expressed their willingness to support only those credit-programmes which are based on the Grameen model.[9] The Grameen Trust established with a mandate of extending financial and technical assistance to Grameen Replicators, was supporting 70 projects in 30 countries in Asia, Africa, Europe and the Americas in the year 2000. It has been estimated that the Grameen Bank lending model has been replicated in 56 countries including developed nations as Canada and U.S.A.

Strengths of the Grameen Bank Model

The Grameen Bank Model did demonstrate a number of positive contributions. These institutions functioned by and large with well defined corporate missions, often enlarging their service/ product baskets to include both credit and non-credit functions. Alleviation of poverty by raising the income level and providing employment opportunities to the rural poor remained the major thrust of their operations. The gender emphasis for larger and wider coverage of women beneficiaries was loud and clear in their operations. More significantly, participative approach in the decision making formed the nucleus of their operations. At the same time, decision making at the group and branch levels was transparent and accountable. Above all, the group, mostly consisting of five members formed the basis of their structural design. Again, homogeneity rather than heterogeneity formed the basic principle of group formation. Team spirit both within and outside the group was strong among the members. Further, group-based lending was the focal approach of these institutions. The group with the help of the branch and its field worker carried out all credit and deposit related functions. Besides, these institutions had introduced multiple savings and credit products to serve different needs of their rural clients.

Significantly enough, linkages between and among members, groups, centres/kendras and the branches were observed to be well defined with strong bondage. Again, the procedural simplicities

in the sanction and disbursement of credit made these institutions flexible. For example, a member of the group could raise loan in a particular group meeting without making much paper work and visiting the branch office. Use of collateral security was totally absent in these institutions. In other words, the loans were collateral free. Instead, the group guarantee provided the risk coverage of a loan. Innovative approach to cover lending risk through insurance premium on the borrower loan was also observed in these institutions. Disciplined repayment ethics with weekly equated instalments were the cornerstone of these institutions. As a result of procedural simplicities and lower administrative expenses, the transaction cost appeared to be quite low. Resource cost was also low on account of heavy dependence on donor fund as also low interests on their saving products. Non- credit functions in terms of education, health and hygiene as also family welfare measures were equally dominant. Monitoring and supervision mechanism from the top also seemed to be efficient. Further, low NPAs (non-profiting assets) due to high recovery rate and wider interest spread, the financial health of these institutions appeared to be sound.[10]

Weaknesses of the Grameen Bank Model

A closer scrutiny of the operations of the microfinance model in Bangladesh revealed a number of weaknesses in terms of both conceptual framework as well as operational designs adopted to achieve their missions. There was no doubt that they had introduced a wide range of credit products to serve different credit needs of their clientele. However, none of these credit products showed to be based on the concept of the project approach. As a result, there seemed to be hardly any regard for economic rational in assignment of the investment cost, margin money, bank loan, economic life of the assets, repayment period, grace period, etc. by these institutions. All such decisions seemed to be loaded with naked arbitrariness. Needless to say, this adversely affected the interests of the borrowers of the robbing/depriving them of what could have been their legitimate. Besides, given the low level of transaction and resource cost as also low

risk in view of almost negligible default rate, the monopoly profit through high interest rates seemed to be as exploitative as traditional moneylenders.

In the process, the microfinance models in Bangladesh contrary to their loud claims appeared to have become a mere substitute of traditional moneylenders. More important, with most of the lending portfolios under consumption segments, the micro-credit programmes did not seem to generate much productive assets and promote incremental income. It created conditions and laid traps for mass rural indebtedness. Again, given the high investment cost and low yield levels as also low price realisation, most of the agricultural based investments showed a relatively lower financial rate of return in the range of 10 per cent. This did not compare favourably with the high interest rate being charged by most of the borrowers through income generated outside the investment. With low rate of return, investments in activities based on borrowing from these institutions thus seemed to be non-sustainable.

With the increasing presence of these institutions, the credit accessibility level of the rural mass in Bangladesh has certainly increased in recent years. However, the accessibility continues to be restricted to the relatively better sections, leaving aside the vast chunk of the hard-core poor. Besides, it may be recalled that these institutions had introduced an inbuilt insurance premium in some of the credit products to be charged from the borrowers as a risk cover. However, with default rate as low as 2-3 per cent and almost no beneficiary showing to have benefited out of the scheme in the preceding few years, the perceived risk seemed to be a mere instrument of seeking zero cost fund. The insurance premium charged on the credit products had thus no economic rational, and was, therefore, not warranted. It must be admitted that such an insurance premium on the loan amount became an additional cost for the borrower.[11] Given the low rate of return, it further narrowed and eroded the viability of the investment. Further, the operations of the microfinance institutions in Bangladesh fell outside the ambit of the control over these institutions and being left free to accept public deposits, the

depositors interests and risks remained unprotected. Transparency of the accounting system also seemed to be blurred in some cases. The miscellaneous head of account without much break-up was observed to be as high as 50 per cent of the total expenditure. Most important, these institutions seemed to be donor-dependent with almost 50-60 per cent of their resources emanating from donations. Once this specific source dries up, the sustainability of these institutions would become a big question mark.

The Indian microfinance experience, based primarily on self-help groups of rural poor, represents an experience which differs quite significantly, at the level of policy, institutional ramifications and organisational specificities from the dominant Bangladesh MFIs model. It has been observed that more autonomous and self-managed mode of operations of SHGs could imply freedom from excessive dependence on the MFIs and, therefore, greater manoeuvrability so as to respond better to the needs and special circumstances of poorer individuals within groups. The global debates on the differential income impact of micro-credit programme acquire resonance in the Indian context in the light of the older experience with self-employment initiative for the poor and the rich legacy of Indian scholarship on this question may hold significant lessons which unsettle established microfinance orthodoxies. It has been suggested that conversion of SHGs into channels for the delivery of the Swarnajayanti Gram Swarozgar Yojana (SGSY) credit imply a loss of flexibility of the earlier SHG-bank linkage programme under attack from the exclusive enterprise focus of the SGSY. It is under the question mark whether the diminishing volume of institutional credit to the designated weaker sections within priority sector lending, and the greater profit orientation of the commercial banking structure, since the inception of the banking sector reforms, bode well for the agenda of expanding the access of the poor to the institutional credit despite the mounting statistics on the number of SHGs linked to banks with every passing year.

The microfinance model in Bangladesh despite a few weaknesses did demonstrate a number of strong positive

attributes in terms of operational simplicities, better accessibilities, wider outreaches, emphasis on women empowerment and availability of a wide range of credit and non-credit services. After crossing over their infancy, they have emerged as alternative players in the rural financial credit market of Bangladesh. With restricted outreach of the formal credit agencies in India, microfinance models of Bangladesh do offer a few lessons to us in our efforts to tackle the twin problem of mass poverty and unemployment.

Self-Help Groups, Swarnajayanti Gram Swarozgar Yojana and Poverty Eradication

Poverty and unemployment anywhere are danger for peace and prosperity everywhere. Despite efforts made over past few decades, rural poverty in India continues to be significant. While the anti-poverty programmes have been strengthened in successive years, and while in percentage terms poverty level has reduced from 56.44 per cent in India's population in 1973-74 to about 26 per cent in 2003-04, it is needed to redress the situation quickly. It is in this context that the self-employment programmes assume significance, for they alone can provide income to the rural poor on a sustainable basis.[12]

Anti-poverty programmes have been dominant features of government initiatives in the rural areas. The programmes have been reviewed and strengthened in the successive years in order to sharpen their focus on reduction of rural poverty. The results achieved in the meanwhile are worth noting. Some States have been more successful in reducing their poverty (rural) during 1973-74 to 2003-04. These States are Andhra Pradesh, Goa, Gujarat, Karnataka, Kerala, Rajasthan, Tamil Nadu and West Bengal. However, the cause of concern is that the estimated number of the poor is still about 244 million which has led to further review and restructuring of the anti-poverty programme.[13] The Swarnajayanti Gram Swarozgar Yojana is the result of such latest review and restructuring of the programmes.

Swarnajayanti Gram Swarozgar Yojana

A new programme known as 'Swarnajayanti Gram Swarozgar Yojana' (SGSY) has been launched from April 1999. The SGSY is a holistic programme covering all aspects of self-employment such as organisation of the poor into self-help group, training, credit, technology, infrastructure and marketing. The SGSY is funded by the Centre and the States in the ratio of 75 : 25.

With the coming into force of the SGSY, the earlier programmes—Integrated Rural Development Programme (IRDP), Training of Youth for Self-Employment (TRYSEM), Development of Women and Children in Rural Areas (DWACRA), Supply of Improved Toolkits to Rural Artisans (SITRA), Ganga Kalyan Yojana (GKY) and Million Shallow Tubewells (MST) are no longer in operation now.

The objective of the SGSY is to bring the assisted poor families (Swarozgaris) above the poverty line in three years by providing them income generating assets through a mix of bank credit and government subsidy. The SGSY aims at establishing a large number of micro-enterprises in the rural areas, building upon the potential of the rural poor. It is rooted in the belief that rural poor in India have competencies and, given the right support, can be successful producers of valuable goods/services. It means ensuring that the family has a monthly net income of at least Rs. 2,000. Subject to availability of funds, the effort was to cover 30 per cent of the poor families in each Block by March 2004.

Towards the end/objective, the SGSY is conceived as a holistic programme of micro-enterprises covering all aspects of self-employment, viz. organisation of the rural poor into self-help groups (SHGs) and their capacity building, planning of activity clusters, infrastructure build-up, technology, credit and marketing.

Under the SGSY the beneficiaries are known as 'Swarozgaris'. The Swarozgaris can be either individuals or groups. The SGSY lays emphasis on the group approach, under which the rural poor are organised into self-help groups. In either case, the list of 'below poverty line' (BPL) households identified through BPL census, duly approved by the Gram Sabha forms the basis for identification

for assistance under the SGSY. The self-help groups should also be drawn from the BPL list approved by the Gram Sabha.

The SGSY focuses on the organisation of the poor at grassroots level through a process of social mobilisation for poverty eradication. The SGSY's approach to organise the poor stems from the conviction that there is a tremendous potential within the poor to help themselves and that the potential can be harnessed by organising them. Social mobilisation enables the poor build their own organisations—self-help groups in which they participate fully and directly and take decisions on all issues concerning poverty eradication. Simultaneously SHGs have the advantages of the assistance—be it in terms of credit or technology or market guidance—reaching the poor faster and more effectively.

The SGSY is different from earlier programmes, in terms of the strategy envisaged for its implementation, and has been conceived as a holistic programme of self-employment covering all aspects of self-employment, viz. organisation of the rural poor into self-help groups and their capacity building, training, planning of activity clusters, infrastructure build-up and technology and marketing support.

The BPL families in rural areas constitute the target group of the SGSY. Within the target group, special safeguards have been provided to vulnerable sections, by way of reserving 50 per cent benefits for SCs/STs, 40 per cent for women and 3 per cent for disabled persons.

Assistance under the SGSY to individual Swarozgaris or self-help groups is given in the form of subsidy by the government and credit by the banks. Subsidy under the SGSY to individuals is uniform at 30 per cent of the project cost, subject to a maximum of Rs. 7,500. In respect of SCs/STs the subsidy is 50 per cent of cost, subject to a maximum of Rs. 10,000. For groups of Swarozgaris the subsidy is 50 per cent of the cost of the scheme, subject to a ceiling of Rs. 1.25 lakh. There is no monetary limit on subsidy for irrigation projects, subsidy is back-ended.

The SGSY is financed on 75 : 25 cost sharing basis between the Centre and the States. The SGSY is being implemented by the

District Rural Development Agencies (DRDAs), with the active involvement of Panchayati Raj Institutions (PRIs), the banks, the Line Departments and the non-government organisations (NGOs).

Activity Clusters : Planning Selection

There are two key aspects of the SGSY, namely Activity Clusters and the Group Approach. Each Community Development Block has to concentrate on 4-5 key activities based on local resources, occupational skills of the people and availability of markets so that the swarozgaris can draw sustainable incomes from their investments. Selection of these activities has to be done with the approval of the Panchayat Samitis at the Block level and District level. These key activities should preferably be taken up in clusters so that the backward and forward linkages may be effectively established. The SGSY also focuses on the organisation of the poor at grassroots level through a process of social mobilisation for poverty eradication. Social mobilisation enables the poor build their own organisations (SHGs) in which they participate fully and take decisions on all issues that will help them in coming above the poverty line. A SHG may consist of 10-20 persons belonging to families below the poverty line, and a person should not be a member of more than one group. In the case of disabled persons, this number may be a minimum of five (5).

Physical Progress of SGSY

Between April 1, 1999 and March 31, 2006, about 19 lakh SHGs have been organised under SGSY. Of these, 10 lakh SHGs have passed Grade-I and 6.22 lakh Grade-II. About 3.09 lakh SHGs have taken up economic activity. The percentage of SHGs taking up economic activity out of the SHGs which have passed Grade-II is around 50 per cent in 2005-06. Similarly, the number of SHG swarozgaris assisted has also increased from 3.47 lakh to 5.87 lakh during this period. Of course, the number of individual swarozgaris assisted has declined from 5.9 lakh to 2.67 lakh during the same period. The percentage of SC/ST community members assisted

under the programme has increased from 44 per cent to 85 per cent, the percentage of women from 44 to 58 and the percentage of disabled from 0.91 per cent to 24.91 per cent (Table 5.5).

Financial Progress of SGSY

Between April 1999 and March 2006, an amount of Rs. 8223.20 crore was allocated for the SGSY out of which a sum of Rs. 7494.75 crore (91%) was utilised. The percentage of utilisation to funds available increased from 49 per cent during 1999-2000 to 89 per cent in 2005-06. The utilisation of funds towards training and skill development too increased from 3 per cent to 3.64 per cent during this period. With regard to the credit mobilised, a sum of Rs. 1,056 crore was provided to this programme in 1999-2000 which went up to Rs. 1755.27 crore by March 2006. The percentage of credit support increased from 32.96 in 1999-2000 to 61 in 2003-04 and declined to 16.84 in 2005-06. In tune with the growing emphasis on group approach, the investment support towards the group has been making steady progress. This seems in the ratio of investment on SHGs individuals which has almost gone up by seven times from 0.24 to 1.84 during this period. Similarly, the per capita investment under this programme has increased from Rs. 17,000 to Rs. 25,000 (Table 5.6).

SGSY in East Champaran District (Bihar)

The targets and achievements of the SGSY in East Champaran district of Bihar in 1999-2000 have been presented in Table 5.7. Table 5.7 reveals that all the banks working in the district with their 176 branches had fixed the target of Rs. 1,265 lakh for SGSY through SHGs in 1999-2000. Altogether 3,076 applications were received under SGSY, out of which 2,164 (70.37%) application were accepted and a sum of Rs. 390 lakh (3.83%) was distributed under the SGSY in the year 1999-2000.

Table 5.5 : Physical Progress of SGSY (1999-00 to 2005-06)

Sl. No.	*Items*	*Years*							*Total*
		1999-00	*2000-01*	*2001-02*	*2002-03*	*2003-04*	*2004-05*	*2005-06*	
	1	2	3	4	5	6	7	8	9
1.	SHGs formed since 01-04-1999	292426	515691	950078	1348951	1740917	1863763	1863565	7226440
2.	No. of SHGs passed Grade II	125402	214011	176002	189634	204959	577021	576339	2063368
3.	No. of SHGs passed Grade I	74234	101291	54040	96020	90491	103403	103196	622675
4.	SHGs taken up economic activities	29017	26317	30576	35317	50574	68741	68532	309074
5.	% of SHGs taken up economic activities to Grade II	39.09	25.98	56.58	36.78	55.89	66.48	66.41	49.64
6.	SHGs Swarozgaris assisted	347912	318803	364676	404419	576639	592382	587555	3192386
7.	Individual Swarozgaris assisted.	585956	687349	572792	411848	319785	265376	267285	3110391
8.	Total Swarozgaris assisted	933868	1006152	937468	816267	896424	857758	854840	6302777
9.	Per capita investment (in rupees)	9307	11954	10788	8884	6620	8788	8823	8145.5
10.	% of SHGs Swarozgaris assisted	37.25	31.69	38.9	49.54	64.33	69.06	68.73	50.65
11.	SC Swarozgaris assisted	278938	310886	284040	249556	275186	481058	479875	2359539
12.	ST Swarozgaris assisted	134944	137850	143619	130260	138281	252038	251385	1188377
13.	Total SC/ST Swarozgaris assisted	413882	448736	427659	379816	413467	733096	731260	3547918
14.	Woman Swarozgaris assisted	416690	409842	385891	382613	469824	500751	499154	3064765
15.	Disabled Swarozgaris assisted	8529	6737	6059	6118	8481	214363	212943	463230
16.	% of SC / ST assisted	44.32	44.6	45.62	46.53	46.12	85.47	85.54	49.78
17.	% of women assisted	44.62	40.73	41.16	46.87	52.41	58.38	58.39	48.63
18.	% disabled assisted	0.91	0.67	0.65	0.75	0.95	24.99	24.91	53.83

Source : Government of India (2006), *Annual Report (2005-06)*, Ministry of Rural Development, New Delhi.

Table 5.6 : Financial Progress of SGSY (1999-2000 to 2005-06)

Items	Years							Total
	1999-00	2000-01	2001-02	2002-03	2003-04	2004-05	2005-06	
1	2	3	4	5	6	7	8	9
1. Total Allocation	1472.33	1332.50	774.50	756.37	1065.83	1410.92	1410.75	8223.90
2. Central Allocation	1105.00	1000.00	581.50	567.9	800.00	1282.96	1282.64	6620.00
3. State Allocation	367.34	332.50	193.00	188.47	265.83	127.95	127.95	1603.19
4. Central Release	869.55	462.11	401.10	504.56	645.12	847.52	844.36	4574.32
5. % of Central Release	78.69	46.21	68.98	88.85	80.64	66.06	65.83	69.10
6. State Release	261.47	200.76	156.07	181.14	192.20	258.86	257.94	1508.44
7. % of State Release	71.18	60.38	80.87	96.11	72.30	202.32	201.34	94.09
8. Opening Balance on 1st April	776.62	854.74	661.58	415.77	287.37	240.56	241.58	3478.49
9. Miscellaneous Receipt	54.33	90.57	80.8	76.66	89.44	52.03	51.99	495.76
10. Total funds available	1961.97	168.18	1299.55	1178.13	1214.13	1398.98	1396.10	10057.04
11. Total funds utilised	959.86	1117.94	970.32	921.11	1044.25	1242.19	1230.07	7494.74
12. % of utilisation to funds available	48.92	69.52	74.67	78.17	86.01	88.79	88.75	74.52
13. % of utilisation to allocation	65.19	83.90	125.25	121.78	97.98	88.04	87.83	91.14
14. % of utilisation on subsidy	36.79	52.67	86.16	80.10	48.35	67.94	67.77	67.47
15. % of utilisation on Infra. Dev.	14.45	20.51	19.79	18.01	4.43	14.41	14.38	13.25
16. % of utilisation on training/skill dev.	3.03	3.62	6.23	5.44	2.36	3.64	3.64	3.50
17. Total credit Target	3205.00	3205.00	3200.87	2525.21	2129.33	10425.44	10426.29	35117.14
18. Credit Disbursed to SHGs	187.30	256.64	318.34	459.08	707.81	1002.55	1001.04	3932.76
19. Credit Disbursed to Individual swarozgaris	869.16	1202.80	1011.34	725.21	593.41	753.79	754.23	5909.94
20. Total credit mobilised	1056.46	1459.44	1329.68	1184.29	1301.22	1756.34	1755.27	9842.70

(Contd.)

Items	Years							Total
	1999-00	2000-01	2001-02	2002-03	2003-04	2004-05	2005-06	
1	2	3	4	5	6	7	8	9
21. % of credit mobilised	32.96	45.54	41.54	46.90	61.11	16.85	16.84	32.72
22. Subsidy Disbursed to SHGs	124.58	167.93	209.94	282.53	444.48	774.11	773.15	2776.72
23. Subsidy Disbursed to individual swarozgaris	417.11	533.92	455.68	323.35	268.51	208.31	208.44	2415.32
24. Total subsidy disbursed	541.69	701.85	665.62	605.88	712.99	982.41	981.59	5192.03
25. Ratio of investment on SHGs *vs.* individual	0.24	0.24	0.36	0.71	1.34	1.85	1.84	0.82
26. Total investment	1598.15	2161.29	1995.30	1790.17	2014.21	2738.76	2736.86	15034.74
27. Credit subsidy ratio	1.95	2.08	2.00	1.95	1.83	1.79	1.79	1.67

Source : Government of India (2006), *Annual Report* (*2005-06*), Ministry of Rural Development, New Delhi.

Table 5.7 : Targets and Achievements of SGSY in East Champaran (1999-2000)

	Name of Bank	*No. of Branches*	*Target (Rs. Lakh)*	*Applications Received (No.)*	*Applications accepted*		*Disbursement*	
					No.	*Amount (Rs. Lakhs)*	*Number*	*Amount (Rs. Lakhs)*
	1	2	3	4	5	6	7	8
1.	State Bank of India	39	430	493	281	68	281	68
2.	Central Bank of India	18	170	291	163	34	163	34
3.	Bank of India	9	90	157	38	10	38	10
4.	Punjab National Bank	8	78	138	57	14	57	14
5.	Allahabad Bank	6	68	147	128	30	128	30
6.	Bank of Baroda	3	35	57	31	7	31	7
7.	Canara Bank	1	12	15	8	2	8	2
8.	Indian Overseas Bank	2	12	53	26	4	26	4
9.	United Bank of India	1	10	18	—	—	—	-
10.	Champaran Kshetriya Grameen Bank	72	300	839	732	52	732	52
11.	Land Development Bank	8	50	853	700	169	700	169
12.	Central Cooperative Bank	3	10	15	—	—	—	—
	Total	176	1265	3076	2164	390	2164	390

Source : Central Bank of India, (2003), *District Credit Plan (2003-04)*, Central Bank of India, Regional Office, Motihari, p. 50.

The targets and achievements of the SGSY in East Champaran district in 2002-03 have been presented in Table 5.8. Table shows that out of the total applications of 6,363 received, 3,706 (58.49%) applications were accepted and 3,555 (56.11%) applications were disposed of after granting the loan of Rs. 72,964 lakh under the SGSY in 2002-03. This amount constituted only 40.02 per cent of the target amount.

Further the bank-wise targets and achievements of the SGSY in East Champaran district in 2006-07 have been produced in Table 5.9. This table shows that all the banks taken together approved 1,257 applications and granted the loan of Rs. 1235.16 lakh under the SGSY. This amount constituted 58.40 per cent of the target amount.[14]

Monitoring of the SGSY

A comprehensive system of monitoring has been adopted under the SGSY. The programme is monitored from central level down to the grassroots levels. At the central level, the Central Level Coordination Committee (CLCC) monitors and reviews the implementation of the programme and lays down policy guidelines for all aspects related to credit linkages for the SGSY. The Performance Review Committee of the Department of Rural Development also reviews the implementation of the SGSY. At the State level, a State Level Coordination Committee (SLCC) monitors the programme. In addition, the progress under the SGSY is monitored periodically through Reports and Returns submitted by DRDA or States. Detailed monitoring formats have been circulated to all the DRDAs. Implementation of the programme is monitored and reviewed through project Director's Workshops and periodic meetings with the State secretaries. At the Block/DRDA level, monitoring is done through field visits and physical verification of assets. Efforts are underway to bring all the DRDA of the country within on-line networks for smooth flow of information from the districts to the centre through States or Union territories.

Table 5.8 : Targets and Achievements of SGSY in East Champaran (2002-2003)

S. No.	Name of Bank	No. of Branches	Target (Rs. Lakhs)	Applications Received (No.)	Applications accepted		Disbursement	
					No.	Amount (Rs. Lakhs)	Number	Amount (Rs. Lakhs)
	1	2	3	4	5	6	7	8
1.	State Bank of India	39	658	1462	1173	239.34	1066	209.29
2.	Central Bank of India	18	236	1072	474	104.04	474	101.78
3.	Bank of India	9	120	439	129	29.78	111	18.89
4.	Punjab National Bank	8	110	793	319	89.00	297	79.00
5.	Allahabad Bank	6	100	647	161	37.00	161	37.00
6.	Bank of Baroda	3	53	217	63	12.18	63	12.18
7.	Canara Bank	2	22	259	61	15.25	61	15.25
8.	Indian Overseas Bank	1	17	—	—	—	—	—
9.	United Bank of India	1	15	93	25	6.25	21	5.25
10.	Champaran Kshetriya Grameen Bank	72	390	1354	1301	251	1301	251
11.	Land Development Bank	9	30	—	—	—	—	—
12.	Central Cooperative Bank	8	70	—	—	—	—	—
	Total	176	1823	6336	3706	793.84	3555	729.64

Source : Central Bank of India, (2003), *District Credit Plan (2003-04)*, Central Bank of India, Regional Office, Motihari, p. 50.

Table 5.9 : Targets and Achievements of SGSY in East Champaran (2006-2007)

S. No.	*Name of Bank*	*No. of Branches*	*Target (Rs. Lakhs)*	*Sanctioned*		*Disbursement*	
				No.	*Amount (Rs. Lakhs)*	*Number*	*Amount (Rs. Lakhs)*
	1	2	3	4	5	6	7
1.	State Bank of India	39	620	1558	290.97	1558	390.97
2.	Central Bank of India	18	250	882	219.14	882	219.14
3.	Bank of India	9	150	125	32.25	125	32.25
4.	Punjab National Bank	8	150	494	122.95	484	120.45
5.	Allahabad Bank	6	140	132	32.15	132	32.15
6.	Bank of Baroda	3	75	70	17.60	70	17.60
7.	Canara Bank	2	50	58	13.85	58	13.85
8.	Indian Overseas Bank	1	30	2	0.14	2	0.14
9.	United Bank of India	1	30	19	4.75	19	4.75
10.	Uttar Bihar Kshetriya Grameen Bank	72	520	1309	49.39	1275	403.86
11.	Land Development Bank	9	50	—	—	—	—
12.	Central Cooperative Bank	8	50	—	—	—	—
	Total	176	2115	4649	1253.19	4587	1235.16

Source : Central Bank of India, (2007), *District Credit Plan (2006-07)*, East Champaran Central Bank of India, Regional Office, Motihari, p. 50.

Evaluation of the SGSY

If debate among the scholars on the comparative efficacy of various forms of poverty alleviation strategies hold important lessons for the global microfinance sector, development within the microfinance sector with specific reference to the shifting conceptualisation of microfinance as an anti-poverty initiative, in turn, pose challenging question to the emerging Indian microfinance experience. If the research perspective critical of the anchoring of the microfinance to micro-enterprise credit delivery constitutes an important insight about the role of microfinance programme in poverty alleviation: how sound is the Government of India's strategy of mandating disbursal of enterprise credit under SGSY scheme for the promotion of self-employment through the existing self-help groups?

The SGSY, successor to the IRDP, TRYSEM and DWACRA, was introduced as a nation-wide self-employment-based poverty alleviation programme in April 1999 and substituted the IRDP, DWACRA, TRYSEM, MST, SITRA, GKY, etc. The SGSY which seeks to use SHGs as channels of delivery of credit-*cum*-subsidy assistance to below poverty line sections, aims to bring every assisted family above the poverty line in three years by creating a monthly income of at least Rs. 2,000 from the activity undertaken, after payment of the bank loan. The SGSY, as enunciated in its guidelines issued by the Ministry of Rural Development, Government of India, declares as a fundamental article of faith, its belief in the latent capacities of the rural poor, expressed in the statement that with the right support, the poor would emerge as successful producers of goods and services.[15] The SGSY in its conceptualisation is, therefore, primarily about injective credit for promotional purposes and it is premised on the expectation that households can use the credit-financed enterprises to make a linear unidimensional movement from below poverty line to above poverty line status.

The SGSY which attempts to capitalise on the group lending process which has been initiated by the NABARD through the launch of SHG-linkage pilot project in 1991, contrasts in many

ways with the SHG-bank linkage programme. The SGSY is striking for the range institutional sectors which have been involved in the selection, planning and monitoring process, the Panchayati Raj Institutions (PRIs), Block development officials, district line department officials, non-government organisations (NGOs) and of course, the SHGs. The SHG-bank linkage scheme involves only the bank, the self-help group and the sponsoring NGO or voluntary organisation. Even while exhorting banks to prioritise the SHG-bank linkage programme within the lending portfolio, the NABARD and the Reserve Bank of India circulars emphasised that the linkage scheme was to be perceived as a credit innovation and not a targeted intervention. The SGSY, in marked difference, is a targeted intervention (like the predecessor—the IRDP), and is charged with the mission of covering 30 per cent of BPL families in a Block within a period of three years. Premised on the understanding that the constituency of SHG was generally the rural poor who were most attracted by low amounts of repeat loans for consumption purpose, the SHG-bank linkage scheme had not specified BPL status for loan recipients, unlike the SGSY. The SHG-bank linkage programme which had reiterated that minimal documentation be gathered from the group, in a relatively debureaucratic manner, had marked a change in bank policy towards weaker section lending for consumption purposes.[16] In contrast the SGSY intended as a self-employment programme ties SGSY loan use to individual or collective enterprises and treats any consumption spending as diversion from permitted purpose.

It is noted, therefore, that certain structural features of the SGSY could potentially threaten the flexibility of SHG-based savings and credit transactions and consequently also the protectional dimension of SHGs. By mandating that bank officials ensure loan finance through SHGs, bank staff could forcing larger amount of loans tied to the end use of enterprise promotion upon women who are neither willing nor able, to engage in loan-financed income generation. This could, in turn, imply the establishment of unviable enterprises by women members of SHGs forced to invest in income earning activities, or subversion of the programme's objectives by SHG

members, camouflaging their consumption needs as self-employment needs. The probability that only those who genuinely need to invest in income generation activities, are borrowing these purposes appear to be higher in the case of the SHG-bank linkage scheme, as consumption related expenditure is permitted here. The SGSY also appears to be redefining the terms of relationship between the commercial bank and the group in more authoritarian and coercive ways as reflected in field reports which indicate that bank officials have tended to make access to the SGSY for the group as an entity contingent upon individual member's payment of balance on older schemes such as the IRDP which their family members might have taken. Group pressures on individual members fuelled by banker's efforts to secure older defaults through the SGSY scheme contain the potential to provoke exclusionary pressure attempting to discipline comembers, also defaulters of the earlier scheme. Yet another features of the SGSY with disquicting implications for the protectional dimensions of SHG-based microfinance has to do with the target-orientation of the programme and the consequent primacy accorded to quantitative assessment such as the number and volume of financial assistance disbursed and number of beneficiaries reached. Field reports indicate that some SHGs have been created with the sole agenda of absorbing the SGSY loan funds, under the aegis of Block and district level administration through the expansionary impulse of the target driven SGSY, and these appear to be short-lived and unsustainable, often time dissolving after the loan has been disbursed, in the absence of sufficient time for and facilitation of intra-group cohesion.[17-18] This would in turn, appear to jeopardise the social mobilisation or the empowerment process, also expected to SHG-based collectivisation of rural women. At this juncture it is noted that the SGSY has provoked the ire of existing micro-finance players who have criticised the programme for its capacity to sabotage the network of self-help groups through the introduction of subsidies, the non-linkage between group-generated savings and external loan amount, the infusion of large amounts of loan finance into group in relatively short period after group formation and the threat of hijack of NGO sponsored groups by Block and district bureaucracy.[19-22]

Policy response to trenchant criticism by Indian researchers of the unsuitability of the poorest for the risks of loan-financed enterprises has taken the form of jettisoning the Antyodaya principle or the priority selection of the poorest within the BPL sections in the SGSY. However, the SGSY continues to be ill-equipped to meet the challenges of the agenda of gauging the suitability of differently placed poor households for various forms of employment programmes depending on their initial asset position or possession of prior entrepreneurial experience, training or skills. Another area of concern relating to the SGSY is the promotion of micro-enterprises lending through SHGs without adequate support to the agenda of ensuring access to protected market for SHGs women. The SGSY's requirement that at least 50 per cent of the SHGs reached in Block office be women's group and the central government's decision to route the SGSY scheme through SHGs in the context where there is a massive policy support behind the creation of women's SHGs, may be perceived as important means of reaching higher volume of institutional credit to women in order to finance their enterprises. However, when it is considered that critical studies of IRDP have revealed that the variety of mechanisms by which the process of selecting enterprises and providing support services, were even more inadequate in the case of women beneficiaries.[23-24] It is disturbing to note that the official guidelines of the SGSY take no note of the additional forms of support that first time women entrepreneurs may need in order to be able to successfully access to markets, manage their enterprises independently and generate sufficient incomes from their chosen activities. Especially on the issue of market access, this is what the guidelines of the SGSY have to say, "It is possible that this might appear to be a formidable proposition and that the field functionaries might feel that they are unequal to the task. Happily this is not so. While to most of us market mechanism may appear unintelligible and a complex task, in reality it means achieving out what sells and what does not. Goods and services are traded everyday in all parts of the country. What is needed is to see what sells in the local markets."[25] Such breezy confidence on the critical issue of marketing belies research on IRDP, which has painstakingly documented the

many ways by which successful market access had evaded grasp of IRDP clients. Although the guidelines envisage an elaborate process of planning at Block and district levels by Block and district committees of the SGSY prior to the choice of enterprises with regard to availability of infrastructure, markets, technology and the capacities of the swarozgaris, early assessment of the SGSY indicates that the notion of comprehensive, holistic planning at the Block and district levels remains much of a fantasy in the SGSY as it did with the IRDP.[26-28]

The prospects for the financial viability of the income generating activities of the poor, on an economy—wide scale, appear even more remote when one factors in analyses that demonstrate the marginalisation of wage employment generation programme, an examination of the pattern of intra-sectoral allocation within the sector of 'rural development' programme (both in Jawahar Rozgar Yojana and Employment Assurance Scheme), which were the most important components within the rural development sector (claiming a share of more than 70 per cent in 1994-95), showed a declining trend in the second half of the 1990s and fell down dramatically to 23.7 per cent in 2001.[29]

In the light of the dwindling resource allocation for wage employment generation in Central Government's expenditure in the late 1990s recalls Nilkanth Rath's argument that the economic feasibility that of the enterprises of the poor depends critically upon wage employment programmes that generate large scale markets for the goods produced by them.[30]

While it is well beyond the scope of this work to attempt to provide a complete assessment of the implications of the SGSY for the protectional dimensions of SHG-based savings and credit transactions, it must be noted that Indian policy makers appear to have not sufficiently factored in findings related to the structural limitations of promotional lendings strategies which have emerged both from the global micro finance experience and from the older IRDP closer home.

By the way of conclusion, it is noted that further evaluation of the efficacy of self-help group based savings and credit transactions, either in promoting the incomes of the poor households through

investment in income generating activities or in protecting households from damaging their precarious economic resources during the period of crises, warrants field studies which can perhaps make an impartial contribution by understanding a mapping of the heterogeneous poor who currently constitute the clientele of the self-help groups as well as the SGSY in India. Studying the differential loan histories of different individuals within groups may offer a clue to understanding which sections of the poor within SHGs are graduating over to time to time income generation and which sections are resorting to more distress related borrowings. One can perhaps seek to further complicate the pattern by situating the SHGs being researched in different contextual settings: areas or regions marked by accountable public institutions relatively to the delivery system *vis-à-vis* more deprived pockets of the country marked by a complete absence or near-breakdown of government provisioning of essential services. It may even be worthwhile to probe the question of whether research on the borrowing and saving pattern of differently placed SHGs members can be used to provide a micro-view of the failure of the welfare State.

Prompt recovery of loans is an important aspect of SGSY, not only to ensure discipline but more importantly as it reflects the success of the self-employment programme. All concerned must, therefore, ensure that the recovery is hundred per cent. To ensure this, the government should take some measure for hundred per cent loan recovery. Moreover a very good monitoring system is adopted for SGSY, that system should be reviewed once in suitable period of intervals.

SGSY is the best tool to eradicate poverty in rural India. The government support and assistance is essential for the success of programme like SGSY. The physical and financial progress of SGSY shows its worst result in recent years. Therefore, the government should come forward to allot huge amount of fund to this programme. The role of NGOs is important for the success of the SGSY, because they are the field workers of this programme. Hence, NGOs should serve the SGSY swarozgaris with an open heart.

Self-Help Groups and Empowerment of Women

India's concern for safeguarding the rights and privileges of women found its best expression in the Constitution of India. Giving special attention to the status of women, Article 14 confers equal rights and opportunities on men and women in the economic, political and social spheres. Article 15(3) empowers the State to make affirmative discrimination in favour of women. In spite of it the credit programmes have ignored women for a long time. Targeting women for credit programmes began to receive serious consideration at the International Women Conference at Mexico City in 1975. In India this universal concern found recognition in the Sixth Five Year Plan (1980-85). Since then a concentrated effort has been made in this direction by rural credit institutions to uplift rural women. This has led the birth of micro credit scheme.

Development has social, economic and political dimensions and is incomplete without developing the women who constitute about 50 per cent of the population. Role of women in development is indispensable and community development is incomplete without women's participation and contribution, but women are not always involved in the process of developmental activities which affect their lives.

The status of women and related issues have attracted the attention of the academicians, political thinkers and social scientists both in developing as well as developed countries. It has been widely accepted that a society built on the inequality between men and women involves wastage of women resources which no country can afford. Thus the effective management and development of women's resources are of paramount importance for the mobilisation and development of human resources. Poverty and deprivation increase gender inequality which favours a policy for empowerment of women. The goals of poverty eradication and empowerment of women can be effectively achieved if poor women could organise themselves into groups for community participation as well as for ascertaining their rights in various services related to their economic and social welfare.

Empowerment is a process of awareness and capacity building, leading to greater participation, the greater decision-making power and control and transformative action. The empowerment of women covers both an individual and collective transformation. It strengthens their innate ability through acquiring knowledge, power and experience.

Empowerment is defined as the one which facilitates change and enables to do what he or she wants. It is a feeling which activates ones psychological energy to accomplish one's goal.

Empowerment is a process whereby women become able to organise themselves to increase self-reliance and to assert their independent right to make choices and control resources, both of which will assist in challenging and eliminating their subordination. It is a participatory process of awareness and capacity building which begins at the levels of home and community, adding to greater participation and decision making power and control, and to transformative action enabling individuals or groups to change balances of power in social, economic and political relations in society.

The dictionary definition[31] links empowerment with self-help groups; "Empowerment can refer to use participation in services and to the self-help movements in which groups take action on their own behalf either in cooperation with or independently of statutory services."

In recent years, the individual approach to poverty alleviation programmes has been increasingly replaced by group mode. SHG is expected to be one of the major programme of poverty alleviation in India. Self-help groups have been instrumental in empowerment by enabling women to work together in collective agency.

Organisation of women in the form of SHGs have laid the seeds for economic and social empowerment of women. The basic strategy adopted to promote empowerment of women through SHGs comprises in organising women SHGs at the village level around savings and rotational credit programmes using their own resources, facilitating regular interaction and exchange of information, linking SHGs with external credit source like banks, cooperative societies, etc., imparting skill training to the members

to manage their credit and take decisions, linking SHGs with rural development programmes thus enabling the members to expand their investment capital and develop leadership qualities and self-confidence.

Group dynamic among the women members empower them to fight against social evils in the community like female infanticide, dowry problem, evils of drinking, corruption, etc. Formation of clutter level committees also empowers women to form network of group and undertake community-based issue with government departments. The experience gained in the group-meetings has also embolden women members to assert their voices not only in the immediate context of their community but also in the larger democratic bodies. The opportunities given to women in the meetings of the federation of the SHGs have also paved way for their participation in the local Panchayat elections.

The number of the women SHGs formed so far constitutes 90 per cent or more of the total number of SHGs. In 1999-2000, 1,16,690 women swarozgaris were assisted which constituted 44.62 per cent of the women swarozgaris. In 2005-06, the number of women swarozgaris swelled to 4,99,154, registering a growth of about 11 per cent during the period 1999-00 to 2005-06. The total number of women swarozgaris assisted was 30,64,765, its 48.63 per cent swarozgaris was assisted during the period under consideration (Table 5.10).

Table 5.10 : Physical Progress of Women Swarozgaris under SGSY (1999-2000 to 2005-06)

Year	*Women Swarozgaris assisted*	*Percentage of Women Swarozgaris assisted*
1	2	3
1999-00	116690	44.62
2000-01	409842	40.73
2001-02	385891	41.16
2002-03	382613	46.84
2003-04	469824	52.41
2004-05	500751	58.38
2005-06	499154	58.39
Total	3064765	48.63

Source : On the basis of Table 5.5 of this chapter.

The assessment of the performance of women self-help groups has brought results with significant implications for policy makers.[32] The assessment highlights the facts that :

(a) Poor women can save if adequately motivated,
(b) Rural poor women need credit,
(c) Rural poor women are bankable,
(d) SHGs are people's institutions and with their support the women can march towards empowerment,
(e) Credit delivery system through SHGs is a cost-effective approach to improve the outreach of banking services, and
(f) SHGs can promote individual/group ventures of income generating programmes under the effective guidance of NGOs.

The analysis of SHGs in terms of outreach and sustainability has revealed mixed results. Outreach has several dimensions like breadth of outreach, depth of outreach and quality of outreach. Breadth of outreach is illustrated by number of members covered and depth of outreach cannot success in covering the difficulties of supplying financial services to the poor. Quality of outreach is reflected in the range of financial services offered, transaction cost incurred by the members and the extent of member satisfaction regarding the conditions of loan and fulfilment of demand for financial services.

Women Empowerment in Bihar

Mass poverty is one of the major critical problems confronting planners in Bihar. There is no denying the fact that the soul of India resides in villages. More than 72 per cent of population of the country lives in villages whereas in Bihar the corresponding figure is 89.5 per cent.

Bihar is the second largest and one of the most populated States in India. It has a geographical area of 94,163 sq. km. with a population density of about 880 per sq. km. The total population of Bihar is 8.29 crore as per the 2001 population census. Out of

the total population of the State about 188 lakh (23%) are the total main workers. Some relevant statistics about the economy of Bihar are given in Table 5.11.

Table 5.11 : Statistics on Bihar Economy

Items	*Figures*
1	2
1. Area	94,163 sq. km.
2. Population	8.29 crore
3. Main Workers	1.88 crore
4. Population Density	888 persons per sq. km.
5. Female literacy rate	33.57 per cent
6. Female literacy in rural areas	30.03 per cent
7. Literacy rate in scheduled caste women in rural areas	5.40 per cent
8. Sex ratio in rural areas	927 females per 1000 males
9. Population density in rural areas	803 persons per sq. km.
10. Average Annual Exponential growth rate (1991-2001)	2.49 per cent
11. Population growth rate (1991-2001)	28.33 per cent
12. Rural population	74,199,596
13. Rural area of Bihar	92,358.40 sq. km.
14. Child population (0-6) in rural area :	
Male	19.93 per cent
Female	20.20 per cent
15. Number of Panchayats	1,138,00
16. Number of Districts	38
17. Death Rate	79 per thousand
18. Infant Mortality Rate	62 per thousand
19. Infant Mortality Rate (Boys)	59 per thousand
20. Per capita income (2003-04)	Rs. 5780

Source : Singh, Indrabhushan and Usha Kumari (2007), "Jeevika Mega Project: Empowerment of Rural Poor in Bihar", *Kurukshetra*, December, pp. 14-15.

The focus of rural development in Bihar has mostly been along the same lines as followed by the Central Government. So the State of Bihar, too, has focused on generation of employment opportunities, upliftment of underprivileged sections by enhancing beneficiary oriented quality of life, apart from providing several basic amenities, improving rural infrastructure and emphasis on agricultural development. Actually, poverty does not simply mean lack of adequate income, it must be viewed as a state of deprivation spanning the social, economic and needs context of people which presents their effective participation, as opportunities for the poor

has remained as one of the important components of poverty alleviation and rural development for which a number of programmes have been initiated in India since the 1970s. The final link of this series of employment oriented programmes (viz. IRDP, TRYSEM, SITRA, FWP, NREP, RLEGP, JRY, JGSY, etc.) is a self-employment programme. Swarnajayanti Gram Swarozgar Yojana (SGSY) is conceived as a holistic scheme of micro-enterprises covering various aspects of self-employment, viz. organisation of rural poor in self-help groups, capacity building, training and skill upgradation, credit and marketing.

Table 5.12 : Workers in Bihar (2001)

Particulars	*Number of Workers (in '000)*
1	2
1. Total main workers	18795
(a) Cultivators	7719
(b) Agricultural Labourers	8114
(c) Livestock, forestry & others	64
(d) Mining & Quarrying	12
(e) Manufacturing, Processing, Servicing and Repairs	
(i) Household industry	292
(ii) Others	276
(f) Construction	89
(g) Trade & Commerce	708
(h) Transport & Storage	188
(i) Other services	1339
2. Marginal Workers	941
3. Non-Workers	44790

Source : Same as Table 5.11, p. 15

Hence the Government of India and also the Government of Bihar adopted various strategies and programmes for rural development and employment generation in the last five decades to meet out these challenges. Poverty is a curse to humanity and the persons suffering from it are not only economically deprived of but are also socially dejected ones, hence, the focus of government policies and plans shifted towards poverty alleviation through area specific and target

oriented programmes from Fourth Plan onward. The yard brought new programmes to cover the failure of earlier ones, but the administrative set-up remained almost the same with minor changes. However, the actual position of beneficiaries (weaker sections like SC, ST, women, handicapped, agricultural labourers, rural artisans, marginal and small farmers living below poverty line) could not improve accordingly and most of them are still not in a position to meet their needs properly. The reasons are the large size of family, illiteracy, ignorance and lack of spirit to work, besides, most of them have no future planning and are mingled with present needs. Moreover, the bureaucratic attitude of the concerned officials, misappropriation in utilisation of assistance and poor involvement of the prospective beneficiaries checked their performance. Thus the earlier programmes could not attain the desired goal successively and became a politically motivated programmes, hence modification was urgently required.[33]

Providing rural households access to financial services, particularly credit, has been a priority agenda for the Central Government since Independence. It was considered an effective tool to earn a sustainable living. As a part of this strategy, several subsidy linked credit programmes were initiated. Within this policy context, the development of India's financial sector inevitably resulted in substantial achievements in enhancing access to credit in rural areas. Though the organised banking has largely undermined the role of the moneylender regarding the provision of credit, yet it is also realised to the credit needs of the formal sector, even though this sector accounted for the bulk of the total employment generated. So the rural poor in the unorganised sector have not yet been able to come out of the clutches of moneylenders charging usurious interest rates. The rural poor generally need finances for mixed purposes (i.e. a mix of production and consumption needs), which are mutually affected by each other. They are poor, so they cannot meet the contingencies of life on their own. In certain circumstances they have to sell or pledge their productive assets (whatever they have) to meet their needs, in the absence of any

outside help. This pushes them into the vicious cycle of debt and impoverishment. The formal credit system generally excludes them for want of a collateral. On the other hand, borrowing from an informal source is very convenient, though the terms are very hard. As a result, the credit needs of the rural poor are only partially met by formal credit agencies. Presently, the overall share of the organised sector in credit flow to the rural poor is only around 16 per cent. Hence, a system would have to be put in place, which is flexible and responsive to the financial needs of the poor and is capable of supplying timely and adequate credit. Banking policies and procedures need to be reviewed to enable banks to adopt a more proactive approach to lending to economically viable activities in the informal sector. For this generally the services of cooperatives and non-banking financial intermediaries are dependent upon for on-lending to finance informal sector activity. Another important mechanism through which banks can meet the credit needs of the informal sector is the self-help groups which provide micro credit for informal sector activities.

Dr. Azad[34] undertook a study of SHGs in Sabour Block of Bhagalpur district (Bihar). On the basis of random sampling method four villages—Farka, Khankita, Chanderie and Sabour were selected. From each village one SHG, altogether four SHGs were selected. From each SHG 10 women members, altogether 40 respondents and 40 non-SHG members were selected for measuring the impact of SHGs regarding socio-economic aspects. The data were collected through schedule and questionnaire.

Table 5.13 reveals that the majority of groups (84%) were organising two meetings in a month for effective working of groups. Most of the groups (45%) were saving Rs. 25-30 per month per member. About 42 per cent members were taking loan for agricultural activities, besides goat (9%), cow/buffalo (16%), poultry (8%), Bidi making and others (7%). In the case of loan recovery, 71 per cent members have exerted group pressure if loan were not paid timely.[35]

Table 5.13 : Operational Mechanism of SHGs in Sabaur Block, District Bhagalpur (Bihar)

Operational Mechanism	Variable	Per cent
1	2	3
1. Number of meeting of SHGs	Once in a month	16
	Twice in a month	84
2. Per month saving of SHGs (in rupees)	10-25	20
	25-30	45
	30-35	20
	35 & above	15
3. Members initial deposits for opening bank accounts	Rs. 500 & above	100
4. Internal loan towards different activities	Goat	09
	Cow / buffalo	16
	Poultry	08
	Bidi Making	18
	Agri. activities	42
	Others	07
5. Loan not paid in time	(a) Group pressure of late payment	71
	(b) Low level	29

Source : Azad, Chandra Prakesh, (2006), "Empowerment of Women through Self-Help Groups: A Study of Sabour Block of Bhagalpur District", *Journal of Regional Studies*, Vol. 16-17, No. 31-34, January 2005-December 2006, p. 59.

The result of impact on socio-economic status through SHGs shows that the total number of SHGs were not having positive result as compared to the total non-member of SHGs. Only 9 per cent of the total numbers has their annual income. Expenditure patterns also shows that the status of women were found insignificant on education, housing facilities, consumption and size of holding.

The SHGs in Sabour have not produced any positive result. Efforts are made on this line. The problems of SHGs in Sabour Block of Bhagalpur district are multifarious and multi-dimensional. These problems can be solved by changing the attitude of society, family and nation towards the weaker sections of the society, poor men and women.

Bihar Rural Livelihood Promotion Project

The Government of Bihar initiated a project in 2006 on rural

livelihood promotion with the support from the World Bank to rural poor men and women. The name of the project is Bihar Rural Livelihood Promotion Project under Bihar Rural Livelihood Promotion Society (BRLPS). The BRLPS is the spearheading agency for the implementation of the project. This project has been named 'Jeevika' in Hindi. Its headquarters is in the Vidyut Bhawan, Patna. Now Jeevika has been designed to address rural poverty in Bihar through the collaboration of the poor, the Government of Bihar and the World Bank.[36]

Objectives: The objectives of the project are:

- To improve rural livelihood and enhance economic and social empowerment of the rural poor men and women.
- By developing organisations of the rural poor and producers, to enable them to access and negotiable better services, credit and assets from public and private sector agencies and financial institutions.
- To invest in capacity building of public and service providers.
- To play a catalytic role in promoting development of microfinance and agribusiness sectors.

Creating an enabling environment for implementing and scaling up innovations for rural livelihood development and service delivery is one of the objectives of the Bihar Rural Livelihood Project. One of the components of the project is also to support innovations by various institutions, entrepreneurs, NGOs, etc. whose main objective is to improve rural livelihoods.

The main objective of the Bihar Innovation Forum is primarily to showcase and support various innovations which show potential in Bihar for scaling up. It is also envisaged that this forum would be working on the lines of a development market place.

The BRLP is the life-saving drug to cure BIMARU (Bihar, Madhya Pradesh, Rajasthan and Uttar Pradesh) State of Bihar which is suffering from serious ailments of economic backwardness, women problems, lowest saving rate, lowest rural industrialisation,

lack of technical and legal information, lack of social mobilisation, slow mobilisation, social strife, dirty politics, parochial thoughts, narrow populist policies, deteriorating education, vote grabbing endeavours, thoroughly corrupt bureaucracy and crime infested scenario. The BRLP is not a shadow or carbon copy of IRDP of the Government of India, but it is a mega and multidimensional challenging project. The BRLP is a 'rainbow project' of the 'Sushasan' Government of Bihar. The policy maker of BRLP should consider the Tenth Five Year (2002-07) advice: "Inclusion of an identifiable women component plan in the programmes of the respective ministries right from the planning process and to monitoring and the promotion of benefit to women, and the promotion of the self-help groups"[37] The Approach Paper to the Eleventh Five Year Plan strategy for gender balancing takes care of the special needs to upliftment of rural downtrodden women, and needed participation of rural women and neglected needy persons in all planning and projects. The BRLP should consider the Bangladesh Nobel Peace Prize Winner's concept of rural development.

Empowerment of Women in Nagaland

"Anitoli was once one of the helpless housewives solely depending upon her husband's income. Many other women inhabitants of her colony—the Agricultural Colony, Kohima were still worse off. Their husbands scanty daily wage income forced them to hand to mouth existence. Only pastime of these helpless housewives was to gather at one place after finishing their daily chores and gossip. They very much wanted to do something, to be able to earn but fell very helpless."[38]

The story of their lives would have continued this way but for the concern shown by the Project Officer of Cooperative Education Project of the National Cooperative Union of India (NCUI). A beginning was made by organising a motivational meeting in their colony and inviting them all to come and listen to how they too can start earning something on their own by forming a self-help group.

This really provided them the opportunity they were looking for and soon ten of their group responded to form their own self-help group, which was registered on the 20th April, 2006. Soon their group became active. They started holding meetings at least once in two weeks. They would all attend these meetings as the absentee would have to pay a fine of five rupees. Cooperatives Education Project officials helped them to learn more about income generating activities that they could undertake. They were also invited to participate in various seminars conducted by National Cooperative Union of India-Cooperative Education Field Project (NCUI-CEFP), Kohima. This training programme was conducted in collaboration with the Nagaland State Industries Department.

The group then not only started making woollen shoes and earn a steady income but also to go beyond. One of their group member Ms. Hekali was invited by the Land Resource Development Council as a Master Trainer to train a group of women SHG Tsunoyn village for a week. For this she earned a handsome amount of Rs. 500 per day.

Later, the group was also trained in woollen carpet making. The other achievements of this SHG is in making of banana chips, potato chips, preparing *papads/rotis* from sticky rice and making pickles. They have mastered the art of stitching jute bags and are skilled in other handicrafts besides their traditional handloom items.

This SHG now has a steady income of their own. They have no difficulty in contributing Rs. 50 per month to their fund as each member's monthly income at present ranges from Rs. 500 to 600. Their total savings have accumulated to over Rs. 40,000 not a mean feat considering that these very women at one time were in awe of talking any official for help. At that time they felt terribly shy to sell the things made by them. No more now, they not only participate enthusiastically in various exhibition-*cum*-sales conducted by NCUI-CEFP, but also conduct sale of pickles, other processed foods, woollen items etc. once in a week at their premises. Products made by their SHG are sold as hot cakes.

This group also has another advantage. Being urban based, the educational status of members is from seventh to tenth

standard. This plus point has also been a contributing factor to the fast growth of the SHG. Two of the group members have also honed skills in piggery. Two piglets purchased from the group fund are being reared by these two members. These would fetch a price of Rs. 15000 per pig. Half of the sale amount will go to the group fund.

Thus each member of the group has to participate in one activity or the other to earn some money of their own from which they also pay their monthly contribution of Rs. 20 to the SHG fund. They have opened their bank accounts, learnt office maintenance, budget making, etc. They have participated in various skill development programmes conducted by the NCUI-CEFP. The project personnel make arrangements to organise such programmes in collaboration with various other Department, of the Nagaland State Government, like Land Resources Development, Industries, Horticulture and Agriculture. The leadership development programmes are mobilised by the lady mobiliser of the CEFP. The success of this SHG speaks in terms of their chairman having been chosen to represent the State Department of Cooperatives to give a demonstration on jute bag making at the Farmer's conference. The conference held in June 7-8, 2006 was graced by the Chief Minister of Nagaland as a chief guest, where Ms. Anitoli, the Chairman of this Likuphy SHG proudly held the demonstration. Thus the group has gained confidence in attending functions with prominent presence of high level State officials and VIPs. Not only that, Ms. Anitoli has also participated and gave a talk about her SHG on the International Women's Day on March 8, 2007 to motivate many more to follow her footsteps.

The story of this tribal women's self-help group from a small colony of Kohima town is truly a motivating story for other groups of women. How insecure and helpless they felt when they were unable to earn even a single paise. Once determined and with help from NCUI-CEFP, they quickly mastered various skills to produce items having demand in the market and also picked up the nuances of financial matters. And with regular upgradation of skills they became conscious about education of their children.

They are also more aware about healthcare of their own-selves and of the family and want to conduct healthcare programmes for the community. They have learnt the lesson may be a bit late. The lesson they want to pass on to other women is that early to learn and early to work together makes one healthy, wealthy and wise.

Microfinance

India, the second fastest growing economy, powered by service sector growth, aided by high quality intellectual capital and the boom in the manufacturing sector, still has about 27 crore people, predominantly ruralites, below the poverty line.

The trickle down theory of growth obviously is not working in favour of the starving masses. Farm sector depends on the vagaries of monsoon, in the absence of an efficient irrigation system. Ruralites suffer from low skill and jobless growth.

The agrarian economy has an important place in India even though it is no longer the sector which contributes the highest percentage to the growth rate. Indian rural scene is rather dismal; with agriculture deteriorating into a rather unglamorous and unremunerative sector. There is an urgent need to strengthen the social infrastructure so as to fight poverty and illiteracy, and simultaneously strengthen the physical infrastructure like health services, roads, irrigation facilities, quality agricultural inputs processing units, produce storage units, marketing, etc. Also bank credit has to be delivered timely and cost effectively.

In India, the rural credit has not been expanding. In fact it has recorded a negative growth rate in the recent past, following the unwillingness on the part of the bankers to provide finance to the rural sector. The growth in the micro-credit is very slow. The subsidies of the agriculture sector hardly reach the needy. Agricultural income remains untaxed, allowing a minority sector of farming population to cover all the benefits. This is the gloomy side of the Indian economy.

Bankers have been playing a very crucial role in this regard. Social banking has produced the first green revolutions. Still much more collective effort is needed from the government, banks and

voluntary organisations to uplift the poor and the downtrodden in rural India.

The significant contribution of institutional finance in agricultural and rural development and economic transformation is well documented. In the technology-led growth of agriculture over the last four or five decades, non-technological factors such as prices, markets and credits have played a critical role. Among these non-technological factors credit has played a critical role. In the fast changing economic environment and agricultural, scenario characterised by increasing market orientation and globalisation, rural financial system is confronted with new challenges to finance vast investment needs of high-tech high-value agriculture, income diversification in rural areas, risk mitigation and inclusive growth. Therefore, the recent renewed-thrust on rural financial system needs to be accelerated with a more systematic approach to provide effective credit support to regions, farmers and other sections of the rural community, particularly those with poor resource base, to enable them to exploit new market opportunities and step up growth rate in agriculture.[39]

In the existing multi-agency approach to rural finance, despite high density of the retail outlets of formal credit institutions, some recent innovations in delivery system, and some renewed thrust on rural finance, the problem of outreach, availability of adequate credit at the right time at reasonable cost and almost at door step continue to be elusive for a vast majority of the farmers. Despite progressive institutionalisation of rural credit availability, credit delivery systems and adequate absorptive capacity of the rural populace.

Credit is not only one of the critical input in agriculture, but is also an effective means of rural development. A large number of agencies, including cooperatives, regional rural banks, commercial banks, non-banking financial institutions, self-help groups and a well-spread informal credit outlets together constitute the Indian rural credit delivery system. One of the objectives of the credit policy is to minimise the role of non-institutional sources, mainly the money-lenders in the flow of agricultural credit. Several

initiatives have been taken in this regard since Independence.[40] Some major milestones in rural credit are the acceptance of Rural Credit Survey Committee Report (1954), nationalisation of major commercial banks (1969 & 1980), establishment of regional rural banks (1975), establishment of National Bank for Agriculture and Rural Development (NABARD : 1982) and the ongoing reforms in the financial sector since 1991.[41] Simultaneously, several measures like establishment of Lead Bank Scheme, direct lending for the priority sectors, banking sectors linkage with the government sponsored programmes targeted at the poor, Differential Rate of Interest Scheme, the Service Area Approach, the SHG-Bank linkage Programme were undertaken. In recent years, initiatives like Kisan Credit Card Scheme, Special Agricultural Credit Plans and Rural Infrastructural Development Fund Schemes have been introduced to enhance the flow of credit to the rural sector. Several committees have been constituted to suggest ways to increase the availability of institutional credit to the rural areas. These include the Expert Committee on Rural Credit (Chairperson: V.S. Vyas), Committee on Agricultural Credit through Commercial Banks (Chairperson : R.V. Gupta), Committee on Cooperative (Chairperson : Vikhe Patil), Advisory Committee on flow of credit to Agriculture (Chairperson : V. S. Vyas) and Task Force on Revival of Cooperative Credit Institutions (Chairperson : A. Vaidyanathan). The government has accepted and implemented several of their suggestions. However, in spite of these efforts and initiatives, the flow of credit to the agricultural sector remains a factor of concern and the moneylenders continue to play a dominant role in the delivery of credit to rural households, the reach of institutional agencies has remained poor, particularly to the small and marginal farmers. Also empirical studies on the characteristics of borrowers from institutional and non-institutional sources are few and the factors which determine the choice of credit outlook have not been well discussed among the academic and policy makers.

For a scientific and empirical analysis of rural credit delivery, one needs to examine at the micro level the distinguishing characteristics of the rural households. Such an analysis would be

useful in understanding the reasons for approaching one type of credit institution as opposed to others by groups of borrowers. This will also help in reorienting the credit policies and programmes for a better impact.

Trends in Rural Credit

India is the country of villages and agriculture is the occupation of the major chunk of the working population. Being a developing economy, India has to take care of the development of its agricultural and rural sectors. This phenomenon is possible only through extending more and more credit facilities to the rural areas and by assigning the status of priority sector to agriculture. Again, being a poor country India has been facing the lack of capital for rural and agricultural development. There are numerous examples of the adverse impact of negligence of agricultural sector. The most recent is the suicide attempts made by the farmers in Andhra Pradesh, Karnataka and Maharashtra and food shortage in the country.

Actually the priority sector today in India has got three phases—prior to 1969, 1969 to 1990 and 1991 onwards. Before 1969, the commercial banks in India were not interested in financing of the priority sector. After the nationalisation of the major commercial banks in 1969, the commercial banks were assigned the task of financing the priority sector. In 1991, the Government of India adopted the New Economic Policy of Liberalisation, Privatisation and Globalisation under structural adjustment programme. The available data indicate that the priority sector lendings by public sector banks have got decreasing trend since 1991 under financial sector reforms. Thus an alarming and burning issue which requires an urgent attention of the planner, policy makers and executors is: if the public banks withdraw their hands from financing the priority sector, who will provide financial and credit facilities to the priority sector ?

The objective of this section is to evaluate the performance of public sector banks in regard to expansion of banking services to the unbanked area in regional perspective and to evaluate the performance with regard to advances to the priority sector during pre- and post-1991 periods.

The regional disparity in the distribution of bank offices and population has been studied with the help of Genne's coefficient of concentration which has been calculated on the basis of the following formula :[42]

$$\text{G.C.G.} = \frac{1}{100} [(X_1 \cdot Y_2 - X_2 \cdot Y_1) + (X_2 \cdot Y_3 - X_3 \cdot Y_2) + \ldots\ldots + (X_n \cdot 100 - Y_n \cdot 100)]$$

Where,

G.C.C. = Ginni's coefficient of concentration

X_1, X_2............ X_n = Subsequent cumulative percentage of population distributed over States.

Y_1, Y_2............ Y_n = Subsequent cumulative percentage of bank offices distributed over States.

The Ginni's coefficient of concentration has been calculated for 1981, 1991 and 2001 mainly to find the trend therein.

The inter-regional variation in the distribution of bank offices, bank deposits and bank credits have been studied with the help of coefficient of variation. The regional inequality in regard to per capita bank deposit and per capita bank credit has been calculated on the basis of the following formulae:[43]

$$Vwc = \sqrt{\frac{\Sigma(C_i - C)^2 . \frac{P_1}{P}}{C}}$$

$$Vwd = \sqrt{\frac{\Sigma(D_i - D)^2 . \frac{P_1}{P}}{D}}$$

Where,

V_{wc} = Weighted index of regional inequality in respect of per capita bank credit.

V_{wd} = Weighted index of regional inequality in respect of per capita bank deposit.

C_i = Per capita bank credit for the ith state.

C = Per capita bank credit at the national level.

P_i = Population of the ith state.

P = Population of India.

D_i = Per capita bank deposits for the ith state.

D = Per capita bank deposit at the national level.

The indices of regional inequality in respect of bank credit and bank deposit have been calculated for 1981, 1991 and 2001 to find out the trends therein.

For analysing the trends in priority sector advances by the public sector banks, the time series data on the number of accounts and amount of advances (from 1981 to 2006) have been taken from the various issues of the *Economic Survey*, Government of India. The rupee value of the amount has been deflated at 1980-81 prices. The exponential trend equation of the type $Y = ab^x$ has been fitted into the time series data from 1981 to 1990, 1991 to 2000 and 2001 to 2006 on the amount of advances to the priority sector, and also on the advances per account. The student's t-distribution has been applied to test the significance of the estimates.[44] The following formula have been used —

Exponential trend equation : $y = ab^x$

Logar·thm form of equation : $\log y = \log a + X \cdot \log b$

Corresponding normal equations :

$$\Sigma \log y = N \cdot \log a + \log b \cdot \Sigma x$$

$$\Sigma x \cdot \log y = N \cdot \log a \, \Sigma x + \log b \cdot \Sigma x^2$$

Compound growth rate : $GR = 100 \cdot (b - 1)$

$$Syx = \sqrt{\frac{\Sigma \log y^2 - \log a \cdot \Sigma \log y - \log b \cdot \Sigma x \cdot \log y}{N - K}}$$

$$Sb = \frac{Sgx}{\sqrt{\Sigma (x - \overline{x})^2}}$$

$$t = \frac{\log b - 0}{Sb}$$

Where,

y = Amount of rupees of priority sector advances and amount of rupees per account of priority sector advances by public sector banks

X = Number of years

a = Intercept (Parameter)

b = Trend value (Parameter)

CGR = Compound growth rate per cent per annum

Syx = Standard error of estimation

N = Number of years

K = Number of constants in the equation

Sb = Standard deviation of b

t = Student's t-statistics.

The distribution of bank offices and population pressure over States for 1981, 1991 and 2001 has been presented in Table 5.14. The table indicates that there exists an uneven distribution of bank offices which leads to growing inequality among States. For example, in 1981, Gujarat with 4.97 per cent of population had 6.63 per cent of bank offices. The shares of Maharashtra were 9.17 and 10.02 per cent respectively in population and bank offices.

Almost the same trend is evident for 1991 from Table 5.14. Gujarat with 4.88 per cent of population had 6.98 per cent of bank offices. Maharashtra with 9.33 per cent population had 10.72 per cent of bank offices. Bihar on the other hand, with 10.43 per cent of population had only 7.08 per cent of bank offices.

Again in 2001, Gujarat with 4.93 per cent of population had 6.79 per cent of bank office, while Maharashtra with 9.42 per cent of population had 10.65 per cent of bank offices. Bihar, on the other hand, with 8.07 per cent of population had only 4.47 per cent of bank offices.

Table 5.14 also presents a picture of population pressure on the bank offices for 1981, 1991 and 2001. In 1981 the pressure of

population on bank office was observed to be the highest in Assam (39.89 thousand per office), followed by Manipur (35.75 thousand) and Orissa (22.98 thousand). The pressure of population was observed to be the lowest in Punjab (10.59 thousand), followed by Kerala (10.95 thousand). At the national level the population pressure per bank office was observed to be 19.41 thousand persons per office.

> In 1991, the highest pressure of population was observed to be in Manipur (34.47 thousand persons), followed by Tripura (31.92 thousand) and Jammu and Kashmir (30.51 thousand). The minimum pressure of population per bank office was observed to be in Himachal Pradesh (8.53 thousand), followed by Punjab (10.53 thousand) and Gujarat (14.15 thousand). At the national level, the population pressure per bank office was observed to be 20.25 thousand in 1991 which was slightly higher than that in 1981. This also indicates that population is increasing at a faster rate than the rate of increase in the bank office in the country.

In 2001, the population pressure on bank offices was observed to be 22.17 thousand persons at the national level. The highest pressure of population on bank office was observed in Manipur (48.75 thousand), followed by Bihar (40.03 thousand) and Jammu & Kashmir (34.03 thousand). The lowest pressure of population on bank office was observed in Himachal Pradesh (9.41 thousand), followed by Punjab (10.98 thousand) and Gujarat (16.08 thousand persons per bank office).

Further, the Ginnis coefficient of concentration with regard to the regional distribution of bank offices has been found to be 17.53, 15.32 and 4.61 respectively in 1981, 1991 and 2001 (Table 5.17). Though the quantum of regional inequality is small and shows a decreasing trend during 1981 and 2001, it is astonishing that even after 60 years of Independence and 38 years of nationalisation of commercial banks, there exists regional disparity in the distribution of bank offices and population. This unevenness

Table 5.14 : Regional Distribution of Population and Bank Offices in India (1981, 1991 and 2001)

State	1981			1991			2001		
	Population (%)	Bank Office (%)	Population Pressure ('000 Persons per office)	Population (%)	Bank Office (%)	Population Pressure ('000 Persons per office)	Population (%)	Bank Office (%)	Population Pressure ('000 Persons per office)
1	2	3	4	5	6	7	8	9	10
1. Andhra Pradesh	7.81	7.78	19.56	7.86	7.79	20.42	7.37	7.90	20.7
2. Assam	2.82	1.42	39.98	2.64	1.92	27.28	2.59	1.78	32.28
3. Bihar	10.21	6.43	29.93	10.23	7.08	29.24	8.07	4.47	40.03
4. Gujarat	4.97	6.63	14.56	4.88	6.98	14.15	4.93	6.79	16.08
5. Haryana	1.89	2.28	16.04	1.93	2.30	17.00	2.05	2.55	18.17
6. Himachal Pradesh	0.62	1.04	11.58	0.61	1.44	8.53	0.59	1.39	9.41
7. J. & K.	0.87	1.26	13.47	0.91	0.61	30.51	0.98	0.56	39.03
8. Karnataka	5.42	7.89	13.34	5.31	6.60	16.28	5.13	6.69	16.99
9. Kerala	3.71	6.59	19.95	3.44	3.89	17.89	3.10	4.01	17.14
10. Madhya Pradesh	7.62	6.02	24.61	7.83	6.48	24.49	5.88	5.05	25.78
11. Maharashtra	9.17	10.02	17.42	9.33	17.78	17.62	9.42	10.65	19.61
12. Manipur	0.21	0.11	38.59	0.22	0.13	34.47	0.23	0.11	48.75
13. Meghalaya	0.15	0.17	22.51	0.2	0.25	16.17	0.22	0.27	18.16
14. Nagaland	0.11	0.11	19.83	0.14	0.15	19.93	0.19	0.13	32.60
15. Orissa	3.84	2.87	29.98	3.73	3.04	25.09	3.57	2.97	26.66

(Contd.)

Table 5.14 : (Contd.)

State	1981			1991			2001		
	Population (%)	Bank Office (%)	Population Pressure ('000 Persons per office)	Population (%)	Bank Office (%)	Population Pressure ('000 Persons per office)	Population (%)	Bank Office (%)	Population Pressure ('000 Persons per office)
1	2	3	4	5	6	7	8	9	10
16. Punjab	2.44	3.84	10.57	2.39	4.60	10.53	2.37	4.86	10.78
17. Rajasthan	4.99	4.57	21.19	5.2	4.21	25.02	5.50	4.36	27.94
18. Tamil Nadu	7.06	8.49	16.17	6.59	7.50	17.49	6.05	7.58	17.69
19. Tripura	0.30	0.24	24.53	0.33	0.21	31.92	0.31	0.20	34.69
20. Uttar Pradesh	16.21	11.49	27.41	16.47	12.40	26.90	16.17	11.13	32.20
21. West Bengal	7.98	6.28	24.67	8.05	7.77	20.99	7.81	7.42	23.35
22. Others	1.47	4.69	35.45	1.71	3.97	9.09	7.47	9.13	18.02
All India	100.00	100.00	19.41	100.00	100.00	20.25	100.00	100.00	22.17

Source : Basic data compiled from the various issues of Economic Survey, Government of India.

is the reason for the inadequate services provided in different regions in the country.[45]

Table 5.15 presents a detailed picture of credit deposit ratio for 1969, 1981, 1991, 2001 and 2006. It can be seen from the Table that in 1969 Tamil Nadu had got the highest credit-deposit ratio (133.34), followed by West Bengal (113.19) and Maharashtra (101.01). Tripura was observed with the lowest value of credit deposit ratio (4.26), followed by Jammu & Kashmir (4.79) and Nagaland (5.61). In 1981, the credit deposit ratio was observed to be the highest in Tamil Nadu (97.45), followed by Maharashtra (81.82) and Karnataka (77.45). The credit deposit ratio was the lowest in Meghalaya (17.39), followed by Nagaland (30) and Jammu & Kashmir (36.08) in 1981.

Table 5.15 : Regional Distribution of Credit-Deposit Ratio in India

	State	*Credit Deposit Ratio*				
		1969	*1981*	*1991*	*2001*	*2006*
	1	2	3	4	5	6
1.	Andhra Pradesh	100.85	74.25	62.53	64.26	84.31
2.	Assam	38.71	45.83	19.03	32.79	42.03
3.	Bihar	30.80	42.23	39.47	21.10	29.99
4.	Gujarat	48.56	57.57	61.08	43.55	55.73
5.	Haryana	47.46	75.75	59.01	38.25	66.77
6.	Himachal Pradesh	28.19	37.31	35.61	22.32	42.45
7.	J. & K.	4.79	36.08	32.13	20.44	32.90
8.	Karnataka	76.17	77.45	86.80	59.34	81.75
9.	Kerala	65.89	69.14	58.55	41.65	64.34
10.	Madhya Pradesh	58.77	61.01	75.48	47.65	61.29
11.	Maharashtra	101.01	81.82	80.04	84.55	97.71
12.	Manipur	14.51	50.00	72.17	35.85	56.93
13.	Meghalaya	28.41	17.39	17.01	16.08	40.38
14.	Nagaland	5.61	30.00	35.21	15.75	27.12
15.	Orissa	49.51	60.32	78.38	40.80	65.96
16.	Punjab	27.12	44.84	43.95	39.97	57.92
17.	Rajasthan	51.81	70.92	58.12	47.38	83.24
18.	Tamil Nadu	33.34	97.45	98.48	79.00	103.73
19.	Tripura	41.26	44.12	44.93	19.22	29.38
20.	Uttar Pradesh	43.60	46.54	47.67	28.63	41.99
21.	West Bengal	115.19	58.14	52.18	40.19	58.25
22.	Others	73.69	81.44	49.05	71.58	60.93
	All India	77.87	67.57	65.24	55.88	70.50
	Coefficient of Variation	67.30	33.88	40.30	19.54	25.32

Source: Basic data compiled from the various issues of Economic Survey, Government of India.

In 1991, Tamil Nadu had got the highest credit deposit ratio (98.48), followed by Karnataka (88.80) and Andhra Pradesh (82.53). The corresponding lowest value was observed with Meghalaya (17.01), followed by Jammu & Kashmir (32.13) and Himachal Pradesh (35.61).

In 2001, the highest value of credit-deposit ratio was observed with Maharashtra (84.55), followed by Tamil Nadu (79) and Andhra Pradesh (64.26). The lowest value of the credit deposit ratio was observed with Nagaland (15.75), followed by Meghalaya (16.08) and Tripura (19.22).

Finally, in 2006, Tamil Nadu was seen with the highest value of credit deposit ratio (103.73), followed by Andhra Pradesh (84.31) and Rajasthan (83.24), Nagaland, on the other extreme, was found with the lowest value of the credit deposit ratio (27.12) followed by Tripura (29.58) and Bihar (29.99).

At the national level, the values of the credit deposit ratio were observed to be 77.89, 67.57, 65.24, 55.85 and 70.50 for 1969, 1981, 1991, 2001 and 2006 respectively. The coefficients of variation in credit deposit ratio were found to be 67.30, 33.88, 40.30, 19.54 and 25.32 for 1969, 1981, 1991, 2001 and 2006 respectively.

Table 5.16 depicts the State-wise distribution of share of priority sector in the bank credit in 1991, 2001 and 2006. In 1991, Himachal Pradesh had got the highest share (68.8%) in bank credit followed by Manipur (68.5%) and Bihar (67.3%). Maharashtra, on the other hand had the lowest share (24%) in the bank credit followed by West Bengal (29.6%) and Gujarat (39.3%).

In 2001, Bihar had got the highest share (76.6%) for its priority sector in the total bank credit followed by Tripura (71.2%) and Manipur (66.7%). The lowest share in bank credit for the priority sector was observed in Maharashtra (27.1%), followed by West Bengal (31%) and Gujarat (34.7%).

Similarly in 2006, Bihar was observed with the highest share (77.9%) for the priority sector, followed by Tripura (63.8%) and Uttar Pradesh (63%). Maharashtra was seen the lowest share (19.8%) for its priority sector, followed by Gujarat (33.9%) and Haryana (36%). At the national level, the share of priority

Table 5.16 : Regional Distribution of Share of Priority Sector in Bank Credit in India (1991, 2001 and 2006)

	State	*Priority Sector Share in Bank Credit*		
		1991	*2001*	*2006*
	1	2	3	4
1.	Andhra Pradesh	47.50	43.20	48.70
2.	Assam	50.50	40.30	39.20
3.	Bihar	67.30	76.60	77.90
4.	Gujarat	39.30	34.70	33.90
5.	Haryana	66.60	63.10	36.00
6.	Himachal Pradesh	68.80	55.00	59.80
7.	J. & K.	54.10	46.40	49.40
8.	Karnataka	47.00	45.50	45.60
9.	Kerala	47.90	43.80	67.60
10.	Madhya Pradesh	52.70	54.80	60.10
11.	Maharashtra	27.00	27.10	19.80
12.	Manipur	68.50	66.70	38.10
13.	Meghalaya	64.00	47.70	48.50
14.	Nagaland	64.20	53.80	47.00
15.	Orissa	64.60	57.10	46.80
16.	Punjab	61.40	51.20	57.50
17.	Rajasthan	58.60	53.50	50.40
18.	Tamil Nadu	44.60	35.40	40.30
19.	Tripura	66.30	71.20	63.80
20.	Uttar Pradesh	54.10	60.50	63.00
21.	West Bengal	29.60	31.00	35.70
22.	Others	37.70	–	–
	All India	40.40	35.20	37.50
	Coefficient of Variation	23.12	13.07	12.44

Source: Basic data compiled from the various issues of Economic Survey, Government of India.

sector in total bank credit was found to be 40.4 per cent in 2006. The coefficient of variations of State's share of priority sector in total bank credit was found to be 23.12 per cent in 1991 which fall down to 13.07 in 2001 and further to 12.44 in 2006.

The regional distribution of per capita credit and per capita deposit for 1981, 1991 and 2001 has been presented in the Table 5.17. In 1981, the highest per capita deposit (Rs. 1,162) has been observed in Punjab followed by Maharashtra (Rs. 1,025) and Gujarat (Rs. 783). The lowest value of per capita deposit (Rs. 112) has been observed in Manipur, followed by Tripura (Rs. 165) and Orissa (Rs. 166).

Table 5.17 : Regional Distribution of Per Capita Deposit and Credit in India (1981, 1991, 2001)

State	1981		1991		2001	
	Per Capita Credit	*Per Capita Deposit*	*Per Capita Credit*	*Per Capita Deposit*	*Per Capita Credit*	*Per Capita Deposit*
1	2	3	4	5	6	7
1. Andhra Pradesh	260	349	1248	1512	3649	5678
2. Assam	77	169	451	920	1062	3240
3. Bihar	96	226	387	920	578	2741
4. Gujarat	450	783	1697	2779	4418	10149
5. Haryana	372	491	1386	2348	3291	8602
6. Him. Pradesh	177	474	947	2659	2542	11383
7. J. & K.	117	324	356	1109	761	3721
8. Karnataka	364	471	1645	1802	4476	7543
9. Kerala	294	425	1868	2576	3951	9490
10. Madhya Pradesh	139	228	535	1088	2032	4263
11. Maharashtra	839	1025	3023	3776	10496	12414
12. Manipur	56	112	383	531	615	1716
13. Meghalaya	60	346	370	2062	1067	6635
14. Nagaland	78	259	666	1744	573	3641
15. Orissa	100	166	612	781	1401	3435
16. Punjab	521	1162	2142	4673	7035	17600
17. Rajasthan	158	223	622	1070	1901	4012
18. Tamil Nadu	436	447	2054	2086	5941	7528
19. Tripura	73	165	372	827	724	3767
20. Uttar Pradesh	146	313	62	1311	1290	4505
21. West Bengal	409	700	1241	2379	2872	7019
22. Others	3239	3858	8186	7078	11990	16750
All India	506	342	1332	2042	4125	7383

Source: Basic data compiled from the various issues of Economic Survey, Government of India.

Again in 1991, Punjab, Maharashtra and Gujarat have been seen with the first, second and third ranks in per capita deposit with Rs. 4,675, Rs. 3776 and Rs. 2779 respectively, while Manipur, Orissa and Tripura have been seen with the lower values of per capita deposit with Rs. 531, Rs. 781 and Rs. 827 respectively.

Further, in 2001, still again Punjab was found with the highest values (Rs. 17,600) of per capita deposit, followed by Maharashtra (Rs. 12,414) and Gujarat (Rs. 10,149). On the other extreme, Bihar was seen with the lowest value of per capita deposit (Rs. 2,741), followed by Assam (Rs. 3,240) and Jammu and Kashmir (Rs. 3,721).

At the national level, the per capita deposit has shown an

increasing trend as the figure rose from Rs. 342 in 1981 to Rs. 2,042 in 1991 and further to Rs. 7,383 in 2001.

In the case of per capita credit, Maharashtra had got the highest value (Rs. 839), followed by Punjab (Rs. 521) and Gujarat (Rs. 450). The lowest value of per capita credit has been observed with Manipur (Rs. 56), followed by Meghalaya (Rs. 60) and Tripura (Rs. 73) in 1981.

In 1991, the highest value of per capita credit is seen with Maharashtra (Rs 3,023), followed by Punjab (Rs. 2,142) and Tamil Nadu (Rs. 2,054). The corresponding lowest value has been observed with Meghalaya (Rs. 370), followed by Tripura (Rs. 372) and Manipur (Rs. 383).

Again in 2001, the highest value of per capita credit has been observed in Maharashtra (Rs. 10,496), followed by Punjab (Rs. 7,035) and Tamil Nadu (Rs. 59,411). The lowest value of per capita credit has been found with Nagaland (Rs. 573), followed by Bihar (Rs. 578) and Manipur (Rs. 615).

At the national level, like the per capita deposit, the per capita credit has also shown an increasing, as the per capita credit rose from Rs. 506 in 1981 to Rs. 1,332 in 1991 and further to Rs. 4,125 in 2001.

The coefficient of regional inequality in respect of per capita deposit was found to be 22.6009 in 1981 which increased to 116.8267 in 1991 but fell to 0.1318 in 2001. Similarly, the coefficient of regional inequality in respect of per capita credit increased from 22.0369 in 1981 to 47.0960 in 1991, but fell down to 0.1107 in 2001 (Table 5.18).

Table 5.18 : Coefficients of Concentration and Inequalities

Sl. No.	*Particulars*	*1981*	*1991*	*2001*
1	2	3	4	5
1.	Ginnis Coefficient of concentration of Bank offices	17.53	15.32	4.61
2.	Weighted coefficient of Regional Inequality for:			
	(a) Per capita deposit	22.6009	116.8267	0.1318
	(b) Per capita credit	22.0369	47.0960	0.1107

Source: Basic data compiled from the various issues of Economic Survey, Government of India.

Table 5.19 presents the picture of trends in the total amount of priority sector advances by public sector banks during the period 1981 to 1990, 1991 to 2000 and 2001 to 2006. The table reveals that the growth rates were positive in all the 12 sub-sectors of the priority sector during the period 1981 to 1990. During the period 1991 to 2000 the lone negative growth rate was observed with the sub-sector of setting up of industrial estates (Sl. No. 3). During the period 2001 to 2006, the growth rate was found to be negative in the case of small scale organisation for SC/ST for purchase and supply of inputs and marketing of outputs (Sl. No. 11). Considering all the sub-sectors of the priority sector, the growth rate was found to be positive during 1981 to 1990 and 1991 to 2000, but negative during period 2001 to 2006.

Table 5.19 : Trends in Priority Sector Lendings by Public Sector Banks in India (1981 to 2006)

	Sub-sector	*Particulars*	*1981 to 1990*	*1991 to 2000*	*2001 to 2006*
	1	2	3	4	5
1.	Agriculture	GM	6591.93	25252.30	88472.55
		GR	11.80	9.82	19.24
		t	9.715	8.516	8.141
		s	0.001	0.001	0.005
2.	Small Scale industries	GM	5654.62	27097.99	59683.23
		GR	12.78	12.89	9.83
		t	8.344	12.639	9.36
		s	0.001	0.001	0.001
3.	Setting up of industrial estates	GM	54.17	41.12	76.34
		GR	2.42	–9.65	26.76
		t	1.244	14.165	10.438
		s	0.25	0.001	0.001
4.	Small road and transport operations	GM	1334.59	2851.20	4337.13
		GR	13.44	5.96	6.47
		t	2.814	18.309	8.501
		s	0.001	0.001	0.005
5.	Retail Trade	GM	863.36	4217.70	15194.13
		GR	13.32	14.08	32.20
		t	7.778	12.036	15.49
		s	0.001	0.001	0.001
6.	Small Business	GM	474.45	2742.67	7954.99
		GR	22.48	13.69	14.38
		t	8.828	11.76	9.819
		s	0.001	0.001	0.001

(Contd.)

Table 5.19 : (Contd.)

Sub-sector	Particulars	1981 to 1990	1991 to 2000	2001 to 2006
1	2	3	4	5
7. Professional and self-employed persons	GM	479.71	1854.34	4333.09
	GR	22.61	8.96	13.50
	t	9.121	12.489	15.899
	s	0.001	0.001	0.001
8. Education	GM	22.71	196.30	3294.56
	GR	16.07	23.91	60.49
	t	7.27	14.175	8.86
	s	0.001	0.001	0.001
9. Consumption Loan	GM	15.99	68.13	966.72
	GR	5.12	38.96	16.23
	t	1.933	14.853	7.068
	s	0.10	0.001	0.005
10. Small Scale organisations for on lending to other priority sector	GM	5.76	103.76	947.22
	GR	30.63	21.49	26.29
	t	3.55	19.332	1.505
	s	0.001	0.001	0.80
11. Small scale organisations for SC/ST for purchase/supply of inputs marketing of outputs	GM	3.95	28.17	151.91
	GR	52.80	18.71	-45.23
	t	2.171	12.907	0.339
	s	0.20	0.001	0.80
12. Housing Loans	GM	52.75	1367.29	42997.27
	GR	13.06	46.84	7.48
	t	0.31	18.681	1.965
	s	0.80	0.001	0.20
Total	GM	15613.00	67429.73	232294.75
	GR	12.70	13.10	22.15
	t	5.999	11.489	11.90
	s	0.001	0.001	0.001
Priority sector credit as% of total bank credit	GM	41.64	36.91	42.47
	GR	2.96	0.32	–1.16
	t	5.999	8.613	4.362
	s	0.001	0.001	0.02

Notes : 1. GM = Geometric mean in rupees crores.
2. GR = Compound growth rate per cent per annum.
3. t = Student's t-statistics.
4. S = Level of Significance.

Source: Basic data compiled from the various issues of Economic Survey, Government of India.

Table 5.20 presents the picture of trends in amount of rupees per account of priority sector lendings by public sector banks during the periods 1981 to 1990, 1991 to 2000 and 2001 to 2006. Out of the 12 sub-sectors, 4 sub-sectors namely small scale industries (Sl. No. 2), setting up of industrial estates (Sl. No. 3), retail trade (Sl. No. 5) and small scale organisation for SC/ST for purchase and supply of inputs and marketing of outputs (Sl. No. 11), have been observed with the negative growth rates during the period 1981 to 1990. During the period 1991 to 2000, the growth rate of lending in the case of setting up of small industrial estates (Sl. No. 3) has been found negative, and all the rest growth rates have been found positive. Similarly, during the period 2001 to 2006 all the growth rates except the one—small organisations for SC/ST for purchase and supply of inputs and marketing of inputs (Sl. No. 11) have been found positive.

Table 5.20 : Trends in Priority Sector Lendings by Public Sector Banks in India

	Sub-sector	*Particulars*	*1981 to 1990*	*1991 to 2000*	*2001 to 2006*
	1	*2*	*3*	*4*	*5*
1.	Agriculture	GM	2328.63	12808.79	46774.36
		GR	1.04	12.49	12.58
		t	2.716	0.766	9.983
		s	0.05	0.025	0.001
2.	Small Scale industries	GM	34789.97	99329.90	346508.75
		GR	–2.58	15.55	3.07
		t	4.119	12.95	1.899
		s	0.005	0.001	0.20
3.	Setting up of industrial estates	GM	413565.87	320688.24	53985.48
		GR	–2.12	–26.85	14.18
		t	1.394	9.933	4.243
		s	0.20	0.001	0.001
4.	Small road and transport operations.	GM	23811.78	42811.09	97834.63
		GR	1.39	9.50	14.13
		t	1.388	6.926	11.498
		s	0.20	0.001	0.001
5.	Retail Trade	GM	3811.42	9872.26	47981.85
		GR	–4.22	18.06	18.52
		t	7.847	6.559	8.409
		s	0.001	0.001	0.001

(*Contd.*)

Table 5.20 : (Contd.)

	Sub-sector	Particulars	1981 to 1990	1991 to 2000	2001 to 2006
	1	2	3	4	5
6.	Small Business	GM	2708.07	6398.96	40631.82
		GR	1.25	17.29	25.75
		t	1.542	9.598	9.512
		s	0.001	0.001	0.05
7.	Professional and self-employed persons	GM	3034.75	10120.75	44752.05
		GR	7.49	18.14	5.65
		t	6.42	9.413	3.225
		s	0.001	0.001	0.20
8.	Education	GM	3031.66	24442.01	11873.77
		GR	6.36	17.49	12.34
		t	6.433	7.184	1.967
		s	0.001	0.001	0.20
9.	Consumption Loan	GM	983.09	2166.99	54785.61
		GR	8.82	18.46	19.47
		t	0.999	6.299	9.336
		s	0.40	0.001	0.001
10.	Small Scale organisations for on lending to other priority sector	GM	7126.74	59286.57	316449.05
		GR	34.10	11.69	39.68
		t	3.32	9.12	2.301
		s	0.02	0.001	0.10
11.	Small scale organisations for SC/ST for purchase/supply of inputs marketing of outputs	GM	5942.06	26323.01	175917.11
		GR	-97.22	8.50	-4.53
		t	2.311	3.161	0.639
		s	0.05	0.02	0.60
12.	Housing Loans	GM	3095.25	25976.53	344907.65
		GR	14.06	8.98	3.91
		t	2.195	9.785	9.187
		s	0.10	0.001	0.001
	Total	GM	7640.42	21441.11	78246.10
		GR	14.68	18.17	16.08
		t	3.19	6.414	9.698
		s	0.01	0.001	0.001

Notes : 1. GM = Geometric mean in rupees.
2. GR = Compound growth rate per cent per annum.
3. t = Student's t- statistics
4. S = Level of Significance.

Source: Basic data compiled from the various issues of Economic Survey, Government of India.

One clear cut implication of the financial sector reforms for the banking system and priority sector lendings has been revealed as the negligence of the priority sector by the public sector banks. It is evident from the fact that the percentage share of the priority sector credit in the total bank credit increased at the rate of 2.96 per cent and 0.32 per cent per annum during the periods 1981 to 1990 and 1991 to 2000 respectively, but during the period 2001 to 2006, it has been found falling at the rate of 1.16 per cent per annum. Thus the impact of the financial sector reforms on the priority sector lending has been very much adverse.

Microfinance and Rural Development

Microfinance refers to the provision of financial services to lower income groups, which also include self-employed people. Grameen Bank in Bangladesh introduced the concept of microfinance and now it is a worldwide movement as it has been replicated in different countries. This is the approach which focused on reducing poverty by providing financial services and other services through institutions which are funded by various donors and government subsidies.

Microfinance is one of the most sustainable and effective tool to provide an access to institutional credit to the poor sections of the society. Whereas microcredit refers to availability of loans in small quantities, microfinance has a broader meaning and includes other financial services like savings insurance, etc.

Realising the importance of credit in the development process, the Government of India and the Reserve Bank of India have taken various steps in this regard and have encouraged banks to make timely and adequate finance available to poor for agriculture as well as allied activities making institutional credit to the poor.

Organisations like MYRDA, NABARD have made microfinance an undividable part of Indian rural development. Also many funding agencies and NGOs are involved in this work of microfinance. There are also many other small institutions which are working extensively in the field of microfinance.

Along with NGOs, the corporate participation in this field have given new radical direction to this revolution of microfinance.

The most successful region of the microfinance is the southern part of India. Andhra Pradesh has become the example of this issue. If one takes into account the overall figure for microfinance in all over India then around 55 per cent is only in Andhra Pradesh.

There are many parts of India which are performing very poorly in the case of microfinance, but at the same in which it is expanding, its branches will soon be reaching to each and every household.

As per recent information of NABARD, one can say that microfinance has proved as a boon for the rural poor :

- More than 8.5 lakh of SHGs have been formed and are functioning successfully in India.
- Innumerable of poor families got sustainable financial services through SHGs.
- Besides the big donor agencies like NABARD and SIDBI, etc., there are 2,800 partner NGOs working extensively in this field of microfinance.
- Many foreign agencies are working comprehensively in this field such as CARE-CASHE.
- Huge participation of corporate icons in microfinance are also witnessed like HLL's project—Sakti and ITC's Women Empowerment.

As in any commercial activity, risk is inherent in microfinance particularly when there is no collateral to fall back upon. Today the risk management in microfinance has assumed greater significance. As banks are preparing to comply with related base norms, the portfolio of microfinance is primarily exposed to credit risk. This is nothing but default/diminution in the credit amount released and operational risk which is the risk of loss resulting from inadequate or failed internal process, people and system or from external events. An element of market risk, which is prevalent in normal commercial activity is significantly absent, perhaps owing to lower value of the product output which was marketed through retail arrangement. The primary risk type in microfinance activities is the operational risk.

As lending through SHG by the commercial banks is on the increasing trend, there is a need to adopt a robust portfolio approach in this regard, since the SHG lending outside the purview of individual credit risk rating framework will help in monitoring the outstanding SHG lending portfolio. There is no doubt that lenders may spread their risk when they go to this particular sector.

A study conducted by the Indian Banks Special Unit for Microfinance, Usilampatti, covering southern districts of Tamil Nadu, revealed that the identified factors having high risk are clubbing too many government programmes, higher than required loan size, frequent switch over of the field staff, lack of monitoring non-transparent deals devoid of good governance, etc. by the SHG/NGO.[46]

Some of the risk mitigating measures in the microfinance through SHG are as follows :

- Encouraging short-term loans to build credit track record history.
- Better to maintain peer pressure by making the loan available only for part of the SHG group so that it is not shared by all in the group.
- SHGs to take up restructuring exercise.
- Migration from group to individual loan after imparting certain amount of training.
- Active SHG leaders are to be identified as Field Official to prevent the staff turnover, but rotation of leaders should be ensured.
- Transparency and good governance are put in place for ensuring end use of funds.
- Proper management information system (MIS) is to be ensured for regular flow of information on the functioning of the unit financed through microfinance so as to have close supervision or monitoring.
- A structured risk assessment model may be evolved to capture the risk at least on a half-yearly basis.
- In a tie up with a national insurance company, micro insurance product may be offered to the SHGs as a cover to protect life/non-life risks.

- Quality internal audit system should be put in place and the important needs to be explained to the SHG members.
- Identify the auditable risks faced by microfinance institutions and try to minimise the non-auditable risks.
- Create industry-wise benchmarks on the basis of historical performance.

There is a need to make microfinance lending through MFIs an attractive business proposition for potential lenders, as the huge demand for financial services by the poor can largely be satisfied through mobilising capital from the formal sector. In addition to credit/financial outputs, injecting managerial inputs into the activities of the target groups would be required, as credit alone may not yield the expected results. This is possible only through close interaction with the target groups. Expansion of micro-credit programme by retaining all the distinctive aspects is also a challenge to be squarely met.

Microfinance is the key *mantra* for a sustained and long-term economic growth in India. The same is in sharper focus today with the government taking keen interest to ensure a comprehensive and visible upliftment of rural people through effective implementation of various schemes. Therefore, it is clear that the microfinance is the most important factor to attain sustainable rural development.

Microfinance in India

Historically, there has been observed a concentration of MFIs/SHGs in southern States of India mainly on account of proactive role played by the State Governments. However, the NABARD has taken up intensification in 13 identified States which account for about 70 per cent of the rural poor population, viz. Uttar Pradesh, Orissa, West Bengal, Madhya Pradesh, Rajasthan, Chhattisgarh, Jharkhand, Bihar, Uttarakhand, Assam and Himachal Pradesh. Consequently, the share of cumulative SHGs credit linked in southern States declined from 71 per cent in March 2001 to 54 per cent in March 2005. During 2005-06 the number of SHGs credit linked increased significantly in some of the major priority States like Maharashtra

(60,324), Orissa (57,640), West Bengal (43,553), Uttar Pradesh (42,263), Rajasthan (38,165), Assam (25,215) and Chhattisgarh (12,722) (Table 5.21). During 2002-06, the number of SHGs credit linked in 13 States of priority constituted 54.4 per cent of the all India credit linkage of 6,20,109 SHGs. At present there are over 2.2 million SHGs credit linked with banks. Out of these, there are over a million SHGs which are now over three years old. These SHGs have not only availed of loans but have also gone in for repeat loans. It is being emphasised that a number of the older SHGs would now be in a position to graduate into micro-enterprises by taking to income generating activities. Though micro-enterprises are not a panacea for the complex problem of chronic unemployment and poverty, yet promotion of micro-enterprises is a viable and effective strategy for achieving significant gains in incomes and assets of poor and marginalised people.

Table 5.21 : Cumulative Growth in SHGs-Bank Linkage in Priority States

(as on 31st March)

	States	*2002*	*2003*	*2004*	*2005*	*2006*
	1	2	3	4	5	6
1.	Assam	1024	3477	10706	31234	56449
2.	Bihar	3957	8161	16246	28015	46221
3.	Chhattisgarh	3763	6763	9796	18569	31291
4.	Gujarat	9496	13875	15974	24712	34160
5.	Himachal Pradesh	5069	8875	13228	17798	32920
6.	Jharkhand	4198	7765	12647	21531	30819
7.	Maharashtra	19619	28065	38535	71146	131470
8.	Madhya Pradesh	7981	15271	27095	45105	57125
9.	Orissa	20553	42272	77588	123256	180896
10.	Rajasthan	12564	22742	33846	60006	98171
11.	Uttar Pradesh	33114	53696	79210	119648	161911
12.	Uttarakhand	3323	5853	10908	14043	17588
13.	West Bengal	17143	32647	51685	92698	136251
	Total Priority States	141804 (31)	249462 (35)	397464 (37)	667761 (41)	1005372 (45)

Note : Figures within brackets indicate percentage share of priority States in total number of SHGs credit linked.

Source : NABARD, (2006), *Progress of SHG-Bank Linkage* (2005-06), NABARD, Mumbai.

Graduation of SHG members to take up micro-enterprises requires intensive training on various aspects of management including understanding the market structure, fine-tuning of skills and entrepreneurship management. During 2005-06, a focused and location specific Micro Enterprises Development Programme (MEDP) on skill upgradation and development for sustainable livelihood for members of matured SHGs was launched. The MEDP aims at facilitating quick inputs to members of matured SHGs on technical skills in enterprises, basic entrepreneurial inputs and aspects covering markets. The active participation of women (90%) and timely loan repayment (95%) continue to be prominent features of the programme. The programme has enabled an estimated 24.25 million poor households in the country to get access to microfinance from the formal banking system, as on 31st March, 2005, registering a growth of 45 per cent over the previous year.

In line with the announcement in the Union Budget for 2006-07, a new refinance scheme, viz. separate line of credit for financing farm and investment activities through SHGs was introduced by the NABARD. A sum of Rs. 500 crore was earmarked for providing refinance under the scheme during 2006-07. Under the scheme, term loan and cash credit limit to SHGs extended by scheduled commercial banks, regional rural banks and cooperative banks, exclusively for farm production and investment activities covering agriculture and allied activities, are eligible for 100 per cent refinance from the NABARD. Consumption credit up to 30 per cent of overall limit is also eligible for the purpose.

Out of the three models emerged under the SHG-Bank Linkage Programme over two years, 80.7 per cent of the SHGs were financed by banks under model II, involving NGOs and government agencies. The performance of SHGs in terms of bank loans and refinance over a period of time can be well understood from Table 5.22, whereas the linkage position—agency-wise has been given in Table 5.23 and model-wise linkage position in Table 5.24.

Table 5.22 : SHG-Bank Linkage Programme

(*Amount in Rupees Crore*)

Year	SHGs Financed by banks		Bank Loan		Reference	
	During the year	Cumulative	During the year	Cumulative	During the year	Cumulative
1	2	3	4	5	6	7
1992-99	33	33	57	57	52	52
1999-00	82	115	136	193	98	150
	(148)	(247.9)	(138.1)	(238.1)	(88.4)	(188.4)
2000-01	149	264	288	481	245	395
	(82)	(129.9)	(111.8)	(149.2)	(150)	(163.3)
2001-02	198	461	545	1026	395	790
	(33)	(74.9)	(89.5)	(113.4)	(61.4)	(100)
2002-03	256	717	1022	2049	622	1413
	(30)	(55.4)	(87.4)	(99.6)	(57.5)	(78.8)
2003-04	362	1079	1856	3904	705	2118
	(41)	(50.4)	(81.5)	(90.6)	(13.3)	(49.9)
2004-05	539	1618	2994	6898	968	3086
	(49)	(50)	(61.4)	(76.7)	(37.2)	(45.7)
2005-06	620	2239	4499	11398	1068	4154
	(15)	(38.3)	(50.3)	(65.2)	(10.3)	(34.6)

Note : Figures in brackets show annual percentage growth.

Source : NABARD (2006), *Progress of SHG-Bank Linkage* (2005-06), NABARD, Mumbai.

Significant progress has been made during the year 2005-06 that witnessed sustained expansion of the programme with credit linkage of 0.6 million non-SHGs by the banking system, taking the accumulation number of such SHGs from 1.6 million on March 31, 2005 to 2.2 million on March 31, 2006. Banks extended loans of Rs. 4,499 crore during 2005-06, registering a growth of 50.3 per cent over the previous year. The average per SHG bank loan increased from 44,624 in 2004-05 to Rs. 50,920 in 2005-06, reflecting deepening of the credit access among the SHGs. The programme continued to enlist the massive support of the rural poor families, thus benefiting through SHGs increased from 24.3 million as on March 31, 2005 to over 32.9 million as on March 31, 2006, registering a growth of 35.4 per cent.

The SHG-bank linkage programme is now considered by the banking system as a commercial proposition, with advantages of

Table 5.23 : Linkage Position (Cumulative)—Agency-wise (As at the end of March)

Agency	Number of SHGs ('000)			
	2004-05	2005-06	Percentage Variation	
			2004-05	2005-06
1	2	3	4	5
1. Commercial Banks	843 (52)	1188 (53)	57 (60)	41 (61)
2. Regional Rural Banks	564 (35)	740 (33)	39 (30)	31 (29)
3. Credit Cooperative Bank	211 (13)	310 (14)	57 (9)	46 (10)
Total	1618 (100)	2238 (100)	50	38
4. Commercial Banks	4159	6987	84	68
5. Regional Rural Banks	2100	3322	64	58
6. Credit Cooperative Bank	640	1087	73	70
Total	6899 (100)	11396 (100)	77	65

Source : NABARD, (2006), *Progress of SHG Bank Linkage (2005-06)*, NABARD, Mumbai.

lower transaction costs and higher coverage of rural clientele by the bank branches. Commercial banks have maintained good progress in financing SHGs as their share increased from 52.2 per cent in 2004-05 to 53.1 per cent in 2005-06 (Table 5.23). The share of cooperative banks in SHG linkage increased marginally from 13 per cent to 13.9 per cent over the period, while that of regional rural banks declined from 34.8 per cent to 33 per cent. The number of SHGs financed by cooperative banks increased sharply from 2,11,137 at the end of March 2005 to 3,10,230 by the end of March 2006, reflecting significant interest being evinced by many cooperative banks.

Continuous efforts are being made to promote linkage of microfinance institutions (MFIs) with banks. With a view to promoting flow of commercial loans from banks to MFIs, a scheme was launched by NABARD during 2005-06 to provide financial support to banks towards rating of MFIs. This scheme has since been made more liberal and extended up to March 31, 2008. A

Table 5.24 : Position of SHG-Bank-Linkage (Model-wise)

Model		As on March 31, 2005		As on March 31, 2006	
		No. of SHG ('000)	Bank Loan (Rs. crore)	No. of SHG ('000)	Bank Loan (Rs. crore)
1		2	3	4	5
1.	SHGs Promoted, guided and financed by banks	343 (21)	1013 (15)	449 (20)	1637 (14)
2.	SHGs promoted by NGOs and financed by banks using NGOs Govt. agencies and financed by banks	1158 (72)	5529 (80)	1646 (74)	9200 (81)
3.	SHGs promoted by NGOs and financed by banks using NGOs formal agencies as financial intermediaries	117 (7)	356 (5)	143 (6)	561 (5)
	Total	1618 (100)	6898 (100)	2238 (100)	11398 (100)

Notes : 1. Figures in brackets indicate percentage to total.
2. Figures may not add up to their respective totals due to rounding off.

Source : NABARD, (2006), *Progress of SHG Bank Linkage* (*2005-06*), NABARD, Mumbai.

scheme called Capital/Equity Support to MFIs from Microfinance Development Fund (MFDF) was announced by NABARD. The scheme provides for capital/equity support to various types of MFIs by NABARD to enable them to leverage capital/equity for accessing commercial and other funds from banks for providing financial services at an affordable cost to the poor and to enable MFIs to achieve sustainability in their credit operations over a period of three to five years.

In order to examine the issues relating to allowing banks to adopt agency model by using infrastructure of civil society organisations, appointment of banking correspondents to function as intermediaries between the lending banks and the beneficiaries

and identifications of steps to promote MFIs, an In-House group (Chairman H.R. Khan) was set up in the Reserve Bank of India. The group submitted its final report in July 2005. Based on the recommendations of the group, and with the objective of ensuring greater financial inclusion and increasing the outreach of the banking sector, banks have been permitted to use the services of non-governmental organisations/self-help groups, microfinance institutions and other civil society organisation as intermediaries in providing financial and banking services and business correspondent models.

MFIs hold significant potential, but they also need to be challenged to make an increasing contribution to scale consistent with cost sustainability and efficiency of operations. National Microfinance Information Bureau (NMIB) may be established by the NABARD to gather information on business correspondents. The business facilitators correspondents may have the contractual relationship with only one bank and NMIB may also facilitate sharing of such information. The NABARD may also capture and share data/information on the MFIs and NGOs associated with SHG-Bank linkage and MFI-Bank linkage programme.

With the aim of knowing the appropriate functioning of MFIs, their rating is required. Basically, the rating tools attempt to access whether the MFI is operating on sound lines and on sustainable basis. Rating is a prerequisite for extension of financial arrangements. Rating can also give a comparative position of the MFI in relation to its peers. The following non-financial parameters are to be examined while arriving at the rating of MFIs :

(a) Governance — Whether board members actually participate in the meetings and take major policy decisions.
(b) Qualification and competence of top management.
(c) Human Resource Policies – Well laid out recruitment and training system.
(d) Systems and producers — Well laid down policies for processing and authorisation.

(e) Organisational structure.
(f) Product Range – In tune with the requirement of client group.
(g) Geographical spread.

With the intention of strength ending the MFI system in the country, the following proactive measures may be introduced :

(a) Introduction of a separate accounting and auditing standard system for MFIs so that it would establish a uniform accounting system which is less stringent than the system applicable to ordinary business firms;
(b) MFIs should be managed by professionals to enable MFIs maintain a high degree of professionalism in their operations;
(c) MFIs should make a clearly specified policy statement that includes periodical voluntary disclosure of operations, activities, financial position for the benefit of the public;
(d) MFIs should, in their own, consent to have a rating for their business activities, so that the members of the public would have required information on them; and
(e) MFIs should strive to build internal reserves out of operational surpluses to enable them to absorb loan losses, withstand adverse shocks and go through difficult periods.

Microfinance needs to be explored in the light of the new paradigm described above. The Reserve Bank of India and the NABARD recognise the growing importance of microfinance and are committed to enable its healthy growth. However, several issues, both in regard to regulation as well as development of MFIs need to be considered and must be comprehensively addressed. While the report of Khan Committee would provide a good starting point for taking a view on development aspects, in particular the CGAP's guiding principles on regulation and supervision on microfinance providing a valuable and globally relevant framework in regard to the regulatory issues. The proposed forum for a consultative process on the MFIs would also

be useful in evolving an appropriate framework for development of the MFI sector, no doubt, a very well-crafted balance between the regulation and growth objectives would be warranted in formulating out approach to a regulatory regime, keeping in view the big challenge of financial inclusion of a large segment of the Indian population.

Evaluation of Microfinance Programmes

Microfinance institutions aim to provide credit to the poor who have no access to commercial banks. In general, these institutions receive financial support from Western donors, NGOs or commercial banks, who lend to microfinance institutions, often against below market interest rates. The microfinance institutions, in turn, lend this money to domestic small companies and poor agents. The size of the loans varies but is often small. According to MixMarket (*www.mixmarket.org*) the average loan size in 2005 was only about $ 470.

In addition to loans, microfinance institutions also provide a wider range of financial services. Moreover, they also play an important role in training potential borrowers how to run a firm and deal with health provision. These non-credit services have become more important during recent years.

A recent survey among 518 microfinance institutions in Africa, Latin America, Eastern Europe and Asia reveals that the majority of the microfinance borrowers are served by institutions in South and East Asia. The largest microfinance institutions are found in countries such as India, Bangladesh, Indonesia and Thailand. Bank Rakyat in Indonesia serves over 3.3 million clients; Grameen Bank, ASA, and BRAC all located in Bangladesh have 4 to 5 million active borrowers. In India, large microfinance institutions are SHARE (8,14,000 active borrowers) and Spandan (7,72,000 borrowers) (*www.mixmarket.org*). Surprisingly the extension of services of microfinance to poor people (outreach) in the most populated countries in Asia such as India and China is relatively low.[47]

Microfinance institutions use innovative methods to reduce

lending costs. The main problem with lending to the poor is that information costs are high as compared to the size of the loan. It is generally known that information costs of lending may be high since lenders are not able to distinguish projects with respect to their risk profiles when allocating credit (adverse selection problem) and borrowers may be able to apply the funds to different uses other than those agreed upon with the lender (moral hazard problem). Commercial banks use several methods to reduce these costs, such as screening potential borrowers and monitoring the progress of the project. These methods, however, are too costly if a bank would lend small amounts of money to potential poor clients in remote areas. Moreover, commercial banks often ask borrower to pledge collaterals. However, the latter solution assumes that collateral is available, which is often not the case, particularly not for the poor in many developing countries.

Microfinance institutions also use methods of screening and monitoring to reduce the cost of lending yet, these methods are adjusted to local circumstances enabling them to offer small-sized loans without incurring too high costs. The most well known example is the use of group lending with joint liability. With joint liability lending, the group of borrowers is made responsible for the repayment of the loan of an individual group member, i.e. all the members of the group are jointly responsible and liable. The advocates of group lending argue that joint liability lending provides clear incentives to borrowers to monitor and screen each other. Moreover, the monitoring and screening of group members is efficient and cheap, because members usually live close to each other and/or have social ties (also referred to as social capital). When social ties are present, group members are supposed to be well informed about each other's projects and that this information is almost freely available. Ideally, then the microfinance institutions does not need to take care of the monitoring and screening of group members.

Despite the focus on group lending in the academic literature on microfinance, microfinance institutions often provide individual based lending. In fact, at the moment there is a strong movement from group based lending to individual-based lending system. Even

well known microfinance institutions which traditionally were focusing on group lending, such as the Grameen Bank of Bangladesh, have started individual-based lending, the information costs are reduced by means of regular contacts between the borrower and the microfinance institutions (relationship lending), and by making future loans dependent on regular repayments (so-called dynamic incentives). Nevertheless, group loans are still the most important in terms of the amount of borrowers that receive a loan. According to a study by Lapenu and Zeller,[48] based on a survey among 1,500 institutions around the world carried out in 1999, 68 per cent of borrowers of microfinance institutions receive a loan through group lending programmes.

The advocates of microcredit argue that microcredit can help to substantially reduce poverty.[49] Access to credit can contribute to a long-lasting increase in income by means of a rise in investments in income generating activities and to a possible diversification of sources of income; it can contribute to an accumulation of assets; it can reduce the vulnerability due to illness, drought and crop failures and it can contribute to a better education, health and housing of the borrower. In addition, microcredit can contribute to an improvement of the social and economic situation of women. Finally, microcredit may have positive spillover effects such that its impact surpasses the economic and social improvement of the borrower.

Notwithstanding the predominantly positive view on microcredit can contribute to a substantial reduction in poverty. Many critics show that microfinance does not reach the poorest of the poor,[50-51] or that the poorest are deliberately excluded from microfinance programmes since they lack confidence or they value the loans to be too risky.[52] The poorest of the poor, the so-called core poor, are generally too risk averse to borrow for investment in the future. They will, therefore, benefit only to a very limited extent from microfinance schemes. Second, the core poor are often not accepted in group lending programmes by other group members, because they are seen as a bad credit risk.[53-54] Third staff members of microfinance institutions may prefer to exclude the core poor since lending to them is seen as extremely risky. Finally,

the way microfinance programmes are organised and set up may lead to the exclusion of the core poor. Examples for this exclusion are the requirement to save before a loan can be granted, the minimum amount of loan that needs to be accepted and the requirement a firm is registered before the loan can be granted.[55]

Several critics also argue that group loans lead to high transaction costs. The main advantages of group loans according to the advocates of microfinance is that group loans drastically reduce monitoring costs, since group members live in the same village and know each other well. Therefore, they are able to assess the riskiness of a project against low costs (some even believe that in group lending programmes monitoring is almost costless). Additionally, group members can prevent any moral hazard behaviour without costs by using social sanctions. This, however, ignores the fact that group members sometimes live far away from each other, and need to spend time and energy to assess each other's projects. Moreover, most microfinance schemes have regular group meetings. During these meetings, information about the projects is exchanged and repayment problems are discussed. These group meetings often imply high transaction costs.[56-57] Obviously, then these costs may reduce the positive income generating effect from access to credit.

In additions, it has been argued that sometimes size of the needed loan exceeds the maximum amount that can be borrowed in terms of a group loan. This especially hampers the future growth of these agents who have invested in successful and growing projects[58-59]. Group loans are rigid and often it is very difficult to adapt the loan to the desired credit needs of individual borrowers within the group. Finally, some authors criticise the impact of microcredit on women. Many microfinance schemes have a clear focus on women. Research shows that women are more reliable and have higher payback ratios. Moreover, women use a more substantial part of their incomes for health and education of their children.[60] Thus woman play a very important role in reducing poverty within households. However, the critics argue that often women are forced to handover the loan to men, who subsequently use the loan for their own purposes. This may lead to an additional

burden for women if they are held responsible for the repayment of the loans.[61]

The theoretical discussions about the impact of microfinance on the poverty reduction calls for thorough empirical research. Therefore, it is surprising that there are only a few solid empirical studies available on the possible poverty reducing effects of microcredit. A major problem is how to measure the contribution of microcredit. Three issues are of importance : first, which contribution is seen as the most important (improvement of income, accumulation of assets, empowerment of women, etc.); second, does microcredit reach the core of the poor or does it predominantly improve income of the better-off poor; and third, do the benefits outweigh the cost of microfinance schemes.[62] The latter issue deals with the question of the extent to which subsidies to microfinance organisations are justified.

Most studies measure the impact of microcredit by comparing recipients of microfinance with a control group that has no access to microcredit. This approach may be problematic. However, first, changes of the social and/or economic situation of the recipients of microcredit may not be the result of microfinance. For instance, it is well known that relatively rich agents are less risk averse than relatively poor agents. This may induce rich agents to apply for microcredit whereas poor agents do not apply. In this situation, an ex-post comparison of income of the two groups may lead to incorrect conclusion that microfinance has stimulated income. Second, in order to improve the probability of microfinance being successful, microfinance organisations may decide to develop their activities in relatively more wealthy regions. Obviously, this biases any comparison between recipients of microfinance and the control group.[63-64]

The empirical literature on the outreach of microfinance in terms of the numbers (breadth) and socio-economic level (depth) of clients who are served by microfinance institutions is vast. However, most of these studies suffer from being anecdotal and case study driven. Moreover, only some of the outreach studies are published in established referred international scientific journals so that it is difficult to value their quality.

Nevertheless, some conclusions can be drawn based on the existing literature.

Most studies conclude that microcredit positively contributes to poverty reduction. Microcredit, therefore, may help to solve the poverty problem. This seems to be good news. However, there is much discussion about the question of the extent to which microfinance reaches the core poor. Here a new measurement problem arises, i.e. how to identify the core poor. Nevertheless, Khandker[65] and Eda Rural Systems[66] find that the extremely poor benefit more from microfinance than the moderately poor. On the other hand, several other studies indicate that it is the 'better off' poor rather than the core poor who stand to benefit most. Evidence for this is given in the works of Hulme and Mosley[67] and Copestake.[68]

It is also important to know what costs are involved in making microfinance a successful instrument to combat poverty. Even if microcredit positively contributes to a reduction in poverty, it is unclear to what extent these results cannot be reached by other more cost-efficient instruments. Providing microfinance is a costly business due to high transaction and information costs. Recent research shows that most microfinance programmes are still depending on donor subsidies to meet the high costs, i.e. they are not financially sustainable[69]. A controversial question is whether these subsidies are justified. Unfortunately, this question cannot as yet be answered due to a lack of solid empirical research.

After having reviewed the debate on microfinance and poverty, the conclusion must be that it is still unclear whether microfinance substantially contributes to a reduction of world poverty. Nor is it clear whether microfinance is the most efficient method to reduce poverty. Much more solid empirical research is needed.

In addition, it should be noted that the outreach of microcredit is still small. Despite the enormous increase in microcredit to poor borrowers, in 2004 only 6 per cent of borrowers with an income below $ 365 were able to borrow from microfinance institutions.[70] It is not to be expected that microfinance, without additional

measures in the area of education, health and infrastructure, is able to substantially reduce poverty.

Moreover, recently, we observe a trend towards a further commercialisation of the microfinance sector. Among other things, this has led microfinance organisations to decide on providing a wider range of financial services. We also see a move from traditional group lending to individual loans. This move seems to be bad news for the poor, since the fraction of poor borrowers and female borrowers in the loan portfolio of individual-based institutions is lower than that for group based institutions. At the same time, individual-based microfinance institutions seem to perform better in terms of profitability, as has recently been in a study by Cull and others. Due to the trend of commercialisation of the sector, financial sustainability of microfinance institutions is becoming more and more important at the expense of using credit to help overcome poverty.

To some extent, the trend towards financial sustainability is counteracted by establishing special programmes for the core poor. Especially in Bangladesh, programmes have been initiated to specifically support the core poor, for instance, by the well-known institutions of BRAC and ASA. These programmes not only focus on credit, but also aim to provide a broad range of services for the poor, such as training, health provision and more in terms of the general social development of this category of poor. Yet, the impact of these programmes is still unclear, and the outreach is small, at least for the moment.

Fortunately, there is another, potentially hopeful development. The involvement of traditional commercial banks in microfinance is growing rapidly around the world. In several developing countries large State banks and private banks have started to provide microfinance services. In Pakistan, for instance, a number of private commercial banks have moved into microfinance. In Malaysia, Nepal and Thailand there are programmes stimulating commercial banks to become involved in microfinance. In India the National Bank for Agricultural and Rural Development (NABARD) recently initiated a programme to involve private banks in microfinance. According to recent studies, the growth of

microfinance in India is led by a number of commercial banks such as ICICI, HSBC and ABN AMRO together with private venture capital funds and social venture capitalists.[71,72]

A possible advantage of the move of commercial banks into microfinance may be that these banks can provide credit to the poor, without being dependent on donor subsidies. Commercial banks have diversified portfolios and are able to use profits from lending to wealthy clients to finance (subsidised) loans to the poor, i.e. cross-subsidisation would take place. At the same time, however, one may question why commercial banks would do this. To some extent this trend can perhaps be explained by the increased attention to socially responsible entrepreneurship, at least among the large western banks. Probably more importantly, however, will be the fact that these commercial banks will try to use subsidised loans to the poor as an instrument to enlarge their future profit making portfolio, based on the assumption that lending to them will make them more wealthy clients in the future who can afford to pay market-based interest rates.

A potential disadvantage of the increased involvement of commercial banks is that traditional microfinance institutions are confronted with increased competition in the market for micro loans. While increased competition may lead to increased efficiency and stimulate financial sustainability, it may also reduce the scope for lending to the core poor. Moreover, increased competition and increased supply of loans may result in higher levels of indebtedness of the clients as they may take up multiple loans from different sources at the same time. This may lead to lower repayment rates, endangering the long-term sustainability of the programme.[73] Lower repayment rates, in turn, may lead to less favourable credit contracts for the poorest borrowers for instance, because interest-rates are raised, which may lead them to drop out from the loan portfolio of microfinance institutions. Research shows that borrowers are likely to benefit from increasing competition among microfinance institutions, it also leads to lower levels of welfare for the poorer borrowers.[74]

The trends of commercial banks entering the market for microfinance appears to be one of the most important challenges

for the microfinance business in the near future. The potential of this trend in terms of reducing poverty is still unclear, however. Further research into this important issue is, therefore, highly desirable.

Summary

The Self-Help Groups (SHGs) are small informal and homogeneous groups of not more than 20 members each. The group has been recommended to be informal to keep them away from bureaucracy and corruption, unnecessary expenditure and profit constraints. The size of 20 members has been made mandatory, because any group larger than this would have to be registered under the Indian legal system.

The exponential trend equation of the type $Y = ab^x$ has been fitted into the time series data on the number of SHGs linkage, amount of bank loan to SHGs, amount of refinance assistance to SHGs from NABARD, and the amount of loan per SHGs.

The number of SHGs linked with banks increased from 255 in 1992-93 to 22,38,565 in 2005-06. The amount of bank loans to the SHGs during the period under consideration increased from Rs. 2.9 million to Rs. 1,13,975 million. Similarly, the amount of refinance assistance to the SHGs from NABARD increased from Rs. 2.7 million in 1992-93 to Rs. 41,597 million in 2005-06.

The number of SHGs linked with banks increased from 255 in 1992-93 to 6,20,109 in 2005-06 on year after year basis. The amount of bank loans to the SHGs increased from Rs. 2.9 million in 1992-93 to Rs. 49,090 million in 2005-06. Similarly, the amount of refinance assistance increased from Rs. 2.7 million in 1992-93 to Rs. 10,677 million in 2005-06. Finally, the average amount of loan per SHG increased from Rs. 11,373 in 1992-93 to Rs. 79,164 in 2005-06.

The SHG-bank linkage has increased at the rate of 90.90 per cent per annum during the period 1992-93 to 2005-06. While the amount of the bank loan increased at the rate of 121.37 per cent per annum, the amount of refinance assistance to the SHGs from the NABARD increased at the rate of 104.60 per cent per annum

during the period under consideration. Finally, the amount of average bank loan per SHG increased at the rate of 15.96 per cent per annum during the period from 1992-93 to 2005-06.

The number of villages covered by the Grameen Bank of Bangladesh Project increased from 363 in December 1980 to 1,88,125 in August 1990. The number of the branches of the bank increased from 25 to 741 during the same period. The number of members of the bank increased from 0.15 lakh in December 1980 to 7.90 lakh in August 1990. The number of groups of the bank increased from 2,935 in 1980 to 98,073 in 1988. The number of borrowers of the bank was 0.15 lakh in 1980 which rose to 4.72 lakh in 1988.

In 1980, the bank had disbursed the loan of Taka 1.71 crore. The corresponding figure for 1988 was Taka 128.44 crore. The cumulative amount of loan disbursed increased from Taka 2.01 in August 1990. The savings in group fund increased from Taka 0.15 crore in December 1980 to 57.45 taka crore in August 1990. The savings in the emergency fund of the bank increased from Taka 1.26 crore in 1985 to Taka 11.16 crore in 1990. The loans from group fund (cumulative disbursement since inception) increased from Taka 2.23 crore in 1985 to Taka 30.91 crore in August 1990.

As of July 2004, the Grameen Bank of Bangladesh has 37 million borrowers, 96 per cent of whom are women. With 1,267 branches the Grameen Bank provides services in 46,000 village covering more than 68 per cent of the total villages in Bangladesh.

A new programme known as 'Swarnajayanti Gram Swarozgar Yojana' (SGSY) has been launched in India since April 1999. The SGSY is a holistic programme covering all aspects of self-employment such as organisation of the poor into self-help groups, training, credit, technology, infrastructure, and marketing. The SGSY is funded by the Centre and the States in the ratio of 75 : 25.

With the coming into force of the SGSY, the earlier programmes Integrated Rural Development Programme (IRDP), Training of Youth for Self-Employment (TRYSEM), Development of Women & Children in Rural Areas (DWACRA), Supply of Improved Toolkits to Rural Artisans (SITRA), Ganga Kalyan Yojana (GKY) and Million Shallow Tubewells (MST) are no longer in operation now.

Under the SGSY the beneficiaries are known as 'swarozgaris'. The swarozgaris can be either individuals or groups. The SGSY lays emphasis on the group approach under which the rural poor are organised into self-help groups. In other case, the list of 'below poverty line' (BPL) households identified through BPL census, duly approved by the Gram Sabha forms the basis for identification for assistance under the SGSY. The self-help groups should also be drawn from the BPL list approved by the Gram Sabha.

Between April 1, 1999 and March 31, 2006, about 19 lakh SHGs have been organised under SGSY. Of these, 10 lakh SHGs have passed Grade I and 6.22 lakh Grade-II. About 3.09 lakh SHGs have taken up economic activity. The percentage of SHGs taking up economic activity, out of the SHGs which have passed Grade-II, is around 50 per cent in 2005-06. The number of SHG swarozgaris assisted has also increased from 3.47 lakh to 5.87 lakh during this period. Of course, the number of individual swarozgaris assisted has declined from 5.9 lakh to 2.67 lakh during the same period. The percentage of SC/ST community members assisted under the programme has increased from 44 per cent to 85 per cent, the percentage of women from 44 to 58, and the percentage of disabled from 0.91 per cent to 24.91 per cent.

Between April 1999 and March 2006, an amount of Rs. 8223.20 crore was allocated for the SGSY, out of which a sum of Rs. 7494.75 crore (91%) was utilised. The percentage utilisation to funds available increased from 49 per cent during 1999-2000 to 89 per cent in 2005-06. The utilization of funds towards training and skill development too increased from 3 per cent to 3.64 per cent during this period. With regard to the credit mobilised, a sum of Rs. 1,056 crore was provided to this programme in 1999-2000 which went up to Rs. 1755.27 crore by March 2006. The percentage of credit support increased from 32.96 in 1999-2000 to 61 in 2003-04 and declined to 16.84 in 2005-06. In tune with the growing emphasis on group approach, the investment support towards the group has been making steady progress. This sums the ratio of investment on SHGs *vs.* individuals which has almost gone up by seven times from 0.24 to 1.84 during this period.

Similarly, the per capita investment under this programme has increased from Rs. 17,000 to Rs. 25,000.

All the banks working in East Champaran district of Bihar with their 176 branches had fixed the target of Rs. 1,265 lakh for SGSY through SHGs in 1999-2000. Altogether 3,076 applications were received under SGSY, out of which 2,164 (70.37%) applications were accepted and a sum of Rs. 390 lakh (30.83%) was distributed under the SGSY in the year 1999-2000.

Out of the total applications of 6,363 received in 2002-03, 3,706 (58.49%) were accepted and 3,535 (56.11%) applications were disposed of after granting the loan of Rs. 729.64 lakh under the SGSY in 2002-03. This amount constituted only 40.02 per cent of the target amount.

All the banks taken together approved 1,257 applications and granted the loan of Rs. 1235.16 lakh under the SGSY in 2002-03 in East Champaran district. This amount constituted 58.40 per cent of the target amount.

Empowerment is a process of awareness and capacity building leading to greater participation, the greater decision making power and control and transformative action. The empowerment of women covers both an individual and collective transformation. It strengthens their innate ability through acquiring knowledge, power and experience.

The number of the women SHGs formed so far constitutes 90 per cent or more of the total number of SHGs under SGSY. In 1999-2000 1,16,690 women swarozgaris were assisted which constituted 44.62 per cent of the women swarozgaris. In 2005-06, the number of women swarozgaris swelled to 4,99,154 registering a growth of about 11 per cent during the period 1999-2000 to 2005-06. The number of swarozgaris assisted in 2005-06 constituted 58.39 per cent. During the period of 6 years from 1999-2000 to 2005-06, the total number of women swarozgaris assisted was 30,64,765, its 48.63 per cent swarozgaris was assisted during the period under consideration.

The majority of the self-help groups in Sabour Block of Bhagalpur district in Bihar were organising two meetings in a month for effective working of groups. Most of the groups (45%)

were saving Rs. 25-30 per month per member. About 42 per cent members were taking loan for agricultural activities, besides goat (9%), cow/buffalo (16%), poultry (8%), Bidi making and others (7%). In the case of loan recovery, 71 per cent members have exerted group pressure if loans were not paid timely.

The Government of Bihar initiated a project in 2006 on rural livelihood promotion with the support from the World Bank to rural poor men and women. The name of project is Bihar Rural Livelihood Promotion Project (BRLP) under Bihar Rural Livelihood Promotion Society (BRLPS). The BRLPS is the spearheading agency for the implementation of the project. This project has been named 'Jeevika' in Hindi. Its headquarters is in the Vidyut Bhawan, Patna. Now Jeevika has been designed to address rural poverty in Bihar through the collaboration of the poor, the Government of Bihar and the World Bank.

The BRLP is not a shadow or carbon copy of the IRDP of the Government of India, but is a mega and multidimensional challenging project. The BRLP is a 'rainbow project' of the 'Sushasan' Government of Bihar.

The success story of the tribal women's Self-Help Group from a small colony of Kohima town is truly a motivating story for other groups of women. How insecure and helpless they felt when they were unable to earn even a single paisa. Once determined and with the help from NCUI-CEFP, they quickly mastered various skills to produce items having demand in the market and also picked up the nuances of financial matters. And with regular upgradation of skills they are treading on the path of success. They became conscious about education of their children. They are also most aware about health care of their own-selves and of the family and want to conduct health care programmes for the community. They have learnt the lesson may be a bit late. The lesson they want to pass on is that early to learn and early to work together makes one healthy, wealthy and wise.

India is the country of villages and agriculture is the occupation of the major chunk of the working population. Being a developing economy, India has to take care of the development of its agricultural and rural sectors. This phenomenon is possible only through

extending more and more credit facilities to the rural areas and by assigning the status of priority sector to agriculture. Again, being a poor country, India has been facing the lack of capital for rural and agricultural development. There are numerous examples of the adverse impact of negligence of agricultural sector. The most recent is the suicide attempts made by the farmers in Andhra Pradesh, Karnataka and Maharashtra and food shortage in the country.

At the national level the population pressure per bank office was observed to be 19.41 thousand persons in 1981 in India. The corresponding figure for 2001 was found to be 22.17 thousand persons per office.

The values of the credit deposit ratio at the national level were observed to be 77.89, 67.57, 65.24, 55.85 and 70.50 for 1969, 1981, 1991, 2001 and 2006 respectively.

The share of priority sector in total bank credit was found to be 40.4 per cent in 1991 which declined to 35.2 per cent in 2001 and to 37.5 per cent in 2006. The coefficient of variation of State's priority sector's share in total bank credit was found to be 23.12 per cent in 1991 which fell down to 13.07 per cent in 2001 and further to 12.44 per cent in 2006.

The per capita deposit at the national level has shown an increasing trend, as the figure rose from Rs. 342 in 1981 to Rs. 2,042 in 1991 and further to Rs. 7,383 in 2001. Like the per capita deposit, the per capita credit also has shown an increasing trend at the national level, as the per capita credit rose from Rs. 506 in 1981 to Rs. 1,332 in 1991 and Rs. 4,125 in 2001.

The coefficient of regional inequality in respect of per capita deposit was found to be 22.6009 in 1981 which increased to 116.8267 in 1991 but fell down to 0.1318 in 2001. Similarly, the coefficient of regional inequality in respect of per capita credit increased from 22.0369 in 1981 but fell down to 0.1107 in 2001.

The growth rates of amount (in rupees) of priority sector lending by public sector commercial banks were positive in all the 12 sub-sectors during the period 1981 to 1990. During the period 1991 to 2000, the lone negative growth rate was observed with the sub-sector of setting up of industrial estates. During the period 2001 to 2006, the growth rate in the case of small

organisations of SC/ST for purchase and supply of inputs and marketing of outputs was found negative and all the rest growth rates were found positive.

In the case of amount of rupees per account of priority sector lendings out of the 12, 4 sub-sectors namely small scale industries, setting up of industrial estates, retail trade, and small organisations for SC/ST for purchase and supply of inputs and marketing of outputs, have been observed with negative growth rates during the period 1981 to 1990. During the period 1991 to 2000, the growth rates of lendings in the case of setting up of small industrial estates has been found negative, and all the rest growth rates have been found positive. Similarly, during the period 2001 to 2006, all the growth rates except the one small organisations for SC/ST for purchase and supply of inputs and marketing of outputs have been found positive. The percentage share of the priority sector credit in the total bank credit provided by the public sector banks has been found increasing at the rate of 2.96 per cent and 0.32 per cent per annum during the periods 1981 to 1990 and 1991 to 2000 to 2006 it has been found falling at the rate of 1.16 per cent per annum. Thus the impact of the financial sector reforms on the priority sector lendings has been very much adverse.

In India, economic reforms with human face have been accepted as the guiding principle of sustainable development keeping the poor at the centre stage, the policies need to be reoriented so as to develop and optimise the potential of such a large segment of the population and enable them to contribute in the growth process significantly in terms of output, income, employment and consumption. After the pioneering efforts of the last ten years or so, the microfinance scene in India has reached a take-off point. With some efforts substantial progress can be made in taking MFIs to the next orbit of significance and sustainability. This needs innovative and forward looking policies, based on the ground realities of successful MFIs. This combined with a commercial approach from the MFIs in making microfinance financially sustainable, will make this sector vibrant and help achieve its single minded mission of providing financial services to the rural poor.

It is necessary to recognise that in India we have to focus on extending financial services in both rural and urban areas for ensuring financial inclusion of all segments of the population. At the same time, one should avoid the temptation of creating one set of banking and financial institutions to cater to set the poor or the unorganised and another for the rest. The medium to long-term objective should be to ensure inclusion of all segments in the mainstream institutions while taking advantage of the flexibility of multiplicity of models of delivering a wide range of financial services. In this light, a comprehensive framework to revive the cooperative credit system, revitalise the regional rural banks and reorient commercial banking systems needs to get a high priority while simultaneously encouraging and enabling the growth of microfinance movement in India, which has been very successful. It is required to build on its strengths and extend it to vast areas which are inadequately covered by both banking and micro-credit entities.

Microfinance broadly defined, needs to be explored in the light of the new paradigm described. the Reserve Bank of India and the NABARD recognised the growing importance of microfinance and are committed to enable its healthy growth. However, several issues, both in regard to regulation as well as development of the MFIs need to be considered and must be comprehensively addressed. While the report of the Khan Committee would provide a good starting point for taking a view on developmental aspects, in particular, the CGAP's guiding principles on Regulation and Supervision of Microfinance provide a valuable and globally relevant framework in regard to the regulatory issues. The proposed forum for a consultative process on the MFIs would also be useful in evolving an appropriate framework for development of the MFI sector. No doubt, a very well-crafted balance between the regulation and growth objectives would be warranted in formulating our approach to a regulatory regime, keeping in view the big challenge of financial inclusion of a large segment of the Indian population.

It is unclear whether microfinance contributes to a reduction in poverty or is the most efficient method to reduce poverty

without additional measures in areas such as education, health and infrastructure. The entry of commercial banks into microfinance may increase the competition for traditional microfinance institutions and reduce lending to the core poor, even if it improves financial sustainability.

The trend of commercial banks entering the market for microfinance appears to be one of the most important challenges for the microfinance business in the near future. However, the potential of this trend in terms of reducing poverty is still unclear. Further research into this important issue is, therefore, highly desirable.

REFERENCES

1. Ramanathan, A., (2006) (quoted by), "Paradigm Shift in Rural Banking: A Case of Microfinance Movement in India Through SHG-Bank Linkage Programme", in Kasturi Nageshwara Rao (Ed.), *Rural Credit and Microfinance*, The ICFAI University Press, Hyderabad.
2. Croxton, Fredrick E. *et al.* (1973), *Applied General Statistics*, Prentice Hall of India, New Delhi.
3. Harper, Malcolm, (2002a), "Promotion of Self-Help Groups under the SHG-Bank Linkage Programme in India", paper presented at the seminar on *SHG-Bank Linkage Programme* at New Delhi, November 25-26, published by Microcredit Innovation Department, NABARD, Mumbai.
4. Harper, Malcolm, (2002 b), "Self-Help Groups and Grameen Bank Groups: What are the Differences", in Thomas Fisher and M.S. Sri Ram (eds.), *Beyond Micro-credit: Putting Development Back into Micro-Finance*, Sage-Vistar Publications, New Delhi.
5. Montgomery, R., D. Bhattacharya and David Hulme, (1996) "Credit for the Poor in Bangladesh, The BRAC, Rural Development Programme and the Government Thana Resource Development & Employment Programme", in David Hulme and Paul Mosley (eds.), *Finance against Poverty*, Vol. II, Routledge, London and New York.
6. Karmakar, K.G., (1991) *Rural Credit and Self-Help Groups* (*Micro-Finance Needs and Concepts in India*), Sage Publications, New Delhi.
7. Abdullah, Shahnaz T., Rafique Bhuyan, Antony Fielding, and Y.W.

Mullineax, (2005) "Micro-credit and Its Role in Affecting Decision Making of Loan use and Empowerment of Women: A Comparative Study of BRAC and Grameen Bank in Bangladesh", *Journal of Insurance & Risk Management*, Vol. 4, Issue 7, December.

8. Kalpana, K., (2004a) "The Shifting Trajectories in Micro-Finance – the Silver Bullet for Empowerment: Some Questions", Working Paper No. 191, Madras Institute of Development Studies, Chennai.
9. Jain, Pankaj and Mick Moor, (2003) "What makes Micro-credit Programmes Effective? Fashionable Fallacies and Workable Realities," IDS working paper 177, Institute of Development Studies, Brighton, Sussex, England.
10. Yunus, Mohammad, (2000) "How Donor Funds Better Reach Grassroots Micro-credit Programme: Working towards the Micro-credit Summits Goal and Core Theme?" *The Bangladesh Development Studies*, Vol. 26, No. 273, June-September.
11. Jha, T.N., (2002) "Micro-credit Finance Models in Bangladesh: Lesson for India", *Yojana*, February.
12. (a) Das, H.C.L., (2001) "Priority Sector Lending by Public Sector Banks under Financial Sector Reforms in India", in Amalesh Banerjee and S.K. Singh (eds.) *Banking and Financial Sector Reforms in India*, Deep & Deep Publications, Delhi.
(b) Das, H.C.L., (2007) "Trends in Priority Sector Lendings by Public Sector Banks in India," paper presented at *67th Conference of the Indian Society of Agricultural Economics*, at Lucknow, November 5-7.
13. Selvakumar, M. and R. Sundar, (2007) "Swarnajayanti Gram Swarozgar Yojana (SGSY) – Tool for Poverty Eradication," *Kurukshetra*, December, pp. 18-19.
14. Das, H.C.L., (2007) "Swarnajayanti Gram Swarozgar Yojana and Self-Help Groups in East Champaran", paper presented at the U.G.C. sponsored regional seminars on *Swarnajayanti Gram Swarozgar Yojana: Its Impact on the Socio-Economic Dimension of Rural People of Bihar*, B.R.A. Bihar University, 30.09.2007 to 01.10.2007.
15. Government of India, (1999) *Swarnajayanti Gram Swarozgar Yojana: Guidelines*, Ministry of Rural Development, New Delhi.
16. NABARD, (1992/1999), "Guidelines for the Pilot Project for Linking Banks with Self-Help Groups," *Circular*, dated February 26, 1992,

No. DPD F.S. 463192-A/91-92, Development Policy Department, Available as Annexure-2 of NABARD, 1999.

17. Kalpana, K., (2004a) "The Shifting Trajectories in Micro-Finance Discourse: A critical Reading of the Anti-Poverty Dimensions of Micro-Finance Programmes", *Working Paper No. 189*, Madras Institute of Development Studies, Chennai.
18. Kalpana, K., (2004b) "Micro-Finance – The Silver Bullet for Empowerment: Some Questions", *Working Paper No. 191*, Madras Institute of Development Studies, Chennai.
19. Sinha, Sanjay, (2000) "Poverty Reduction through Micro-Finance", *The Economic Times*, August 15, Kolkata.
20. Harper, N., (2002a), "Promotion of Self-Help Groups under the SHG-Bank Linkage Programme in India", Paper presented at the seminar on the *SHG-bank Linkage Programme*, New Delhi, November 25-26, Published by the Micro-credit Innovation Department, NABARD, Mumbai.
21. Harper, M., (2002b), "Self-Help Groups and Grameen Bank Groups: What are the Difference", in Thomas Fisher and M.S. Sriram (Ed.), *Beyond Micro Credit: Putting Development Back into Micro-Finance*, Vistar Publications, New Delhi.
22. Malhotra, Rakesh, (2000) "SGSY: An Improvisation in Anti-Poverty Programmes", at *http:// www.alternativefinance. org.uk/cgi-bin/summary p1 2ed=150&view=html language = 57 source lang=E.*
23. World Bank, (1990) *World Development Report (1990)* Oxford University Press, New York.
24. Kabeer, N. and R.K. Murthy, (1996) "Compensating for Institutional Exclusion. Lesson from Indian Government and Non-Government Credit Intervention for the Poor", IDS discussion Paper 356, Institute for Development Studies, Susex, Brighton.
25. Government of India, (1999) *op. cit.*
26. Ghosh, Imon, (2001) "An overview of the SGSY guidelines and findings from a Field Study", *http:// www.alternativefinance. org.uk/ egi-bin/summary p 12ed=150&view=html language=E source lang=E.* Accessed September 2007.
27. Nair, M.K.S. and P.M. Mathew. (2002) *Poverty Alleviation Programme and Structural Changes in the Rural Economy*, Project Report, sponsored by Planning Commission, Yojana Bhawan, New Delhi.

28. Reddy, Gangi Y. (2000) "Swarnajayanti Gram Swarozagar Yojana (SGSY) in Rajasthan, A Few Observations", *Indian Association of Social Science Institutions, IASSI Quarterly* Vol. 19, No. 1, July-September.
29. Moogi, Jos and Mahendra S. Dev, (2002) "Social Sector Priorities: An Analysis of Budget and Expenditures in India in the 1990s", *IDS Working Paper 164*, Institute of Development Studies, Sussex, Brighton.
30. Rath, Nilkanth, (1985) "Garibi Hatao: Can IRDP Do It?" *Economic and Political Weekly*, Vol. 20, No. 6.
31. Thomas, M. and J. Pierson, (1995) *Dictionary of Social Work*, Collin Educational Publishers, London.
32. Nagrajan, B.S. and N. Lalitha, (1999) A Critical Study of Women Self-Help Groups in Selected Districts of Tamil Nadu (A Report), Project funded by ICSSR, New Delhi, Gandhi Gram Rural Institute (Deemed University), Gandhigram University, Tamil Nadu.
33. Singh, Indrabhushan and Usha Kumari, (2007) "Jeevika Mega Project: Empowerment of Rural Poor in Bihar", *Kurukshetra*, December, pp. 14-15.
34. Azad, Chandra Prakash, (2006) "Empowerment of Women through Self-Help Groups: A Study of Sabour Block of Bhagalpur District", *Journal of Regional Studies*, Vol. 16-17, Nos., 31-34, January 2005 – December 2006, pp. 58-59.
35. *Ibid.*, p. 59.
36. Singh, Indrabhushan and Usha Kumari, (2007) *op. cit.*, p. 17.
37. Planning Commission, (2002) *Tenth Five Year Plan (2002-07)*, New Delhi.
38. Sood, Archna, (2007) "March of A Women's SHG in Kohima", *Kurukshetra*, Vol. 56, No. 1, November, p. 43.
39. Tiwari, S.K., (2007) "Trends in Rural Finance" Rapporteur's Report, 67th Annual Conference of the Indian Society of Agricultural Economics, *Indian Journal of Agricultural Economics*, Vol. 62, No. 3, July-September, p. 551.
40. Kumar, Anjani, Dhiraj K. Singh and Prabhat Kumar, (2007) "Performance of Rural Credit and Factors Affecting the Choice of Credit Sources", *Indian Journal of Agricultural Economics*, Vol. 62, No. 3, July-September, p. 297.
41. Vyas, V.S., (2004) Report of the Advisory Committee on Flow of Credit

to Agriculture and Related Activities from the Banking System, Submitted to Reserve Bank of India, Mumbai.

42. Gupta, B.N., (1990) *Statistics*, Sahitya Bhawan Publication, Agra.
43. Williamson, J.G., (1965) "Regional Inequality and Process of National Development: A Description of Pattern," *Economic Development and Cultural Change*, Vol. 13, Chicago, (U.S.A.).
44. Croxton, Fredrick E. *et al.*, (1970) *Applied General Statistics*, Prentice Hall of India, New Delhi.
45. Sinha, S.P., (1979) "Agricultural Credit: Development and Prospects", *Commerce*, Vol. 139, No. 3577, Annual Number.
46. Anand, V. Vijay, (2008) "Microfinance for Rural Development", *Yojana*, February, p. 64.
47. Weiss, J. and H. Montgomery, (2004) "Great Expectations: Microfinance and Poverty Reduction in Asia and Latin America", *Oxford Development Studies*, Vol. 33, Nos. 3-4, pp. 391-416.
48. Lapence, C. and M. Zeller, (2001) "Distribution, Growth and Performance of the Evolving Microfinance Institutions in Africa, Asia, and Latin America,", FCND discussion paper 114, International Food Policy Research Institute (IFPRI), Washington D.C. (USA).
49. Littlefield, E., J. Mordeech and S. Hashemi, (2003) "Is Microfinance an Effective Strategy to Reach the Millennium Development Goals." CGAP Focus Note 24, *http//www.cgap.org*.
50. Scully, N., (2004), *Microcredit: No Panacea for Poor Women*, Global Development Research Centre, Washington D.C., *http//www. gdrc.org/icm/wind/micro.html*.
51. Simanowitz, S., (2002) "Microfinance for the Poorest: A Review of Issues and Ideas for Contribution of Impact", *Impact-Improving the Impact of Microfinance on Poverty: An Action Research Programme, http//www.microfinancegateway.org/content/article /detail/3395*.
52. Ciravegna, D., (2005) *The Role of Micro Credit in Modern Economy: The Case of Italy, www.flacso.or.cr/fileadmin/documents/FLACSO/auciravegna 2DOC.*
53. Hulme, D. and P. Mosley, (1996) *Finance against Poverty*, Routledge, London.
54. Marr, A., (2004) "A Challenge to the Orthodoxy Concerning Microfinance and Poverty Reduction", *Journal of Microfinance*, Vol. 5, No. 3, pp. 293-304.

55. Kirkpatrick, C. and M. Maimbo, (2002) "The Implications of the Evolving Microfinance Agenda for Regulatory and Supervisory Policy," *Development Policy Review*, Vol. 20, No. 3, pp. 293-304.
56. Armendariz, De Aghion B. and J. Morduch, (2000) "Microfinance Beyond Group Lending", *Economics of Transitions*, Vol. 8, No. 2, pp. 401-20.
57. Murray, I. and E. Lynch, (2003) "What Do Microfinance Customers Value?" *Women's World Banking: What Works, http//www.womesworldbanking.org/English/PDF/Focus%20 Note%201%30 What% 20 customers% value, April,04.pdf.*
58. Khawari, A., (2004) "Microfinance: Does It Hold Its Promises? A Survey of Recent Literature", *HWWA Discussion Paper* 276, Hamburg Institute of International Economics, Hamburg, *http//www.hwwa.de/Forschung/Pubicationen/Discussion Paper/204/276 pdf.*
59. Madajewiez, M., (2003) *Does the Credited Contract Matter? The Impact of Lending Programmes on Poverty in Bangladesh*, Columbia University Press, New York.
60. Pitt, M.M. and S.R. Khandkar, (1998) "The Impact of Group-based Credit on Poor Households in Bangladesh: Does the Gender of Participants Matter?", *Journal of Political Economy*, Vol. 106, No. 5, pp. 958-96.
61. Goetz, A.M. and R.S. Gupta, (1996) "Who Takes the Credit? Gender, Power and Control over Loan Use in Rural Credit Programmes in Bangladesh", *World Development*, Vol. 24, No. 1, pp. 45-63.
62. Dunford, C., (2006) *Evidence of Microfinance's Contribution to Achieving the Millennium Development Goals: Freedom from Hunger, http// microfinancegateway.org/files/35795_file_ Evedence _on_ MDGS_Dunford.pdf.*
63. Karlan, D., (2001) "Microfinance Impact Assessment: The Perils of Using New Members as Control Group", *Journal of Microfinance*, Vol. 3, No. 2, pp. 75-85.
64. Armendariz De Aghion, B. and J. Morduch, (2005) *The Economics of Microfinance*, MIT, Press Cambridge. M.A.
65. Khandkar, S.R., (2005) "Microfinance and Poverty: Evidence Using Panel Data from Bangladesh", *The World Bank Economic Review*, Vol. 19, No. 2, pp. 283-86.
66. Eda Rural Systems, (2001) *The Maturing of Indian Microfinance: A Longitudinal Study*, Eda Rural Systems, New Delhi.

67. Hulme, D. and P. Mosley, (1996), *op. cit.*
68. Copestake, J., P. Dawson, J.P. Fanning, A.M. Kay, K. Wright-Revolledo, (2005) Monitoring the Delivery of the Poverty, Outreach and Impact of Microfinance: A Comparison of Methods using Data from Perce", *Development Policy Review*, Vol. 23, No. 6, pp. 701-33.
69. Cull, R., A. Demirgtic-Kunt, and J. Morduch, (2007) "Financial Performance and Outreach: A Global Analysis of Leading Microbanks", *Economic Journal*, Vol. 117, No. 1.
70. Daliy-Harries, S., (2006) *State of the Microcredit Summit Campaign Report 2006*, Microcredit Summit Campaign, Washington D.C.
71. Lakshman, N., (2006) "India's Banks Are Big on Microfinance", *Business Week*, August, 22.
72. Iyer, P.R., (2006) "ICICI Joins Hands with Three VCs to Fund Microfinance Institutions, *The Economic Times*, June 5.
73. Vogelgesang, U., (2003) "Microfinance in Times of Crisis: The Effects of Competition, Rising Indebtedness and Economic Crisis on Repayment Behaviour", *World Development*, Vol. 31, No. 12, pp. 2085-2115.
74. McIntosh, C., A. De Janvry Sadoulet, (2005) "How Rising Competition among Microfinance Institutions Affects Incumbent Lenders?" *Economic Journal*, Vol. 115, No. 506, pp. 987-1004.

6

Summary, Conclusions and Suggestions

Summary

The key to the success of the different anti-poverty and other welfare programmes lies in the evaluation and participation of community based organizations at the grassroots level. People's participation in credit delivery and linking formal credit institutions to borrowers through intermediaries of Self-Help Groups (SHGs) have been recognized as supplementary mechanism for providing credit support to the rural poor.

The first official interest in informal group lending in India took shape during 1986-87 when the National Bank for Agricultural and Rural Development (NABARD) supported and funded an action research project on Savings and Credit Management of Self-Help Groups of Mysore Resettlement and Development Agency (MYRADA). In 1988-89, the NABARD undertook a survey of 43 Non-Government Organizations (NGOs) spread over 11 States in India to study the functioning of SHGs and possibilities of collaborations between the Banks and SHGs in the mobilization of rural savings and improving the delivery of credit to the rural poor.

Alternative to the SHGs, the other type of group lending, although in smaller number is through groups of Grameen Bank

Group (GBG) model of Bangladesh. The groups are much smaller, i.e. of five members to start with thrift. However unlike in the SHGs, the GBG does not manage its resources, the individual savings are deposited in the bank and the members get loan directly from the bank. The GBG only helps the Bank in screening the borrowers and assuring repayment. Although the bank gets benefits the GBG does not develop much skill in financial management. In fact, it does not have much financial resources to manage. Although 0.5 per cent of loan amount is deducted to develop a group fund, it is negligible in comparison to at least 2 per cent per month of rate of interest. As propensity to save (voluntary) for the poor people is much less than the compulsion to pay interest (involuntary), the forced saving in the GBG is much less than the SHGs. The interest earned in the group after all belongs to its members. The GBG groups permanently remain dependent on the banks or the promoter NGOs but so many SHGs have been found to become independent of banks for their credit requirements.

A majority of the NGOs in India promote SHGs only and the commercial banks lend to the SHGs or to the NGOs or federation for 'on lending' to the SHGs. Very few NGOs like Adithi in Bihar, Activities for Social Alternatives (ASA) in Tamil Nadu, Loylam Bank of Rural Development and Organization (RDO) in Manipur and Society for Helping and Awakening Rural Poor through Education (SHARE) in Andhra Pradesh follow the Grameen Bank model for group lending.

Microfinance refers to the entire range of financial and non-financial services, including skill upgradation and entrepreneurship development, rendered to the poor for enabling them to overcome poverty. In the context of designing programmer for the poor, microfinance is recognized and accepted as one of the new development paradigms for alleviating poverty through social and economic empowerment of the poor with special emphasis on empowering women. The operational framework of microfinance, therefore, especially rests on the premise that (a) formation of self-employment enterprise is a viable alternative means of alleviating poverty, (b) lack of access to capital assets or credit

acts as a constraint on the existing and potential micro-enterprises, and, (c) the poor are capable of saving despite their poor income-level. In essence therefore, microfinance may be referred to as an institutional mechanism of providing credit support in small amount and usually limited with small groups along with other complementary support such as training and other related services to the people with poor resources and skills for enabling them to take up economic activities.

The concept of microfinance is now several decades old its institutions provide small credits and other financial services to low income households and very small informal business. With constant innovations to meet the specific needs of the people they serve, microfinance institutions offer a menu of options. Through group lending they are able to provide credit with minimal reliance on collateral to group members who take terms borrowing and are jointly responsible for loan repayment.

Many microfinance institutions are owned and operated by non-governmental organizations which review grants and sometimes loans from multilateral development agencies, private charities, government and similar institutions. In some parts of the world they follow the model of financial co-operatives, funding their lendings from members deposits and capital contributions. While some have grown into formal self-sustaining financial institutions, most remain informal and dependent upon donor funds.

But after years of experience with microfinance, surprisingly little is known about it. There are no comprehensive and authoritative data on the size of the industry or the population served. Stylized facts, however, can be drawn from studies at the country and regional levels. These suggest that while the industry comprises a very large number of institutions—in tens of thousands by some estimates—the number of people served and amount of money involved are small. Most microfinance activities are concentrated in a handful countries and only a few large institutions carry out a significant portion of the transactions.

The term rural development connotes overall development of rural areas with a view to improve the quality of life of rural

people. In this sense it is a comprehensive and multidimensional concept and encompasses the development of agriculture and allied activities, village and cottage industries and crafts, socio-economic infrastructure, community services and facilities and above all, the human resources in rural areas. As a phenomenon, rural development is the end result of interactions between various physical, technological, economic, socio-cultural and institutional factors. As a strategy, it is designed to improve the economic and social well-being of a specific group of people—the rural poor. As a discipline, it is multi-disciplinary in nature representing an intersection of agricultural, social, behavioural, engineering and management sciences.

Precisely, rural development may be defined as a process leading to sustainable improvement in the quality of life of the rural people especially the rural poor.

Rural sector requires institutional credit to take up economically viable projects. But it needs to be noted that the credit alone cannot deliver the goods. There is what is called the credit absorption capacity of the region. This depends on the implementation of economically viable schemes. Hence, the formulation of economic plans should precede the preparation of credit plans. There are certain agencies like the co-operatives, regional rural banks and farmers service societies which are most appropriate to serve the rural population, but their performance needs to be toned up. Of course cheap credit needs to be discouraged.

Credit is an important input in the development process. It is an accelerator of development. Ensuring the provision of timely and sufficient credit to as large a segment of rural population as possible has been one of the major policy initiative, which has guided the formulation of public policy in India. The rural credit system in India has evolved through different phases as a result of these initiatives and there has been a substantial broadening of the infrastructure for credit delivery resulting in increased outreach and reduction is the influence of informal agencies as evidenced by the increase in the share of institutional sources of the cash debts of rural households from 7.3 per cent in the early 1950s to 64 per cent in 1991 as per the All India Debt and Investment Survey.

II

Rural development involves raising the socio-economic status of the rural population on a substantial basis through optimum utilisation of social resources both natural and human.

The term 'rural development' is of focal interest and is widely acclaimed in both the developed and developing countries of the world. Rural development as a concept connotes overall development of rural areas with a view to improve the quality of life of rural people. In this sense it is a comprehensive and multi-dimensional concept and encompasses the development of agriculture and allied activities, village and cottage industries and crafts, socio-economic infrastructure, community services and facilities and above all, the human resources in rural areas.

Today the term rural development has come to an agreement to boost the all-round economic development in rural sector for faster economic development and welfare of common masses. There has been considerable discussion of the need for and the nature of shift in emphasis and approach called for in rural development in keeping with the objective of overall development policy for speedy elimination of backwardness in rural areas and economic incentives to reduce the disparities between the haves and have-nots in rural sector.

The emphasis on rural development in most of the developing countries is understandable. The majority of the population lives in the rural areas. As such their backwardness would be retarding growth in other sectors and in the economy as a whole. The growth of towns and cities will be possible if it is backed by prosperity in rural areas. Rural backwardness is the major cause for the falling demand for most products.

The administration in the urban areas has been finding it difficult to provide employment to the rural labour force migrating to towns and cities. The social consequences of rural exodus like growing slums is too serious to be ignored by the urban administrative authorities.

Another disturbing trend in the rural areas is that the surpluses

generated in the rural areas are being invested in the urban areas for various reasons.

Rural development embraces such things as agricultural development, growth in income, better and expanded employment opportunities reduction in poverty, more equitable distribution of income and wealth, improved human development index and environmental protection in rural areas.

India has achieved tremendous progress since the First Five Year Plan even though the targets fixed in each Plan might not have been fully met. Between 1951 and 2004, production of food grains had increased by 316 per cent, production of oilseeds by 400 per cent, that of sugarcane by 412 per cent and of cotton by 366 per cent. The increase in the production of wheat has been really spectacular by over 1100 per cent.

During the first decade of planning (1951-1961) when the First and Second Five Year Plans were implemented, the annual rate of growth in agriculture was 3.5 per cent. During the next two decades of planning (1961-1981) despite spectacular progress made under the IADP and HYVP, the overall progress in agriculture was dismal. The average annual rate of growth declined to 2.2 per cent and 1.7 per cent respectively during 1961-1971 and 1971-1981 mainly because of the weather and poor monsoon condition. But condition improved during the fourth decade of planning (1981-1991). The growth rate in the 1980 was highly respectable (3.9%). The compound growth rate of agriculture for the period 1991-2001 was 2.8 per cent.

During 2002-03 the annual compound growth rate of agricultural production declined deeply to –7.2 per cent. The Tenth Plan had fixed a target growth rate of 4 per cent in agriculture to achieve 8 per cent growth in GDP. But the actual growth rate in agriculture and allied sector was only 2.3 per cent while the actual growth rate in GDP was 7.6 per cent.

During the pre-green revolution period wheat recorded most impressive growth in yield—from 7 quintals per hectare in 1950-1951 to nearly 11 quintals per hectare in 1964-65. The annual rate of growth was 2.1 per cent yield per hectare in the case of wheat improved from 6.6 quintals in 1950-51 to 9.1 quintals in

1964-65, a modest annual rate of growth of 1.3 per cent. Among non-foodgrains, cotton, and sugarcane recorded low growth rates during this period.

The production of foodgrains increased from 196.8 million tonnes in 2000-01 to 216.1 million tonnes in 2006-07. The production of cereals increased from 185.9 million tonnes in 2000-01 to 201.9 million tonnes in 2006-07. Rice witnessed the production of 85 million tonnes in 2006-07. Similarly wheat witnessed the production of 69.7 million tonnes in 2006-07. Pulse recorded the production of 11.1 million tonnes in 2000-01 to 14.2 million tonnes in 2006-07. Oilseeds recorded the production of 18.4 million tonnes in 2000-01 to 23.9 million tonnes in 2006-07. The production of sugarcane increased from 206 million tonnes in 2000-01 to 345.3 million tonnes in 2006-07.

During the post-green revolution period, however, the most spectacular growth rate was recorded by wheat (3.2 per cent per annum). Potato recorded an impressive growth rate of 3.1 per cent per annum. Pulses recorded a growth rate 0.1 per cent per annum and oilseeds a mere 1.2 per cent per annum. This shows that the new biochemical technology was particularly suited to wheat production, but was not effective in the case of other crops.

In the post-independence period, the attempts of the Union as well as State Governments in the field of institutional change or land reforms have been found concentrated on the following four aspects :

1. Abolition of zamindari system,
2. Ceiling on landholdings,
3. Consolidation of holdings, and
4. Tenancy reforms.

After independence high priority was accorded to the abolition of intermediary tenures (zamindari). Accordingly every State enacted its own legislation to abolish this tenure system on the payment of compensation. Basically, the law provided for the State takeover of the estates of the zamindars on payment of compensation and offering their ownership to cultivators on their

payment of fixed sums. The process of legislative action commenced in 1948 and was completed in 1954, by which time most States had adopted necessary legislations.

An important part of land reforms relates to the fixation of a ceiling or an upper limit on landholdings and also by implications defining a floor level or lower limit on landholdings. The laws enacted by the State legislatures presupposed ceiling on existing landholdings which preserved middle landholders and rich peasants. With more than 60 per cent of the total households on average owning only up to 2 acres each and together holding as little as 7 per cent of the total land, and 5 per cent of the upper group holding 42 per cent of the land, the ceiling fixed by the principal States holds significance.

Legislation for ceiling on existing land holdings and unit of application has been enacted in two phases. During the first phase, which lasted up to 1972, ceiling legislation largely treated landholder as the unit of application. After 1972, it was decided to have family as the basis of holdings. Further, the ceiling limit was also reduced to bring about a more equitable distribution of this scarce asset.

Since the inception of ceiling laws on landholdings and up to 31st March, 2003, total quantum of land declared surplus in the entire country was 73.73 lakh acres, out of which 65.01 lakh acres have been taken in possession, and a total area of 53.93 lakh acres has been distributed among 54.47 lakh beneficiaries.

Consolidation of holdings stand for the substitution by exchange of fields among the farmers in an area in such a way as to make the holding held by each of them more compact. On consolidation, the number of fragments in the holdings is reduced. The fields are made contiguous with each other.

The legislation pertaining to the consolidation of holdings exist at present in most of the States. A significant feature of the consolidation work is the uneven progress made in the different States, the bulk of the consolidated area being associated for Punjab, Haryana, and Madhya Pradesh.

As consolidation operations have not made much headway in many States, consolidation of landholdings is especially important in the States like Assam, Bihar, and West Bengal. Some of the

factors working against consolidation are: (a) fear of displacement among tenants and share croppers, (b) advantage of having land in fragmented parcels in the event of floods, and other natural calamities, and (c) apprehension that the bigger farmers would get a better deal. As far as possible, the holdings of small and marginal farmers need to be consolidated in such a way that they form contiguous block of land so that the exploitation of ground water for them as well as provision of various agricultural services and inputs become economical.

The sad social and economic plight of tenants and also their sheer number call for serious attention and concerted efforts for the improvement of their lots. Broadly speaking, tenants can be divided into (a) tenants-at-will, (b) sub-tenants, and (c) occupancy or permanent tenants. While the occupancy tenants enjoy fixation and security of rent and can get reimbursement of improvement made on the land, the other categories especially tenants-at-will continue to suffer from serious disabilities. In number, tenants constitute 12.7 per cent of the total agricultural population and tenant households constitute 23.6 per cent of the total cultivating households in India. The percentage of the area leased out forms 20 per cent of the total cultivated area though this ratio varies from 27 per cent in Punjab to 6.7 per cent in Madhya Pradesh.

The various States in India have enacted tenancy reform legislation to protect the poorer tenants of different categories. These measures pertain to Regulation of Rent Security of Tenures and Conferment of Ownership on Tenants.

From the mid-1980s when liberalization started entering the Indian economy at first steadily and then with thunderous gale force from 1991, land reform went off the radar screen of the Indian polity. As a general proposition, it may be said that land reforms should remain an essential element of national agricultural and rural development strategies not only because land-based agricultural occupation must continue to provide livelihood to a vast majority of rural population, but also because macro-economic growth in most contexts has failed to create improved prospects for the rural poor to acquire assets, gainful employment or increase their income and quality of life.

Poverty and unemployment anywhere are danger to peace and prosperity everywhere. In India the rate of poverty is higher in rural areas than of the urban areas and is pervasive among the landless labour class in rural areas as compared to the land owning class. About 26.5 per cent of people in rural areas are living below the poverty line. About 3.3 per cent families in the rural areas are suffering from hunger. The percentage of hungry people is high in West Bengal (10.4%), Orissa (8%), Assam (7.1%) and Bihar (6%). In India 13.4 per cent of population are living in food insecurity. About 27.3 per cent million people had to suffer some degree of hunger and as many as 23 per cent of the population remained under-nourished as of late 1990s.

About 27 per cent of India's populations live below poverty line. The poverty estimate in 2004-05 based on Uniform Recall Period (URP) consumption distribution (27.5%) is comparable with the poverty estimates of 1993-94 which was 36 per cent. The poverty estimate in 2004-05 based on Mixed Recall Period (MRP) consumption distribution (21.8%) is roughly but not strictly comparable with the poverty estimate of 1999-2000 which was 26.1 per cent.

The Panchayati Raj Institutions (PRIs) need to play an important role in the development of primary sector. The 73rd Constitutional Amendment has envisaged that development of agriculture is one of the responsibilities of the Panchayats. The Panchayati Raj Acts of many States have assigned duties and responsibilities to the Panchayati Raj Institutions for the promotion of agriculture.

Information and Communication Technology (ICT) has lifted India out of the gloom in last 15 years. It has not just created wealth for the country but for more importantly, it has created confidence in the country. Youngsters in India no longer consider themselves to be inferior to anyone else in the world. Urban middle class youngsters no longer believe that one has to born rich to be highly successful in the country and thus entrepreneurship is thriving. India is on the move. But this confidence permeates to rural areas. ICT can help in this area but it would require a lot of efforts one must not forget that ICT is at best a tool. One needs to use it to make difference.

Rural India comprises 72 per cent of the country's population but its share in the total national income is currently about 45 per cent. Rural India is characterised by low income levels, poor quality of life and a weak base of human development. Rural-urban divide is quite apparent in all spheres of human life. What worries most the policy planners is that the magnitude of disparity has accentuated during the post-reform period due to change in the income growth trajectories of rural and urban areas.

The share of rural areas in NDP at factor cost has steeply declined from 62.95 per cent in 1970-71 to 48.09 per cent in 1999-2000, whereas the corresponding percentage for urban areas has remarkably increased. Today the urban population may earn about three-fifths of the national income. Thus in terms of generation of GDP, the centre of gravity has shifted from rural to urban areas, whereas majority of people still earn their livelihood in rural areas.

At current prices in 1973-74, the monthly per capita consumption expenditure (MPCE) in urban areas was about 43 per cent higher than that of the rural areas, whereas in 2004-05, it was higher by 52 per cent.

Urban India has better outcome of almost all health indicators. Fertility rate, infant death rate under 5, mortality rate and crude death rate are much higher in the rural areas than those in the urban areas. In the case of birth delivered in medical institutions, it has been observed that in 2005-06, as against 69.4 per cent deliveries made in medical institutions in urban areas, such deliveries in rural areas were only 31.1 per cent. Similarly, percentage of birth assisted by professionals in rural areas was just half that of urban areas. Percentage of a total unmet need to family planning was also higher in the rural areas than that of the urban areas.

In 2004, as against 74.1 per cent urban households lived in pucca houses, only 25.5 per cent households in rural areas had this facility. In the case of drinking water only about 28 per cent rural households had tap water facility whereas 71 per cent urban households had this facility. Against 93.1 per cent urban households having electricity, the corresponding percentage for

rural households was only 55.7 per cent. Moreover availability and reliability of electricity is higher in urban areas than that in the rural areas. Only 25.9 per cent rural households had toilet facility while the corresponding percentage in the urban areas was 83.1. In 2004, only 5.7 per cent of rural households had LPG cooking gas facility, whereas in urban areas 48 per cent of households used LPG as a source of cooking energy. Thus the urban population has much better access to these basic amenities than the rural population.

Disparity between rural and urban households also exists in the case of access to the durable consumer assets like radio, television, bicycle, motorcycle, scooter, car, banking services, and telephones. In the case of even possession of radio and bicycle the percentage of rural households are lower than that of urban households. In the case of access to television, as against 64.1 per cent urban households having the asset, the corresponding percentage in rural areas is only 18.9. In 2001, only 5.3 per cent of rural households possessed motorcycle/scooter while the corresponding figure for the urban areas was 24.7 per cent. Teledensity measured by number of telephones per 100 people was only 1.33 in the rural areas against 26.88 in the urban areas. Further, it has been observed that about 50 per cent of urban households availed the banking services, while the corresponding figure for the rural areas was only 30.1 per cent.

There is a need to adopt two types of policies to reduce rural-urban disparity first, the policy which helps to generate sustained income and employment and also abate the undesirable flow of rural workforce to the urban areas; and second, which helps to raise the socio-economic status of rural populace and enlarge their capability to participate actively in the developmental activities. There is a need for both qualitative and quantitative changes in the rural areas. In the quantitative form, it must be reflected in more production more income and more employment. In qualitative form, it must be reflected in the form of institutional changes in the areas of health, education, environment, transport and social welfare. Economic growth *per se* is necessary but not sufficient condition for economic development. What matters

more is the broad-base of the growth and its equitable distribution. Economic growth would be more effective in eliminating rural poverty and deprivation when it works with the indicators of human development in the multiplicative form.

Mohan Das Karamchand Gandhi or Mahatma Gandhi, as he is popularly known, appeared on the political scene when the national movement for the freedom was gaining momentum. This spiritualised the Indian politics and economies truly and fully during his lifetime.

Gandhiji had a comprehensive plan for the regeneration of Indian villages. The main plank of his programme was the *charkha* (spinning wheel) movement. The slogan was 'Sarvodaya through spinning'. Subjugated India could not depend upon foreign masters to initiate genuine plans for economic development, and therefore, Gandhiji clearly saw that the solution of the mass poverty in the villages lays in teaching the villages self-help. He wanted honest work to be provided for them, not relief or charity. To Gandhiji charkha thus became a symbol of economic independence as well as political emancipation.

Gandhiji conceived decentralisation as an integral part of the social and productive organisation. Highly mechanized factory was inconsistent with the non-violent structure of society since centralization cannot be sustained without adequate force. He favoured cottage industries from the point of view of decentralization as well as distribution.

Gandhiji's ideas on machines and technological civilization grew out of deep conviction that the modern machine civilization was at the root of all tensions and frustration, which bring about aggression, violence and war. He saw how technology always led to the multiplication of want and as state of culture in which material wants are the king. His conviction in regard to machines and technology was logical if accepted the moral postulates underlying that approach. Employment of large-scale machinery in an acquisitive society, he believed, would give rise to greed and avarice. Gandhiji conceived an ideal society in which there would not be much scope for glaring inequalities of wealth and income.

In so far as these existed in the present day society, the rich were duty-bound to act as the trustees. According to Mahatma Gandhi, "the rich man will be left in possession of his wealth of which he will use what he reasonably requires for his personal needs and will act as a trustee for the remainders to be used for the rest of the society." His belief in non-violence ruled out expropriation of the wealthy by the use of force. He extolled the principle of voluntariness enjoyed by non-violence.

If the modern India has to get rid of poverty, unemployment, under-employment, disparity in personal income, attitudes militating against hard work, and corruption in the highest riches—both political and administrative, it will have to return to Gandhi for redemption. His thought has immense relevance to India of today and tomorrow. He visualized the growth of the Indian economy on the basis of its own resource-endowments and its own techniques or techniques evolved to suit the country's conditions of scarce capital and redundant labour. He accorded the top priority to self-reliance and called for an organization of economic production on a widely decentralized basis which would utilise local endowment talents to the maximum.

The National Community Development Programme (NCDP) was launched in 1952. Its aim was to bring about the overall development of the rural community with people's participation in the development process.

The Government of India on its part decided to provide technical and other services in a coordinated fashion. An institutional structure was provided in the form of Panchayati Raj, cooperatives and village schools. The approach to rural development was holistic one.

The Intensive Agricultural District Programme (IADP) launched in 1960, aimed at concentrating resources in agriculturally better placed areas. The essence of IADP strategy has been to attain foodgrains self-sufficiency in favourable areas with maximum irrigation facilities and minimum natural hazards, providing simultaneously all the requisite essential inputs and services which were needed. Thus a package approach to step up agricultural production was evolved.

The policy of growth centres in India is concerned more with the development of areas rather than with their rates of growth. However, the growth pole theory is inapplicable to all developmental situations and is too rigidly linked to industrialization.

Integrated Rural Development Programme (IRDP) is a synergistic approach aiming at total development of the area and the people by bringing about the necessary institutional attitudinal changes and by delivering a package of services through extension methods to encompass economic field as well as establishment of the required special infrastructure and services in the areas of health and nutrition education and literacy, basic civic amenities, family planning, etc. with an ultimate objective of improving quality of life in the rural areas.

One of the lessons learnt during the period of experimentation in India is that rural development must focus on manageable areas in which development activity can be responsive to the specificity of natural endowment and social order. But planning at the micro level faces a number of problems. It cannot be effective unless attention is paid to production programmes and skill development, provision of minimum needs and a programme for institutional support.

Providing Urban Amenities in Rural Areas (PURA) consists of four connectivities: physical, human, electronic, knowledge and thereby leads to economic connectivity to enhance the prosperity of clusters of villages in the rural areas. The economic connectivity would generate a market and the production establishments for servicing the market. The PURA has all the dimensions to become a business enterprise which has global dimensions but operating in every nook and corner of our country. The PURA entrepreneur has to have the skill for evolving a business plan with banks and also create infrastructural support such as educational institutions, health centre, and small scale industries, transportation services tele-education, tele-medicine, e-governance services in the region integrating with the governmental rural developmental schemes such as road, communication and transport and also with national and global markets to sell the products and services.

The intention of the Panchayati Raj Institutions (PRIs) is to translate the Gandhian dream of village self-governance (Gram Swarajya) and making them an effective tool of rural development and construction. The new PRIs, however, have assured the vibrant grassroots democracy through the 73rd Constitutional Amendment. This constitutional amendment clearly speaks of the meaning of the decentralized governance. Decentralization of economic power to the grassroots level, therefore, becomes essential not only for the sake of ensuring people's democracy, but also for higher growth and equality. Decentralized planning and associated devolution of powers to the village Panchayats are new institutional arrangement which can be effectively utilized to meet the needs of rural people in changing environment.

The Village Development Board (VDB) of Nagaland is a unique rural planning and development institution which is based on the rich traditional heritage of the community life of the Nagas. The concept of VDB was first introduced in 1976 in Ketsapo village in Phek district of Nagaland in the form of a committee to manage the village funds generated from the common property resources, a task which was customarily performed by the village council (VC). It was, therefore, only a delegated power till 1980 when the concept of VDB was adopted and introduced in the entire State with the enactment of the VDB rules. Today the VDB, which was started in a remote village on an experimental basis as a developing agency of the village council, has grown into a massive board comprising 1,083 VDBs operating in the entire State covering 2,16,503 households, spread over 52 community development Blocks. This has pioneered the grassroots level organization for decentralized planning and rural development.

III

In the past decade the world has realized that the poor are bankable and poor women are the trustworthy in providing financial services. Over time, the notion of micro-credit has broadened into microfinance which includes not only savings and credit, but also insurance and pension and even housing. The challenge of

future is that the low-income people are inclusive to financial systems. Microfinance can be robustly sustainable. When the model is right, the growth of microfinance is fast.

Recently the attention for microfinance and its role in reducing poverty was further increased when Prof. Mohammad Yunus received the Nobel Peace Prize. According to the Nobel Peace Committee, microfinance can help people to break out of poverty which in turn is seen as an important prerequisite to establish long lasting peace. This has led to an almost euphoric attitude among policy makers and aid organizations about potential poverty reducing effects of microcredit.

Microfinance refers to the entire range of financial and non-financial services, including skill upgradation and entrepreneurship development, rendered to the poor for enabling them to overcome poverty. In the context of designing programme for the poor, microfinance is recognized and accepted as one of the new development paradigms for alleviating poverty through social and economic empowerment of the poor with special emphasis on empowering women. The operational framework of microfinance rests on the premises that formation of a self-employment enterprise is a viable alternate means of alleviating poverty, lack of access to capital assets credit acts as a constraint on the existing and potential micro enterprises, and the poor are capable of saving despite their poor income level. In essence, therefore, microfinance may be referred to as an institutional mechanism of providing credit support in small amount and usually limited with small group along with other complementary support such as training and other related services to the people with poor resources and skills for enabling them to take up economic activities.

Microcredit is delivered through Self-Help Groups (SHGs). A Self-Help Group is a registered/unregistered group of micro-entrepreneurs having homogenous social and economic background, voluntarily coming together to save small amounts regularly. They mutually agree to contribute to a common fund to meet their emergency needs on mutual help basis. The group members use collective wisdom and peer pressure to ensure proper end-use of credit and timely repayment thereof. In fact peer pressure has been recognized as an effective substitute for collaterals.

Microfinance providers in India can be classified under three broad categories: formal, semi-formal and informal. The formal banking sector constitutes the first category, while the semi-formal group consists of a variety of microfinance institutions and self-help groups. Informal providers on the other hand, are not legal entities and include moneylenders and various social workers. Today semi-formal and informal lenders dominate the scene.

In order to provide an institutional mechanism in the private sector for promoting rural savings as well as channelizing adequate credit for promoting rural viable economic activities, setting up of Local Area Banks (LABs) in the private sector has been allowed with an area of operation restricted to two or three contiguous districts.

In view of the effectiveness of routing financial assistance to the poor through the Self-Help Groups, the Union Government has accorded priority to coverage of SHGs by banks with help from the NABARD and the Small Industries Development Bank (SIDBI).

The Swarnajayanti Gram Swarojgar Yojana (SGSY) aims at establishing a large number of micro enterprises in rural areas of the country. The objective of the scheme is to bring every assisted family above the poverty line in three years by providing them income-generating assets through a mix of credit and government subsidy.

For sustainable development in the rural areas in consonance with rural people's wishes and aspirations, huge investments are being made by the Ministry of Rural Development, Government of India, through different programmes. A pre-poor policy in terms of which the rural poor are treated as a net resource replete with their own ideas and experience well in tune with the local conditions, forms an integral part of development strategy. In the process, the most disadvantaged sections of the society receive high priority.

The plethora of self-employment programmes for the rural poor have been merged into a single holistic programme called Swarnjayanti Gram Swarozgar Yojana (SGSY). It is conceived as a holistic programme of micro enterprises covering all aspects of self-employment.

Gainful employment, food security and strengthening of infrastructure in rural areas is a must for national renewal for a resurgent India. The Sampoorna Grameen Rojgar Yojana (SGRY) has been launched to attain these objectives. The scheme envisages an annual expenditure of Rs 10,000 crore.

The peoples partnership particularly of targets groups of various rural development programmes is sought to be promoted not only through institution of Gram Sabha, but also through execution of works by people themselves under different programmes of the Ministry of Rural Development.

The Union Budget 2007-08 of India focused on the agriculture and rural development with the Government's efforts to impart growth, equity and social justice. The highlight of the budget was a 31 per cent hike in allocation towards the Bharat Nirman Programme for upgrading rural infrastructure from Rs. 18,696 crore to Rs. 24,603 crore and substantial increase in farm credit.

Farm credit target for 2007-08 was fixed at Rs. 2,25,000 crore and 50 lakh new farmers were to be brought into the banking fold. Interest subvention for short-term crop loans of 2 per cent would continue for which a budgetary provision of Rs. 1,677 crore was made. Regional Rural Banks were to take up a branch expansion programme with at least one branch in 80 uncovered districts.

The National Rural Employment Guarantee Scheme (NREGS) is one of the major flagship programmes of the Government of India launched in February 2006. Though the scheme being demand driven, there is inter-State variation in its implementation. The Government of India has expanded NREGS from 200 districts to 330 districts. This 130 additional districts would be covered for which the government had provided Rs. 12,000 crore in the 2007-08 budget. From April 1, 2008 the NREGS has been extended to all the remaining districts of the country.

The Union Budget 2007-08 makes a refreshingly bold departure from the traditional track by refocusing on rural development and agriculture, because if these crucial segments

were cold shouldered, the development and progress of the country would remain uneven and unpleasant. A country with large population has to be nearly self-sufficient in essential food items, otherwise supply constraints could upset macroeconomic stability and growth prospects. Hence, agriculture must top the agenda of the policy makers and must hold the first charge on the resources of the country. Given the inescapable reality that inflation has reared its ugly head in recent months the Union Budget 2007-08 has truly trained its gun on tackling inflation. The budget attempts to do it through creating salutary and stable environment for farm sector and rural regeneration so that supply constraints could be overcome and there is no binding constraint for India's growth trajectory.

IV

Self-Help Group (SHG) is an association of body of people which is homogeneous, has a common aim and whose members in one way or the other help one another. It is a micro cooperative. All or a majority of members of an SHG may be drawn from the low income strata, for instance SHGs have come to encompass a wide range of activities, to overcoming problems of addiction and ensuring safe sex. While the SHGs in the developing countries have been dealing with disabilities apart from other activities, the most important job it has taken up is the propagation of microfinance. It has been increasingly realized. That lending to an SHG offers unique opportunities, since the recovery rate is between 90 and 100 per cent.

The proportion of all rural households borrowing from formal credit agencies has been steadily increasing, as revealed in the All India Debt and Investment Survey Reports (1951,1961, 1971, and 1981) from 7.2 per cent in 1951 to 17.3 per cent in 1961, 29.2 per cent in 1971 and 61.2 per cent in 1981. Also the percentage of non-cultivator borrowers depending on non-formal sources of credit (agriculturist money lender, professional money lender, landlord and trader) continued to be above 50 per cent. The dependence of the rural poor on non-institutional sources of credit

is one of the causes that perpetuate their poverty and restrict surplus generation to maintain their meagre economic activity and households.

There is a clear inverse relationship between the incidence of poverty reflected by asset holding of the households and the need to incur debt for household expenditure. There is also a positive relationship between the wealth of the household and the debt contracted for productive purposes (crop loan, etc.).

It is discernible that the cooperative credit institutions were virtually the only institutions providing credit for agricultural activities till 1970-71, when the commercial banks made a beginning in the area. With the spread of their branches the commercial banks moved fast by 1988-89 when they adopted service area approach, they claimed more than 41 per cent of the share in disbursement of agricultural credit and about 54 per cent in outstanding agricultural credit. The market share of the regional rural banks in agricultural credit by this time was a mere 5 per cent but the credit had gone entirely to the rural poor. The demand for credit had risen fast from year to year and the figures of annual disbursements for agricultural purpose moved from Rs. 7,438 million in 1970-71 to Rs. 91,062 million in 1988-89 until the concept 'Service Area Approach' was implemented. And now the disbursements have shot up to Rs. 15,74,800 million in 2005-06.

Dependence of rural households on non-institutional sources of credit was as high as 92.8 per cent in 1951 just four years after India's independence, which declined to 82.7 per cent in 1961 and further to 70.8 per cent in 1971 when cooperative credit institutions made their presence felt on the rural scene after acceptance and implementation of recommendations of the All India Rural Credit Survey Committee in 1954 and entry of major private sector banks after their nationalization in the year 1969. Access of rural households to formal credit institutions sharply increased to 61.2 per cent in 1981, partly because of enabling measures initiated by the Reserve Bank of India to direct public sector banks towards rural lending and partly because of the establishment of the Regional Rural Banks from the year 1975 onwards—specifically to cater to the credit needs of rural poor

households. However, in the year 1991, there was only marginal increase in the institutional sources of credit from 61.2 per cent in 1981 to 64 per cent in 1991, while dependence of rural households on professional money lenders in particular declined from 46.4 per cent in 1951 to 8.3 per cent in 1991. Role of agricultural moneylenders had also decreased progressively from 47 per cent in 1961 to 7.1 per cent in 1991. The performance of commercial banks was very spectacular between 1971 and 1981 but it showed little improvement in 1991. Cooperatives had shown good performance from 1961 to 1981 but its performance declined in 1991.

The goal of the Government of India as announced by the Finance Minister in the budget speech in 2004, to double the flow of farm credit in three years (2004-05 to 2006-2007), was achieved in two years only. Actual flow of credit during the year 2006-07 exceeded the target of Rs. 17,50,000 million set for the year by Rs. 1,50,000 million. During April to December 2006, about 53,37,000 new farmers as against the target of 5 million, were linked with the institutional credit system. For the year 2007-08 the target of farm credit disbursement was fixed at Rs. 2,250,000 million (28.6 per cent over the target of 2006-07), and an addition of 5 million new farmer borrowers.

Total disbursements progressively increased from Rs. 6,20,450 million in 2001-02 to Rs. 9,54,252 million in the year 2005-06, reflecting a rise by 153.8 per cent. Commercial Banks and regional rural banks recorded phenomenal rise by 216 per cent and 189 per cent respectively as compared to 58 per cent by cooperatives. While there has been progressive rise in each successive year in the case of cooperatives, commercial banks and regional rural banks, there has been spectacular increase during 2004-05 and 2005-06 in respect of commercial banks and regional rural banks. The share of cooperatives in the total disbursements of short-term and long-term credit progressively declined from 37.91 per cent in 2001-02 to 23.65 per cent in 2005-06 whereas that of the commercial banks recorded progressive increase from 54.13 per cent to 67.41 per cent during the corresponding years. The regional rural banks accounted for 7.82 per cent increases in

2001-02, which progressively rose to 9.91 per cent in 2004-05, but declined by one percentage point in the following year. The flow of agricultural credit for the banking system as a whole during 2005-06 has surged to Rs. 18,04,860 million reflecting 128 per cent of the target of Rs. 14,10,000 million which was set for the year.

The proportion of short-term credit to enable farmers to conduct seasonal agricultural operation was around 63 per cent as against 37 per cent of long-term credit for investment purposes.

Under the service area approach to rural financial services, the annual growth target was between 12.5 and 24 per cent during 2000-01 and 2003-04. The growth was spectacularly high at 54.5 per cent during 2004-05 which declined to 44.6 per cent in the following year. Disbursements of credit as against targets ranged from 92.1 per cent to 117.3 per cent during the six-year period. Achievements were higher than 100 per cent only in the last two years.

Public sector banks recovery to demand under direct agricultural advance was 69.3 per cent during the year 2000-01 which gradually increased during the following three years. It, however, phenomenally rose to 84.1 per cent in the year 2004-05. During the five years period, the demand (loan amount to be recovered) and percentage of recovery to demand have progressively increased in the successive years whereas overdue amount has increased until the year 2003-04, and then it steeply declined by Rs. 29,620 million in the following years.

During the seven years period from 2000 to 2006, the public sector banks outstanding credit to priority sectors increased by 221.9 per cent from Rs. 1,274,780 million as on 31st March, 2000 to Rs. 41,03,790 million as on 31st March, 2006, whereas that of the private sector banks shot up by 480.2 per cent from Rs. 1,83,680 million to Rs. 1,065,660 million during the period under consideration. Priority sector advances of public sector banks as group accounted for over 43 per cent of net bank credit in four years as against the target of 40 per cent which, however, declined from 42.8 per cent to 40.3 per cent in three years. In this respect private sector banks as a group has less than that of targeted 40 per

cent during initial three years, but they showed impressive performance (42.8% to 47.3%) in the following four years.

Agricultural advances by the public sector banks during the period rose by 242 per cent from Rs. 452,960 million to Rs. 15,49,000 million whereas that of the private sector banks increased significantly by 799 per cent from Rs. 40,230 million to Rs. 361,850 million during the period under consideration. The share of agricultural advances in the net bank credit by the public sector banks ranged between 14.3 per cent and 15.7 per cent, whereas that of the private sector banks varied from 8.3 per cent to 14.2 per cent during the period under consideration. Neither public sector banks, nor private sector banks as a group could achieve the targeted agricultural credit of 18 per cent of net bank credit.

During 2005-06, all public sector banks (except State Bank of India and State Bank of Patiala) were able to meet the priority sector target for agriculture. None of the private sector banks could meet the sub-target for lending to agriculture.

During the period from 2001-02 to 2005-06 banks provided 5,90,93,000 Kisan Credit Cards to farmers to facilitate them to purchase farm inputs and other requirements. Share of the commercial banks was 37 per cent as against the shares of cooperatives and regional rural banks at 51 per cent and 12 per cent respectively.

The refinance provided by NABARD to banks has significantly increased from Rs. 45,210 million in 1998-99 to Rs. 86,223.7 million in 2005-06. Only the commercial banks availed significantly increased of refinance in the successive years. Share of refinance in the total agricultural loans disbursed by cooperatives was as high as 50.3 per cent followed by commercial banks at 31.4 per cent, whereas regional rural banks accounted for 18 per cent.

As on the 31st March, 2006, the number of SHGs linked with Banks were as high as 2,238,565 as compared to 10,79,091 in 2004 and 1,618,546 in 2005. Credit disbursed to these SHGs was also as high as Rs. 113,975.3 million in 2004 and Rs. 68,984.6 million in 2005. Share of commercial banks in respect of number

of SHGs linked with banks and credit disbursed was the highest followed by the regional rural banks and cooperatives.

The commercial banks falling short of achieving priority sector/agricultural lending targets have since 1995-96 till 2005-06 deposited Rs. 287,499.5 million with NABARD under Rural Infrastructure Development Fund at very reduced interest rate. The NABARD has so far disbursed a sum of Rs. 322,893.3 million to support 2,44,651 projects in various parts of the country.

The share of irrigation development projects in terms of number was the highest at 38.7 per cent followed by social sector and rural roads, whereas in terms of amount disbursed, the irrigation development project accounted for as high as 34.3 per cent share, followed by rural roads, rural bridge and social sector.

Despite all the noble efforts on the part of the governmental agencies, access to financial services for all at affordable rates remained a distant dream. Remoteness of the rural area and poor infrastructure leads to market inefficiencies and a huge gap between demand and supply of credit. Problem is compounded by the fact that the rural population is still largely illiterate and not so technology driven (technology itself comes at cost). For the overall development of the country these problems related to rural credit should be addressed in proper way. Steps are required at both policy level and organizational level to solve these problems

V

The Self-Help Groups (SHGs) are small informal and homogenous groups of not more than 20 members. The group has been recommended to be informal to keep them away from bureaucracy and corruption, unnecessary expenditure and profit constraints. The size of 20 members has been made mandatory, because any group larger than this size would have to be registered under the Indian legal system.

The exponential trend equation of the type $y = ab^x$ has been filled into the time series data on the number of SHGs linkage, amount of bank loan to SHGs, amount of refinance assistance to SHGs from NABARD, and the amount of loan per SHG.

The number of SHGs linked with banks increased from 255 in 1992-93 to 6,20,109 in 2005-06 on year after year basis. The amount of bank loans to the SHGs increased from Rs. 2.9 million in 1992-93 to Rs. 49,090 million in 2005-06. Similarly, the amount of refinance assistance increased from Rs. 2.7 million in 1992-93 to Rs. 10,677 million in 2005-06. Finally, the average amount of loan per SHG increased from Rs. 11,373 in 1992-93 to Rs. 79,168 in 2005-06.

The SHG-Bank linkage has increased at the rate of 90.90 per cent per annum during the period 1992-93 to 2005-06. While the amount of the bank loan increased at the rate of 121.37 per cent per annum, the amount refinance assistance to the SHGs from the NABARD increased at the rate of 104.60 per cent per annum during the period under consideration. Finally, the amount of average bank loan per SHG increased at the rate of 15.96 per cent per annum during the period from 1992-93 to 2005-06.

The number of villages covered by the Grameen Bank of Bangladesh project increased from 363 in December 1980 to 1,88,125 in August 1990. The number of the branches of the bank, increased from 25 to 741 during the same period. The number of members of the bank increased from 0.15 lakh in December 1980 to 7.90 lakh in August 1990. The number of male and female members of the bank increased from 0.55 lakh and 1.13 lakh in December 1985 to 0.75 lakh and 7.15 lakh respectively in August 1990. The number of groups of the bank increased from 2,935 in 1980 to 98,073 in 1988. The number of borrowers of the bank was 0.15 lakh in 1980 which rose to 4.72 lakh in 1988.

In 1980, the bank had disbursed the loan of 1.71 lakh crore. The corresponding figure for 1988 was Taka 128.44 crore. The cumulative amount of loan disbursed increased from Taka 2.01 crore in 1980 to Taka 681.07 crore in August 1990. The savings in group fund increased from Taka 0.15 crore in December 1980 to Taka 57.45 crore in August 1990. The savings in the emergency fund of the bank increased from Taka 1.26 crore in 1985 to Taka 11.16 crore in 1990. The loans from group fund (cumulative disbursement since inception), increased from Taka 2.23 crore in 1985 to Taka 30.91 crore in August 1990.

As of July 2004, the Grameen Bank of Bangladesh has 37 million borrowers, 96 per cent of whom are women. With 1,267 branches the Grameen Bank provides services in 46,000 villages covering more than 68 per cent of the total villages in Bangladesh.

A new programme known a 'Swarnajayanti Gram Swarozgar Yojana' (SGSY) has been launched in India since April 1999. The SGSY is a holistic programme covering all aspects of self-employment such as organization of the poor into Self-Help Groups, training, credit, technology, infrastructure and marketing. The SGSY is funded by the centre and the States in the ratio of 75 : 25.

With the coming into force of the SGSY the earlier programmes—Integrated Rural Development Programme (IRDP), Training of Youth for Self-Employment (TRYSEM), Development of Women & Children in Rural Areas (DWACRA), Supply of Improved Toolkits to Rural Artisans (SITRA), Ganga Kalyan Yojana (GKY) and Million Sallow Tubewell (MST) are no longer in operation now.

Under the SGSY, the beneficiaries are known as 'swarozgaris'. The swarozgaris can be either individuals or groups. The SGSY lays emphasis on the group approach under which the rural poor are organized into Self-Help Groups. In either case, the list of 'below poverty line' (BPL), householders identified through BPL census, duly approved by the Gram Sabha forms the basis for identification for assistance under the SGSY. The Self-Help Groups should also be drawn from the BPL list approved by the Gram Sabha.

Between April 1, 1999 and March 31, 2006 about 19 lakh SHGs have been organized under SGSY. Of these, 10 lakh SHGs have passed Grade I and 6.22 lakh Grade II. About 3.09 lakh SHGs have taken up economic activity. The percentage of SHGs taking up economic activity, out of the SHGs which have passed Grade II is around 50 per cent in 2005-06. The number of SHG swarozgaris assisted has also increased from 3.47 lakh to 5.87 lakh during this period. Of course, the number of individual swarozgaris assisted has declined from 5.9 lakh to 2.67 lakh during the same period. The percentage of SC/ST community members assisted under the programme has increased from 44 per cent to 85 per

cent, the percentage of women from 44 to 58, and the percentage of disabled from 0.91 to 24.91.

Between April 1999 and March 2006 an amount of Rs. 8223.20 crore was allocated for the SGSY out of which a sum of Rs. 7494.75 crore (91%) was utilized. The percentage utilization to funds available increased from 49 per cent in 1999-2000 to 89 per cent in 2005-06. The utilization of funds towards training and skill development too increased from 3 per cent to 3.64 per cent during this period. With regard to the credit mobilized, a sum of Rs. 1,056 crore was provided to this programme in 1999-2000 which went up to Rs. 1755.27 crore by 2006. The per cent of credit support increased from 32.96 in 1999-2000 to 61 in 2003-04 and declined to 16.84 in 2005-06. In tune with the growing emphasis on group approach, the investment support towards the group has been making steady progress. This sums in the ratio of investment on SHGs *vs.* individuals which has almost gone up by seven times from 0.24 to 1.84 during this period. Similarly, the per capita investment under this programme has increased from Rs. 17,000 to Rs. 25,000.

All the banks working in East Champaran district of Bihar with their 176 branches had fixed the target of Rs. 1,265 lakh for SGSY through SHGs in 1999-2000. Altogether 3,076 applications were received under SGSY, out of which 2,164 (70.37%) applications were accepted and a sum of Rs. 390 lakh (30.83%) was distributed under the SGSY in the year 1999-2000.

Out of the total applications of 6,363 received in 2000-03, 3,706 (58.49%) were accepted and 3,535 (56.11%) applications were disposed of after granting the loan of Rs. 729.64 lakh under the SGSY in 2002-03 this amount constituted only 40.02 per cent of the target amount.

All the banks taken together approved 1,257 applications and granted the loan of Rs. 1235.16 lakh under the SGSY in 2002-03 in East Champaran district. This amount constituted 58.40 per cent of the target amount.

Empowerment is a process of awareness and capacity building to greater participation, the greater decision making power and control and transformative action. The empowerment of women

covers both an individual and collective transformation. It strengthens their innate ability through acquiring knowledge, power, and experience.

The number of women SHGs formed so far constitutes 90 per cent or more of the total number of SHGs under SGSY. In 1999-2000, 1,16,690 women swarozgaris were assisted which constituted 44.62 per cent of the women swarozgaris. In 2005-06, the number of swarozgaris swelled to 4,99,154 registering a growth of about 11 per cent during the period 1999-2000 to 2005-06. The number of swarozgaris assisted in 2005-06 constituted 58.39 per cent. During the period of 6 years from 1999-2000 to 2005-06 the total number of women swarozgaris assisted was 30,64,765; its 48.63 per cent swarozgaris was, assisted during the period under consideration.

The majority of the Self-Help Groups in Sabour Block of Bhagalpur district in Bihar were organizing two meetings in a month for effective working of the groups. Most of the groups (45%) were saving Rs. 25 to Rs. 30 per month per member. About 42 per cent members were taking loan for agricultural activities, besides goats (9%), cows/buffaloes (16%), poultry (8%), Bidi, making and others (7%). In the case of loan recovery, 71 per cent members have exerted group pressure if loans were not paid.

The Government of Bihar initiated a project in 2006 on rural livelihood promotion with the support from the World Bank to rural poor men and women. The name of the project is Bihar Rural Livelihood Promotion Project (BRLP) under Bihar Rural Livelihood Promotion Society (BRLPS). The BRLPS is the spearheading agency for the implementation of the project. This project has been named 'Jeevika' in Hindi. Its headquarters is in the Vidyut Bhawan, Patna. Now Jeevika has been designed to address rural poverty in Bihar through the collaboration of the poor, the Government of Bihar, and the World Bank.

The BRLP is not a shadow or carbon copy of the IRDP of the Government of India but it is a mega and multi-dimensional challenging project of the Sushasan 'Government of Bihar'.

The success story of the tribal women's Self-Help Group from a small colony of Kohima town is truly a motivating story for

other groups of women. How insecure and helpless they felt when they were unable to earn even a single paisa. One determined and with the help of NCUI-CEFP, they quickly mastered various skills to produce items having demand in the market and also picked up the nuances of financial matters. And with regular upgradation of skills they are treading on the path of success. They became conscious about education of their children. They were also more aware about health care of their ownselves and of their families and want to conduct health care programmes for the community. They have learnt the lesson may be a bit late. The lesson they want to pass on is that early to learn and early to work together makes one healthy, wealthy and wise.

India is the country of villages and agriculture is the occupation of the major chunk of the working population. Being a developing economy, India has to take care of the development of its agricultural and rural sectors. This phenomenon is possible only through extending more and more credit facilities to the rural areas and by assigning the status of priority sector to agriculture. Again, being a poor country, India has been facing the lack of capital for rural and agricultural development. There are numerous examples of the adverse impact of negligence of agricultural sector. The most recent is the suicide attempts made by the farmers in Andhra Pradesh, Karnataka and Maharashtra, and food shortage in the country.

At the national level, the population pressure per bank office was observed to be 19.41 thousand persons in 1981 in India. The corresponding figure for 2001 was found to be 22.17 thousand persons per office.

The values of the credit deposit ratio at the national level were observed to be 77.89, 67.57, 65.24, 55.85, and 70.50 for 1969, 1981, 1991, 2001 and 2006 respectively.

The share of priority sector in total bank credit was found to be 40.4 per cent in 1991, which declined to 35.2 per cent in 2001 and to 37.5 per cent in 2006. The coefficient of variation of States, priority sectors share in total bank credit was found to be 23.12 per cent in 1991, which fell down to 13.07 per cent in 2001 and further to 12.44 per cent in 2006.

The per capita deposit at the national level has shown an increasing trend as the figure rose from Rs. 342 in 1981 to Rs. 2,042 in 1991 and further to Rs. 7,383 in 2001. Like the per capita deposit, the per capita credit also has shown an increasing trend at the national level, as the per capita credit rose from Rs. 506 in 1981 to Rs. 1,332 in 1991 and to Rs. 4,125 in 2001.

The coefficient of regional inequality in respect of per capita deposit was found to be 22.6009 in 1981, which increased to 116.8267 in 1991, but fell down to 0.1318 in 2001. Similarly, the coefficient of regional inequality in respect of per capita credit increased from 22.0369 in 1981 to 47.0960 in 1991 but fell down to 0.1107 in 2001.

The growth rates of amount (in rupees) of priority sector lendings by public sector commercial banks were found to be positive in all the 12 sub-sectors during the period 1981 to 1990. During the period 1991 to 2000, the lone negative growth rate was observed with the sub-sector of setting up of industrial estates. During the period 2001 to 2006, the growth rate in the case of small organizations for SC/ST for purchase and supply of inputs and marketing of outputs was found negative and all the rest growth rates were found to be positive.

In the case of amount of rupees per account of priority sector lendings, out of the 12, 4 sub-sectors, namely small scale industries, setting up of industrial estates, retail trade, and small organizations for SC/ ST for purchase and supply of inputs and marketing of outputs have been observed with negative growth rates during the period 1981 to 1990. During the period 1991 to 2000, the growth rate of lendings in the case of setting up of industrial estates has been found negative, and all the rest growth rates have been found positive. Similarly, during the period 2001 to 2006, all the growth rates except the one small organizations for SC/ST for purchase and supply of inputs and marketing of outputs have been found positive.

The percentage share of the priority sector credit in the total bank credit provided by the public sector banks has been found increasing at the rate of 2.96 per cent and 0.32 per cent per annum during the periods 1981 to 1990 and 1991 to 2000 respectively, but during the period 2001 to 2006 it has been found increasing

at the rate of 1.16 per cent per annum. Thus the impact of the financial sector reforms on the priority sector lendings has been very much adverse.

In India economic reforms with human face have been accepted as the guiding principle of sustainable development. Keeping the poor at the centre stage, the policies need to be reoriented, so as to develop and optimize the potential of such a large segment of the population and enable them to contribute in the growth process significantly in terms of output, income, employment and consumption. After the pioneering efforts of the last 10 years or so the microfinance scene in India has reached a take-off point. With some efforts substantial progress can be made in taking MFIs to the next orbit of significance and sustainability. This needs innovative and forward looking policies, based on the ground realities of successful MFIs. This combined with a commercial approach from the MFIs in making microfinance financially sustainable, will make this sector vibrant and help achieve its single-minded mission of providing financial services to the rural poor.

It is necessary to recognize that in India we have to focus on extending financial services in both rural and urban areas for ensuring financial inclusion of all segments of the population. At the same time one should avoid the temptation of creating one set banking and financial institutions to cater to the poor or the unorganized and another set for the rest. The medium to long term objective should be to ensure inclusion of all segments in the main stream institutions while taking advantage of the flexibility of multiplicity of models of delivering a wide range of financial services. In this light, a comprehensive framework to revive the cooperative credit system, revitalize the regional rural banks and reorient commercial banking system needs to get a high priority while simultaneously encouraging and enabling the growth of microfinance movement in India, which has been very successful. It is required to build on its strengths and extend it to vast areas, which are inadequately covered, by both banking and microcredit entities.

Microfinance broadly defined, needs to be explored in the light of the new paradigm described. The Reserve Bank of India and

the NABARD recognize the growing importance of microfinance and are committed to enable its healthy growth. However, several issues, both in regard to regulation as well as development of the MFIs need to be considered and must be comprehensively addressed. While the report of the Khan Committee would provide a good starting point for taking a view on developmental aspects, in particular, the CGAP's guiding principles on regulation and supervision on microfinance provide a valuable and globally relevant framework in regard to the regulatory issues. The proposed forum for a consultative process on the MFIs would also be useful in evolving an appropriate framework for development of the MFI sector. No doubt, a very well-crafted balance between the regulation and growth objectives would be warranted in formulating our approach to a regulatory regime, keeping in view the big challenge of financial inclusion of a large segment of the Indian population.

It is unclear whether microfinance contributes to reduction in poverty or is the most efficient method to reduce poverty without additional measures in areas such as education, health and infrastructure. The entry of commercial banks into microfinance may increase the competition for traditional microfinance institutions and reduce lending cost to the core poor, even if it improves financial sustainability.

The trend of commercial banks entering the market for microfinance appears to be one of the most important challenges for the microfinance business in the near future. However, the potential of this trend in terms of reducing poverty is still unclear. Further, research into this important issue is, therefore, highly desirable.

Conclusion

The financial sector reforms since 1991 and the emphasis on implementation of prudential norms, income recognition, asset classification provisioning norms and Capital Risk Weighted Ratio (CRWR), were instrumental in compelling the commercial banks to concentrate on the financial efficiency and economic viability

through rationalization of their operating system, consideration of their branch network, which resulted in relocation of many bank branches, concentrating on core strengths reducing the surplus staff as also the computerization of operations.

Over time, the flow of credit to agriculture and rural sector has expanded impressively. The ground level credit flow had registered an increase (in real terms with 1993-94 prices) from Rs. 13,915 crore in 1991-92 to Rs. 49,401 crore in 2003-04 and further to Rs. 92,125 crore in 2005-06. The estimated annual compound growth in credit to the agriculture sector in real terms was 14.5 per cent (with 14.1 per cent growth in production credit and 14.9 per cent growth for investment credit during the above period. While the annual growth rate in production and investment credit flow (in real terms) during 1991-92 and 2003-04 were 11.5 per cent and 10.5 per cent respectively, their respective growth rates during 2003-04 and 2005-06 were 31.3 per cent and 45.1 per cent. However, the maximum growth in credit flow were registered during 2004-05 and 2005-06 when agricultural credit was doubled during two years instead of the targeted three years.

The analysis of agency-wise credit flow indicates that the cooperative banks were the major source of agricultural credit in 1991-92, constituting 53.7 per cent of the total ground level credit flow of Rs. 13,915 crore (in real terms with 1993-94 prices), followed by commercial banks at 41.2 per cent (Rs. 5,731 crore), and regional rural banks at 5.1 per cent (Rs. 712 crore). Though cooperative banks had dominated agricultural credit supply during the early reform period, commercial banks and regional rural banks recorded impressive growth rates. As a result, in 2005-06, the share of cooperative banks in the total institutional credit flow receded to 21.9 per cent and that of commercial banks advanced to 69.7 per cent. Although the quantum of disbursement for cooperative banks increased, it could not keep pace with commercial banks in enhancing the credit flow due to several reasons including its poor financial health, dual control, lack of internal controls and corporate governance norms and excessive dependence on other financial institutions.

The reasons for the massive increase in the credit flow for commercial banks and regional rural banks could be attributed to the linkage of Self-Help Groups with banks in 1992, introduction of the scheme of Kisan Credit Cards (KCC) in 1998, formulation of the Special Agricultural Credit Plans (SACP) by the public sector banks since 2004-05, and monitoring under the scheme of doubling of credit in 2004.

Despite impressive growth in direct credit to farmers from the scheduled commercial banks between 1991-92 and 2003-04, country to expectation, credit disbursement to small and marginal farmers has not been encouraging. However, for small farmers and other farmers respectively, the number of accounts increased from 44.4 lakh and 36.7 lakh in 1991-92 to 48 lakh and 43.8 lakh in 2003-04. The percentage of marginal farmers to total farmers came down from 42.8 in 1991-92 to 39.8 in 2003-04, while the same for other farmers increased from 25.9 to 28.7. Further, the annual average growth rate in the number of accounts and the amount of credit outstanding during the period between 1991-92 and 2003-04 were 0.62 per cent and 6.2 per cent respectively. One important observation from the above findings is that the credit per account had increased without any increase in the number of accounts. Further increase in credit flow favoured the richer farmers.

While analyzing the pattern of credit flow, it is observed that the proportion of bank deposits and credit shares have moved in favour of the South-West and North regions. While the share of loans in the total disbursement of credit for agriculture and allied activities were the maximum for the south region (47.9 per cent in 1990-91 and 43.7 per cent in 2001-02), it was the minimum for North-East regions (0.4 per cent in 1990-91 and 0.5 per cent in 2001-02). The population per rural branch, which was estimated at 16,355 and 16,402 respectively in the North-East and Eastern regions in 1991, increased to 22,158 and 21,208 respectively in 2005. Further, when the number of savings accounts for every 100 persons in rural areas of the North-East region had shown a marginal rise from 16.1 in 1991 to 16.4 in 2005, during the same period, the number of savings accounts in the eastern region had declined from 17.7 to 16.9. Similarly in the case of the number of

credit account for every 100 persons in rural areas the number reduced from 4.4 and 7.2 in North-East and Eastern regions in 1991 to 3.2 and 4.2 respectively in 2005.

Although with the rise in net bank credit, the credit flow for priority sector by the scheduled commercial banks had increased in percentage terms it remained stagnant at around 36 per cent over the last 14 years. While the net bank credit of the scheduled commercial banks increased from Rs. 1,45,250 crore (in real terms at 1993-94 prices) in 1991 to Rs. 5,75,090 crore in 2005 at an annual compound growth rate of 10.3 per cent, the advances to priority sector increased from Rs. 53,125 crore to Rs. 2,05,000 crore at annual compound growth rate of 10.1 per cent. As a result, the gap between these two has been widening. Further, the zig-zag trend i.e. downward during 1991-1996 and upward during 1996-2005, in the priority sector lending as a per cent to the net bank credit of the banks during the period between 1991 and 2005 shows that no consistent effort has been made to step up advances in favour of the priority sector. With the new norms for the priority sector announced by the Reserve Bank of India in 2007, it is expected that the commercial banks would be able to achieve the targets fixed.

The credit deposit ratio, which is an important indicator of deployment of the resources of bank, had been showing a downward zig-zag movement during the last 14 years. The deposits and credit of the scheduled commercial banks in rural areas which were Rs. 36,961 crore and Rs. 22,168 crore (in real terms at 1993-94 prices) in 1991, increased to Rs. 56,254 crore respectively, in 2005. Thus the credit deposit ratios had declined from 60 per cent in 1991 to 51.6 per cent in 2005.

However, the credit deposit ratios of the banks in urban areas had increased from 62.3 per cent in 1991 to 68 per cent in 2005. When the pattern of the credit deposit ratios for rural and urban areas are observed, it is found that the credit deposit ratios of the banks operating in urban areas are positioned above the overall credit deposit ratio and that of the rural areas are positioned well below the overall credit deposit ratios.

While the credit deposit ratio of the rural branches of the scheduled commercial banks declined during the period between 1991 and 2004, that of the urban offices had shown some improvement with declining and increasing trend in some years during the same period. However, the credit deposit ratio for rural and urban areas increased from 43.6 per cent and 60.4 per cent in 2004, to 51.6 per cent and 68 per cent respectively in 2005. During the period between 1991 and 2005, while the annual growth rates in the volume of deposits and credits for urban areas were 10.2 per cent and 10.9 per cent respectively, the same for the rural areas were 8 per cent and 6.9 per cent respectively. Thus while in urban areas the growth rate of credit was higher than that of deposits, in rural areas the growth ratio in deposits was higher than that of credit.

The Indian banking system has acquired a wide outreach, judged in terms of expansion of branches and the growth of deposits and credit. The expansion of the branch network peaked in the phase of social banking during the 1970s and 1980s. Although the Narsimham Committee had recognized the need for continuing with the expansion of banking infrastructure in rural areas, in the process of executing financial reforms, the importance of rural financial infrastructure has got neglected and the number of branches of the scheduled commercial banks declined steadily in rural areas and increased in urban areas. For instance, in 1991 there were 35,206 rural branches out of the total 60,220 branches of the scheduled commercial banks. But in 2006, while the total number of branches of the scheduled commercial banks was 69,471, the number of rural branches had reduced to 30,579. Thus the financial system has become increasingly urban centric. Urbanized staff members of commercial banks perceive rural postings as a punishment and serve out their mandatory rural postings rather than grudgingly. The Voluntary Retirement Scheme (VRS) in commercial banks has also ensured that rural branches remain undermanned. Rural postings are avoided because of poor infrastructure facilities, lack of communications, poor transport facilities, lack of good educational opportunities and also due to reduction in perks and allowances.

The trend analysis brings out the fact that financial inclusion by way of credit to rural sectors as also marginal and small farmers is a distant dream and demands evolution of appropriate strategies. This aspect has drawn the attention of the government, the Reserve Bank of India and the NABARD in recent years and a series of interventions have been initiated to enhance credit flow in favour of priority sectors and the disadvantaged sections of the society.

In order to increase credit flow to the agriculture sector, the policy of doubling of agricultural credit in three years was introduced in 2004-05. In 2004, the Government of India constituted a Task Force to revive the rural cooperative credit institutions under the chairmanship of Prof. A. Vaidyanathan. In order to expand the outreach of the banking services, banks made available basic banking 'no-frills' account with low or nil minimum balances as well as low or no charges in 2005. The regional rural banks were also specifically advised to allow limited overdraft facilities in 'no frills' accounts without any collateral or linkage to any purpose.

For opening account with banks, procedures have been simplified by introducing the concept of 'Know Your Customer' (KYC) drill. In January 2006, banks were permitted to utilize the services of NGOs, SHGs and other Civil Society Organizations (CSOs) as intermediaries in providing financial and banking services through the use of Business Facilitators (BF) and Business Correspondence (BC) models. The BC model allows banks to do 'cash in cash out' transactions at the location of the business correspondence and also permits branch banking. With the objective of providing revolving credit to the rural people, banks in rural and semi-urban areas have been advised to provide a General-Purpose Credit Card (GCC) facility. For all borrowers having a principal amount of less than Rs. 25,000 and whose accounts have become Non-Performing Assets (NPA), banks have been requested to offer a One Time Settlement (OTS) scheme. It is expected that such a provision will restore the borrowing relationship of small borrowers with the formal system and thereby obviate the need to go back to informal system. In 2007, a multi-lingual website in 13 Indian languages on all matters concerning

banking was launched by the Reserve Bank of India for credit counselling and financial education. In 2007-08, two funds, Financial Inclusion Fund (FIF) for promotional interventions and Financial Inclusion Technology Fund (FITF) for meeting cost of technology adoption were proposed to be established with the NABARD.

Complementing its core financing and developmental functions in tune with the emerging challenges, the NABARD has been pioneering innovative rural interventions for ensuring sustainable development and prosperity. In its long journey for the development of farm and non-farm sectors through credit and other support services, initiatives such as Potential Linked Credit Plans (PLCPs), District Development Offices (DDOs), Participatory Watershed Development Programme (PWDP), non-farm-sector promotional programmes, Self-Help Group-Banks Linkage Programmes, Rural Infrastructure Development Fund (RIDF), Kisan Credit Card (KCC), Swarozgar Credit Card, Consultancy Services, Tribal Development Programmes, Farmers Club, etc., have contributed immensely. The initiatives of the bank centre around (i) exploring innovative investment opportunities, (ii) investing partners for financial/technical assistance, (iii) creating infrastructure base, (iv) developing leadership, entrepreneurship and capacity building, (v) educating the rural masses, (vi) building sound network of rural financial institutions, (vii) continuous innovations in delivery procedures and systems, (viii) credit planning, and (ix) support Research & Development activities in the area of agriculture and rural development. In order to augment the much needed institutional credit, the NABARD included financing of housing in rural areas as an eligible activity for extension of refinance under investment credit to financial institutions since April 1, 2001 subject to a maximum of Rs. 5 lakh for a dwelling unit.

The major initiatives of NABARD, which have had a direct impact on the rural credit delivery mechanism have touched and transformed the lives of millions of rural people.

The SHG-Bank linkage programme, which comes as a corporate strategy in 1992, aims at improving access of the weaker

and other sections of the society from formal financial institutions. It has been built around a simple but basic aspect of human nature—'the feeling of self worth'. The ability of people to pool their micro-savings provide collective social collaterals for banks to lend against and add to the SHGs funds and the collective alteration of funds to meet the emergent credit needs of the SHG members rates, which reflect risk and management cost of funds are the unique features of this movement which has enabled banks to assist in meeting the credit needs of the very poor people without sacrificing their fund and has helped the rural women especially to empower themselves both economically and financially. Over the last 15 years or so, the microfinance initiative of NABARD has passed through various stages like pilot testing (1992-95) mainstreaming (1996-98) and expansion (1998 onwards) and has assumed the shape of a microfinance movement in the country by linking around 30 lakh SHGs with the formal banking system by March 2007. Further the programme has enabled an estimate 394 lakh poor households to gain access to funds from the formal banking system. Studies conducted by various experts show that the programme has indeed helped in the social and economic empowerment of rural folk, especially women, causing significant upscaling of social capital while at the same time delivering crucial financial services. Today it has extended banking services to people hitherto underserved by the banking system.

Absence of ability to provide adequate collateral security acts as a major hurdle for landless/tenant farmers in securing loans. The inability of this section of farmers to provide collateral often excludes them from the purview of formal credit cover. Keeping this in view, a pilot project on financing Joint Liability Group (JLG) was initiated for developing effective credit products for such clients, which reduce the risk and transaction costs for the banks and also introduce a greater degree of flexibility for the credit users to determine their credit needs and priorities. Joint Liability Groups (JLGs), to be established under the pilot project, will be a group of 5-10 member clients who are together informally recognized by the bank as a group. The group members offer an undertaking to the bank that enables them to jointly receive such

amounts as deemed eligible by the bank for pursuing any activity, individually or jointly, as found suitable by the group. The group serves as collective guarantor for loans extended to individual member by executing joint liability agreements, making them severally and jointly liable for repayment of loans to the group. Although the JLG credit model was pilot tested for mid-segment farmers, the concept could very well be extended to tenant farmers oral leases/share croppers also.

With a view to promoting the scheme on a large scale, banks may be allowed to adopt 'Agency Model' by involving, civil society organizations, NGOs, Farmers Club, Village Knowledge Centre, Panchayats, various users Groups such as Water Users' Association etc. Their services could also be made use of for performing various non-financial functions for the bank such as borrower identification preliminary appraisal, promotion and monitoring of JLGs, etc.

An approach similar to TPGs or JLGs was also adopted in Andhra Pradesh, with the initiative of the State Government. The programme called Rythu Mitra Groups (RMGs), which envisages bringing about holistic development in the lives of small/marginal/landless farmers through collective action. RMGs are expected to serve as a conduit for technology transfer, facilitate access to market information and market, assess input requirements, etc. for its members. NABARD provides resource and grant assistance for conducting training and capacity building initiatives to different stakeholders. During the year 2006, 4,437 RMGs were financed by 18 commercial banks, 9 RRBs, and 9 DCCBs involving ground level credit flow of Rs. 28.11 crore. About 62,000 farmers have been assisted under this pilot project.

During the year 1998-99, the NABARD introduced the Kisan Credit Card (KCC) scheme in conjunction with the cooperative banks, commercial banks and regional rural banks to smoothen and strengthen the credit delivery system and more particularly, to make available timely and hassle-free Crop loans to the farmers. As on 28 February, 2007, 665.6 lakh KCCs had been issued by the banking system. Of the total 665.6 lakh cards, the cooperative banks accounted for the target share of 49 per cent, followed by

commercial banks (38%) and regional rural banks (12%). Recognising it as an accepted mechanism for delivery of credit to farmers, the banking system has been routing crop loans through the Kisan Credit Cards. To cover the KCC holders against accidental death/permanent disability and practical disability upto Rs. 50,000 and Rs. 25,000 respectively, an insurance scheme was formulated by the General Insurers' Association of India (GISA) in close coordination with the NABARD Banks have been advised to implement the scheme with effect from the kharif 2001 season. All the KCC holders are required to be covered under the scheme by payment of a nominal premium amount. With a view to making KCC more user-friendly and comprehensive, the NABARD has further enlarged the scope of the scheme to cover long-term loans and consumption loans along with crop loans.

The joint studies conducted by the NABARD and the financing banks on the implementation of the KCC scheme have confirmed that the scheme was well received by the farmers and bankers and the flexibility in operation has resulted in improved loan recoveries. For many banks some ground level constraints like adoption of selective approach in identifying beneficiaries, reluctance to extend KCC facility to mono crop areas, levy of costly charges and levy of stamp duty by some of the State governments for issuing loans under KCCs, were observed.

The Swarozgar Credit Card (SCC) scheme was introduced in 2003 for facilitating hassle-free availability of credit for meeting investment and working capital requirements of small borrowers and rural micro-entrepreneur. As on 31st March, 2007, the banking system had issued 6.79 lakh cards involving credit limits of Rs. 2,700 crore.

With an objective of quicker completion of on-going rural infrastructure projects, the rural infrastructure development fund (RIDF) was set up with the NABARD during 1995-96 with an initial corpus of Rs. 2000 crore. In the Union Budget for 2006-07, the XII tranche for RIDF was announced with an allocation of Rs. 60,000 crore. As on 31st March, 2007, the cumulative number of projects sanctioned rose to 2,44,025 and the amount sanctioned increased to Rs. 61,539.87 crore. Although initially it was meant

mainly for incomplete projects in irrigation, rural roads and rural bridges, the scope has now been extended to cover major infrastructure projects in various sectors like irrigation, roads, bridges, power, marketyards, godowns cold storage, informational technology, primary education and health systems.

The rural microfinance institutions which have emerged as a powerful tool for fighting poverty may be made a part of the financial system for effective delivery of rural financial services. The banks need to gear up their rural branches for facilitating bank linkages of SHGs where the programme has not shown satisfactory progress. The Business Correspondence as recommended by the Internal Group of Microfinance (Khan Committee), may also be put in place which will increase banking outreach.

The performance of Indian agriculture during 2007-08 has struck a disappointing note with the growth rate for the whole year estimated at only 2.6 per cent. The budget for 2008-09, therefore, endeavoured to embody specific plans, programmes and policy directives and it allocated funds to crucial areas to yield expected results. Despite the fact that agriculture in India has been a very vital sector of national economy and its 4 per cent annual growth rate is necessary to boost the Indian economy, agricultural growth has been decelerating and stagnating since several years.

The 2008-09 budget of the Government of India specifically focused on provision of bank credit, financial inclusion, waiver of loans, creation of irrigation potential, crop insurance plan, health management and subsidized supply of fertilizer.

Agricultural credit was doubled in the two years during 2004-06 as against three years and has now reached the level of Rs. 240,000 crore by March 31, 2008. The target for 2008-09 has been set at Rs. 280,000 crore. Short-term crop loan will continue to be disbursed at interest rate of 7 per cent per annum.

The recommendations of the Vaidyanathan Committee on revival of the short-term cooperative credit structure are under implementation in 17 States. The Union and State Governments have reached an agreement on the content of package to implement

the recommendations of the Vaidyanathan Committee on the revival of the long-term cooperative credit structure.

As recommended by the Committee on Financial Inclusion, every commercial bank including regional rural banks would add at least 250 rural household accounts every year at each of their rural and semi-urban branches and banks are allowed to appoint individuals such as retired bank officers, ex-servicemen, etc. as business facilitators or business correspondent or credit counsellor. Bank should embrace the concept of Total Financial Inclusion. NABARD, SIDBI and NHB can augment resources of scheduled commercial banks to the extent they fall short of their obligations to under the priority sector and achieve financial inclusion. The 2008-09 budget provides a fund of Rs. 5,000 crore to NABARD, Rs. 2,000 crore to SIDBI, and Rs. 1,200 crore to NHB.

All scheduled commercial banks have been asked to meet the entire credit requirements of SHG members, viz. income generating activities, social needs like housing, education, marriage, etc. and debt swapping.

The borrowers eligibility criteria under the differential rate of interest scheme at 4 per cent per annum is now fixed as annual family income of Rs. 18,000 in rural areas and Rs. 24,000 in urban areas.

Under the loan waiver and relief package, small and marginal farmers (with holdings up to 2 hectares), there would be a complete waiver of all loans overdue as on December 31, 2007, and which remained unpaid until February 29, 2008. For other farmers there would be a One-Time Settlement (OTS) scheme. Under the OTS, a rebate of 25 per cent would be given against the payment of the balance 75 per cent. Loan rescheduled in 2004 and 2006 through special packages and these rescheduled in the normal course would also be eligible for a waiver or an OTS. The debt relief scheme would be implemented by June 30, 2008 and the covered farmers would be entitled to fresh farm loans from banks in accordance with normal rules. The total value of overdue loans being waived is estimated at Rs. 50,000 crore and the OTS relief at Rs. 10,000 crore. The scheme is likely to benefit about three crore small and marginal farmers and one crore other farmers.

After the six decades of independence, it is now high time that the farm and rural development programmes should be identified, formulated and implemented by beneficiaries and Panchayati Raj Institutions (PRIs) at village and Block levels and monitored on a monthly basis by PRIs and government departments at district level. Beneficiaries and PRIs need to be trained to do a quality job. Local academic institutions and students pursuing post-graduate studies may be involved to evaluate the performance and end results of these programmes. Members of Legislative Assemblies (MLAs) and Members of Parliament (MPs) in their respective constituencies must identify factors constraining progress and initiate measures to improve the performance in consultation with concerned officials of Union and State Governments. While wide publicity on the performance of these programmes and problems should be given in local dailies for the benefit of local population, concerned State legislative assemblies and Lok Sabha may consider debating on the performance and problems in nutshell on a quarterly basis.

There is an imperative need for effective coordination, full commitment of State Governments and financial institutions, better transparency, good governance, and enforcing strict accountability while implementing the farm and rural development programmes involving huge amount of subsidy, credit and insurance payments.

Suggestions

Keeping in mind the constraints being faced by SHGs/micro-credit movement, the following suggestions are being made :

(1) An important issue in microfinancing the small and marginal farmers is their total credit requirements, i.e. productive credit as well as consumption credit demands. Neglect of any credit requirement, to ignore the poor households jeopardizes the credit for production as well. Therefore, both types of loan should be considered simultaneously, if necessary.

(2) A proper identification of beneficiary under government sponsored schemes be made and the credit institution should ensure adequate and continuous supply of credit, supervision and follow–up action after disbursement of loans.
(3) The credit institutions should strengthen the field and credit disbursing staff in their rural branches motivate and involve them in processing applications for sanctioning credit to marginalized farmers with better work norms and ethics.
(4) The credit limit for crops and other allied activities should be increased with the increase in prices of inputs.
(5) Proper and integrated formation of different schemes should be made, so that different activities like crop loan, minor irrigation, dairy, poultry and other activities may come on one forum.
(6) Credit institutions should develop schemes in which provisions be made to get marketing finances so that distress sale may be avoided. Provisions to purchase tools and other agricultural implements for creating sources of supplementary income for small and marginal farmers should be made.
(7) The security oriented certificates documents should be minimized and a real flexibility in terms and conditions of loans to small and marginal farmers be evolved so that they could get credit timely on concessional terms.
(8) Provisions of rescheduling of loan repayment should be made regularly in the case of natural calamities and personal genuine difficulties.
(9) The short-terms credit of small and marginal farmers primarily comes from cooperatives. State Governments should regularly contribute their share to cooperative credit institutions so that there should not be dearth in flow of credit to small and marginal farmers, because cooperatives are easily accessible source of microfinance in rural India.
(10) Regional rural banks were established for easy accessibility, sanction and disbursal of loans in rural credit system.

Keeping this in view, maximum branches of these banks were established in remote rural areas to provide adequate credit facilities to the small and marginal farmers. Directive should be given by the apex body to follow the potential linked plan especially meant for small and marginal farmers.

(11) The credit institutions should strictly follow 'service area approach', so that the beneficiaries of the area may get benefit of the credit.

(12) Commercial banks and regional rural banks should make household survey on its own and on that basis needy beneficiaries be identified and credit be disbursed to them only.

(13) Central as well as State Governments should avoid the populist programmes like 'waiving the loans', which have adversely affected the psychology of the borrowers in the rural areas and discouraged loan repayment.

(14) Preference and encouragement should be given to the cases of recovery. Some concession/incentives should be provided in the case of 100 per cent recovery.

(15) Where banks and cooperatives have not reached SHGs, linkage may be promoted.

(16) Generally, farmers of larger landholding groups are found reluctant to gain self-help groups. They should also be motivated to form SHG not for taking loans due to their better economic conditions, but for better interest earnings from SHGs.

(17) Proper training should be provided to at least one woman among the SHGs to understand banking operations and also to maintain records properly.

(18) To boost the moral and expand the business of SHGs, frequent visit of bank officials and personnel of NGOs, rotational leadership exhibition and sale promotion of their products and subsidies should be encouraged/ ensured.

(19) The credit disbursement is not an end in itself, but credit generated additional income should be used in repayment of loan as well as to improve their living conditions. Thus,

resources like counselling, advising, extension, insurance and larger amount of funds are subsequently needed.

There has been a massive mobilization of women taking place as a result of the SHG movement. The growth of SHGs incidentally has occurred during the period of economic reforms. The SHG movement has a good potential to serve both as a human face of the economic reforms as well as contribute towards women emancipation. There is a major onus on all actors involved in SHG promotion and development to further intensify their efforts in enabling SHGs to reach a mature stage. There is a need of major investment in capacity building of SHGs and proactive policies to help overcome the constraints by SHGs to integrate rural poor and women fully into the developmental programmes aimed at empowerment of rural poor particularly the women.

Bibliography

Abdullah, Shahnaz T.; Rafique Bhuyan; Antony Fielding; and Y.W. Mullineux (2005), "Micro-credit and Its Role in Affecting Decision Making of Loan Use and Employment of Women: A Comparative Study of BRAC and Grameen Bank in Bangladesh", *Journal of Insurance and Risk Management*, Vol. 4, Issue 7.

Abiad, V.G. (1995), *Grass Root Financial System Development*, Asia-Pacific Regional Agricultural Credit Association, Bangkok.

Adams, Dale W.; G.H. Graham; and J.D. Von Pischke (Eds) (1984), *Undermining Rural Development with Cheap Credit*, Westview Press, London.

Akoten, John E. (2006), "The Determinants of Credit Access and Impact of Micro and Small Enterprises", *Economic and Cultural Change*, Vol. 54, No. 4.

Anand, V. Vijay (2008), "Microfinance for Rural Development", *Yojana*, February.

Anjaria, J.J. (1952), *An Essay on Gandhian Economics*.

Anonymous (1978), "Mahatma Gandhi on Rural Development", *India Farming*, October-November.

Armendariz De Aghion, B. and J. Morduch (2000), "Microfinance Beyond Group Lending", *Economics of Transactions*, Vol. 8, No. 2.

Armendariz De Aghion, B. and J. Morduch (2005), *The Economics of Microfinance*, MIT Press, Cambridge, M.A.

Athreya, V. *et al.* (1983), "Identification of Agrarian Classes—A Methodological Essay: Empirical Material from South India".

Arbejols Paper, No. 21, Memeo, Sociology Institute, Copenhagen University.

Aurora, S.S. (2005), *Microfinance India Conference and A Look at the Expanding Market*, Financial Sector Team, Policy Division, DFID, United Nations Capital Development Fund (UNCDF), Issue 13, June.

Azad, Chandra Prakash (2006), "Empowerment of Women through Self-Help Groups : A Study of Sabour Block of Bhagalpur District", *Journal of Regional Studies*. Vol. 16-17, Nos. 31-34, January 2005, December 2006.

Azad, R.N. (1983), "Integrated Rural Development" in S.K. Sharma (Ed.), *Dynamics of Development*, Concept Publishing Co., New Delhi.

Aziz, Abdul (1989), "Approaches to Micro Area Development Planning" in I.S. Sundaram (Ed.), *Rural Poverty and Area Planning*, B.R. Publishing Corporation, New Delhi.

Banerjee, Amalesh and S.K. Singh. (Ed.) (2001), *Banking and Financial Sector Reforms in India*, Deep & Deep Publications, New Delhi.

Basu, Kaushik (1984), *The Less Developed Economy—A Critique of Contemporary Theory*, Oxford University Press, New Delhi.

Bhaduri, Amit (1973), "A Study In Agricultural Backwardness Under Semi-Feudalism", *The Economic Journal*, Vol. 83, No. 329.

Bhalla, G.S. and G.K. Chaddha (1983), *Green Revolution and the Small Peasants (A Study of Income Distribution among Punjab Cultivators)*, Concept Publishing Co., New Delhi.

Bhatt, Ela, R. (2008), "Foreword", *Yojana*, January.

Bishops, C.E. and W.D. Taussiant (1970), *Agricultural Economic Analysis*, Oxford University Press, London.

Brahmanand, P.R. (1987), "Prelude Towards an Economic Philosophy of Rural Development in India," in P.R. Brahmanand and V.R. Panchamukhi (Eds.), *Dimensions of Rural Development in India*, Himalaya Publishing House, New Delhi, Bombay.

Brahmanand, P.R. and C.N. Vakil (1956), *Planning for an Expanding Economy*, Allied Publishers, Bombay.

Brahmanand, P.R. and V.R. Panchamukhi (1987), *Dimensions of Rural Development in India*, Himalaya Publishing House, New Delhi, Bombay.

Brouman, F.J.A. (1984), "Informal Savings and Credit Arrangements in Developing Countries: Observations from Sri Lanka", in Dale W. Adams, G.H. Graham and J.D. Von Pischke (Eds), *Undermining Rural Development with Cheap Credit*, Westview Press, London.

Brouman, F.J.A. (1989), *Small, Short and Unsecured Rural Finance in India*, Oxford University Press, New Delhi.

Chambers, Robert (1983), *Rural Development : Putting the Last First*, Longman Press, London.

Ceravegna, D. (2005), *The Role of Micro-Credit in Modern Economy: The Case Study of Italy*, www. Flacso. Or. Cr/ file admen / documents/ FLACSO / cu/ Ceravegna 2. DOC.

Copestake, J., P. Dawson, J.P. Fanning, A.M. Kay, and K. Wright Revolledo (2005), "Monitoring the Delivery of the Poverty, Outreach and Impact of Micro-finance: A Comparison of Methods using Data from Peru", *Development Policy Review*, Vol. 23, No. 6.

Croxton, Fredrick. E., Dudley J. Cowden, and Sidney Klein (1973), *Applied General Statistics*, Prentice Hall of India Pvt. Ltd., New Delhi.

Cull, R.; A. Demigetic; Kunt and J. Morduch (2007), "Financial Performance and Outreach: A Global Analysis of Leading Micro Banks", *Economic Journal*, Vol. 117, No. 1.

Daley-Harris, S. (2006), *State of the Micro-credit Summit Campaign Report 2006*, Micro-credit Summit Campaign, Washington DC, USA.

Das, H.C.L. (1993), *Agricultural Efficiency in India*, Mittal Publications, New Delhi.

Das, H.C.L. (2001), "Priority Sector Lending by Public Sector Banks under Financial Sector Reforms in India", in Amalesh Banerjee and S.K. Singh (Eds.), *Banking and Financial Sector Reforms in India*, Deep & Deep Publications, New Delhi.

Das, H.C.L. (2007a), "Micro-credit Delivery Through Group Lending in India and Bangladesh : Some Lessons for India", Paper presented at *90th Conference of Indian Economic Association*, University of Kashmir, Srinagar (J & K), October 25-27.

Das, H.C.L. (2007b), "Swarnajayanti Gram Swarozgar Yojana in

East Champaran", Paper Presented at UGC Sponsored Regional Seminar on *Swarnajayanti Grameen Swarozgar Yojana: Its Impact on the Socio-Economic Dimensions of Rural People of Bihar.* P.G. Department of Economics, M.J.K. College, Bettiah, (BRA Bihar University), September 30 to October 01.

Das, H.C.L. (2007e), "Trends in Priority Sector Lending by Public Sector Banks in India", Paper Presented at *67th Conference of Indian Society of Agricultural Economics*, November 07, Lucknow.

Das, H.C.L. and S.K. Jha (1985), "Economic Ideas of Mahatma Gandhi", Paper presented at the *68th Conference of Indian Economic Association*, Ahmedabad, December 28-30.

Dasgupta, Rajaram (2001), "An Informal Journey through Self-Help Groups", *Indian Journal of Agricultural Economics*, Vol. 56, No. 3, July-September.

Das Gupta, R.; N.B. Shete; K.D. Rao and D.P. Khankhoji (2001), *Maharashtra Rural Credit Project: Ongoing Evaluation XI*, National Institute of Bank Management, Pune, (Unpublished Report).

Datt, Ruddar (2002), "Second Generation Reforms: Need for Changing Growth Strategy", In *Second Generation Economic Reforms*, Deep & Deep Publications, New Delhi.

Datt, Ruddar (2002), *Second Generation Economic Reforms*, Deep & Deep Publications, New Delhi.

Datt, Ruddar (2005), "PURA – A Neo-Gandhian Approach to Development", In P. Jagdish Gandhi (Ed.). *Dr. Kalam's, PURA Model and Social Transformation*, Deep & Deep Publications, New Delhi.

Datt, Ruddar and K.P.M Sundarm (2006), *Indian Economy*, S. Chand & Co., New Delhi.

Desai, Bhupat M. and N.V. Namboodiri (1996), "Whither Financial Institution", *Economic and Political Weekly*, Vol. 31, No. 31, August 03.

Deva, S. (1984), "Problems of Rural Development in Green Revolution Areas", *Social Scientist*, No. 130, March.

Dhingra, I.C. (1992), *The Indian Economy: Resources, Planning, Development and Problems*, Sultan Chand & Co., New Delhi.

Dreze, Jean and A. Sen (Eds.), (1977), *India Development: Selected Perspectives*, Oxford University Press, New Delhi.

Durban, E.F. (1963), *Problems of Economic Planning*, Oxford University Press, New York.

Dunford, C. (2006), *Evidence of Microfinance Contribution to Achieving the Millennium Development Goals: Freedom from Hunger*, http: // Microfinance gateway. Org/ files / 35795. File-Evidence-on-MDGs-Dunford pdf.

Eda Rural Systems (2001), *The Maturing of Indian Microfinance: A Longitudinal Study*, Eda Rural System, New Delhi.

Encyclopaedic Edition (2003), *The New International Webster's Comprehensive Dictionary of the English Language.*

EPW. (2004), "Microfinance: Productive Linkages", *Economic and Political Weekly*, March 6.

F.A.O. (1977), *Joint of Report the Expert Consultations, Policies, and Institutions for Integrated Rural Development*, Colombo and Nairobi.

Fisher, Thomas and M.S. Sri Ram (2002), *Beyond Micro-Credit: Putting Development Back into Microfinance*, Sage-Vistar Publications, New Delhi.

Gandhi, M.K. (1936), "Rural Development", *Harijan*, April 4.

Gandhi, M.K. (1936), *Harijan*, August 29.

Gandhi, M.K. (1942), *India of My Dream.*

Gandhi, P. Jagdish (Ed.), (2005), *Dr. Kalam's PURA Model and Social Transformation*, Deep & Deep Publications, New Delhi.

George, Susan (1977), *How Other Half Dies?* Harper Publications, New York.

Ghosh, Imon (2001), "An Overview of the SGSY Guidelines and Findings from Field Study," at http:// www. Alternative Finance. Org. uk / egibin / Summary P 12 id = 153 & view-html 1 & Language = e source lang = E, Accessed September 2007.

Goetz. Am. and R.S. Gupta, (1996), "Who Takes the Credit? Gender Power and Control Over Loan Use in Rural Credit Programmes in Bangladesh", *World Development*, Vol. 24, No. 1.

Government of India (1962), *Report of the Committee of Panel on Land Reforms*, Ministry of Agriculture, New Delhi.

Government of India (1976), *Report of the National Commission on Agriculture*, Ministry of Agriculture, New Delhi.

Government of India (1999), *Swarnajayanti Gram Swarojgar Yojana: Guidelines*, Ministry of Rural Development, New Delhi.

Gupta, B.N. (1990), *Statistics*, Sahitya Bhawan Publications, Agra.

Hansen, V.M. (1980), *Human Settlement Process*, Ballinger. Publishing Co., Cambridge.

Harper, Malcolm (1998), *Profit for the Poor*, Oxford & IBH Publishing Co., New Delhi.

Harper, Malcolm (2002a), "Promotion of Self Help Groups under the SHG-Bank Linkage Programme in India", Paper Presented at the Seminar on *SHG-Bank Linkage Programme*, November 25-26, New Delhi, Published by Micro Credit Innovation Department, NABARD, Mumbai.

Harper, Malcolm (2002b), "Self-Help Groups and Grameen Bank Groups: What are the Difference?" In Thomas Fisher and M.S. Sri Ram (Eds.), *Beyond Micro Credit: Putting Development Back into Microfinance*, Sage-Vistar Publications, New Delhi.

Haq, Mahbub Ul (1971), "Employment and Income Distribution in the 1970s: A New Perspective", *Pakistan Economic and Social Review*, June-December.

HDFC (1997), *Source Book on Reputed India's Practices of Microfinance*, Housing Development Finance Corporation Ltd., Mumbai.

Hermes, Niels and Robert Lensink (2007), "Impact of Microfinance: A Critical Survey", *Economic and Political Weekly*, February 10.

Higgins, Benjamin (1974), *Economic Development: Problems, Principles, and Policies*, Universal Bookstall, New Delhi.

Hoff, K. and J.E. Stiglitz (1990), "Introduction: Impact Information and Rural Credit Markets—Puzzle and Policy Perspectives", *The World Bank Economic Review*, Vol. 4, No 3.

Hott, S.I. and H. Ribe (1991), "Developing Financial Institutions for the Poor and Reducing Barriers in Access for Women", *World Bank Discussion Paper 117*, The World Bank, Washington DC, USA.

Hulme, D. and P. Mosley (1996), *Finance Against Poverty*, Routledge, London.

Huppi, M. and G. Fider (1990), "The Role of Groups and Credit Cooperatives in Rural Lending", *The World Bank Research Observer*, Vol. 5, No. 2, July.

Imnayongdang (1996), *Levels of Rural Development in Nagaland: A Spatial Analysis*, A.S., Prakashan, Meerut.

International Cooperative Alliance (1966), *The Role of Cooperative in Social and Economic Development.*

Iyer, P.R. (2006), "ICICI Joins Hands Three VCs to Fund Microfinance Institutions", *The Economic Times*, June 05.

Jain, Pankaj and Mick Moore (2003), "What Makes Micro-Credit Programmes Effective. Fashionable Fallacies and Workable Realities", *IDS Working Paper 177*, Institute of Development Studies, Brighton, Sussex. England.

Jha, T.N. (2002), "Micro Credit Finance Models in Bangladesh; Lessons for India", *Yojana*, February.

Jhingan, M.L. (1988), *The Economics of Development and Planning*, Konark Publications, New Delhi.

Jhingan, M.L. (2005), *The Economics of Development and Planning*, Vrinda Publications, New Delhi.

Jhunjhunwala, Ashok and Roshni Menon (2007), "ICT to Empower Rural India", *Yojana*, August.

Joshi, Deepali Pant (2002), "Rural Credit", *Yojana*, January.

Kabeer, N. and R.K. Murthy (1996), "Compensating for Institutional Exclusion & Lesson from Indian Government and Non-Government Credit Intervention for the Poor", *IDS Discussion Paper 356*, Institute for Development Studies, Sussex, Brighton (UK).

Kalpana, K. (2004a), "The Shifting Trajectories in Microfinance Discourse: A Critical Reading of the Anti-Poverty Dimensions of Microfinance Programmes", *Working Paper No. 189*, Madras Institute of Development Studies, Chennai.

Kalpna, K. (2004b), "Microfinance The Silver Bullet for Empowerment: Some Questions", *Working Paper No. 191*, Madras Institute of Development Studies, Chennai.

Karalay, G.N. (2005), *Integrated Approach to Rural Development: Policy, Programme and Strategies*, Concept Publishing Co., New Delhi.

Karlan, D. (2001), "Microfinance Impact Assessment: The Perils of Using New Members as Control Group", *Journal of Microfinance*, Vol. 3, No. 2.

Karmakar, K.G. (1999), *Rural Credit and Self-Help Groups*, Sage Publications, New Delhi.

Khandkar, S.R. (2005), "Microfinance and Poverty: Evidence Using Panel Data from Bangladesh", *The World Bank Economic Review*, Vol. 19, No. 2.

Khandkar, S.R.; B. Khalily and Z. Khan (1995), "Grameen Bank Performance and Sustainability", *World Bank, Discussion Paper* 306, The World Bank, Washington DC, USA.

Khawari, A. (2004), "Microfinance: Does It Hold Its Promise? A Survey of Recent Literature", *HWWA Discussion Paper 276*, Hamburg Institute of International Economics, Hamburg, http://www.a.de/For schung / Publications / Discussion paper / 2004/276.pdf.

Khusro, A.M. (1973), *Economics of Land Reforms and Farm Size in India*, Allied Publishers, Calcutta.

Kirkpatrik, C. and M. Mainmbo (2002), "The Implications of the Evolving Microfinance Agenda for Regulatory and Supervisory Policy", *Development Policy Review*, Vol. 20, No. 3.

Koch, E. and Soctjipto (1991), "Target Groups at a Glance: Linking Banks and Self-Help Groups after Three Years", *Savings and Development*, Vol. 17, No. 4.

Kota, Ina (2007), "Microfinance: Banking for the Poor", *Finance & Development*, Vol. 44, No. 2, June.

Kropp, E.M.T. Mars; B. Pramod; B.R. Quinons; and H.D. Siebel (1989), *Linking Self-Help Groups after Three Developing Countries*, Asia Pacific Regional Agricultural Credit Association, Bangkok.

Kumar, Anjani; Dhiraj K. Singh, and Prabhat Kumar (2007), "Performance of Rural Credit and Factor Affecting the Choice of Credit Sources", *Indian Journal of Agricultural Economics*, Vol. 62, No. 3, July-September.

Kumar, B. Das (1988), "Spatial Framework for Rural Development in India, *Khadigramodyog*, February 01.

Lakshman, N. (2006), "Indian Banks are Big on Microfinance", *Business Week*, August 22.

Ledgerwood, Joanna (1999), "Microfinance Handbook: An Institutional and Financial Perspective". *Sustainable Banking with the Poor*, The World Bank, Washington DC, USA.

Leland, H. and D. Pyle (1977), "Information Assymetrics, Financial Structure and Financial Intermediaries", *The Journal of Finance*, Vol. 32, No. 2.

Lele, Uma (1992), "Design of Rural Development: Lessons from Africa", in I.C. Dhingra (Ed.), *The Indian Economy—Resources, Planning Development and Problems*, Sultan Chand & Co., New Delhi.

Lepene, C. and M. Tellor (2001), "Distribution, Growth and Performance of the Evolving Microfinance Institutions in Africa, Asia and Latin America", *ECND Discussion Paper 114*, International Food Policy Research Institute, (IFPRI), Washington DC, USA.

Lewis, John P. (1970), *Quiet Crisis in India: Economic Development and American Policy*, Asia Publishing House, Bombay.

Littlefield, E.J. Morduch and S. Hashimi (2003), "Is Microfinance an Effective Strategy to Reach the Millennium Development Goals? CGAP, *Focus Note 24*, Http://www.cgap.org.

LKr, Lanushshi and Tashmenta Jamir (2006), "Village Development Board—Quest for Revolutionising Rural Development in Nagaland", *Proceedings of the Eighth Annual Conference of the North Eastern Economic Association*, Mizoram University, Aizawl, Mizoram, November 16-17.

Llanta, Gilberto (1990), "A Symmetric Information on Rural Financial Markets and Interlinking of Transactions through the Self-Help Groups," *Savings and Development*, Vol. 14, No. 2

Mahajan, Vijay and Bharati Gupta Ramola (2004), "Microfinance in India: Banyan Tree and Bonsai", *Basix Quarterly Review*, October.

Marr, A. (2007), "A Challenge to the Orthodoxy Concerning Microfinance and Poverty Reduction", *Journal of Microfinance*, Vol. 5, No. 2.

Madajeweez, M. (2003), *"Does the Credit Contract Matter? The Impact of Lending Programmes on Poverty in Bangladesh*, Columbia University Press, New York, USA.

Malhotra, Rakesh (2000), "SGSY: An Improvisation in Anti Poverty Programmes", at http://www.alternative finance. org.uk/cgi-bin/ summary p 12 Ed = 150& view=html 1 Language=57source Lange= E.

Mentosh, C. and A. De Janvry Sadoulet (2005), "How Rising Competition among Microfinance Institutions Affects Incumbent Lenders?", *Economic Journal*, Vol. 115, No. 506.

Meir, G.M. (1991), *Leading Issues in Economic Development*, Oxford University Press, New Delhi.

Micro-Credit Summit (1997), "Declaration and Plan of Action", February 2-4, 1997.@http://www.microcredit Summit. org/ declaration. html. last accessed October.

Minhas, B.S. (1974), *Planning and the Poor*, Oxford University Press, New Delhi.

Misra, R.P. and K.V. Sundaram (Ed.), (1979), *Rural Area Development: Perspectives and Approaches*, Sterling Publications, New Delhi.

Misra R.P. and K.V. Sundaram (1980), *Multilevel Planning and Integrated Rural Development in India*, Heritage Publications, New Delhi.

Misra, R.P; K.V. Sundaram; and V.L.S. Rao (1976), *Regional Development Planning in India*,. Vikas Publishing House, New Delhi.

Misra, S.K. and V.K. Puri (2001), *Indian Economy*, Himalaya Publishing Co, Mumbai.

Mitra, S.K. (1992), "Rural Development: Need for Holistic Approach", *The Economic Times*, November 21.

Mittal, Mukta (1995), *Rural Development in India*, Anmol Publications, New Delhi.

Montgomery, R.; D. Bhattacharya; and David Hulme (1996), "Credit for the Poor in Bangladesh, the BRAC, Rural Development Programme and the Thana Resource Development and Employment Programme," in David Hulme and Paul Mosley (Eds.), *Finance Against Poverty*, Vol. ll, Rutledge, London and New York.

Mooji, Jos, and Mahendra S. Dev (2002), "Social Sector Priorities: An Analyses of Budget and Expenditure in India in the 1990s", *IDS Working Paper 164*, Institute of Development Studies, Sussex, Brighton, U.K.

Mosley P. and R.P. Dahal (1985), "Lending to the Poorest: Early Lessons from the Small Farmers Development Programme, Nepal", *Development Policy Review*, Vol. 3, No. 2.

Mukharjee, Suman K. (2002), *Test Book of Economic Development*, Orient Longman, Kolkata.

Mundle, Sudipto (2005), "Ethics and Development", *India Economic Bulletin*, Asian Development Bank, Vol. 3, No. 1, January.

Murray, I. and E. Lynch (2003), "What Do Microfinance Customers Value?" *Women's World Bank: What Works*; @ http:/ /www. Woman's world banking. Org./ English / PDF/ Focus% 20 NoG% 20% 30 what% 20 customers% value / April 04/ pdf.

NABARD (1992/1997), "Guidelines for the Pilot Project for Linking Banks with Self Help Group", *Circular*, dt. February 26, 1992, DPD, F.S. 4631/92- A/91-92, Development Policy Department, available as Annexure 2 of NABARD, 1999.

NABARD (1995), *Report of the Working Group on Non-Governmental Organizations and Self-Help Groups*, Mumbai.

NABARD (1999), *Report of the Task Force on Supportive Policy and Regulatory Framework for Microfinance*, Mumbai.

NABARD, *Annual Report (2006-07)*, National Bank for Agriculture and Rural Development, Mumbai.

Nagayya (2000), "Microfinance for SHG", *Kurukshetra*, Vol. 48, No. 11, September.

Nagrajan, B.S. and N. Lalitha (1999), *A Critical Study of Women Self-Help Groups in Selected Districts of Tamil Nadu (A Report)* Project Funded by ICSSR, New Delhi, Gandhi Gram Rural Institute, (Deemed University), Gandhigram, Chennai.

Naidu, M. Venkatah (2002), "Rural Reconstruction", *Yojana*, January.

Nair, M.K.S. and P.M. Mathew (2000), "*Poverty Alleviation Programme and Structural Changes in the Rural Economy*," Project Report Sponsored by Planning Commission, Yojana Bhawan, New Delhi.

Nair, Tara S. (2001), "Institutionalising Microfinance in India", *Economic and Political Weekly*, Vol. 36, No. 4, January 27.

Namboodari, N.V. and R.L. Shiyani, (2001), "Potential Role of Self-Help Groups in Rural Financial Deepening", *Indian Journal of Agriculture Economics*, Vol. 56, No. 3, July-September.

Narayansamy (2005), "Micro Credit and Rural Enterprises", *Journal of Rural Development*, Vol. 4, No. 3.

Norwegian Peace Committee (2006), "The Nobel Peace Prize 2006", *Press Release*, Oslow, October.

Nehru, Jawaharlal (1951), *China Builds for Democracy*.

Owusu, K. Ppuku and William Tetteh (1982), "An Experiment in Agricultural Credit: The Small Farmer Group Lending in Ghana", *Savings and Development*, Vol. 6, No. 1.

Parikh, K.S. and Radhakrishna (2005), *Indian Development Report* (2004-05), Oxford University Press, New Delhi.

Patel, Amrit (2007), "Rural Financial Institutions in India: Touching the Lives of Millions", *Kurukshetra*, Vol. 55, No. 12, October.

Patnaik, B.K. (2007), "Rural Poverty and Need for Primary Sector Development", *Kurukshetra*, Vol. 55, No. 9, July.

Pearce, David W. *et al.* (1990), *Sustainable Development, Economy and Environment in Third World*. Oxford University Press, London.

Pearsall, Judy (Ed.), (2000), *Concise Oxford English Dictionary*, Oxford University Press, London.

Pitt, Mark M. (2003), "Empowering Women with Microfinance", *Journal of Economic Development and Cultural Change*, Vol. 54, No. 4.

Pitt, Mark M. and S.R. Khandkar (1998), "The Impact of Group based Credit on Poor Household in Bangladesh: Does The Gender of Participants Matter?" *Journal of Political Economy*, Vol. 106, No. 5.

Planet Finance (2000), *Country Study: India*, July, @ http://www. Plant Finance, org.

Planning Commission (1969), *Fourth Five Year Plan (1969-74): A Draft Outline*, Government of India, New Delhi.

Planning Commission (1970), *Fourth Five Year Plan (1969-1974): Final*, Government of India, New Delhi.

Planning Commission (1973), *Report of The Task Force on Agrarian Relations in India*, Government of India, New Delhi.

Planning Commission (1978), *Report of the Working Group on Block Level Planning*, Government of India, New Delhi.

Planning Commission (1980), *Sixth Five Year Plan (1980-1985)*, Government of India, New Delhi.

Planning Commission (1985), *Seventh Five Year Plan (1985- 1990)*, Vol. II, Government of India, New Delhi.

Planning Commission (2002a), *National Human Development Report*, Government of India, New Delhi.

Planning Commission (2002b), *Tenth Five Year Plan, (2002-07)*, New Delhi.

Planning Commission (2003), *Vision 2020*. Government of India, New Delhi.

Prabhu, R.K. and H.R. Rao (1948), *The Mind of The Mahatma*, J.C. Cooper & Co., Bombay.

Rajan, Raghuram (2006), "Separate and Unequal", *Finance and Development*, Vol. 43, No 1, March.

Rajsekhar, D. (1996), "Problems and Prospects of Group Lending in NGO. Credit Programme in India", *Savings and Development*, Vol. 20, No. 1.

Rajnish, Shalini (2002), *Rural Development through Democratic Decentralisation*, Deep & Deep Publications, New Delhi.

Ramnathan, A. (2006), "Paradigm Shift in Rural Banking: A Case of Microfinance Movement in India through SHG—Bank Linkage", In Kasturi Nageswar Rao (Ed.), *Rural Credit and Microfinance*, The ICFAI University Press, Hyderabad.

Rao, K.D.; R. Dasgupta; and Khankhoji (2001), *OBC in the New Millennium – Banking with the Poor*, National Institute for Bank Management, Pune.

Rao, Kasturi Nageshwar (2006), *Rural Credit and Microfinance*, the ICF AI University Press, Hyderabad.

Rath, Nilkantha (1985), "Garibi Hatao: Can IRDP Do it?" *Economic and Political Weekly*, Vol. 20, No. 6.

Ravi Kumar, Ratna (206), "A Premier on Microfinance: The Paradox of Plenty in Poverty", *Journal of Chartered Accountants*, Vol. 54, No. 11.

Ray, Debraj (2004), *Development Economics*, Oxford University Press, New Delhi.

Reddy, Ganji Y. (2000), "Swarnjayanti Gram Swarozgar Yojana (SGSY) in Rajasthan: A Few Observations", *Indian Association*

of Social Science Institutions/ASSI Quarterly, Vol. 19, No. 1, July-September.

Reddy, Sudhakar (2000), "Rural Non-Farm Employment", *Journal of Rural Development*, Vol. 19, No. 1.

Reddy, Y.V. (2003), "Microfinance: Reserve Bank's Approach", Address to Reserve Bank of India at the *Microfinance Conference*, Organized by the Indian School of Business, Hyderabad, August 06.

Registrar General & Census Commissioner of India (2004), Census of India (2001), Series–1: India, Final Population, New Delhi.

Robinson, M.F. (2001), *The Microfinance Revolution Sustainable Finance for the Poor*, Open Society Institute and World Bank, Washington D.C., USA.

Rosalenda (2005), "Problemising Microfinance as an Empowerment Strategy for Women Living in Poverty", *Journal of Gender, Technology and Development*, Vol. 5, No. 4.

Scully, N. (2004), *Micro Credit: No Panacea for Poor Women*, Global Development Research Centre, Washington DC, USA. http:// www. gdrc.org/icm/wind/mene html.

Seers, Dudley (1969), "The Meaning of Development", Paper Presented at the *Eleventh World Conference of the Society of International Development.*

Selva Kumar, M. and R. Sundar, (2007), "Swaranjayanti Gram Swarozgar Yojana (SGSY)—Tool for Poverty Eradication," *Kurukshetra*, December.

Semanawitz, S. (2002) "Microfinance for the Poorest: A Review of Issues and Ideas for Contribution of Impact", *Improving the Impact of Microfinance on Poverty*, http:// www. Microfinance gateway. arg/ content/ articles / detail/ 3395.

Sengupta, S. and H. Gagadhar (1979), "Agrarian Potties and Rural Development in West Bengal", In Jean Drege and A. Sen. (Eds.), *India Development: Selected Regional Perspective*, Oxford University Press, New Delhi.

Shah, Dilip (2007), "Central Budget 2007-08 and Rural Development in India", *Kurukshetra*, April.

Sharma, B.D. (1978), *Tribal Development: The Concept and the Frame*, Prachi Prakashan, New Delhi.

Sharma, S.K. (Ed.) (1999), *Dynamics of Development.*, Concept Publishing Co., New Delhi.

Sharma, S.K. and S.L. Malhotra (1980), *Integrated Rural Development : Approach, Strategy and Perspective*, Abhinav Publication, New Delhi.

Shylendra (2004), "The SHG-Bank Linkage Programme", *Journal of Rural Development*, Vol. 23, No. 04.

Singh, Indrabhushan and Usha Kumari (2007) "Jeevika Mega Project: Empowerment of Rural Poor in Bihar", *Kurukshetra*, October.

Singh, Katar (1999), *Rural Development: Principles, Policies and Management*, Sage Publications, New Delhi.

Singh, Roshan *et al.*, (2001), Rural Development and Cooperatives", *Yojana*, July.

Singh, S.N. and C.B. Kumar (2007), "Rural Development and Poverty Alleviation through Decentralised Planning in India", *90th Conference Volume*, Indian Economic Association, University of Kashmir, Srinagar (J&K), October 25-27.

Singh, S.P. (2007), "Growing Rural Urban Disparities in India", *Kurukshetra*, November, Vol. 56, No. 1.

Sinha, Sanjay (2000), "Poverty Reduction through Microfinance", *The Economic Times*, August 15, Kolkata.

Sinha, Subodh Kumar and Rajiv Kumar (2007), "Grass Root Democracy and Governance", *90th Conference Volume*, Indian Economic Association, University of Kashmir, (J & K), October 25-27.

Singh, S.P. (1979), "Agricultural Credit: Development and Prospects", *Commerce*, Vol. 139, No. 3577, Annual Number.

Smith, D.H. and K. Pillhiemer (1983), "Self–Help Groups as Social Movement Organization: Social Structure and Social Change", *Research in Social Movement, Conflicts and Change.*

Sood, Archana (2007), "March of a Women SHG in Kohima", *Kurukshetra*, Vol. 56, No. 1, November.

Srinivasan, P.V. (2002), "Poverty and Agricultural Research", *India Development Report 2002*, Oxford University Press, New Delhi.

Srivastava, A.K. (1986), *Integrated Rural Development Programmes in India*, Deep & Deep Publications, New Delhi.

Stiglitz, J.F. (1990), "Peer Monitoring and Credit Movements", *The World Bank Review*, Vol. 4, No. 3.

Stiglitz, J.E. and A. Wiess (1981), Credit in Markets with Imperfect Information", *American Economic Review*, Vol. 71, No. 3.

Stohar, Walter and Frang Stodtlines (1980), "An Evaluation of Regional Policies – Experiences in Market and Mixed Economies", In V.M. Hansan (Ed.), *Human Settlement Process*, Ballinger's Publishing Co., Cambridge.

Subramanian, R. (Ed.), (1988), *Rural Development an Inside Look at Problems and Prospects*, Yatan Publication, New Delhi.

Sundaram, I., Satya (2002), *Rural Development*, Himalaya Publishing House, Delhi.

Sundaram, K.V. (1979), "Some Recent Trends in Rural Area Development Planning in India", In R.P. Mishra and K.V. Sundaram (Ed.). *Rural Area Development: Perspective and Approaches*, Sterling Publications, New Delhi.

Sumacher, E.F. (1974), *Small* is *Beautiful*, Sphere Book Limited, London.

Taylor, D.B.F. (1990), *Spatial Aspects of Kenya's Rural Development Strategy: Spatial Aspect of Development*, John Willy and Sons, New York.

Tendulkar, D.G. (1950), *Mahatma: Life of Mohan Das Karamchand Gandhi*, J.C. Cooper & Co. Bombay.

Thomas, M. and J. Pierson (1995), *Dictionary of Social Works*, Coltin Educational Publishers, London.

Tiwari, S.K. (2007), "Trends in Rural Finance, Reporters Report," 67th Annual Conference of Indian Society of Agricultural Economies. *Indian Journal of Agricultural Economics*, Vol. 62, No. 3, July-September.

Todaro, Michail P. (1977), *Economic Development in The Third World*, Longman Press, London.

Todaro, Michail P. *et al.* (2003), *Economic Development*, Pearson Education, Washington DC, USA.

United Nations (1986), *Savings for Development: Report on the Third International Symposiums on the Mobilization of Personal Savings in Developing Countries*, New York, USA.

United Nations (1998), "United Nations General Assembly Resolution – 52/194, Passed in December 1997 (1998)", in Countdown 2005, *Newsletter of the Micro Credit Summit Campaign*, Vol. I, No. 3, February-March.

Unnithan, T.K.N. (1950), *Gandhi and Free India.*

Uppal, J.S. (1969A), "Attitude of Farm Families towards Land Reforms, *Journal of Developing Areas*, Vol. 4, No. 1.

Uppal, J.S. (1969), "Implementation of Land Reforms in India", *Asian Survey*, Vol. 9, No. 5.

Vazqueg, Franciso (2005), "Pros and Cons of Microfinance", *IMF Survey*, Vol. 34, No. 5, March 21.

Veil, Laurance A. (1976), India's Second Revolution, McGraw-Hill Publications, New York, USA.

Venkatappiah, B. (1962), "Small Farmers Development Agency", *Address to the 29th Annual Conference* of The Indian Society of Agricultural Economics, December 30.

Vidyarthi, Chaman Ram (1990), "The Philosophy of Rural Development", In Narendra Prasad (Ed). *Constraints on Rural Development*, Amar Prakashan, New Delhi.

Vogelgesang, U. (2003), "Microfinance in Times of Crisis: The Effects of Competition, Rising Indebtedness and Economic Crisis on Repayment Behaviour", *World Development*, Vol. 31, No. 12.

Von Piscke, J.D. (1992), *Finance at the Frontier—Debt Capacity and the Role of Credit in the Private Economy*, The World Bank, Washington DC, USA, (EDI Seminar Series).

Vyas, V.S. (2004), *Report of the Advisory Committee on Flow of Credit to Agriculture and Related Activities from the Banking System*, Submitted to Reserve Bank of India, Mumbai.

Vyas, V.S. (2005), *Food Security In Asian Countries In The Context, of Millennium Goals*, Academic Foundations, New Delhi.

Vyas, V.S. (2005), "Food Security In India", In V.S. Vyas (ed.). *Food Security in Asian Countries in the Context of Millennium Goals*, Academic Foundations, New Delhi.

Weiss, J. and H. Montgomery (2004), "Great Expectation: Microfinance and Poverty Reduction in Asia and Latin America", *Oxford Development Studies*, Vol. 33, Nos. 3 & 4.

Weitg, Rahnan (1971), *From Peasant to Farmer*, Columbia University Press, New York, USA.

Williamson, J.G. (1965), "Regional Inequality and Process of National Development: A Description of Pattern", *Economic Development and Cultural Change*, Vol. 13, Chicago, USA.

World Bank (1975), *Rural Development Sector Policy Paper*, Washington DC, USA.

World Bank (1983), *Indonesia Rural Credit Study*, Washington DC, USA.

World Bank (1990), *World Development Report* (1990), Oxford University Press, New York, USA.

World Bank (1997), "Emerging Issues in Development Economics", *World Bank Policy and Research Bulletin*, October-December.

World Bank and NCAER (2005), *Rural Financial Access Survey (2003)*, New Delhi.

Yaron, J. (1992), "Successful Rural Finance Institutions", *World Bank Discussion Paper 150*, Washington DC.

Yunus, Mohammad (2000), "How Donor Funds Better Reach Grassroot Micro Credit Programme: Working towards the Micro Credit Summits Goal and Core Theme?" *The Bangladesh Development Studies*, Vol. 26, No. 2 & 3 June-September.

Zellor, M.G.; G. Shriider; J. Von Braun; and Hiedhues (1997), *Rural Finance for Food Security for the Poor : Implications for Research and Policy*, Food Policy Review 4, International Food Policy Research Institute, Washington D.C., USA.

Zellor, Manfred and Manohar Sharma (1998), *Rural Finance and Poverty Alleviation*, (Food Policy Report) Research Institute, Washington DC, USA.

Index